A SEA OF LANGUAGES: RETHINKING THE ARABIC ROLE IN MEDIEVAL LITERARY HISTORY

EDITED BY SUZANNE CONKLIN AKBARI
AND KARLA MALLETTE

A Sea of Languages

Rethinking the Arabic Role in Medieval Literary History

UNIVERSITY OF TORONTO PRESS
Toronto Buffalo London

ISBN 978-0-8020-9868-9

Library and Archives Canada Cataloguing in Publication

A sea of languages : rethinking the Arabic role in medieval literary history / edited by
Suzanne Conklin Akbari and Karla Mallette.

Includes bibliographical references.
ISBN 978-0-8020-9868-9

1. Literature, Medieval – Arab influences.   2. Comparative literature – Arabic and
European.   3. Comparative literature – European and Arabic.   I. Akbari, Suzanne
Conklin   II. Mallette, Karla

PN682.A67S42 2013   809'.02   C2013-901477-2

University of Toronto Press gratefully acknowledges the financial assistance of the Centre for Medieval Studies, University of Toronto in the publication of this book.

University of Toronto Press acknowledges the financial assistance to its publishing program of the Canada Council for the Arts and the Ontario Arts Council.

University of Toronto Press acknowledges the financial support of the Government of
Canada through the Canada Book Fund for its publishing activities.

In memoriam, María Rosa Menocal
For Sara and Eva, benevolent despots and beloved daughters

Contents

In Memoriam

We lost a singular voice when María Rosa Menocal died on 15 October 2012: someone with a unique ability to speak to both contemporary global events and the long train of history they trundle behind them. I first contacted María when I was a graduate student at the Centre for Medieval Studies at the University of Toronto. She responded swiftly and generously, with the capaciousness of spirit for which she was known, and remained an informal advisor and an inspiration for me throughout my professional career; she played the same role for many. It seemed right to honor her with a conference at Toronto – an institution that has trained so many fine philologists through the years – since her first book used philological method to turn some of the assumptions of philology on their head. The conference, "The Persistence of Philology: Rethinking Comparative Literary History on the Twentieth Anniversary of The Arabic Role in Medieval Literary History," took place at the University of Toronto in 2007.

As those who have read María's work know, she was passionate about music. In part to honor the role that music plays in a later book of hers – *Shards of Love*, with its cover art adapted from the Derek & the Dominos album "Layla and Other Assorted Love Songs," and its unforgettable explication of Eric Clapton's vocal performance on the song "Layla" – we planned a concert in conjunction with the conference. The ensemble Alpharabius performed medieval Arab and European music, and members of the Toronto opera company Queen of Puddings brought us selections from an opera based on the life of Jaufré Rudel, a troubadour poet who traveled from Europe to the Holy Land only to die in the arms of his beloved ("Amour de loin," with music by Kaija Saariaho and libretto by Amin Maalouf, 2000). For both Suzanne and me that evening is a sublime memory: a glowing moment on a cool Toronto spring night, when we scholars put aside all the idiolects of discipline and were drawn along on a musical pilgrimage from one shore of the Mediterranean to the other. In retrospect, this evening seems to encapsulate what María did better than any scholar of her generation: not dodge the bullets or evade the mines of history, but write about history with an emotional honesty and depth that allowed us to understand it – even convinced us to love it – despite its difficulty. María captured the urgency that drew many of us to the study of literature; like a skilled singer, she was able to use raw emotion to give a ragged edge to sweetest melody, and the most memorable insights of her scholarship are at once historical and emotional truths.

As scholars of medieval literature, we meet death again and again in the texts and documents we study. We know its brutality, but we also know that death doesn't silence the spirit and that the works that great writers and thinkers leave behind are the best consolation for their loss. The essays in this volume honor María by continuing the work begun by her, as the papers delivered at the 2007 conference did. It is with profoundly bittersweet gratitude that we send our unintentional festschrift out into the world to make our debt to her apparent.

Karla Mallette

Acknowledgments

This volume had its origins in a workshop at the University of Toronto which we convened to take stock of the impact of María Rosa Menocal's work upon our shared fields of Medieval Studies and Comparative Literature and within the fields of national literary history that are our specialty. As the planning progressed, it became increasingly clear to us how wide-spread the ripples generated by Menocal's work really were, extending far beyond literary history into musicology and art, Jewish and Islamic Studies, and informing the new research paradigms that were beginning to be formulated within the framework of Mediterranean Studies. *A Sea of Languages* is a crystallization of a turning point in this field of study, and (we hope) will provide a suggestive stimulus for its next stages of development.

We are grateful to the Social Sciences and Humanities Research Council of Canada for its support of the workshop, and also to the Chancellor Jackman Program for the Arts (now the Jackman Humanities Institute) at the University of Toronto, which co-sponsored the workshop. The Jackman Program also sponsored "Cross-Cultural Musical Currents," with performances by two ensembles. The consort Alpharabius presented selections of medieval Arabic and Romance music, and John Hess directed a program drawn from the opera *L'Amour de loin*, with a score by Finnish composer Kaija Saariaho and libretto by Lebanese novelist Amin Maalouf; members of Queen of Puddings Music Theatre sang, and Linda Hutcheon introduced the performance. It is a pleasant duty to acknowledge these contributors, who both beguiled us and illustrated some of the scholarly insights that we had discussed in the papers presented at the workshop. Additional thanks are due to the Centre for Medieval Studies, the Pontifical Institute for Mediaeval Studies, the Departments of English, French, Italian, Spanish and Portuguese, and Near and Middle Eastern Civilizations, the Centre for Jewish Studies, and the Centre for Comparative Literature at the University of Toronto. We would also like to thank those graduate students who helped to prepare the manuscript (Andrew Reeves and Elizabeth Watkins) as well as those who worked at the original workshop (Alice Cooley, Jennifer Gilchrist, and Clare Snow) under the able supervision of Sara Akbari.

A SEA OF LANGUAGES: RETHINKING THE ARABIC
ROLE IN MEDIEVAL LITERARY HISTORY

1 The Persistence of Philology: Language and Connectivity in the Mediterranean

SUZANNE CONKLIN AKBARI

Mare Magnum est quod ab occasu ex Oceano fluit et in meridiem vergit, deinde ad septentrionem tendit; quod inde magnum appellatur quia cetera maria in conparatione eius minora sunt. Iste est et Mediterraneus, quia per mediam terram usque ad orientem perfunditur, Europam et Africam Asiamque disterminans.

– Isidore, Etymologies 13.16.1 (ed. Lindsay 2.98)

[The Great Sea is the one that flows from the Ocean out of the West, turns to the South, and finally stretches to the North. It is called "great" because the other seas are smaller in comparison with it. This is also called the "Mediterranean" because it flows through the "middle of the land" (*media terrae*) all the way to the East, separating Europe, Africa, and Asia.]

– (trans. Barney et al. 277)

Homer was more Mediterranean than Greek.

– Ezra Pound ("New Paideuma" 255)

The Mediterranean is an inland sea, but the term can also be used in a broader sense: to describe the geographical region that includes the sea, its islands, and the surrounding lands; to describe the cultural environment thought to be typical of this part of the world, even – as in the quotation from Pound above – a characteristic way of thinking and feeling, one determined by the nature of the region itself. While the form of national history has long been dominant, the attractions of conceiving of Mediterranean history synthetically, as a complex whole made up of many parts, have only recently begun to be felt. This impulse appeared with dramatic force in the mid-twentieth century, in the influential study by the *Annales* historian Fernand Braudel, *The Mediterranean and the Mediterranean World in the Age of Philip II*. This work not only had a dramatic impact on studies of the sixteenth century, which was Braudel's particular focus, but also appealed to scholars who were eager to move beyond the framework of national history both within the field of early modern studies and also in other periods as well.[1] Simultaneously, impelled largely by new work in comparative archaeology and anthropology, over the last decades Mediterranean Studies has become an increasingly important area in studies of the ancient world, especially in the disciplines of classics and history (Harris, "Mediterranean and Ancient History"; Alcock, "Alphabet Soup"). It is therefore unsurprising that when, in 2000, Peregrine Horden and Nicholas Purcell published their wide-ranging study of the Mediterranean, *The Corrupting Sea*, which extends from prehistory through the early Middle Ages, it engendered a profoundly challenging and complex set of responses.

Horden and Purcell were explicit both about the audacious breadth of their undertaking and its debt to Braudel's *Mediterranean and the Mediterranean World*, which they refer to as "our project's great inspiration and progenitor" ("Four Years" 358). In the book, Horden and Purcell attempt to demonstrate the "unity and distinctiveness" of Mediterranean culture (*Corrupting Sea* 9), an effort which has continued in a more extended form through their lengthy and cogent responses to the many critiques that the book has elicited ("Four Years"; see also Purcell, "Boundless Sea"; Horden and Purcell, "New Thalassology"). In this sense, Horden and Purcell's work on the Mediterranean has been less an intervention than a series of proposals and responses, part of an exceptionally fertile dialogue – or, better, a symposium – on ways in which Mediterranean culture can be seen as wholly "distinctive" ("New Thalassology" 732–4), having special qualities that set it apart from any analogues. At the same time, the debate engendered by Horden and Purcell's work has created a powerful counterargument that sees the Mediterranean not as unique but as representative of a particular form of cultural and economic connectivity. In this view, espoused most articulately by David Abulafia, the model of cultural interaction that can be traced in the premodern Mediterranean can be seen as representative of a whole series of other "Mediterraneans," including not only other similarly interconnected seascapes but also other geographically distinctive environments that facilitate trade and cultural exchange, such as the Silk Road or the Sahara Desert (Abulafia, "Mediterraneans"; on thalassology and the Silk Road, see Whitfield, "Perils of Dichotomous Thinking").

Horden and Purcell themselves point out the striking differences to be seen in the ways in which various disciplines have responded to their provocative work. While the impact of *The Corrupting Sea* is clearly evident in the fields of anthropology, archaeology, and ancient history, its effect has been less dramatic – or, at least, has been much slower to appear – in the fields of late medieval and early modern history, including cultural and literary history ("Four Years" 349–53). In part, this discrepancy may be due to disciplinary divisions within academic institutions, especially in the case of literary history, where the framework of national literature is still of paramount importance, at least in terms of institutional structures such as departmental boundaries, fellowship programs, and so on. This rigidity has begun to be challenged, however, not only through the medium of Comparative Literature and World Literature, where a range of synthetic frameworks for reading literature and language have been introduced, but also through the emergence of new conceptions of how one might place literary and linguistic histories in their broader context, one that emphasizes inter-cultural and cross-linguistic exchange. In this effort, the work of María Rosa Menocal has been seminal, not only in terms of her own specific contributions to the field of Iberian studies but also in broader terms, in the ways in which her work has inspired methodologies that reach beyond the narrow framework of national histories.

In 1987, Menocal published a study that would have a decisive impact on the practice of medieval literary history, and particularly on the study of medieval and early modern Spanish literature and culture. *The Arabic Role in Medieval Literary History* challenged standard paradigms of European literary and intellectual history in a simple but forceful way, illustrating how, for earlier generations of scholars, arguments regarding the role of the Arabic language in the emergence of Romance vernacular poetics had largely fallen on deaf ears. This lack of receptivity was not due to any weaknesses in the arguments, for the textual evidence was strong; rather, it was due to an unwillingness to acknowledge the permeability of the cultural veil that separated Christian and Muslim communities on the Iberian peninsula during the Middle Ages. Largely due to Menocal's influence, literary historians began to reconsider their assumptions about the interrelation of cultures not only in the territories that would become the modern nation of Spain, but in Europe more broadly. A new understanding of literary history began to emerge, one in which the Christian writers of medieval Spain took inspiration from the poetry, music, and philosophy of the Arabs. Comparable work on the art and literature of Sicily soon began to emerge, providing yet another example of the fruitful interactions between Christian and Muslim culture in the medieval Mediterranean. In addition, the study of the interplay of Romance languages and Arabic in medieval Spain soon expanded into an increased focus on the even more complex communications between Hebrew and these languages, as the different roles of Christians, Jews, and Muslims in medieval Spain came into sharper focus. Instead of a crude model of linguistic and literary succession, in which one dominant culture simply wiped out the other like waves on a beach, a more complex model came into view, offering a sharper image of the polyvalent cultures that existed in the contact zones of the pre-modern world.

The importance of Menocal's work, then, is twofold. Both through her initial intervention in *The Arabic Role* and in her subsequent writings on the flowering and subsequent fall of the culture of al-Andalus and the emergence of Castilian Spain (especially the widely popular *Ornament of the World* and the richly evocative *Arts of Intimacy*, co-authored with Jerrilynn Dodds and Abigail Krasner Balbale), Menocal has brought the complexity of one particular region – medieval Spain – into brilliant, vibrant view. At the same time, however, Menocal has opened the door to a whole new way of thinking about European literary history, through the lens of a comparative philology nuanced by a deep understanding of the intellectual and cultural history of the region. It is crucial not to lose sight of this broader contribution to be found in Menocal's work, for it is here that her insights dovetail with other work on the dynamic intercultural exchange that took place in the medieval Mediterranean. Spain was far from being the only crossroads of intercultural and cross-linguistic contact: Sicily, both under Muslim rule and, later, under Norman Christian rule, was another such point of contact. In addition, other centres provided a comparable nexus for the meeting of cultures, as illustrated (for example) in Goitein's magisterial work on the expansive "Mediterranean society" that could be reconstructed through the documents found in the Geniza of medieval Cairo – a dramatic locus of "connectivity" inexplicably neglected by Horden and Purcell (Bagnall 340–1). The territories of the Crusader Kingdom of Jerusalem also formed a region of cross-cultural interaction whose literary history, as witnessed in the local redactions of romances and universal chronicles, we are only just beginning to understand. Finally, brilliant work has been done by Susan Einbinder in exploring the ways in which Jewish communities in France and Italy interacted with their local Christian neighbours. While at times this interaction ended in violence and exclusion, at other times moments of cultural connection clearly took place, witnessed by the literary forms that remain from both communities on each side of the religious divide.

In approaching comparative literary history in the new light offered by Menocal's groundbreaking work, some scholars have taken inspiration from the methodologies that have emerged from postcolonial studies. Representative work of this kind can be found in the collaborative volumes on this topic edited by Jeffrey Jerome Cohen: Horden and Purcell single out the first of Cohen's two volumes, *The Postcolonial Middle Ages*, to introduce their account of how territories and frontiers had become "taboo" in recent studies of pre-modern discourse ("New Thalassology" 722n1), while the second of Cohen's volumes, *Cultural Diversity in the British Middle Ages*, pushes the geographical dimension even farther, positing a reading of England not as the pre-modern avatar of the modern nation-state but rather as part of a broader formation that Cohen identifies as an "archipelago." As in *The Postcolonial Middle Ages*, in *Cultural Diversity* Cohen seeks to reposition the national, metropolitan centre so that "it is no longer the world's umbilicus, but one center among many" (*Cultural Diversity* 7). In his recent survey of postcolonial approaches to medieval literature, Simon Gaunt also highlights the usefulness of Cohen's approach, though he emphasizes the practical limitations that all too often constrain such efforts: in spite of the *desire* to move beyond national parameters, as evinced in Cohen's avowed intention to reposition England as only "one center among many," in practice "the training of most medievalists within disciplinary structures that are largely determined by modern national languages and literatures means that little scholarship ranges beyond the confines of one literary tradition" ("Can the Middle Ages Be Postcolonial?" 165). Gaunt proposes that the solution to this difficulty lies, in the first instance, in the improved training of graduate students in a range of medieval languages: students must learn to "work across different languages" and "understand the dissemination and use of different languages in the Middle Ages" (172). Beyond this, collaborative research can expand the field of study even farther, bridging the gaps that separate national literatures, or even clusters of interrelated national literatures.

Perhaps one of the most suggestive and potentially fruitful recent moves from within postcolonial studies has centred on the role of religion in dividing and unifying groups within the borders of the ethnic community, the language group, or the nation. In their probing essay "What Was Postcolonialism?," Vijay Mishra and Bob Hodge interrogate the grounds on which religion serves as a vector of identity within postcolonial experience. Their insights, although developed on the basis of modern cultural formations, offer potentially useful ways of viewing pre-modern religious experience in the contact zones around the Mediterranean. Building on the work of Gauri Viswanathan, Mishra and Hodge propose that religious conversions must be seen not merely as "acts of incorporation into centers of power" and therefore "an aberration," but rather – at least in the case of voluntary conversions – as "intentional acts aimed at correcting … inequities of class, race, and sex in culture" (Mishra and Hodge 392). Such recognition of "the enduring force of religion in culture" illustrates its instrumental role, the ways in which religion could serve as one vector among many in the movement of the individual person (or the communal group) across cultural and political boundaries. Significantly, this aspect of the pre-modern Mediterranean is identified by David Abulafia as among the most significant omissions from Horden and Purcell's capacious study, *The Corrupting Sea*. Abulafia notes that their account of "the nature of cultural and religious exchanges" is very limited, especially with regard to "the relationship between those exchanges and trade" (65–6), and goes on to focus particular attention on "the confrontation between Islam and Christendom in the Mediterranean," which in Abulafia's view "needs to be re-examined from the perspective of trade" (69). Like Mishra and Hodge, but from the very different position of the medieval historian, Abulafia highlights the vector of religion in the Mediterranean "connectivities" that form the heartstrings of Horden and Purcell's "corrupting sea." In their response to Abulafia's critique, Horden and Purcell acknowledge that this remains "an undeveloped aspect of the subject" ("Four Years" 371).

More recently, a second theoretical position has begun to rival postcolonial approaches to the complex cultural interactions of the pre-modern Mediterranean region: that is, cosmopolitanism. Although we are only beginning to see studies that explicitly place Menocal's work on al-Andalus in the context of cosmopolitanism, nonetheless it is already clear that some of the idealization of the multi-faith, multicultural environment of medieval Spain bears a strong affinity to idealizing impulses in cosmopolitan theory. This can be seen not only in the occasionally facile celebration of the *convivencia* of medieval Spain (a notion sharply critiqued in Brian Catlos's account of "conveniencia"), but also in what William Granara has memorably named the "Andalusian chronotope." In "Cosmopolitanism and Medievalism," John Ganim surveys a range of examples of what he labels "utopian cosmopolitanism" (5, 7), including evocations of Granara's "Andalusian chronotope" in Tariq Ali's 1993 *Shadows of the Pomegranate Tree*. For Ganim, works such as Ali's novel posit a conflict between "utopian cosmopolitanism" and a "repressive theocracy" (5), whether Muslim or Christian. While this conflict may not be happily resolved within the confines of the novel, Ganim suggests that it nonetheless serves the function of resolving the conflict of cosmopolitan and theocratic in the imaginary of the modern reader: such works "insist that the medieval past is not origin or lost paradise, but a continual double of the present" in which "history turns back on itself" (10–11). The pre-modern figure of exile and resistance thus becomes an avatar of the modern "cosmopolitan intellectual" (11). Ganim points out the unsettling way in which Menocal's more recent books, *Ornament of the World* and *The Arts of Intimacy*, "seem almost as if they could stand in for the scenarios" described in the novels he surveys (10). While this is arguably a simplification of Menocal's work, Ganim nonetheless offers a glimpse of what is potentially lost in the joyful rediscovery of the shared cultural past of al-Andalus: that is, a history of violent conflict and exclusion, a past that David Nirenberg has worked particularly hard to maintain in scholarly view.[2]

While cosmopolitanism has had a relatively lengthy history in the context of ethical philosophy, its role in the remapping of literary history is comparatively recent. For our purposes, the most important figure in this effort is Sheldon Pollock, who has offered an articulate, ambitious reading of how cosmopolitanism can be used as a lens through which to view large cultural formations, with a particular focus on the role of language and literature. In "Cosmopolitan and Vernacular," Pollock argues that cosmopolitanism can be posited against vernacularity in a binary opposition that reveals how sacred or administrative languages, such as Sanskrit or Latin, operated in contrast to the vernacular languages that would ultimately supplant them. While "cosmopolitan" is "unbounded and potentially infinite in extension," "vernacular" is "practically finite and bounded by other finite audiences" (17). While "cosmopolitan" "assumes the universal intelligibility and applicability of a very particular and privileged mode of political identity, citizenship in the *polis*," "vernacular" by contrast "refers to a very particular and unprivileged mode of social identity" (20). While Pollock's primary focus is the interplay of the cosmopolitan language of Sanskrit and the Asian vernaculars that would ultimately take its place, he chooses to embed his analysis in a comparative study of what he calls "Latinitas" (as a counterpart to the "Sanskrit cosmopolis" [29]) and the romance vernaculars that grew up in its shadow. While there is much to dispute in Pollock's argument (which he develops at greater length in his 2006 monograph *The Language of the Gods in the World of Men*), his work is nonetheless useful precisely in the same way as is Horden and Purcell's *Corrupting Sea*. In each case, the generalizations and sweeping narrative generate many points of friction and a range of critical responses; nonetheless, the effort bears fruit in that it helps to clarify what sort of questions ought to be asked, and what sort of inquiries need to go forward.

A third approach, which is central to much of the work engendered by Menocal's pioneering study and, more specifically, to many of the essays gathered in this volume, centres on the role of philology. Throughout the period of imperial expansion, from the eighteenth through the early twentieth centuries, the study of philology was deeply intertwined with the foundation myths of nations: national philology became the handmaiden of colonial ideology. Yet other kinds of nationalist philology were also possible, as Karla Mallette has established in vivid detail in her most recent work, *European Modernity and the Arab Mediterranean*. For several southern European nations, in contrast to their northern counterparts, philology was instead a way to craft a myth of nation that explicitly drew upon the cultural and linguistic plurality of the Mediterranean. In Italy, Spain, and Malta, Mallette suggests, Orientalist philology provided the tools to invent a myth of the nation that posited the Arabic language and even Islamic culture as not external to European culture, but constitutive of it. Philology provides a way into deep intellectual history, as well, in Stuart Elden's recent work on the notion of and the terminology surrounding the concept of "territory." Elden's approach to his topic is narrow but extremely deep, ranging from Roman antiquity to the present day, focusing on the many connotations of the term *territorium* and the vocabulary that developed around it. By means of this central, philological thread, Elden is able to illuminate the complex web of political, ethical, and linguistic filiations that have governed the discourse used to express the nature of the power that is held *over* land and possessions, as well as the nature of the power that is expressed *through* the medium of land and possessions. As Elden makes clear, it is essential to regard territory not just as "a word" or "a concept," but as "a practice": through the expression of the discourse of territory, territory itself is called into being. In the broadest possible terms, territory functions transhistorically and transnationally; at the same time, Elden cautions, territory must be understood in its local context, "in its historical, geographical and conceptual specificity" (14).

This seemingly paradoxical union of the general and the specific, the global and the local, is essential to any study of the pre-modern Mediterranean. Inspired by the impact of María Rosa Menocal's work – both by the foundations she has explicitly laid in her own publications, and in the call to action she has implicitly evoked through her foregrounding of the "Arabic role" in European literary history – the essays in this volume seek to illuminate some of the most provocative questions currently in play within medieval and early modern studies. The postcolonial, the cosmopolitan, and, above all, the philological are central to the essays gathered in *A Sea of Languages*. While Menocal's work has focused on medieval Iberia, its effects have been felt much more broadly – and its impact often acknowledged more explicitly – in scholarship generated within fields lying outside of Hispanic Studies, especially in the emergent field of Mediterranean Studies. The essays in this volume reflect a tension that persists between these two fields: like any form of scholarship grounded in a national language and history, Hispanic Studies is at odds with the self-consciously transnational formation of Mediterranean Studies. Spain, however – thanks to its insularity well into the modern period, and thanks to the developmental delay that resulted in part from its isolation – is a special case. In the Spanish context, national history is by definition Mediterranean: the waves of conquest that brought Greeks, Romans, Vandals, and Umayyad Muslims to its shores, followed by the centuries of convivencia during the Middle Ages, make the Iberian peninsula a Mediterranean in microcosm, a polity and a history unimaginable without the broader backdrop of Mediterranean history.

Yet the conditions of Spanish history have contributed to a paradoxical insistence on Spain's exceptionalism and separation (from other parts of Europe, from other shores of the Mediterranean) on the part of Hispanists. Scholars of the literary history of Spain have expanded our understanding of what it means to create literature within a given national context by insisting on the multiplicity and complexity of the Spanish literary tradition. They have not responded coherently, however, to the fundamental provocation of Mediterranean Studies to work beyond the category of the modern nation, to see local microhistories and the macrohistory of the sea in indissoluble and essential continuity. In compiling this volume, we have aimed to juxtapose essays showcasing the important interventions of scholars working within the discipline of Hispanic Studies alongside works that contextualize that scholarship and propose new directions, methodologies, and foci for future scholarship. In this respect, Menocal's *Arabic Role in Medieval Literary History* has proved to be foundational to this volume, whose essays use Menocal against the Mediterranean and the Mediterranean against Menocal. Menocal's interventions provide a blueprint for a literary approach to the Mediterranean that responds energetically to the well-established Mediterranean scholarship of social and economic historians, while Mediterranean scholarship serves in turn to challenge Hispanists to think beyond the limitations of national literary formations.

Spain has a unique position in the Mediterranean, at once peripheral and metropolitan. Its marginality – its geographical distance from the centers of Arab civilization and European civilization alike – and the paradoxically cosmopolitan nature of its literary and intellectual history make it a fascinating test case for some of the fundamental insights of Mediterranean scholarship. To put it another way, our central purpose in this volume is to frame Spain: that is, to point out what is exemplary and what is anomalous about Spanish history, highlighting Spain's role as a gateway or frontier in the medieval history of cultural, religious, and linguistic encounter in the Mediterranean region. We draw Spain more fully into the Mediterranean setting by putting Hispanists into dialogue with scholars working on Mediterranean topics from other shores of the sea. The opening sequence of essays provides a range of ways to approach the connectivity and mobility of medieval Mediterranean culture, while the second sequence focuses on the Spanish context, enriched by the broader framework of Mediterranean Studies. Taken together, these two juxtaposed angles of approach produce a dialectical account of both Spain and the Mediterranean, in which Spain is at once a special case and the very paradigm of medieval connectivity.

As Isidore of Seville makes clear in his great encyclopedia, the *Etymologies*, the Mediterranean is more than a sea: it is the space that makes the whole world coherent. In the passage that appears as an epigraph to this introduction, Isidore for the first time gives the Great Sea the name we know it by, "Mediterranean":

> The Great Sea is the one that flows from the Ocean out of the West, turns to the South, and finally stretches to the North. It is called "great" because the other seas are smaller in comparison with it. This is also called the "Mediterranean" because it flows through the "middle of the land" (*media terrae*) all the way to the East, separating Europe, Africa, and Asia. (Trans. Barney et al. 277)

Horden and Purcell suggest that not until the nineteenth century do we witness the real "invention" of the Mediterranean, "as a region and not just a sea": only at this time, they claim, "did it become ... a full-fledged geographical expression" ("New Thalassology" 728). Without taking away from the historical specificity of that nineteenth-century moment and its role in the emergence of a modern conception of the region, it is worth pointing out the extent to which, already for Isidore, the Mediterranean was much more than just a great sea.

In this seminal passage, written by the Spanish bishop not long after the fall of the Roman Empire, and not long before the first Islamic armies would enter the Iberian peninsula to establish a new kind of rule and a new kind of society, the "Great Sea" is already a principle of order, embracing within its watery arms the four cardinal directions. It unites West, South, North, and East; but it also divides, separating out the continents of Europe, Africa, and Asia into distinct parts. In the medieval world maps appearing in the works of Isidore, which display the conventional "T-O" form, the Mediterranean appears as the letter T dividing what the map rubrics call "the three parts of the world." The T also evokes the figure of the Cross on which Christ was crucified, a remembrance made explicit on some monumental world maps that actually inscribe the head, hands, and feet of Jesus at the corners of the ecumene. Yet Isidore's evocation of the Mediterranean is at once global and local, for the description of the Great Sea immediately transitions into an account of the regions proximate to it. For the Spanish bishop, these regions are the parts of Iberia. Isidore begins his detailed account of the Mediterranean Sea with the local, stating that "the curve of its first part, which washes the Spanish regions, is called Iberian and Balearic. Then comes the Gallic part ..." (13.16.2; ed. Lindsay 2.98, trans. Barney 277). Once he finishes his catalogue of the various watery regions of the Mediterranean, Isidore begins to enumerate the regions of the surrounding land, which in his presentation also constitutes the "Mediterranean," the so-called middle land of the world: "And just as the land, though it is a single thing, may be referred to with various names in different places, so also this Great Sea is named with different names according to the region; for it is called Iberian and Asiatic from the names of provinces, and Balearic, Sicilian, Cretan, Cypriot, Aegean, Carpathian from the names of islands" (13.16.5; ed. Lindsay 2.98, trans. Barney 277–8). For Isidore, the Mediterranean is general, the central form that gives the whole world its shape; yet it is also specific, particular to the Spanish bishop's own homeland.[3] Here, the global and the local appear as two sides of the same coin.

A Sea of Languages consists of two strands of essays, with a cluster titled "Philology in the Mediterranean" followed by a second cluster titled "The Cosmopolitan Frontier: Andalusi Case Studies." The strong transnational impulse of the opening strand is evident in Sharon Kinoshita's exploration of the various romance vernaculars of the pre-modern Mediterranean. In "Beyond Philology: Cross-Cultural Engagement in Literary History and Beyond," Sharon Kinoshita illustrates the disturbing narrowness of the nationalist narratives through which French literary history is too often read. Grounding her analysis in a reading of the foundational text of the French "nation," the *Chanson de Roland*, Kinoshita shows how this epic continues to provide the basis for contemporary readings of medieval engagements with Islam, even those that explicitly position themselves within a postcolonial perspective. Instead, Kinoshita argues, we should be looking more closely at the range of medieval French romances and epics that demonstrate the extraordinary fluidity and interpenetration of Mediterranean culture, as well as at material artifacts that reveal the contours of the routes of trade and exchange that crisscrossed the region. This evidence, in Kinoshita's view, reveals the extent to which the Mediterranean was "a transitional space – a contact zone of commercial exchange and cross-confessional interaction." This insight, in turn, requires us to revisit conventional notions of periodization, re-examining the ways in which an explicitly non-Arab, non-Islamic Middle Ages came into being through the self-conscious foundation of the Renaissance subject. This is especially visible in the figure of Petrarch who – at least in his own self-presentation – functions as a kind of "hinge" between periods, drawing a sharp line to separate an abject medieval past from an exuberantly modern future.

In the strand's second essay, "Linguistic Difference, the Philology of Romance, and the Romance of Philology," Simon Gaunt continues to interrogate the nationalist myths of origin that underlie French philology. Unlike Kinoshita, however, he situates his analysis in the borderland of hybrid literary languages, arguing that the mixed vernaculars such as Franco-Italian and Franco-Occitan in which many medieval verse romances and *chansons de geste* were composed were far from being defective, sub-standard expressions of proper, normative French. On the contrary, though an intricate reading of the Catalan-Occitan verse narrative *Frayre de Joy et Sor de Plaser*, Gaunt suggests that such hybrid literary vernaculars functioned as a powerful expression of social and mercantile networks. Building upon his earlier work on the hybridized literary language of Franco-Italian, Gaunt shows how the nationalist philologies that underlie histories of southern France and northern Spain often minimize the extent to which the regions share a common, complex literary and linguistic history.

The next two essays in the "Philology in the Mediterranean" strand move from the literary expression of cultural and social exchange to the field of history of religion. The essays of Tolan and Saleh are essentially dialogic in nature, laying out the different constituencies involved in an assessment of medieval Spain in particular, and the Mediterranean more broadly: not only the medieval communities – Muslim, Christian, and Jewish – that inhabited the region, but also the modern stake-holders, both scholars and non-academics, who continue to participate in imagining what might have been the reality of al-Andalus. In "Forging New

Paradigms: Towards a History of Islamo-Christian Civilization," John Tolan builds upon Richard Bulliet's influential study, *The Case for Islamo-Christian Civilization*, arguing that medievalists are obliged to speak out regarding what they know of the "shared intellectual and cultural inheritance" of the "linguistically and religiously hybrid societies that ringed the Mediterranean." Tolan is cautious about drawing any simple lessons from the pre-modern past in order to inform the post-modern present; he is, however, acutely aware of the dangers that lie both in the idealization of the Andalusian past, and in its denigration by those who subscribe to the pernicious 'clash of civilizations' model popularized by Samuel Huntington.

In "Reflections on Muslim Hebraism," Walid Saleh explores the vulnerability of the scattered Muslim communities that struggled to maintain a toe-hold in fifteenth-century Spain. As Saleh shows, these Muslims lived in an increasingly tense and fragile environment as the inevitable final expulsions got closer and closer. Through the case-study of a late medieval Arabic manuscript written by a Muslim in a predominantly Christian environment, Saleh allows us to glimpse a community in crisis, acutely aware of the way in which it has been cut off from the central body of the community of Muslims or *umma*, and the extent to which knowledge of Islamic law and theology as well as facility in learned Arabic had declined in the last few generations. For such Muslims, attempts to refute anti-Islamic polemics entailed an increasingly direct engagement with the Bible, a text towards which they were "ambivalent": in Saleh's words, "The Bible was a shadow of the Qur'an, always accompanying it, and always impossible to ignore." Saleh makes a special appeal to scholars working in his own field of Islamic Studies to pay more attention to the moments of cultural, theological, and linguistic engagement on the part of Islamo-Arabic authors with Jewish and Christian texts. For Saleh himself, this project entails a detailed study of the history of Bible in Islam, work that complements the growing field of studies of the Qur'an in the western tradition pioneered by Marie-Thérèse d'Alverny and continued today by Thomas Burman.

With Paulo Horta's "'Mixing the East with the West': Cosmopolitan Philology in Richard Burton's Translations from Camões," we turn to the remarkable nineteenth-century explorer and diplomat who prided himself on his ability to pass unnoticed across religious, cultural, and linguistic borders. Horta focuses on Burton's largely unknown, as-yet unpublished translations of Camões's *Lusiads*. Like his wildly popular translation of *The Thousand and One Nights*, Burton's rendering of Camões's narrative of national might and imperial conquest inhabits a curious cultural space, one which seeks to recreate the qualities of a people within the English language by making philology the privileged vehicle of ethnography, both of these in the service of a renewed imperialism. Burton's engagement with the Portuguese experience of empire, especially as seen in his work on Camões, reveals more than a simple desire to build the structure of a British Empire upon the foundations laid by the Portuguese; instead, "the cosmopolitan travel and sensibility" of Camões and his fellow explorers provided "a positive model" for "reform and reinvigoration of … an ailing British imperial enterprise." What Burton admires most of all in Camões, however, is the "Mediterraneanism" he finds in his Portuguese fellow cosmopolitan. In Burton's self-reflective engagement with Camões, we observe "the palimpsest quality of the imperial philologies, Portuguese and English, which would bridge the Mediterranean and 'Oriental' worlds."

The cluster's final essay, Karla Mallette's "Reading Backward: *The Thousand and One Nights* and Philological Practice," begins with a word-history of the term "philology" itself, offering a "bouquet" of definitions of the word. Mallette continually evokes the metaphorical and allusive, anchoring her argument with a glittering through-line that is perhaps most visible in her naming of the renowned Galland manuscript of the *1001 Nights* not as "it," but as "her," thus metonymically linking it to the voice of the storyteller Shahrazad. On closer examination, however, these feminine sites of narrative origin prove to function as intermediaries through which the *Nights* gives voice to the suppressed history of Abbasid Baghdad, a dark tale of betrayal by the Barmakids followed by their subsequent accusation and massacre. Mallette's reading – an audacious "reading backward" – provides a way to read history against the grain by means of the medium of literary regeneration and fecundity, following the thread of philology through the labyrinth of interlocked tales.

Mallette's "Reading Backward" brings the first sequence of essays on "Philology in the Mediterranean" to a close. The second sequence, "The Cosmopolitan Frontier: Andalusi Case Studies," opens with Ross Brann's "Andalusi 'Exceptionalism,'" an exploration of the faith communities that inhabited medieval Spain: the Jewish population of Sefarad, and the Muslim population that struggled to survive as modern Christian "Spain" came into being. In "Andalusi 'Exceptionalism,'" Brann offers a comparative analysis of the imagined communities of Muslim "al-Andalus" and Jewish "Sefarad," illustrating the extent to which nationalistic celebrations of the region, rooted in climate theory and geographical idealizations, were shared across cultural and religious boundaries. He shows the ways in which both modern scholars and pre-modern poets have described the territory of medieval Spain in terms of "exceptionalism," asserting that this land – whether identified as "Sefarad" or "al-Andalus" – was fortunate in its climate, its geographical situation, its cultural excellence, and the quality of its artistic achievements. Even after the expulsion of Jewish and Muslim communities, Brann shows, a strong nostalgia continued to be expressed for the "paradise" that had been left behind, and which persisted only in memory.

Ryan Szpiech's contribution, "The *Convivencia* Wars: Decoding Historiography's Polemic with Philology," explores the complex history of the fields of study — history and philology — that have attempted to take stock of the multicultural, multi-faith environment of pre-modern Spain. Szpiech gives an expansive account of the intertwined genealogies of philology, historiography, and philosophy in the wake of the Enlightenment, highlighting the ways in which the study of the languages and culture of medieval Iberia has been inflected by the profoundly different methodologies that competed for primacy. Szpiech argues that a fuller understanding of this history allows us to "frame the discussion in new terms that do not reduce the question of interaction between the faiths of medieval Iberia to a facile one simply of tolerance or intolerance, but instead emphasize the importance of methodology in determining the outcome of historical and philological research." Philological approaches, in Szpiech's view, must be explicitly situated as literary analysis, on the one hand, and as a mode of history, on the other. Only with such a fully self-conscious, self-reflective approach can philological study of pre-modern Spain — and, by extension, Mediterranean societies more broadly — avoid the Scylla of teleological myths of the nation, and the Charybdis of an artificial and idealized convivencia.

Cynthia Robinson turns to the intersection of pictorial art and religious text in northern Spain to explore how Muslim devotional practices fertilized the cultural productions of the Christian *Reconquista*. "'In One of My Body's Gardens': Hearts in Transformation in Late Medieval Iberian Passion Devotions" hauntingly conveys how medieval Christian artists incorporated Islamic materials into the most intimate of religious milieux, the representation of Christ's Passion. Like Ryan Szpiech in the preceding essay, Robinson interrogates the value of the often over-idealized notion of Spanish convivencia, seeking to displace it with a more nuanced way of reading devotional materials from a cross-cultural perspective. Her interpretation of the Passion narrative written by the Franciscan Françesc Eiximenis models how a comparative devotional reading can bridge the divide that separated fifteenth-century Muslim and Christian faith communities. Castilian readers of Eiximenis's narrative were encouraged to meditate on the stainless heart of Mary, rather than on the broken body of Christ as was typical of Latin Passion texts written in European lands north of Spain. Christ's body appears not as abject or in a state of humiliation, inviting compassionate sorrow and pain, but rather as a "vessel devoid of all human content," analogous to the pure heart evoked in the devotional poems of Ibn 'Arabi. For Eiximenis, the heart of the worshipper comes to mirror the heart of Christ and the heart of his Mother, united through "the mimetic identification of lover with divine beloved."

Robinson's exploration of the cross-cultural exchange of devotional imagery finds its musical counterpart in Dwight Reynolds's masterful study of the movement of musical motifs among diverse ethnic and religious communities. In "Arab Musical Influence on Medieval Europe: A Reassessment," Reynolds draws upon Menocal's arguments concerning medieval literary history in order to illustrate the extent to which musical history conforms to and deviates from larger patterns of cultural interaction. For the field of musicology, as for the field of Romance philology, medieval Spain was long a site of contention: the "Arab hypothesis" was hotly disputed within both fields of study, with the claim frequently being put forth that not only the lyric content but also the melodic forms of the Occitan and Catalan troubadours had been derived from Arab sources. Reynolds persuasively demonstrates the ample opportunities for such cross-cultural transmission, based on historical sources concerning performance practices and the movement of musicians and poets among courts both Muslim and Christian. Yet while we can clearly trace shared poetic themes, metaphors, and lyrical motifs, other areas of overlap are more difficult to find. These include the use of end rhyme, whose origins still remain somewhat obscure, and the close correspondence of melodic changes with shifts in rhyme – a standard feature among Arab musical poets, but unattested within the surviving corpus of troubadour poetry. Reynolds demonstrates that both the "European nationalist" vision of the development of music in medieval Spain and the "Arab hypothesis" that posits transmission from Muslims in al-Andalus to passively receptive Christian Europeans are equally misguided: "Instead, the evidence points to complex genealogies and patterns of cross-fertilization which resist being captured in simple master narratives."

The complexly interwoven courts of Muslim and Christian rulers surveyed by Reynolds are mirrored in the equally intricate relations that linked medieval Spain with Sicily. In "Sicilian Poets in Seville: Literary Affinities across Political Boundaries," William Granara surveys the poetry of Sicilians who made their way in the late eleventh century to the Abbadid court at Seville during the Norman Conquest of Sicily, focusing particularly on the Siculo-Muslim poet Ibn Hamdis. Although Muslim Sicily is often seen as a satellite state of medieval al-Andalus, Granara challenges this view, arguing that the web of filiation between the two regions was both complex and variable. While both Sicily and al-Andalus might loosely be described as "frontier" cultures, Granara makes clear the extent to which the two domains differed from one another, and how the nature of those "frontiers" varied over time. Granara uses the paired concepts of philology and "worldliness" in order to describe the interactions that can be charted in the shared history of Spain and Sicily: following Edward Said's formulation, Granara juxtaposes a philology that entails "a detailed, patient scrutiny" and "a lifelong attentiveness" to the use of language and rhetoric with a "worldliness" that serves as a foundation for "humanistic praxis." In Granara's view, the relationship of the exiled Sicilian poet Ibn Hamdis to his Andalusian patron al-Muʻtamid Ibn ʻAbbad was based neither in an established, historical link between Sicily and Spain, nor in a shared religious outlook, nor in a common ethnic origin; instead, their bond was founded on the "worldliness" that each man recognized in the other, forming a substrate of mutual understanding expressed through the medium of poetic sensibility.

Granara illustrates how audiences in Seville might have understood the exilic poetry of their Sicilian guests as a harbinger of the fate that might await the Abbadids of al-Andalus at the hands of some future conqueror. David Wacks's essay, "Vidal Benvenist's *Efer ve-Dinah* between Hebrew and Romance," turns to the aftermath of this future event. Wacks contributes to a radical realignment of literary history by arguing that Iberian Hebrew literature must be read in tandem with medieval Arabic texts, and that both participated in the early formation of Spanish vernacular literature. While *Efer ve-Dinah* has most commonly been studied within Hebrew literary traditions, Wacks shows the many ways in which the text can be fruitfully situated within vernacular traditions, juxtaposing it with texts such as the French *Floire et Blancheflor* and the Castilian *Grisel y Mirabella*: in sum, this narrative mixture of prose and poetry should properly be read "not only as Hebrew *mahberet*, but also as European novella or romance." While the beleaguered Jewish community of early fifteenth-century Zaragoza clearly lived under enormous pressure, to which they responded with an increasingly desperate "proto-nationalism," writers such as Benvenist also lived in a world of thriving Romance vernacularity: "this was a Jewish community that shared a common vernacular culture, language, and literature with their Christian neighbors … these are authors working in the Romance world." Wacks shows how the Hebrew story of tragic love and misguided marriage found in *Efer ve-Dinah* may have laid the foundations for the rise of Hispanic "malmaridada" narratives such as those composed by Lope de Vega and Cervantes, thus establishing the Hebrew building blocks for some of the best-known literature of Spain's "Golden Age."

In "The Shadow of Islam in Cervantes's 'El Licenciado Vidriera'," Leyla Rouhi turns to the greatest figure of Golden Age Spain, reconstructing Cervantes's curiously ambivalent relationship to the Arab past of his emphatically Christian nation. Cervantes's traditional place as a founding father of Spanish literary history, often couched explicitly in nationalist terms, is challenged in Rouhi's reconstruction of the nostalgic longing for al-Andalus that emerges from the pages of Cervantes's short story. In "'The Finest Flowering': Poetry, History, and Medieval Spain in the Twenty-First Century," María Rosa Menocal draws upon her profound knowledge of the Andalusian past and its place in Spanish and European narratives of national history in order to articulate the nature of the lessons that the past can teach the present. Menocal offers an elegant philological reading of the past that does not flatten its difference while still making clear its relevance to the present. She shows how poetry – as a representative of all the arts – is simultaneously able to illuminate and contradict the apparently self-evident "facts on the ground" revealed by conventional modes of historical analysis. In Menocal's words, "poetry reveals the sometimes unbearable contradictions that political and ideological discourse rarely tolerates"; as a result, poetry is able to convey "a very different story and one which is at least as true," so that we twenty-first-century readers are able to "learn things about society from aesthetic forms that would otherwise be unknowable."

With the retrospective vision of Menocal's "Finest Flowering," the second sequence of essays in *A Sea of Languages* comes to a close. The volume concludes with co-editor Karla Mallette's "Boustrophedon," an essay that is Janus-faced, at once retrospective and prospective. It looks back in an elegiac remembrance of the remnants of Mediterranean literature and culture that are the focus of *A Sea of Languages*, but it also looks forward in what can only be called a philological manifesto, aiming to take some initial steps towards "a literary theory of the Mediterranean." As "Boustrophedon" makes clear, the editors' undertaking in this volume has also led us to try to articulate in direct, even polemical, terms what kinds of avenues a "new philology" might pursue, based on the foundations established by the essays contained in *A Sea of Languages*. In this respect, "Boustrophedon" emphatically looks not just backward, but forward. Like Simon Gaunt in his survey of postcolonial approaches to the Middle Ages, Mallette highlights the need for broader linguistic training of the students who will make up the next generations of scholars. She goes on, moreover, to highlight the special role that might be played by the philologist, asking what strategies literary historians might use to write the history of a region in which linguistic formation has always been multiple, dynamic, even mercurial. If in recent years literary historians have learned crucial lessons from social and economic historians, now, Mallette argues, philologists must bring a peculiarly *literary* sensibility to bear on medieval Mediterranean history in order to define the next phase of research. Our vision of the history we study is, at times, clouded by the instruments we use to analyse it, as Ryan Szpiech demonstrates in detail in his essay in this volume. In order to produce a fresh account of the medieval Mediterranean, we must devise a new template for our analyses, a new repertoire of images that we might use to interpret medieval texts. Mallette identifies linguistic complexity as the central challenge of writing Mediterranean literary history, and points out that the analytic metaphors that philologists have used to characterize pre-modern texts have not done justice to this complexity. Though they have worked admirably to enable sophisticated descriptions of specific literary historical problems – the evolutionary descent of the Romance languages from late Latin, for instance – the arboreal metaphors of traditional philological scholarship occlude the sorts of readings proposed by the essays in *A Sea of Languages*.

It is crucial, however, to point out that one potentially very fruitful approach to comparative literary studies, Franco Moretti's recent work on genre, is founded precisely on the same arboreal metaphors that have long formed the backbone of philological method. Significantly, Moretti explicitly situates his own literary-historical methodology in the context of Braudel's historiography, in an approach that is at once narrowly formalist (25n14) and yet capacious enough to take in the "longue durée" (13–14). Through three conceptual models – the graph, the map, and the tree – Moretti establishes formalist frameworks through which it is possible to see the big picture of comparative European literary history.[4] Moretti's model of the tree, unlike its counterpart in conventional philology, is polyvalent: it is both "interconnected *and* branching," illustrating "syncretism *and* divergence" (79; emphasis in original). The formal variations within a given genre are not to be characterized simply in terms of conformity to a norm or departure from it, but rather in terms of the dialectical relationship of both processes: "Convergence … only arises *on the basis of previous divergence* … Conversely, a successful convergence usually produces *a powerful new burst of divergence*" (80). Moretti's approach to modern genres, which centres on the emergence and development of the novel, works equally well as a way of dealing with medieval genres, especially the capacious and sprawling genre of medieval romance. One could imagine a Mediterranean genre theory that would select a text that appears in a large number of redactions across a wide range of vernacular languages – for example, *The Book of John Mandeville*, the hugely popular *Roman de Fierabras*, or Orosius's universal chronicle of world history – and use it to take a broad sample of the dissemination of a particular narrative form across the languages and cultures that cluster about the shores of the Great Sea and inhabit its many islands. Such a comparative mode of reading would be broad but not deep, in a strategic choice to sacrifice sharpness of the individual reading in order to catch a glimpse of the movement of narrative forms and thematic motifs as they crystallize in a range of different milieux.

Such work, however, still lies ahead, and it is very different from what we hope to have achieved in the present volume: one might describe it as the horizontal counterpart to the vertical mode of philology, which twists and turns its way into the subterranean past – and into imagined futures – like Ariadne's twine. If an approach to the pre-modern Mediterranean patterned on Moretti's work on genre will allow us to map the labyrinth and even to superimpose on it all the other possible architectural models to which it might correspond, a philological approach of the sort we have proposed in *A Sea of Languages* offers a way to penetrate the hidden core of the maze – or, perhaps, to find the way out. In order to capture the interplay of languages in the medieval Mediterranean, in order to describe the significance of historical events which social, economic, and now literary historians have so meticulously excavated in recent decades, we need more robust rhetorical and symbolic strategies to represent a historical complexity characterized in particular by linguistic density and connectivity. This is a task that necessarily falls to the specialists: philologists, familiar with the material history of writing and the rhetorical strategies and image banks used by the writers of the past. In the closing pages of *A Sea of Languages*, Mallette presents the "boustrophedon" text – in which alternate lines run from left to right and from right to left – as a model for alternate ways of viewing texts and textual generation. It would be all too easy to read teleologically, moving from the ninth-century riddle that attests to the earliest traces of Italian vernacular to the Arabo-Romance novel of the twenty-first century: instead, we propose a reading that circles back to the point of origin, and then turns about to face the future.

This move might be seen as a corrective counterpart to Petrarch's famous ascent of Mont Ventoux, the moment in which he self-consciously inscribed himself within an ancient lineage extending back through Augustine, Seneca, and Cicero to the passionate epic heart of Greek verse. On the mountaintop, Petrarch imagined himself to be standing wholly outside of the clutter of the intervening ages, united with the classical authors who were – in this imagined community of letters – his beloved friends. Here, he could be free of the Islamo-Arabic heritage that permeated the medieval Mediterranean, a legacy that – as Tolan, Kinoshita, and Mallette all remind us – Petrarch so energetically sought to repudiate. It is fitting that Petrarch would ascend the mountain in order to shake off these medieval bonds: as both Braudel and Horden and Purcell tell us, in terms of climate, "every mountaintop is outside the Mediterranean" (Braudel, *Memory* 26–7; Horden and Purcell, "New Thalassology" 734). No matter how much Petrarch worked to inscribe himself within a pure linguistic and literary lineage, positing a philological umbilicus connecting him to ancient Greece by way of the glories of Rome, he was not able to suppress completely the traces of the Mediterranean, with all its complex and impure cross-cultural heritage. Even for the father of all poets, Homer, the many shores of the Great Sea were constantly in corrupting flux, leading both soldiers and sailors astray.[5] In spite of – or, perhaps, because of – his heroic efforts to be the poetic heir to Homer, Petrarch may also have been "more Mediterranean than Greek."

NOTES

1 Braudel made an additional, posthumous contribution to the developing field of Mediterranean Studies in *Les Mémoires de la Méditerranée* (based on an unpublished draft manuscript written in 1968–9).

2 Contrasting "anti-semitic" and "philo-semitic" approaches to the pre-modern past, Nirenberg argues that both of these "miss what I think is the more important conclusion: that both exclusion and inclusion are inseparable faces of a debate over Islam that appears in tandem with the idea of Europe itself" (Nirenberg, "Islam and the West" 24). For a sensitive appreciation of Menocal's work and its important place within what Nirenberg identifies as the "philo-semitic" mode of scholarship, see Nirenberg, "Islam and the West" 18–20. For a more polemical engagement with the political stakes riding on idealizations of the multi-faith, multi-cultural medieval past, see Nirenberg, "Hope's Mistakes."

3 Isidore's special emphasis on the place of Spain within world geography can also be seen in his account of the nations and languages of the world; similar nationalist impulses within universal histories or encyclopedias can be found in the work of the English writers Bartholomaeus Anglicus and Robertus Anglicus. On Isidore and Bartholomaeus, see Akbari, *Idols in the East* 42–6, 64; on Bartholomaeus and Robertus, see Akbari, "Diversity of Mankind" 162–3.

4 On mapping, especially the labyrinthine schematic, see Moretti 43, 55–7; on the verticality of the tree model, see 69–70, 91.

5 On the role of Homer in the conception of the "corrupting sea," see Horden and Purcell, *Corrupting Sea* 24–5, 43; "New Thalassology" 724; and "Four Years" 359: "Our Mediterranean is partly discourse, with the *Odyssey* as its creator – but only partly."

PART ONE

Philology in the Mediterranean

2 Beyond Philology: Cross-Cultural Engagement in Literary History and Beyond

SHARON KINOSHITA

I.

One of the things I most appreciate in the work of María Rosa Menocal is her insistence on the specificity of the Middle Ages. This is most in evidence in her lovely elegiac essay "Horse Latitudes" in *Shards of Love*, in which she evocatively conjures the "messy, cacophonous" (43) world of "riotous pluralities and often-chaotic poetics" (10) foreclosed in 1492. In that vision, the pre-modern stood for the overlapping complexities of a multilingual and multiconfessional Spain not yet straitjacketed by the rectilinear Humanist rationality Walter Mignolo calls the "Darker Side of the Renaissance." A look back at *The Arabic Role in Medieval Literary History*, however, reveals this suspicion of early modernity to be an abiding element in her thinking: already in 1987, she linked the Renaissance privileging of classical antiquity to "the critical notion, which remains strong today, of the essential continuity and unity of Western civilization from the Greeks through fifteenth-century Italy." It is, as she points out, "*a notion of history formulated as much to deny the medieval past and its heritage* as to establish a new and more worthy ancestry." Moreover, "the depiction of the medieval world as a dark age ... is still operative in many spheres to this day" (5, emphasis added). Menocal's own Middle Ages inverts this narrative in significant ways. Where other medievalists are sometimes tempted to vindicate their object of study by laying claim to a pre-cocious Humanism (in, for example, the so-called twelfth-century Renaissance), she instead highlights the *dis*continuities – the epistemic rupture handily summed up in the events of 1492. Menocal's point, of course, was that the "othering" of the Middle Ages evident in the "depiction of the medieval world as a dark age" goes hand-in-hand with the repression of "the Arabic role" in the history of the medieval "West." Having no place in the narrative of "the essential continuity and unity of Western civilization," the Arabic role in medieval literary history remained, in 1987, largely unspoken and unthinkable – invisible to all but a small group of specialists of medieval Iberia.

A central focus of Menocal's work, then, has been her repeated explication of the cultural complexity of the Iberian peninsula. From *Shards of Love* (1994) to her crossover bestseller, *Ornament of the World* (2002), to her lovely co-authored volume, *The Arts of Intimacy* (Dodds et al. 2008), she works against the tide of the explicit or implicit equation "Spain" with "Castile" and "Castilian." In her hands, "medieval Spanish literature" encompasses Arabic and Hebrew, Catalan and Galician as well as Castilian; the Iberian peninsula was a multilingual space in which different literary cultures entered into dialogue and intertwined. Directed toward a wide and varied audience, her books and essays have contributed significantly to the deprovincialization of medieval Iberian studies. If "[t]he story of the Middle Ages has largely been told from a northern European perspective" that takes the histories of France and England as normative while "push[ing] the Iberian Middle Ages to an exotic, orientalized fringe," then Menocal's work helps assure that "Iberomedievalism" no longer occupies a "'primitive,' 'backward,' or 'belated' position in relation to other 'national' disciplines of Western European medieval studies" (Dagenais and Greer 440), but becomes a place from which to launch a post-national literary history of the Middle Ages. This is especially so since, in the more than twenty years since the publication of *The Arabic Role in Medieval Literary History*, the emergence of postcolonial theory and cultural studies has given us a new lexicon – terms like hybridity, contact zones, and transculturation – to facilitate our apprehension of the aspects of Andalusian culture that Menocal had to work so hard to articulate, against the grain, in 1987. Many of the concerns announced there have, in the intervening years, become central to medieval scholarship in general, reconfiguring our sense of the *bon à penser*.

If Menocal's vision of the multilingual and multiconfessional landscape of al-Andalus has sometimes been suspected of undue romanticism, it comes as a strategic counterbalance to other contemporary representations of the Middle Ages in modern media and public discourse. As recent studies have shown, the familiar demonization of the Middle Ages as "a period of superstition, social and economic backwardness, political chaos, and cultural inferiority" has been given new life in the "odd field of policy studies called 'neomedievalism'," in which the Middle Ages – though ultimately beside the point – have been exploited as a repertoire of analogies touching on "the 'medieval' nature of contemporary non-state actors, including terrorists," with real-world repercussions in the formation of policy and legal judgments around such questions as the use of torture (Spiegel, drawing on Holsinger; see also Lampert-Weissig). And nowhere are these allusions to the violence of the medieval world more insidious than in the neo-Orientalist representations of the Arabic or Islamic worlds, deploying a discourse of uneven temporalities consigning the non-western Other to a medieval past at odds with modernity, rationality, and liberal democracy (Davis).

Thinking about the Arabic role in medieval literary history, therefore, poses a double challenge: moving beyond the "sheer knitted-together strength" of Orientalist discourse (Said, *Orientalism* 6), on the one hand, and the automatism of the modern othering of the Middle Ages (Leupin), on the other. Prying our thinking out of these well-worn discursive grooves in ways that do not simply invert the binary demands constant critical rigor and scrupulous attention to historical, cultural, and textual specificity. Issues surrounding the history and politics of *convivencia* in medieval Iberia provide one set of salutary critical questions. For Michelle Hamilton, the character of the go-between common to Arabic, "Judeo-Andalusi," and Castilian literatures aptly figures the possibility of thinking otherwise: a product of the Middle Ages, "that 'other' time … into which contemporary thinkers, politicians, and pundits are fond of placing all that is evil, dark, and barbarous," in the Iberian Peninsula, "that 'other' space … between Europe and Africa and not clearly belonging to either," Celestina and her sisters inhabit "the in-between spaces in which different social, linguistic, ethnic, and cultural groups intermingle[d]" (1–2).

The remainder of this essay explores some of the ways this transgressive spirit could productively reenergize our study of medieval literature. Where Iberomedievalists have focused on the lyric and the frame tale, we begin with a different language and genre: the Old French *chanson de geste*. Examining postcolonial uses and abuses of the *Chanson de Roland*, we revisit the way recent readings have transformed this foundational text of the French Middle Ages into an overdetermined site for the expression of hostile Christian-Muslim relations. Then, turning to a lesser-known epic, the *Charroi de Nîmes*, we explore how a "thick" understanding of medieval Mediterranean material culture might contribute to the elaboration of a post-national, postcolonial philology. From there, we return to the problem of periodization. Beginning with Petrarch and continuing the story through the writings of sixteenth-century Italian Humanists, we follow Menocal's lead in suggesting that, seen through the problematic of Christian-Muslim difference, questions concerning the period divide between the Middle Ages and early modernity produce answers that radically challenge "the critical notion … of the essential continuity and unity of Western civilization" (*Arabic Role* 5).

II.

How might the questions raised in *The Arabic Role* and Menocal's subsequent work translate outside the field of Iberomedievalism? Her expansion of the idea of "Spanish" literary history to include Arabic, Catalan, Galician, and Hebrew provides a useful model for rethinking other multilingual or multiconfessional sites. Karla Mallette, for example, has reimagined the literary history of Norman and Hohenstaufen Sicily (1100–1250) through the collocation of texts in Arabic, Latin, French, and Sicilian – a reflection of the linguistic and cultural complexity of a place where, in 1149, a cleric at the royal court covered his mother's tombstone with epitaphs in three languages and four scripts (Latin, Greek, Arabic, and Judeo-Arabic), noting the date of her death according to the Latin, Orthodox, Muslim, and Jewish calendars.[1]

How questions of multilingualism, multiconfessionalism, and cultural contact might play out in the field of Old French is less immediately obvious. Here, other strategies are called for. A good place to start is literary representations of the Islamic world – specifically, the use and abuse that has been made of *the* canonical work of the medieval French tradition, *La Chanson de Roland*.[2] I am thinking, in particular, of studies in the emerging field of "postcolonial medievalism" that tend to emphasize the barbarity of its representation of the Saracen "other," taking it as exemplary of medieval Christian attitudes towards Islam and the Islamic world. In an essay on Bernard of Clairvaux's reading of the Song of Songs, for example, Bruce Holsinger identifies the *Chanson de Roland* as:

> one of the most violent and widely diffused pieces of anti-Muslim literature in the years surrounding the First Crusade. Here the religious alterity of the Saracen Abisme, who "fears not God, the Son of Saint Mary," is writ large on his countenance: "Black is that man as molten pitch that seethes." Roland himself gazes upon other such "misbegotten men," who appear "more black than ink is on the pen, / With no part white but their teeth." Samir Marzouki has gone so far as to argue that for the *Roland* author skin color was "un indice moral ainsi qu'un indice social," in which the Saracen, "hâlé par le soleil, était considéré comme laid et par conséquent immoral." (Holsinger 170)

Holsinger's essay belongs to a recognizable moment of interest in medieval depictions of race.[3] There are many rejoinders one could make about the distortions that result when "Saracen" is treated as a predominantly racialized category – a tendency, I have suggested, more revelatory of modern than medieval assumptions.[4] Suffice it to say that Holsinger's essay is not an isolated case. In his 2001 article "On Saracen Enjoyment: Some Fantasies of Race in Late Medieval France and England," Jeffrey Jerome Cohen writes:

> Like monsters, racist representations inevitably conjoin desire and disgust. The Saracens were no exception. The extended visualizations of "lusty, black-skinned people" in the *Chanson de Roland*, for example, brought "the darkness of Africa" queerly close to Christianity, a temptation within a threat. The poem describes both Margariz,

whose beautiful body attracts the lingering eyes of Saracen ladies and Christian men, and Abisme, a Saracen "neirs cume peiz ki est demise" [black as molten pitch] whose skin color and character are inseparable (he enjoys perfidy, murder, and heresy). Another Saracen leader, Marganice, rules over Africa (Ethiopia, Carthage, Alfrere, Garmalie), where he holds "the black race [la neire gent] under his command; / their noses are big and their ears broad" (1917–18; cf. 1933–4: "[they] are blacker than ink / and have nothing white but their teeth"). During battle scenes groups of warriors are described according to the physical difference which sets apart their race: the Milceni, with their large heads and piglike bristles on their spines (3221–3); the Canaanites, who are simply ugly (3238); the fiery desert dwellers of Occian, whose skin is so hard they do not wear armor (3246–51), and who bray and whinny in battle (3526); giants from Malprose (3253); the Argoille, who bark like dogs (3527). (J. Cohen 119–20)

Including more examples and citing the text at greater length than Holsinger, Cohen seems decisively to carry the case against the *Chanson de Roland* as a locus of the medieval racialization and demonization of Islam. Still, for anyone familiar with the *Roland*, his allusion to a "lusty, black-skinned people" who "brought 'the darkness of Africa' queerly close to Christianity" rings a little odd: however one reads the representation of the Saracen Abisme, "black … as molten pitch," who "fears not God, the Son of Saint Mary," "lustiness" is surely not the first attribute that springs to mind. As we see on closer examination, however, Cohen's characterization is itself a quotation, drawn from Gregory Hutcheson and Josiah Blackmore's Introduction to their 1999 volume *Queer Iberia*:

> Ever since the Romans named Iberia's western reaches "Extremadura" – the extreme territories – it has lain on the margins of Europe's consciousness, always the site of difference, always "queer" Iberia. Here it is that the Romans located the *nec plus ultra*, beyond which there was nothingness, or worse, every conceivable monster of the imagination. For the Europe of the *Chanson de Roland*, Iberia was the land of the Saracens, a lusty, black-skinned people that brought the darkness of Africa dangerously close; so too the temptations of the soul's darker side … Roland's Saracens are implicitly defined by a sexuality that exceeds the bounds of a Christian normativity, one that subverts the teleology of sex and emblematizes the shadow side of European culture. Indeed, in Christian accounts of Muslim Iberia, sexual excess seems inevitably to cross with cultural (or racial) otherness, and at times becomes its unique mode of expression. (Hutcheson and Blackmore 1)

The fifteen essays in the volume explore various permutations of "queerness" in a wide of array of Iberian texts and phenomena. As far as I can tell, this is the book's *lone* mention of the *Chanson de Roland* (which does not even figure in the volume's index), yet here, on the very first page, it is called upon to exemplify everything that is most intransigent and reprehensible in medieval "European" culture; its representation of the Saracens is read as allegory of a long history of the European "othering" of the Iberian peninsula, stretching back to Roman antiquity. Moreover, it is as if, by a logic of association, the volume's focus on sexuality and queerness must inevitably permeate the *Roland* as well. Thus Saracens are necessarily "lusty" and "implicitly defined by a sexuality that exceeds the bounds of a Christian normativity."[5]

Returning to Cohen's article: his main topic, let us note, is "the construction of race in *late medieval France and England*" (114, my emphasis), and his reading of the Middle English text *The Sultan of Babylon* shows a responsible degree of historical contextualization.[6] What concerns me is the collateral damage inflicted along the way. From the outset, Cohen unambiguously assumes "Saracen" to be a racialized category, referring to a people "whose *dark skin* and *diabolical physiognomy* were the Western Middle Ages' most familiar, most exorbitant embodiment of *racial alterity* ... a *racialized figure* of ultimate difference who condensed everything inimical to the fragile Christian selfsame,"[7] with the *Roland*, as we have seen, as a key piece of evidence supporting his claim.[8] His description of the poem's Saracens – like Holsinger's – is likely to ring just familiar enough to casual readers to secure their acceptance of his more general, and questionable, characterizations. And in this, I suggest, it resembles nothing so much as the workings of Orientalist discourse. In the following, I take a passage from Said, replacing "the Orient" with "the *Roland*" and "place" with "text":

> In the system of knowledge about the *Roland*, the *Roland* is less a text than a *topos*, a set of references, a congeries of characteristics, that seems to have its origin in a quotation, or a fragment of a text, or a citation from someone's work on the *Roland*, or some bit of previous imagining, or an amalgam of all of these. Direct observation or circumstantial description of the *Roland* are the fictions presented by writing on the *Roland*, yet invariably these are totally secondary to systematic tasks of another sort. (Said, *Orientalism* 177; modifications mine)

The reproduction of Hutcheson and Blackmore's "lusty, black-skinned" Saracens in Cohen's text ominously gestures towards the "sheer knitted-together strength" and "redoubtable durability" that Said attributed to the citational economy of Orientalism itself (Said, *Orientalism* 6).

If my critique of these essays risks seeming rather churlish, it is important to the extent that Bruce Holsinger and Jeffrey Jerome Cohen are – deservedly – two of the most visible and influential scholars of medieval literature working today. And the fact that both focus primarily on medieval *English* gives their work – let's be honest – a much wider audience than that of any critic working in the field of

Old French. Those who teach or write about the European Middle Ages are much more likely to stumble across their accounts of the *Roland*'s depiction of the Saracens as "ugly and therefore immoral" or "lusty" and "black-skinned" than, for example, Michelle R. Warren's nuanced reading of the way Roland's famous oliphant, an artefact "probably [of] Arabic origin" circulating "with a casual familiarity within Frankish culture," belies "the oppositional ideology motivating Christian aggression, and testif[ies] to Frankish desires at odds with the poem's more strident moral claims" (278), or my own argument that the opening scene of the *Chanson de Roland* represents an offer of *parias* (the tribute money eleventh-century kings of Islamic Spain paid to their Christian rivals) – thus alluding to a cultural complexity and an on-the-ground history of accommodationism that, in our present moment, it might be important not to forget (*Medieval Boundaries* 17–24). Cohen's influence is visible, for example, in an essay on "The Crusaders' Perception of Their Opponents" in a 2005 volume on the Crusades:

> In the *Song of Roland*, for instance, the black skin colour and diabolical physiognomy of the enemy were the surface signs of their perfidious nature. They connoted evil in antithesis to the righteousness of the Christians, and left no doubt that the enemy would be the losers in the end. *In a seminal article, Cohen* has used the discourse of psychoanalysis and postcolonialism to explore further the question of race as it was presented in France and England in the Middle Ages. He investigates why the conventional portrayal of the black, demonic Saracen was perpetuated in western literature long after the religious and territorial ambitions that originally motivated it were relevant. An episode from the fourteenth-century *Grandes Chroniques de France* in which the Saracen foot-soldiers don black horned masks, which make them look like devils, in order to frighten the Christians enables him to expose both the constructed nature of racial difference and the writer's tacit admission of its artificiality. Cohen argues that the fantasy rested on a structure of collective pleasure, in which writers and audiences were complicit, and which explained its perpetuation and its resistance to change. (Jubb 227 and 242nn. 8, 10)

This particular case is all the more surprising since its author is a specialist in medieval French. Though other parts of the article, notably the long "case study" on Saladin, are – once again! – much more highly contextualized and nuanced, this use of the *Roland* to establish the genealogy of a racialism found in a fourteenth-century text suggests that the "structure of collective pleasure, in which writers and audiences were complicit," can play a significant role in modern as well as in medieval compositions.

As a scholar of medieval *French*, I am not ready to cede the ground to this vision of an always-already Orientalist Middle Ages. In *The Chansons de Geste in the Age of Romance*, Sarah Kay demonstrates how radically our understanding of gender relations in Old French epic is altered if we take into account the *entire* corpus of nearly 100 poems, rather than allowing the *Chanson de Roland* to stand in for the whole of the genre. *Mutatis mutandis*, the same point may be made about the epic's depiction of the Other. Even beyond the alternate readings of the *Roland* alluded to above, a turn to lesser-known *chansons de geste* immediately gives a different and more varied picture of medieval Christian-Muslim relations. In *La Prise d'Orange*, the conversion of the beautiful Queen Orable (an example of the widespread "Saracen princess" motif) shows the advantage to be gained not by demonizing Saracens but by seducing them – reversing the binary by sleeping with the enemy. More complexly, in *Gui de Bourgogne*, a younger generation represented by the titular protagonist (Charlemagne's nephew) moves from seeing the Saracens as "undifferentiated enemies to be massacred without remorse" to "individual adversaries with whom one can negotiate" to, finally, "respected allies whom one can trust" (Denis, "Les Sarrasins dans *Gui de Bourgogne*" 182). And in a key subplot of *Raoul de Cambrai*, the Saracen king Corsuble turns to his Christian prisoner-of-war and, addressing him as "Crestiie[n]s, frere," offers him his freedom, lifelong friendship, and twenty pack animals laden with "silk cloth, pure gold, and silver coins" ["dras de soie, de or fin, de deniers" (6744)] in return for military assistance (Kinoshita, "Fraternizing with the Enemy" 696–7). In all these cases, reading beyond the canon reveals an aspect of medieval French epic far more complex than the static racialized and anti-Muslim portraits we have been taught to expect.

If reading beyond the canon uncovers wide-ranging literary treatments of cultural difference, reading beyond the literary reveals the degree of the epic's engagement with the complexities of the medieval Mediterranean. In *La Prise d'Orange*, the description of the Andalusian port of Almería ["Aumarie"] as an "African city" ["cité d'Aufrique" (1302)] across the sea seems at first glance to betray a hopeless ignorance of Mediterranean geography and culture. Though mildly surprising, given the prestige Almerían silks enjoyed in the French feudal imaginary (Kinoshita, "Almería Silk"), it otherwise reinforces assumptions concerning medieval Europe's plodding ignorance of the world beyond its borders. Yet in the twelfth century, Almería was, in a sense, "African" – ruled by the Almoravids and Almohads, two North African-based nomadic confederations. And it was also "across the sea" – the most direct link with the southern Rhone valley being the western Mediterranean maritime routes plied by the Genoese. Seen in historical context, then, a phrase we might initially read as a symptom of medieval geographical ignorance instead becomes a window on the complex network of medieval political and economic culture.

Construed as the literary expression of a medieval "European" society shaped by lord-vassal relations, genealogical politics, and an ideology of conquest and crusade, Old French epic and romance are typically read as idealizing a culture of feudal warfare and chivalric refinement in which merchants (famously omitted from the ideology of the three orders) had little role. By the second half of the twelfth century, however, many members of the French-speaking nobility for whom this new vernacular literature was composed were intimately acquainted with a "Mediterranean" society in which *mercatores* – those who buy and sell – were as familiar a part of the landscape as those *oratores*, *bellatores*, and *laboratores* whose function it was to pray, fight, and work.[9] And in fact, against received notions of epic as the genre of fixed and monological feudal ideals, texts like the *Charroi de Nîmes*, comic prequel to the *Prise d'Orange*, gesture towards the world of commercial practices in which merchants were key agents of interaction and exchange: not marginal but *liminal* figures whose stock in trade is the negotiation of religious, political, and cultural divides. In the *Charroi*, Guillaume Fierebrace, a mighty but landless noble repeatedly snubbed by his overlord, the king, decides to seek his fortune in the Saracen south. Setting his sights on the mighty city of Nîmes, he commandeers a wagon-train from a Muslim peasant and conceals men and arms in barrels intended to convey humble goods to market. Struggling to drive the heavily laden oxcarts through the mud, Guillaume makes his way towards Nîmes to conquer the city not by siege but through this Trojan Horse-like stratagem, posing as an English merchant named Tiacre.[10]

Guillaume's choice of disguise is not accidental: as "professional boundary crossers" (Curtin 6), medieval merchants regularly negotiated linguistic, cultural, and confessional divides. So it is no surprise that, in literature, "merchant" is a favoured disguise for noblemen wishing to travel incognito.[11] Successfully making his way inside the city of Nîmes, Guillaume comes under the scrutiny of its pagan king:

King Otrant called him forth: "Where are you from, *fair friend merchant*?" "Lord, we're from mighty England, from the noble city of Canterbury." "Do you have a wife, *fair friend merchant*?" "Yes, a very noble one – and 18 children …" "What's your name, *fair friend merchant*? "Gentle lord, I am called Tiacre, to be sure." The pagan says: "That's a name belonging to a vile people. Brother Tiacre, what goods are you carrying?"

[Li rois Otran l'en apela avant:
"Don estes vos, *beaus amis marcheant*?
–Sire, nos somes d'Angleterre la grant,
De Cantorbiere, une cité vaillant.
–Avez voz feme, *beaus amis marcheant*?
–Oïl, molt gente, et dis et uit enfanz …"
"Com avez nom, *beaus amis marcheant*?

–Beau tres dolz sire, Tiacre voirement."
Dit li paiens: "C'est nom de pute gent.
Tiacre frere, quel avoir vas menant?"]   (1120–5; 1135–8, emphases added)

The fact that the pagan king thrice addresses the foreigner before him as "beaus amis marcheant" is in itself unremarkable: formulaic repetition is central to Old French *chansons de geste*, particularly in moments of heightened formality such as this. Three things, however, call our attention to this particular occurrence. First, formulae – the readymade units that help the poet fill out the metrical line – typically occupy the first hemistich of the decasyllabic verse (as in the *Chanson de Roland*'s opening line, "*Carles li reis*, nostre emperere magnes"), rather than, as here, the second. Then, the adjective "beaus," appropriate to knights and nobles, seems slightly misplaced applied here to the ill-clad and travel-weary merchant. Finally, there is the incongruity of the scene overall: the comic contradiction between the pagan king's almost involuntary recoil at his interlocutor's proper name – "C'est nom de pute gent" – and his immediate recuperation of that name in the fraternal embrace of a new formula, "Tiacre frere." Conditioned by the paratactic logic of the *chanson de geste*[12] and partaking of the twelfth-century tolerance for "opposites" (Bouchard), Otrant's instantaneous shift from a discourse of commerce to a discourse of crusades and back again, leavened with a vocabulary of feudal fidelity (*amis*) and kinship, gives a crudely comic rendition of the mutually beneficial engagement across confessional lines that historian Brian Catlos, riffing on the notion of *convivencia*, has dubbed *conveniencia*.

It is no coincidence that Otrant's warm indulgence towards "Tiacre, frere" surfaces precisely around his interest in the merchant's commodities. Our protagonist's response to the king's closing question moves us beyond philology, into the realm of medieval material culture. For Guillaume knows exactly what the pagan king wants to hear:

My lord, I'm carrying siglaton, cendal, and bouquerant; fine green and blue woolens, silver hauberks and strong, shiny helmets, sharp spears and good, weighty shields; bright swords with resplendent pommels; ink, sulfur, incense, quicksilver, alum, [graine], pepper, and saffran; skins (bazenne and cordoban) and marten skins – good in cold weather.

[Syglatons, sire, cendaus et bouqueranz
Et escarlate et vert et pers vaillant
Et blans heauberz et forz elmes luisanz,
Tranchanz espiez et bons escuz pesanz,

> Cleres espees au ponz d'or reluisanz …
> Encres et soffres, encens et vis argent,
> Alun et graine et poivres et safran,
> Peleterie, bazenne et cordoan
> Et peaux de martre, qui bones sont en tens.]   (1139–43, 1148–51)

Giving pride of place to silks – a key commodity in the Mediterranean economy (Kinoshita, "Almería Silk") – along with fine woolens, shiny arms, spices, minerals associated with the cloth trade, leathers, and furs, Tiacre's catalogue is a virtual casebook for long-distance luxury trade. If it seems strange that a Canterbury merchant should be stocking such items (the fine woolen "scarlets" are the only commodity on the list that might plausibly come from England[13]), Tiacre's inventory is explained by his itinerary, which includes France, Lombardy, Calabria, Apulia, Sicily, Germany, Romagna, Tuscany, Hungary, Galicia, Poitou, Normandy, England, Scotland, Wales, the Crusader States, and Venice (1190–1202). This list itself is a kind of parodic send-up of all the lands Roland claims to have conquered with his sword Durendal in the *Chanson de Roland* (2322–32) – its excess part of the *Charroi*'s tone of comic exaggeration, pitting Guillaume's daring against Otrant's credulity. The spectacle of a Saracen king eager for the goods purveyed by an itinerant Christian cuts at least two ways: emphasizing Latin Europe's appetite for luxury goods flowing from Islamic lands, on the one hand, while underscoring the dominant role Christian merchants had come to play in Mediterranean trade, on the other.

A look at material history reveals, perhaps, an even greater sense of play. This passage in fact amplifies an earlier one in which "Tiacre" had catalogued the goods he was carrying for the inhabitants of Levardi, a town on the road to Nîmes: "siglaton, purple cloth, and silk; / scarlets and valuable green-and-brown; / sharp spears, hauberks, and shiny helmets, / heavy shields and cutting swords" ["syglatons et dras porpres et pailes / Et escarlates et vert et brun proisable, / Tranchanz espiez et hauberz et verz heaumes, / Escuz pesanz et espees qui taillent" (1064–7)]. Here we easily recognize an abridged version of the list Guillaume will subsequently spin out for Otrant, as if the residents of Levardi, lacking Otrant's wealth and discerning royal eye, were not worth the effort of a full elaboration. One phrase, however, deserves a second look: the "vert et brun" of the second line, above. Editor Claude Lachet renders it "pieces of precious green and brown *cloth*" ["de précieux *tissus* verts et bruns"], a reading that fits seamlessly into semantic sequence with the "purple" (silk) and "scarlet" (wool) of ll. 1064–5.

There is, however, another possible reading of "vert et brun": the green-and-brown ceramics widespread in the western Islamic Mediterranean. More modest than the brilliant lustreware produced in the eastern Islamic world (Pancaroglu), it was a popular export from the Maghreb to Latin Europe, where it eventually gave rise to late medieval and early modern Hispano-Mauresque and Maiolica ware.[14] In 1991, excavations in the Sainte-Barbe quarter of Marseille uncovered an early thirteenth-century potters' district dedicated to the production of "green-and-brown" (Amouric et al. 185) – the missing link between twelfth-century ware imported from North Africa and the fourteenth-century *vert et brun* of papal Avignon. The catalogue of the resulting 1995 exposition, *Le Vert et le brun: de Kairouan à Avignon, céramique du Xe au XVe siècle*, casts the potters of medieval Marseilles as objects of a retrospective civic pride. Credited with transforming a "more than three centuries' old ceramic tradition from the other side of the Mediterranean" to Provençal tastes (11), they are cited as precocious exemplars of Marseilles's turn away from her hinterland towards the wider maritime world.

The popularity of *vert-et-brun* evokes a world of exchange in which sites like Marseilles served as Latin Europe's privileged points of access to the economies and cultures of the medieval Mediterranean.[15] For those in the know, the claim of a would-be Canterbury merchant to be carrying ceramics from the southern Mediterranean if not from Marseilles itself to the city of Nîmes must have sounded like an elaborate joke – a wicked jab at the rubes of Levardi, not to be risked with the likes of King Otrant. Meanwhile, for all its comic reversals, the dialogue between Otrant and "Tiacre" serves as a gentle reminder not to underestimate the degree of cross-confessional exchange in the pre-modern Mediterranean.

Rethinking the medieval Mediterranean as a transitional space – a contact zone of commercial exchange and cross-confessional interaction – puts pressure, in turn, on traditional views of the Middle Ages as a transitional time – those perilous centuries during which the legacy of classical antiquity hung in the balance until being reanimated by the "rebirth" emanating from northern Italy in the mid-fourteenth century. And if one were to seek one figure to stand as a hinge between the Middle Ages and early modernity, that figure might be Petrarch. Called upon "with uncommon regularity" to serve as the first "modern" man (Menocal, *Shards of Love* 7–8), Petrarch the Humanist is credited with establishing a new model for what it means to be an author (Nichols, "Medieval Author" 79). In the history of western civilization, this is seen as an important and, of course, positive step. At the same time, Petrarch's own critical self-consciousness is famously rooted in a privileging of classical antiquity over the Middle Ages and its messy vernacularity. Of course, period boundaries are never so simple; the very loudness of the early Humanists' open rejection of all things medieval, as historian Clifford Backman writes, "should make us wary of its genuineness, for people are seldom so absolutely insistent that they have nothing at all to do with a given thing as when they in fact do" (435). As Menocal puts it, noting the paradoxicality of Petrarch's simultaneous condemnation and embrace of vernacular lyric: "it is a pity that we have clung so much to what Petrarch preached (and indeed, fashioned a whole History from it) and so little to what his poetry tells us about the other History, the one made up of the languages of songs …" (*Shards of Love* 49).

And then there is the Orientalist element in Petrarch's thought. Petrarch, as Nancy Bisaha writes,

> completely dismissed Arab learning as valueless and even harmful to Western read-ers. In a 1370 letter criticizing modern medicine Petrarch seized the opportunity to assail the entire "race" and culture of the Arabs[:] "you know what kind of physi-cians the Arabs are, I know what kind of poets they are. There is nothing more charming, softer, more lax, in a word, more base … I shall scarcely be persuaded that anything good can come from Arabia." (170)

Petrarch's anti-Arabism, as Bisaha points out, may have derived in part from his hatred of scholasticism, heavily informed by Arab philosophy; at the same time, his stereotypes of "the Easterner as weak, effeminate, and corrupt, yet also seduc-tive in his cultural attainments" suggest the influence of the classical tradition.[16] That is to say, whatever Orientalism is discernible in Petrarch's thought may be less a mark of medieval prejudice than the result of his "modern" humanistic endeavours.

In fact, the more closely one looks, the more muddled the lines between East and West, self and other, medieval and early modern, appear. In the sixteenth cen-tury, at least one Italian Humanist's understanding of classical Roman architecture was mediated by his experience of medieval Islamic architecture. In 1526, the Ve-netian Humanist Andrea Navagero, ambassador to the court of Charles V, came to Granada, which had been conquered by the emperor's maternal grandparents, the Catholic Kings Ferdinand and Isabel, thirty-four years before.[17] Touring the Alhambra and its adjacent gardens, Navagero recorded his impressions in a series of letters to his compatriot and fellow Humanist, Giovanni Battista Ramusio – today remembered for his publication of travel narratives, including Marco Polo's *Travels*. (The letters were published in 1563 as *Il viaggio fatto in Spagna e in Francia dal magnifico M. Andrea Navagiero*.) As the architectural historian Cammy Brothers has shown, Navagero's perceptions were strongly mediated by classical accounts of palaces and gardens – in particular, Pliny the Younger's description of his villa at Laurentinum: "Both follow the same sequence, beginning with a descrip-tion of the landscape and site, proceeding to an account of the interior and the views, and concluding with the gardens; and both comment on the tranquility and pleasure afforded by the place." So well do Islamic gardens lend themselves to Pliny's general vocabulary that "Navagero's description of the Alhambra could be detailed and accurate without compromising or even challenging the classical literary paradigm."[18] Navagero's account may in turn have influenced a circle of Humanist friends and architects (including Fra Giocondo, Venetian author of the first illustrated edition of Vitruvius, Raphael, Baldassare Castiglione, and Pietro Bembo) then preoccupied with trying to reconstruct ancient villas based on the same textual sources. Thus the unusual features of the Villa della Torre at Fumane in the Veneto – completed 1562 by an architect and for a patron both likely to have read Navagero's letters – may, Brothers suggests, have indirectly been inspired by the Alhambra.[19] In the last quarter of the sixteenth century, Spaniards "saw Vitruvian features in the mezquitas of Córdoba and Seville, and as a result concluded that their origin must be Roman rather than Moorish, or read features of buildings they knew to be Muslim – the entry halls of Moorish buildings in Granada, Moorish plaster ceiling ornamentation – as Vitruvian" (94). One could hardly find a more graphic argument for what historian Richard Bulliet calls "Islamo-Christian civilization" – a rereading of the "prolonged and fateful intertwining" of Latin Christianity and Islam as "sibling societies" born of late antiquity, "enjoying sovereignty in neighboring geographical regions and following parallel historical trajectories."[20] In this perspective, the much-vaunted Humanist recovery of the classical world central to conventional histories of "Western civilization" turns out to have been enabled, to a much greater degree than generally recognized, through an encounter with the Islamic Mediterranean.

This confusion was no one-time aberration. At the turn of the twelfth century, in the wake of their conquest of Jerusalem, the victorious knights of the First Crusade took the Dome of the Rock, built by the Umayyad caliph in 691, to be the Holy of Holies or the Temple of the Lord and the al-Aqsa mosque (also late seventh century) to be the Temple and Palace of Solomon.[21] And in the late nineteenth century, as Karla Mallette has described, the medieval pleasure palaces dotting the outskirts of Palermo were assumed to belong to the period of Islamic rule, stretching from the early ninth to the late eleventh centuries. Only with Michele Amari's deciphering of the inscriptions of La Zisa were these buildings revealed to be the products of Latin Christian rule – built in the twelfth century by the son and grandson of the first Norman king, Roger II.[22] Repeatedly from the twelfth through nineteenth centuries, in other words, the biblical and classical traditions at the core of "western" civilization have been imagined through and confounded with monuments of religious and secular architecture from the Islamic world.

Following up on the messiness rather than the rectilinearity of period divides and their effect on the history of Orientalist representation on occasion yields some rather surprising results. It is easy to assume, for example, that *morismas* – the theatrical spectacles featuring mock battles between Moors and Christians, brought to Spanish America in the late sixteenth or early seventeenth century and still celebrated annually in Zacatecas, Mexico – date to the high period of the Spanish reconquest. Scholarly tradition holds that the first documented battle took place in 1150, at the marriage of Petronilla of Aragon and Count Ramón Berenguer IV of Catalonia. However, these accounts, as Max Harris has shown, may all be traced to a single 1855 text that cites as its source an unpublished manuscript from the early part of that century. Accounts of mock battles between Moors and Christians are in fact rare before 1492, with "the first evidence of a sustained tradition of local performance" being the Corpus Christi processions in fifteenth-century Barcelona:

> I am aware of very few accounts of mock battles between Moors and Christians before 1492. The two earliest reports depend on secondhand nineteenth-century citations of manuscripts now lost, and the first evidence of a sustained tradition of local performances comes from the fifteenth-century Barcelona Corpus Christi procession, which regularly included a dance of Turkish infantry. (Max Harris 31–2 and 252n.4)

As in the case of Petrarch's anti-Arabism, these stagings of Christian-"Saracen" violence characterize, as it turns out, the transitional bridge between the late Middle Ages and early modernity. Taken together, these examples demonstrate the complex interrelation between periodization and the assertion of Christian-Muslim difference: where "common sense" casts medieval Europe as a time-space of religious rigidity and intolerance, historical and philological investigation sometimes yields a counterimage of "riotous pluralities and often-chaotic poetics" (Menocal, *Shards of Love* 10) that demand new models of conceptualization.

III.

In January 2008, an item identified as a nineteenth-century "French claret jug," its surface "relief cut with mythological animals, birds, and vegetable motifs," came up for sale at a provincial auction house in Somerset, England. Initially valued at between £100 and £200, the object ultimately sold for £220,000 – a good deal more than the original estimate but a good deal less than the £5 million at which it was subsequently appraised. For despite the catalogue description, the vessel turned out to be no "French claret jug" at all, but an eleventh-century Fatimid rock crystal ewer, with a "silver gilt and enamel mounting, possibly of Austro-Hungarian origin" – one of only five in existence (L. Harris).

On the one hand, it is unsurprising that the Somerset auctioneers didn't know what they had: what could be more obscure than a vase – however wondrous – carved in eleventh-century Egypt? On the other hand, the ewer would have been instantly recognizable to anyone with even a glancing familiarity with the Islamic decorative arts: similar objects are given pride of place in the Louvre, the Victoria & Albert, and the treasury of San Marco (*Trésors fatimides* 140–2; 231; Blair and Bloom 252–3; Ettinghausen et al. 206–7). Elsewhere I have used the so-called Eleanor vase – another rock crystal vessel (Sasanian rather than Fatimid) mounted in a medieval European frame – to exemplify Latin Europe's simultaneous appreciation and appropriation of the culture of the non-Christian East (Kinoshita, *Medieval Boundaries* 6–7). The Somerset sale, it seems to me, wonderfully metaphorizes the modern misprision of this medieval mode of *translatio*: the silver and enamel frame, "possibly of Austro-Hungarian origin," marks the ewer as European, obscuring the medieval Islamic origins of the object thus "contained."

At the current moment, our critical vocabulary is poorly equipped to conceptualize material and literary objects of multiple provenances, often the products of cultures which prized eclecticism as an expression of political or civilizational strength rather than of aesthetic weakness. Exemplary here is a monument like the Cappella Palatina, the celebrated palatine chapel of the Norman palace in Palermo: a Latin Christian structure whose walls are gilded with Byzantine-style mosaics, topped with a honeycombed *muqarnas* ceiling of Islamic provenance and design. Modern criticism typically cannibalizes the building – treating the mosaics in studies of Byzantine art and the *muqarnas* ceilings in studies of Islamic art, each without reference to the other.[23] Only recently, in works such as William Tronzo's *The Cultures of His Kingdom*, do the political, cultural, and ideological ramifications of this aesthetic of hybridity or juxtaposition emerge, belatedly, as themselves *bon à penser*.

Menocal's vision of the literatures of medieval Iberia represents an early and insistent reconfiguration of literary studies in ways that resonate with recent work in (for example) medieval Mediterranean art and architectural history.[24] The new questions and perspectives enabled by this reterritorialization of disciplinary and conceptual fields remind us that, seen from the vantage point of world history,

> The rise of the West ... no longer seems quite the inevitable development it has widely been assumed to have been, nor does Western civilization appear to have been unique. The line that runs from the Greeks to the Renaissance to the Industrial Revolution is finally an optical illusion, the product of a highly selective historical imagination. (Hodgson 312)

As Garth Fowden writes, "There are roads out of antiquity that do not lead to the Renaissance; and although none avoids eventual contact with the modern West's technological domination, the rapidly changing balance of power in our world is forcing even Western scholars to pay more attention to non-Latin perspectives on the past" (Fowden 9).

NOTES

1 See Mallette, *The Kingdom of Sicily*, and, on the multilingual tombstone, *L'età normanna e sueva in Sicilia. Mostra storico-documentatia e bibliografica* (Palermo, 1994), cited in "Palerme, Eglise de Saint-Michel des Andalous, Inscriptions funéraires," in *La Méditerranée entre pays d'Islam et monde latin: textes et documents*, 148–9.

2 The discussion of the *Chanson de Roland* draws on Kinoshita, "Political Uses and Responses."

3 See *The Journal of Medieval and Early Modern Studies* 31: 1 (2001) – a special issue on "Race and Ethnicity" edited by Thomas Hahn.

4 Kinoshita, "Political Uses and Responses," esp. pp. 272–3.

5 In comparison, Said's characterization in *Orientalism* is judiciously restrained. In the *Chanson de Roland*, he notes, "the worship of Saracens is portrayed as embracing Mahomet *and* Apollo" (61); its author – like other pre- and early modern poets including Ariosto, Milton, Shakespeare, and Cervantes – drew on the "prodigious cultural repertoire" associated with the East (63), representing "the Orient and Islam ... as outsiders having a special role to play *inside* Europe" (71).

6 The *Sultan of Babylon*, Cohen notes, was "probably written around 1400, the year that Geoffrey Chaucer died" (134), a decade after the 1390 crusade to Tunis that included "a contingent of English nobles" (133). For his reading of the text, see "On Saracen Enjoyment," 125–36.

7 Cohen, "On Saracen Enjoyment" 114–15, emphasis added. The second half of the quotation seems to be Cohen's characterization of the representation of the Saracen in Peter the Venerable's *Liber contra sectam sive haeresim Saracenorum*.

8 Never mind that the first example Cohen cites, "from the spurious late-eleventh- or early-twelfth-century 'Letter of [Byzantine emperor] Alexius Comnenus to Count Robert of Flanders Imploring His Aid,'" shows no trace of racialization *per se*: "in the Holy Land Saracens circumcise Christian boys and 'spill the blood of circumcision right into the baptismal fonts and compel them to urinate over them'" (Cohen, "On Saracen Enjoyment" 114 and 136n.4). Cohen draws this quotation from John Boswell, *Christianity, Social Tolerance, and Homosexuality* (279–80, 367–9).

9 On the three orders, see Duby; on French vernacular literature, see Kinoshita, *Medieval Boundaries*, 1–12; on Mediterranean society, see Goitein.

10 Altmann and Psaki read the comedy in this incongruous scene as a critique of crusade ideology.

11 Examples include Floire in the mid-twelfth-century romance *Floire et Blancheflor* (Kinoshita, *Medieval Boundaries* 89–90) and Saladin in *Decameron* 10.9, who, wanting to

gauge for himself the extent of western European preparations for the Third Crusade, comes to Pavia disguised as a Cypriot merchant on his way to Paris. See Kinoshita, "Noi siamo" 41–60.

12 Compare the *Chanson de Roland*, when the titular protagonist reacts to his nomination to the rearguard of Charlemagne's army with both exaggerated courtesy (lines 753–4) and unmitigated rage (lines 762–3) in two successive *laisses*.

13 Scarlets were not necessarily coloured red (the name of the colour deriving from the cloth and not vice versa). It seems to have a double etymology, from the Germanic "scaerlaken" (sheared cloth), influenced by the Arabic *siklatun*, the name of a silk by association since those from Spain were rich red, dyed with kermes (Munro 212–15).

14 Vert-et-brun was a variant of the tin-glaze opaque wares first produced in Iraq, in imitation of imported Chinese white porcelain (Watson 37–8).

15 Note the numbers of Jews from Marseille who found their way to Egypt – some attaining high position in the Jewish community (as in the case of Anatoli, head judge of Alexandria) despite an ignorance of Arabic. Goitein, *A Mediterranean Society* 1:53, 67.

16 Bisaha, *Creating East and West* 170. On the proto-racism common in the Graeco-Roman world from the fifth century B.C.E., see Isaac, *The Invention of Racism* 1.

17 The conclusion of the siege of Granada, Ferdinand and Isabel's expulsion of their kingdoms' Jews, and their funding of Columbus's first voyage form part of the world-historical moment Menocal reads elegiacally, as a moment of foreclosure, rather than proleptically, as the inauguration of modernity.

18 Cammy Brothers, "The Renaissance Reception of the Alhambra" 81. See also 79–80, 81–2, 92–4.

19 These features included its location on an incline and its "formal, architectural uses of water, irrigation, and natural supply." Brothers 94.

20 Bulliet 10, 15. For "twin siblings," see Samir Amin, *Eurocentrism* 26.

21 On crusader misprisions, see Deborah Howard, *Venice and the East* 200.

22 Karla Mallette, *The Kingdom of Sicily*, 17. In the mid-sixteenth century, on the other hand, the Dominican Leandro Alberti, in his *Descrittione di tutta l'Italia e Isole pertinenti ad essa*, had described La Zisa's symmetry and geometrical relations in ways that "suggest an attitude to these Islamic ruins akin to that adopted by Renaissance architects to Roman ruins" (Brothers, "The Renaissance Reception" 82–3).

23 For a rare photograph showing the two parts at the same time, see Jonathan M. Bloom, *Arts of the City Victorious*, Illustration 158.

24 See *Late Antique and Medieval Art of the Mediterranean World*, ed. Eva R. Hoffman.

3 Linguistic Difference, the Philology of Romance, and the Romance of Philology*

SIMON GAUNT

Scholarship on romance, like so much scholarship on medieval literature, has been deeply entrenched in modern narratives of the emergence of national literary histories. Widely regarded as an index of French courtly sophistication that other cultures could import, by translation or adaptation, in order to emulate French models, romance has traditionally been used by literary historians – whether consciously or unconsciously – to demonstrate the centrality and primacy of French literature and culture to European vernacular literary culture more generally.[1] The translation or adaptation of French literature undoubtedly was central to the emergence of medieval vernacular literary cultures in English, German, Spanish and Italian at least, but traditional approaches beg a fair few questions and have also led to the occlusion of a lot of evidence – and a good few texts – that might encourage us to tell the story differently. One obvious question is that of the "Frenchness" of the French language itself; for French was widely used outside France, both as a literary and as a non-literary language, whether France is understood as the medieval kingdom of France or the modern hexagon, and it would be erroneous therefore to assume its use necessarily connotes an association with France.[2] Indeed, several of the earliest landmarks of "French" literature were either composed outside France, in England for example, or owe their transmission, partially or substantially, to manuscripts produced outside France, notably in England and Italy.[3] Similarly, texts that imitate supposedly French models may not do so slavishly, but rather in order to establish an independent tradition, even to contest elements of their "French" sources, rather than simply reproduce them, within a literary context that is far more multilingual and fluid than has sometimes been realized. Powerful cases in point here include: the frequently independent English tradition of romance in French; an Occitan and Hispanic trajectory of romance that quickly diverges from and often contests the French tradition; the substantial Italian transmission of romances in French such as the *Roman de Troie* or *Tristan en prose*, a tradition of transmission that is inextricably imbricated with translation into Italian and anthologization.[4]

The nationalist orientation of most modern literary historical and philological accounts of medieval vernacular literature has increasingly come under scrutiny in recent years. María Rosa Menocal offers a particularly eloquent critique in her chapter "The Inventions of Philology" in *Shards of Love* (91–141). It is paradoxical, she suggests, that literary history has become so entrenched in offering national narratives when many of the founding texts in the discipline of Romance philology (from Dante's *De Vulgari eloquentia* to Auerbach's *Mimesis*) share a utopian commitment to universality, to the movement of texts across borders, and to cultural traffic between languages:

> The strong texts in this Romance philological tradition are clearly marked by an indifference – or often a palpable hostility – to the parallel but opposite features in the national literary traditions: the highly temporal and developmental perspective (how France became France from the ruins and from the primitive dark age); the limitation to a single language, with others in subsidiary positions of "influence"; the neat separation of historical moments that divides in virtually absolute and epistemological terms the "medieval" from the "modern," since the division in national history and consciousness runs along the same fault line. (109)

The tendency to concentrate on a single language or tradition in order to place it centre-stage and then to put other languages and traditions in subordinate positions is of course a direct result of what Hans Ulrich Gumbrecht calls philological desire. Philology, Gumbrecht argues, is driven by a desire for the past, or rather for a particular version of the past, by a desire to retrieve and restore a text, to preserve it, but also to transpose it into the present time and place through critical editions that will situate it in a coherent narrative of the past in relation to the present (*The Powers of Philology* 2–4; 6–7); this in turn entails a clear identification with the text and/or with its supposed author as belonging to the same cultural tradition as the philologist's broader object of study (26). Because post-medieval literary culture has tended to be monolingual and associated largely with so-called national literatures, the overwhelming desire of modern scholarship has been to situate earlier texts in relation to monolingual literary histories, or at the very least to view them as part of their pre-history. There is much to disentangle here if we wish better to understand medieval textual culture, how it is often rooted in multilingualism, rather than in national literary traditions that do not begin to come fully into being until the early modern period. We need to strip away suppositions (if not to say prejudices) that derive from modern scholarly traditions that are rooted, whether consciously or unconsciously, in nineteenth-century national and imperial ideologies.[5]

One important element of an alternative, less Franco-centric history of medieval romance that has yet to be written is the use of hybridized literary languages. This is of course a particularly strong feature of the transmission of French texts in Italy: numerous literary manuscripts survive that mix Italian and French forms to varying degrees.[6] If Romance philology as a discipline has been partly to blame for some of our misapprehensions concerning medieval textual culture (with, for example, its proclivity for tables that compare the morphology of different romance languages in relation to Latin, thereby reifying clear-cut boundaries between languages and dismissing forms that do not fit into the tables as "incorrect"), its methods (whether these be linguistic, codicological, or literary) must surely offer the key to unlocking some of the mysteries of medieval textual production and reception. But rather than dismissing the hybrid language of many so-called Franco-Italian texts as an index either of textual corruption or of authorial or scribal incompetence, as textual criticism in both France and Italy has sometimes tended to do,[7] in recent years scholars have begun to see the linguistic features of these texts as far more knowing and purposeful, as deliberate stylistic choices, marking simultaneously similarity and difference, proximity and distance, identification and uncanny foreignness.[8] Analogies with modern creoles are of course suggestive here, particularly in the linguistic melting pot that was the Mediterranean, since trade inevitably brought a range of Romance idioms into contact with each other (as well as with other languages), especially but by no means exclusively in the key trading ports of Catalonia, Southern Occitania, Genoa, Venice, Naples, Cyprus, Palestine and so on. It is also worth remembering that because French was widely spoken at various points in time in Naples, Sicily, Puglia, Morea, Cyprus, Antioch and Palestine, it was effectively a Mediterranean, not just a Northern European language.

French and Italian are not the only two Romance languages that become hybridized in the production of literary texts. There are several striking *chansons de geste* that mix French and Occitan in a manner that seems quite deliberate;[9] Occitan may also be mixed with Catalan. Occitan texts from or circulating in Catalonia have until comparatively recently received philological attention only from those whose primary interest is in Catalan literature, and they have received virtually no critical attention. However, Catherine Léglu's recent book, *Multilingualism and Mother Tongue,* shows the extent to which there was a vibrant multilingual literary vernacular culture in medieval Catalonia and Aragon that entailed a complex mixture of French, Occitan and Latin, a literary culture that was concurrent with the development of Catalan and the ongoing use in some places of Arabic and also Hebrew.

The short verse narrative *Frayre de Joy et Sor de Plaser* is thought to have been composed in Catalonia in the fourteenth century, but this supposition is not, as far as I can see, grounded in hard and fast evidence.[10] On linguistic grounds at least, the text could equally well date from the thirteenth century, and, as we will see, its place of composition could equally well be Occitania. Interestingly, the text was originally classified in the modern era as Catalan and has only comparatively recently been included in the Occitan corpus;[11] it may therefore be taken as a symptom of what Léglu calls a "courteous border dispute" (102).

Frayre de Joy is related to the "sleeping beauty" theme that is common in European and non-European folklore,[12] but adds an explicit – and frankly creepy – sexual twist. A prologue rejects the use of French in favour of an unspecified alternative language. The exceptionally beautiful daughter of the Emperor of Gint-Senay, Sor de Plaser, dies unexpectedly ("La puncela mori .I. dia" [26]) and her grief-stricken parents, unable to bear the thought of burying her beautiful body and precisely because they have read tales of false deaths, place her body in a tower that can be reached only by a magically guarded bridge of glass which only they can cross. The body fails to decompose but rather retains its beauty, and as the nation goes into mourning the story attracts attention from far and wide. One youth, Frayre de Joy, who is the son of the king of the (fictional) kingdom of Florianda, is smitten by the tales he hears of the dead beauty and enlists the help of Virgil, a well-known Roman magician, in order to gain access to the tower. Unable to believe that one so lovely could be dead, he imagines a smile on her face ("E fo li semblant c'un dolç ris / Li fases" [212–13]) and, interpreting this as encouragement, he takes a series of increasingly intimate liberties with the body, as a result of which Sor de Plaser becomes pregnant. Much to her parents' shock and horror, she gives birth to a baby boy whom they find feeding on her apparently still lifeless breast. They assume a miracle (only a bird or the Holy Ghost could have entered the tower! [284]), and in response to their prayers, Sor de Plaser raises one hand slightly, but remains otherwise dead to the world. At this point, a jay – not just gifted with the power of speech, but an exceptional linguist to boot – appears with a curative herb. He has been sent by Frayre de Joy, having been acquired from Virgil, who in turn had been sent the bird by Prester John. The jay undertakes the delicate task of explaining to Sor de Plaser what has happened and of pressing Frayre de Joy's suit. Initially furious at what has happened to her, Sor de Plaser is quite clear that she has been raped, but she eventually relents when she realizes that Frayre would be quite a catch as a husband and that marrying him legitimizes her baby. Still the path of true love does not quite run smooth: the jay is captured on his way back to Frayre and offered as a present to a lady by her enamored knight. But the jay convinces her that to stand in the way of a courtly go-between is a cardinal courtly sin and so she releases him to complete his mission. All's well that ends well, and there is a splendid double wedding, attended by Virgil, Prester John and the Pope.

This zany text has stylistic and thematic affinities with the Old French Breton *lai* and romance, but it also imports elements from medieval traditions concerning

Virgil and Prester John.[13] Furthermore, like the Old French Breton *lais* (Marie de France's, for instance) with their insistence on the relation or non-relation of three vernacular languages to each other (Celtic, English, and French), *Frayre de Joy* works hard to thematize linguistic difference both on and within its diegetic frame. Its language is basically the *koinè* of literary Occitan, but with frequent Catalan forms and graphies. This leads Catherine Léglu to note that "the poem is composed in an artificial literary idiom, a hybrid mixture of Occitan and Catalan" (100). However, this perhaps needs some qualification in that the linguistic evidence from the two surviving manuscripts, both of which are of Catalan provenance, could equally well suggest that this is an Occitan text for which all surviving evidence of transmission is Catalan, rather than a text composed in a hybrid mixture of Occitan and Catalan;[14] but I would add that literary Occitan itself was already "an artificial literary idiom," one that is notoriously impervious to the dialectical and regional variation we know existed in Occitania and one that had international currency from a very early stage.[15] So there is no doubt that the language of *Frayre de Joy* as it has survived is marked in relation to standard literary Occitan. Léglu's reading of *Frayre de Joy e Sor de Plaser* (one of only two sustained readings in print I know of, the other being by Suzanne Thiolier-Méjean) highlights the text's attention to interculturality – what she calls, using the work of Hélène Cixous, the *entredeux* – and, as she suggests, the text foregrounds linguistic difference throughout. Léglu concludes that "it is tempting to read *Frayre de Joy e Sor de Plaser* as an allegorical narrative of an aggressive conquest, followed by diplomatic activity and an official alliance" (111–12), and she suggests that the text's play on language contributes to this. Léglu is of course right to stress the importance of consent and force to any interpretation of *Frayre de Joy*, and the deftly comic tone of parts of the text fails to occlude entirely just how creepy and sinister Frayre de Joy's necrophilic and predatory heterosexual desire is. However, I nonetheless want to approach the text with some slightly different questions. If the story works to mystify the true nature of Frayre de Joy's coercion of Sor de Plaser, what is the nature of the fantasy it seeks to put in place in order to do this? And how does this relate to the thematization of language within the text? In sketching an answer to these questions I hope to show how this text's treatment of language contributes to a commentary on the romance tradition on which it draws.

Whenever the language of a medieval text seems hybridized by modern standards of linguistic correctness, the question arises as to the extent to which medieval writers, transmitters and readers thought in terms of hard and fast distinctions between languages, particularly between Romance languages. Thus, particularly in the twelfth century, when we have substantial surviving traditions only in French and Occitan among the Romance vernaculars, authors tend often not to refer to the Romance languages in which they composed as "French" or

"Occitan," but to use generic terms such as *romanz* that effectively work to contrast the vernacular with Latin.[16] Was the only important distinction, then, for medieval authors, transmitters and readers that between Latin and the vernacular, with differences between similar and cognate Romance languages that seem vital to us simply paling into insignificance in comparison? Furthermore, Romance languages frequently share the same lexis, with similar grammatical structures, sometimes even phonology and verb morphology. Thus Alison Cornish has suggested that in Italy in the thirteenth and fourteenth centuries scribes were simply copying French texts in a form they felt they and their readers could best understand, giving their material a "linguistic dress" that varied according to context: "the instability of linguistic form suggests that scribes were constantly engaged in subtle, perhaps unconscious acts of translation even when they thought they were simply transcribing" (*Vernacular Translation* 54). In talking about hybrid or hybridized languages, is one then imposing upon texts a sense of linguistic difference that simply is not relevant?

In fact, a considerable body of medieval evidence suggests a strong awareness in some quarters and in some contexts of the difference between different Romance languages, which in turn suggests that texts that mix forms from different languages may be doing so deliberately. Most famously in *De Vulgari Eloquentia*, a text that Menocal and others take as foundational for Romance philology, Dante distinguishes quite explicitly between different Romance vernaculars; and he is by no means the only medieval literary theorist to do so. It is also clear from the handful of treatises composed between the late twelfth and early fourteenth centuries with a view to teaching native speakers of Catalan and Italian how to write correct Occitan (so that they might compose poetry in it) that distinguishing between similar Romance vernaculars was vital to successful literary endeavour,[17] while comments on the relative value or aesthetic properties of different Romance languages make it clear they were considered distinct from each other.[18] But perhaps the most eloquent and interesting evidence concerning linguistic difference is the troubadour Raimbaut de Vaqueiras's famous multi-lingual *descort* (c. 1190).

A *descort* (literally discord) is a lyric that uses a different metrical scheme for each stanza. Raimbaut begins in Occitan, his own language, but announces the conceit of the poem quite explicitly:

> Eras quan vey verdeyar
> Pratz e vergiers e boscatges,
> Vuelh un descort comensar
> D'amor, per q'ieu vauc aratges;
> Q'una dona.m sol amar,
> Mas camjatz l'es sos coratges,

Per qu'ieu fauc dezacordar
Los motz e.ls sos e.ls lenguatges.   (XVI, 1–8)

[Now when I see the meadows, gardens and woods growing green, I wish to start
a *descort* concerning love, since I am discountenanced by it; for a lady who used to
love me has changed heart towards me, which is why I wish to create discord in the
rhymes, the tune and the languages.]

This is the prelude to stanzas in Italian, French, Gascon, and Galician-Portuguese,
all lamenting his lady's cold shoulder. The concluding stanza then moves through
all five languages, picking up rhymes from the corresponding stanzas in each
language:

Belhs Cavaliers, tant es car
Lo vostr' onratz senhoratges (Occitan)
Que cada jorno m'esglaio.
Oi me lasso! Que farò (Italian)
Si sele que j'ai plus chiere
Me tue, ne sai por quoi? (French)
Ma dauna, he que dey bos
Ni per cap santa Quitera, (Galician-Portuguese)
Mon corasso m'avetz treito
E mot gen favlan furtado. (Gascon)   (XVI, 41–50)

[Fair Knight, your powerful lordship is so dear to me that I am distraught all the time.
Alas, what shall I do if the one I cherish above all others slays me and I know not
why? My lady, by the faith I owe you and the head of Saint Quiteria, you have taken
my heart from me and stolen it with your sweet speech.]

The poem's conceit depends, of course, on its audience being able to discern
clear phonological, syntactic and morphological differences among the five Romance vernaculars that are used, but this is not the only reason why the poem
is significant. Its most authoritative modern editor, Joseph Linskill, notes that
"Raimbaut's primary purpose was no doubt to display his linguistic and artistic
virtuosity, and the thought betrays a certain poverty of invention, reflected in the
repetition of ideas," though he goes on to suggest that "such repetitions may
however be deliberate" (196) without elaborating what he thought Raimbaut's
purpose might have been.

It seems clear that linguistic difference is being used by Raimbaut de Vaqueiras
to figure or parallel other types of difference (or discord): formal, sexual, and
emotional.[19] Whereas in another multilingual poem attributed to Raimbaut – the

tenso "Domna, tant vos ai preiada" (III), in which a Genoese-speaking lady sends an Occitan-speaking suitor away with a flea in his ear, rejecting his *proenzalesco*, which is to say both his Provençal ways and his Provençal language – linguistic difference is used to underscore the binary structure of the dialogue,[20] in "Eras quan vey verdeyar" linguistic difference is more layered. Indeed, the *descort* presupposes (and in the last stanza instantiates) a romance community of languages which, though united by shared Latinity, is nonetheless fractured by discernible internal differences.

With this in mind, let us now turn to the opening of *Frayre de Joy*:

> Sitot Francess a bel lengatge
> No-m pac en re de son linatge.
> Car son *erguylos* ses merce,
> E-z *erguyll* ab mi no-s cove,
> Car entre-ls francs humils ay apres;
> Per qu'eu no *vull* parlar frances.
> Car una dona ab cors gen
> M'a *fayt* de prets un mandamen,
> Qu'una faula tot prim li rim,
> Sens cara rima e mot prim.
> Car pus leus, se *dits*, n'es apresa
> Per mans plasenters ab franquesa,
> Per mans *ensenyats* e cortes,
> Don faray sos mans, que obs m'es
> E diray o tot *anaxi*
> Con la dona ha dit a mi,
> Que mas ni *menys* no-n pensaray.   (1–17, Catalan forms in italics)

[Although the Frenchman has a fair language, I do not like at all their sort, for they are proud and merciless, and pride doesn't suit me at all, for I was educated among the modest and the free (*francs*); and that is why I do not want to speak French (*frances*). But a fair lady has given me a precious commission to rhyme a tale for her swiftly, without complicated rhymes or over-subtle words so that it might be learned for recitation more quickly by many pleasant and honest (*ab franquesa*) people, as well as by many educated and courtly people. Wherefore will I execute her commission and speak exactly as the lady commanded me to, without further ado.]

The difference between French and the language the poet uses here instead is primarily ethical and therefore ideological, not because there is anything intrinsically bad about French as a language, but rather because of the overweening pride of the French themselves. We have here a classic example of what Saussure was to call the arbitrary nature of the sign; and as if to drive this home, the poet plays on the etymology of *Francess/frances*, by describing those who are not French as *francs* and praising their *franquesa*. Reflexes of *franc* are thus made to have both positive and negative value. The mother tongue of neither the poet nor his putative patroness is clear. But already in these lines there are Catalan forms; and as Léglu suggests, the Catalan context of transmission, combined with the fact that the concluding lines of the poem suggest a Catalan political context, might hint that one of them at least is Catalan (100–1), which in turn suggests a further implicit element of cultural and linguistic dissonance here: *caras rimas* and *mot prim*, which are specifically excluded by the lady's mandate, are by and large positively marked stylistic features in the Occitan lyric tradition, stigmatized only by those with inadequate poetic training or low expectations.[21] I would not go so far as the text's most recent editor, Suzanne Thiolier-Méjean, who posits (on the basis of thematic elements she identifies with Old French narrative texts and a couple of Gallicisms in the text) a lost French original to an Occitan text that is then reworked by a Catalan scribe (*Une Belle au Bois Dormant* 153). But it is nonetheless clear that the text as we know it holds at least three romance cultures in play with and against each other, linguistically, formally, and thematically.[22]

If the narrative does have its origin in French subject matter, its narration in Occitan may already suggest an outside or sideways look at the story; in which case the text's ironic account of Frayre de Joy's "courtship" of Sor de Plaser and of her eventual acceptance of his suit may in fact be a way of satirizing an inadequate "French" understanding of courtliness. Indeed, several elements in the text point to a critical evaluation of the story's mystification of Frayre de Joy's aggressive and coercive behaviour, and all relate in one way or another to the question of language.

First, and most obviously, the names of the two main protagonists – Frayre de Joy and Sor de Plaser – suggest a linguistic symmetry between them (Frayre/Sor; joy/pleasure) that destines each for the other in a quasi-grammatical manner, a point which is not lost on Sor de Plaser when she is being persuaded by the jay to marry Frayre:

> Ffrayre de Joy, Sor de Plaser,
> Anc noms no s'avengron tan be:
> Lo meu nom ab lo seu s'ave
> Mils que nuyll nom que hanc fos.   (539–42)

[Brother of Joy, Sister of Pleasure, never have two names been better-suited to each other: my name suits his better than that of any man who ever lived.]

It is as if a love affair between words is invoked to supplement à love affair that never took place because the boy was a necrophilic rapist and the girl already a corpse incapable of giving consent. Suzanne Thiolier-Méjean argues that the characters' names play on the convention of *senhals* in troubadour poetry whereby a lady or a male friend is designated using a code-name or "sign" (*Une Belle au Bois Dormant* 125). In the lyric, however, ladies are often designated using a masculine *senhal*, and the gender symmetry of Frayre and Sor makes the device here qualitatively different. If Frayre de Joy and Sor de Plaser's love is primarily a love of/ between words, or grounded in letters – indeed, one might even say a philological love, if one follows Gumbrecht's etymological definition of philology as a love of words (2) – this is reinforced by a twist on the common device of the exchange of rings. After Frayre has had his way with Sor, he notices the ring on her finger:

> E tenia al dit un anell
> Escrit ab letres que desien
> Aycells que legir les sabien:
> "Anell suy de Sor de Plaser,
> Qui m'aura leys pora aver,
> Per amor, ab plazer viven,
> Can ach de joy pres complimen." (230–6)

[And she had on her finger a ring on which letters were engraved for those who knew how to read: "I am Sor de Plaser's ring: he who has me can have her, with love and lively pleasure, when he has had his fill of joy."]

Oblivious to the intense irony of any pleasure here – for Sor de Plaser at least – being far from "lively" in the strictest sense of the term, Frayre takes the ring and exchanges it for his own, which has a complementary inscription:

> "Anell de Frayre de Joy suy,
> Qui m'aura leys amaray,
> No jes a guisa de vilan,
> Mas com a fill de rey presan." (240–3)

["I am Frayre de Joy's, and I will love whoever has me, not in the manner of a peasant, but rather in the manner of the son of a king."]

That Frayre de Joy and Sor de Plaser are destined for each other thereby becomes inscribed on their bodies "for those who know how to read," but Frayre's response to the ring and its inscription may equally be seen as a misreading of the letters on the ring in that he takes the future verbs *aura* and *pora* prophetically and literally, suppressing any agency on Sor's part in favour of powers attributed to the rings themselves. This misreading perhaps has a well-known intertext in Perceval's misreading of his mother's injunction, in Chrétien de Troyes's *Conte du graal*, to exchange rings with a damsel who pleases him: he subsequently does so forcibly with an unwilling damsel, with disastrous consequences when her *ami* thinks she has betrayed him as a result (514–18; 597–791). In each instance, the oafish young man's "gift" of a ring is a courtly smoke-screen to his failure to take account of what the object of his affections may want. The rings may signal Sor's tacit and passive consent,[23] but they may equally well be read as underscoring the fact that her body is appropriated by Frayre without her being consulted, a point that is emphasized when the jay later draws her attention to the ring on her finger, which is now said to read simply "De Frayre de Joy suy" (517), as if the ring has become a bejeweled luggage tag.

Significantly, the inscription on Sor de Plaser's ring also entails reflection on the relationship between joy and pleasure, suggesting that joy must complement pleasure. This reciprocal but rhetorical relationship between joy and pleasure returns under a number of guises in the text:

> Puxs s'en partex forsats, sospiran,
> Soven guardan tench sa via,
> Per ço c'or era l'ora e-l dia
> Que y devia esser l'emperayre;
> Pero soven, no tardan gayre,
> Tornava lay son rich joy prendre,
> Que no volgra donar ni vendre,
> Ne camjar per altre sa via;
> Per ço dits ver tot hom qui-l dia:
> "Plaser ama, plaser desira,
> Pesar fay regart, plaser guia." (244–54)

[Then [Frayre] was obliged to leave, sighing and often turning round as he went on his way, for now was the day and time when the emperor was to visit; but he returned often and without delay to take his rich joy there, for he would not have given or sold or changed his destination for another: this is why men speak the truth when they say: "Pleasure loves, pleasure desires; while worry makes one weary, pleasure guides."]

> Le savis dits: "En corts reyal
> Qui so que desira no pren
> Cant pot, apres pauc s'en repen
> E no y pot hora tornar";

So feits vos que-us veyam preyar
Sol aytant qu'el, vostre plaser,
Vos pusc ab joy viva veser.
Pus mort ab gran trabayll vos vi.   (471–8)

[The wise man says: "He who does not take what he desires when he can in a royal court quickly repents of this when he can't return there." So you should allow us to beseech you so that he might see you alive with joy and for your pleasure.]

The effects of this rhetorical play are again to mystify what is actually happening. In the first passage, Frayre de Joy returns often to the magic tower to take his joy while Sor de Plaser is still comatose, but joy is something his name implies already belongs to him. And he does so, it is suggested, because of the agency of pleasure. In the second passage, which is part of the jay's attempts to persuade Sor de Plaser to accept Frayre de Joy's hand in marriage, it is unclear whose joy is at issue (line 477): Frayre de Joy's at seeing Sor de Plaser alive, or hers at being seen by him. Once again the implication is that the outcome depends on Sor de Plaser's agency or pleasure.

Lacan's aphorism from *Encore* "il n'y pas de rapport sexuel" (21) seems apposite here. *Frayre de Joy e Sor de Plaser* simultaneously articulates and subjects to scrutiny a ubiquitous yet impossible fantasy in which sexual difference is perfectly symmetrical, grounded in reciprocal desire, a fantasy in which man and woman fit together and complement each other. For Lacan "love" in Western culture is the ideological structure that underpins the fantasy that the categories "man" and "woman" not only have ontological reality, but also have a necessary and "natural" relation to each other. However, the sinister undertones and supernatural elements in *Frayre de Joy* (ingenious towers, talking birds, supernatural conception, and magic that brings the dead back to life) underscore the fantasy *qua* fantasy. There is indeed no sexual relation in this boy-meets-girl narrative: the boy has sex with a corpse and the girl is absent from the proceedings. Courtly love, for Lacan, is a "façon de suppléer à l'absence du rapport sexuel" (a "means to supplement the lack of sexual relation" [89]); it represents for man "la seule façon de se tirer avec élégance de l'absence du rapport sexuel" ("the only way to extract oneself elegantly from the lack of sexual relation"), and he cites the troubadour Jaufre Rudel's *amor de lonh* as the paradigmatic example of this (90). Jaufre, at least according to his celebrated *vida*, fell in love with a woman he had never seen only to die the second he laid his eyes on her, thereby perpetuating the illusion that union with her was possible and would have been perfect. The future perfect love from the masculine point of view, according to this paradigm, is precisely one that you cannot have (whether because she is not there or because she is dead), with the result that you can retain the illusion of its perfection. As for Sor de Plaser, the text is unclear about what might constitute "joy" for her: as with Lacan's model in *Encore*, of which Bellini's enigmatic statue of Saint Teresa in ecstasy is emblematic, what woman wants is opaque. Masculine and feminine desire thus do not coincide in *Frayre de Joy*, exposing what Žižek in *The Ticklish Subject* calls the real of sexual difference (273–9), by which he means the actual lack of co-ordination and reciprocity between the masculine and the feminine, between masculine and feminine desire, no matter how much discursive structures (such as courtly love) suggest the contrary.[24] It is thus highly significant that desire is exposed in *Frayre de Joy* as working first and foremost along the signifying chain, as the words "pleasure" and "joy" have a more meaningful relationship with each other than the individuals the words designate; indeed, they procreate, producing a child that will be named (significantly by the jay) "Joy de Plaser" (742) – in other words, a synthesis of the parents' names. As Lacan says at the end of the first seminar in *Encore* devoted to sexual difference and *jouissance*: "Les faits dont je vous parle sont des faits de discours" ("the facts of which I speak to you are discursive facts" [19]): gender and sexuality, in other words, are first and foremost effects of linguistic structures.

Furthermore, the main protagonists are not the only couple in the text whose love appears reciprocal and symmetrical because of their names. The knight who captures the jay and offers it to his lady is called Amors m'Esduy ("love guides me") and his lady Amors mi Pays ("love nourishes me"). Troublingly, perhaps, this couple's names lack the gender symmetry of Frayre and Sor's, though the linguistic symmetry is apparent. Perhaps this suggests the extent to which linguistic structure or embellishment may paper over underlying cracks or conceal murky undercurrents? If Frayre and Sor are made for each other, is it really appropriate for brother and sister to marry (whether these terms evoke biological siblings or religious orders)? And since the double wedding of the two couples at the end of the text is explicitly the work of the jay (819), he is thus the agent of the fantasy that there is a symmetrical sexual relation in the text; so let us turn now to the role of the jay.

In her study of *Frayre de Joy e Sor de Plaser* that accompanies her edition of the text in *Une Belle au Bois Dormant*, Suzanne Thiolier-Méjean suggests (in my view correctly) that the jay represents first and foremost the power of rhetoric (72), but she also assumes (I think quite erroneously) that the jay is really a parrot.[25] Her grounds for this are threefold: first, parrots appear elsewhere as go-betweens in courtly literature, but this is the only jay to play such a role; second, the northern audiences for whom she believes the first version of the text was composed (in French) would not, she thinks, have known what a parrot was, since the bird was not indigenous to northern Europe; finally the phonetic similarities between the words for parrot and jay may have led to confusion. However, the two words are less phonetically similar than they seem on the page (for we have [g] in *papagai*, but [dʒ] in *jai*); while the parrot is not indigenous to anywhere in Europe, so if Thiolier-Méjean's argument were to hold, its presence in literary texts in any romance language would be surprising. However, the fact that parrots were frequently held in captivity at courts throughout Europe suggests that courtly audiences would have been quite capable of giving significance to the fact that in *Frayre de Joy* the messenger-bird is a jay rather than a parrot. Indeed, the cultural significance of both parrots and jays was well-known to medieval readers, in Latin and in the vernacular, through encyclopedias and bestiaries, where we learn that both birds, which are associated with India and the Orient, can be taught to talk. A parrot, of course, repeats what it hears without necessarily understanding it: thus, in the texts in which a parrot persuades a lady to yield to a lover's suit, it may figure the effectiveness of courtly discourse, however conventional it may be. A jay, on the other hand, is noted above all for being a noisy bird. Contact with humans and learning to speak make it even noisier and even more garrulous, which is why the jay frequently represents gossip and slander. It is therefore significant that we have a jay rather than a parrot in *Frayre de Joy*: whereas the parrot represents the effectiveness of a certain kind of artfully deployed rhetoric, the jay represents both an excessive and a duplicitous (though not necessarily less effective) use of language.[26]

Among the jay's many attributes, we are told that it is an exceptional linguist:

> E-l jay anava say e lay
> Ffar e dir tot ço com volia,
> E totes les erbes sabia
> E conexia lur vertuts,
> E portava breus e saluts
> E noves, mils qu'altre missatge,
> E sabia de tot lenguatge,
> E mils que-l mestre encantava.   (335–42)

[And the jay went all over the place to do the bidding of others, and he knew all about herbs and their powers, and he carried letters and greetings, and news, better than any other messenger, and he knew every language and cast spells even better than his master [Virgil].]

Not unlike romance itself, the jay moves between languages and cultures, resolving differences into a single harmonious system or symbolic order, one that offers a fantasy or fictional resolution to the layers of linguistic, cultural

and sexual difference that inhabit this text. That the jay – linguist extraordinaire –
should be agent of romantic, magical apotheosis for Frayre de Joy and Sor de
Plaser (or indeed for Amors m'Esduy and Amors mi Pays), thereby (through marriage) also structuring and instantiating social order, is entirely apposite. Indeed,
such is the uncanny power of language – or the linguist – that the dead may even
be brought back to life: thus the parrot re-animates Sor, thereby subjecting her
inanimate body to a discourse of desire that resubjectivizes her after her rape,
retrospectively suggesting agency where there was none.

Yet the text's resolution of internal (sexual, linguistic, cultural) difference depends on something that comes from outside. Not just a talking animal, the jay
comes from two exotic beings, Virgil and Prester John. Thiolier-Méjean argues
(in my view implausibly) that Virgil and Prester John contribute to the text's predominant Christian ethos (*Une Belle au Bois Dormant* 95–6): Virgil, because of the
kind of spiritual authority that is attributed to him in texts such as Dante's *Commedia*; Prester John, because he is a legendary Christian prince. She thus sees the
text as deeply invested in a Christian ideology of marriage, pointing out that the
wedding at the end is attended not just by Virgil and Prester John, but also by
the pope and numerous archbishops, bishops and prelates (802–8).[27] According
to her reading, Sor de Plaser's fury when she awakes is excessive, so she needs to
calm her hysterical reaction for her social and spiritual integration to be effected
(108–10). But even the most blinkered and misogynous reader would surely realize that raping corpses is problematic and that Sor de Plaser's angry reaction when
she realizes what has happened is, to say the least, understandable. Furthermore,
the Christian associations of Virgil or Prester John are not given any weight in this
text; on the contrary, it is their abilities as magicians that are stressed, and their exoticism: Prester John was believed to reside either in the far reaches of Asia or Africa,
and Virgil, frequently represented as a pagan magician in the Middle Ages,[28] is
the means of contacting Prester John. Rather than simply assimilating Prester
John to hegemonic Christian culture, as Thioler-Méjean does, I am more inclined to see him as a striking figure of the uncanny, a being who is at one and
the same time totally foreign and yet represents familiar values.[29] Thus if *Frayre
de Joy* achieves resolution, like so many other romance texts, through a Christian
marriage that suggests a closed and harmonious system, this marriage is effected by means that call into question the very neatness of the structure that
is produced.

Frayre de Joy thus seems not only to be aware of internal cultural and linguistic
difference within the Romance sphere, but also to be engaging actively with far
more exotic external differences that encompass not only language (the jay's language skills were implicitly acquired as part of his training at the hands of Prester
John and Virgil), but also other significant cultural differences. It achieves this by

foregrounding language, which is at one and the same time that which defines a culture as different (as in the prologue) and that which makes it possible to bridge the gap between apparently irreconcilable differences (as figured by the multilingual jay, whose role as a *missatge*, which means both a message and a messenger, is repeatedly stressed [e.g., lines 629–36]). There is thus potentially an interesting mismatch between the text's cultural openness and its ostensibly conservative and repressive representation of sexual difference and love: the superficially clunking and blinkered naivety of the text's fairy-tale representation of sexual difference may well therefore be knowing and deliberately disingenuous, rather than straight-forwardly crass. When taken together with the text's play on names, words and linguistic difference, perhaps *Frayre de Joy e Sor de Plaser* may be read as a warning against the power of the unbridled rhetoric used to effect sexual unions (the rhetoric of courtly love, in other words) to mislead, a power that is embodied in the magic, garrulous, cheeky, but effective multilingual jay, whose mastery of courtly rhetoric is but one of his linguistic and other skills.

Suzanne Thiolier-Méjean's reading of the text as a cute love story foregrounding Christian values and Catherine Léglu's as a mystification of territorial conquest parallel influential readings and then counter-readings of romance as a whole. Many romances have a wedding as their resolution and dénouement, but since Roberta Krueger's seminal *Women Readers and the Ideology of Gender in Old French Verse Romance* at least, it has been recognized that "happy ever after" endings are not always what they seem and that frequently they mystify territorial conquest or political antagonism. My own reading of *Frayre de Joy e Sor de Plaser* as a playful meditation on different types of difference and the way cultures resolve them clearly allies itself more with the latter approach than the former; but it is equally important, particularly as romance evolves from the early thirteenth century onwards, to consider its international currency: how romances circulate between a range of diverse languages and not just in imitation of French models, and, finally, how linguistic difference in and of itself may carry cultural and ideological freight in romance. The garrulous, multi-lingual jay is an eloquent emblem of this mobility of romance: he comes from elsewhere but belongs nowhere, masters other languages effortlessly but apparently has no native language of his own, and finally he offers an enticing (albeit ultimately implausible) vision of a world in which a variety of different types of difference may be transcended.

NOTES

* This article has benefitted enormously from the questions and observations of the audiences that heard earlier versions as seminar papers at the universities of Cambridge, Glasgow, Manchester, and Warwick during the course of 2011. I should

particularly like to thank Adrian Armstrong, Emma Campbell, Miranda Griffin and Jim Simpson for their invitations to speak, and also Sarah Kay for her comments on one of those earlier versions.

1 For example, Roberta Krueger writes in *The New Oxford Companion to Literature in French*: "Old French romances transmitted their tales of love and chivalry throughout European national literatures by means of translations and adaptations" (709).

2 The most thoroughly researched area of the use of French outside France remains England, and there is a large body of scholarship on Anglo-Norman literature (which might more properly now be termed Anglo-French); but see, for example, Lusignan for recent work on non-literary uses of French. On French in Italy, see most notably Cigni; Cornish, *Vernacular Translation* 70–100; Holtus and Wunderli; and Renzi. On French in the Eastern Mediterranean, see Aslanov, Folena 269–86 ("La romania d'oltramare: Francese e veneziano nel levante"), and Minervini.

3 Most famously, the earliest – and for many, the most important – manuscript of the *Chanson de Roland* is English, and its language is Anglo-Norman French; in the romance tradition, Thomas's *Tristan* and Marie de France's *Lais* were almost certainly composed in England. Italian manuscripts are crucial to the transmission of several major romances in French, for example the *Roman de Troie* and the *Tristan en prose*. For an important recent contribution on French in England in the later Middle Ages, see Butterfield.

4 See Crane on England; Jewers on Occitania and the Iberian peninsula; Cornish, *Vernacular Translation* 74–5 and 89–99 and Delcorno Branca on the *Roman de Troie* and *Tristan* in Italy.

5 In addition to Menocal, Mallette's recent *European Modernity* is a model here.

6 See Holtus and Wunderli 18–36 for a survey of the corpus. A substantial portion of the corpus is composed of *chansons de geste*, on which see Vitullo.

7 Philippe Ménard, for example, writes that the Franco-Italian text of Marco Polo's *Devisement du Monde* is "déformé par de nombreux italianismes," whereas the standard French redaction (which is a reworking of it) is "remarquable … écrite dans une langue dépourvue des graves incorrections et des confusions verbales qui déparent la rédaction franco-italienne. Elle est donc beaucoup plus agréable à lire" (9–10). See further Gaunt, *Marco Polo* 24–6 for a critique of Ménard's approach.

8 For example see Gaunt, "Translating the Diversity" and *Marco Polo*; Cornish, *Vernacular Translation* 70–100. As Holtus and Wunderli note, Franco-Italian (a term which is used somewhat loosely to encompass a range of linguistic practices, from French that is barely distinguishable from standard French to Gallicized Italian) is primarily a *code écrit*, one designed to make texts (some of which date from the relatively distant past) accessible to non-native readers (63; 83).

9 See Gaunt, "Desnaturat son li Frances" on the effects of hybridization here.

10 Thiolier-Méjean says that the text "est selon toute apparence du XIVe siècle" (*Nouvelles courtoises* 37), but it is not clear on what grounds she makes this assertion. She

seems to be relying on Meyer (273), who says that the language and form of the poem suggest the fourteenth century, but does not go into any detail. In fact, some of the linguistic forms found in the poem are already quite archaic by the fourteenth century, while the form and style are reminiscent of numerous thirteenth-century texts. Thiolier-Méjean has published two editions of *Frayre de Joy*: the first in *Une Belle au Bois Dormant médiévale*, the second in *Nouvelles courtoises*.

11 See Paul Meyer 265–6; de Riquer 2:72–6. Thiolier-Méjean brought the text into the Occitan corpus.

12 On its relation to the "sleeping beauty" myth see Zago, though she seems to miss the implications of the fact that everyone in *Frayre* believes Sor is dead, not simply asleep. It is one of three articulations of the story in medieval Romance literatures, the others being in the *Perceforest* and *Blandin de Cornualha*. Meyer discusses the possible relation of *Frayre* to *Perceforest* (274–5).

13 On the myth of Prester John, see Uebel.

14 The two surviving manuscripts both date to the fifteenth century: Paris Bibliothèque Nationale de France, esp. 487 (on which see Meyer 265) and Palma, Biblioteca d'Estanislau Aguiló. The former is a collection of Occitan-Catalan short narratives and romances; the latter a collection of Occitan-Catalan pieces that includes a fragment of the Occitan romance *Flamenca*. Almost all the Catalan forms in the *Frayre* are orthographic (see Thiolier-Méjean, *Une Belle au Bois Dormant* 130–48) and seem to be randomly but evenly distributed across the two manuscripts.

15 On which see Cabré.

16 Well-known examples include Jaufre Rudel III, 31 ("plana lengua romana"), Marie de France, Prologue to the *Lais* 30 (*romaunz*), and the *Roman de Troie* 37 (*romanz*).

17 See, for example, the *Donatz proensals* and the *Razos de trobar*.

18 Most famously, Brunetto Latini writes: "Et se aucuns demandoit por quoi ceste livre est escrit en roman selonc le patois de France, puis que nos [so]mes ytaliens, je diroie que ce est por .ii. raisons: l'une est que nos [so]mes en France, l'autre por ce que la parleure est plus delitable et plus comune a touz languages" ("And if anyone were to ask why this book is written in Romance, according to the idiom of France, since we are Italian, I would say that this is for two reasons: one is that we are in France, the other is that this language is the most delightful and also the most widespread of all the languages" [I, I, 7]).

19 For the best interpretation of this poem's multilingualism, see Brugnolo; but see also Heller-Roazen 87–90.

20 See Gaunt, "Sexual Difference" on this poem.

21 On *car* and *prim* as stylistic terms in troubadour lyric, see Paterson 136–9, 181–4, 201–2.

22 For Meyer (265), *Frayre*'s main interest is that it illustrates the influence of French literature in Catalonia; see also Zago 270 and de Riquer II 72–6.

23 This is how they are read by Zago (272–3).

24 For further exposition on the "real of sexual difference," see my *Love and Death* 157.

25 *Une Belle au Bois Dormant* 99–100; see also "Le motif du perroquet" 1364–6 and "Le langage du perroquet" 272 and 287–9.

26 Brunetto Latini devotes a chapter to the parrot (see *Tresor* I, 168), and a parrot acts as a messenger in another Occitan short verse narrative (see *Las Novas del Papagay* in *Nouvelles courtoises*, 186–205). On the jay, see the discussion in the *Französisches Etymologisches Wörterbuch* 4:21–3. Etymologically related to *graculus* "garrulous" (on the authority of Isidore of Seville), the jay symbolises an "individu bavard." Cf. Chrétien de Troyes's *Cligès* 4380: "Si sont plus gengleor que jai."

27 Zago's reading also gives the poem a highly moral reading and argues that "if Frayre de Joy is to be the perfect lover, it is nevertheless part of the author's intentions to de-emphasize the sexual aspects of that role" (271). Sor's pregnancy, however, would seem to belie this.

28 On Virgil as a magician, compare Guiraut de Calanson, "Fadet juglar" 158–62, edited in Pirot; also Pirot's comments on p. 536 his extensive note on p. 593.

29 See Uebel; also Akbari, *Idols* (52–3, 55–66, 86–8) on how Prester John supplies an alternative center that necessarily decenters.

4 Forging New Paradigms: Towards a History of Islamo-Christian Civilization

JOHN TOLAN

"Leave to us, in Heaven's name, Pythagoras, Plato and Aristotle, and keep your Omar, your Alchabitius, your Aben Zoar, your Abenragel."

María Rosa Menocal uses this citation from Pico della Mirandola as the epigraph to the first chapter of her *Arabic Role in Medieval Literary History*, on "the myth of Westernness in Medieval Literary History." This "myth," which excludes medieval Arabs from "our" common cultural heritage (but includes the Greeks, Romans, Celts, and Germans – and sometimes Hebrews), is first constructed by Italian Humanists in the fourteenth and fifteenth centuries, and other Europeans and Americans through the centuries have added to this ideological edifice, from Petrarch to Chateaubriand and Disraeli – and, one could now add, to Samuel Huntington, for whom two massive entities, "Islam" and the "West," are locked in a titanic "Clash of Civilizations."

The supposed confrontation between Islam and the West, writes Richard Bulliet in his recent book, *The Case for Islamo-Christian Civilization*, "arises not from essential differences, but from a long and willful determination to deny their kinship" (Bulliet vii). Because of this "long and willful determination[,]" the common history of medieval Mediterranean civilization is now in many ways "a forgotten past," as María Rosa Menocal affirms in these pages – not forgotten to current specialists of the medieval Mediterranean world, clearly, but largely absent from the popular visions of European civilizations which leapfrog the medieval millennium, tracing "Western" culture from Greece to Rome to the Renaissance and Enlightenment. This essay is a brief look at the history of this "determination to deny" this kinship and at the efforts of scholars since the nineteenth century (including María Rosa Menocal) to set the record straight. But first, let me insist on the fact that Europeans in the twelfth century made no attempt to deny this kinship.

Medieval Europeans were indeed acutely, at times painfully, aware of their intellectual and cultural debt to the Arabs. In the first quarter of the twelfth century Adelard of Bath writes, in his *Natural Questions*:

> It is difficult for me to speak to you about the nature of animals. I learned about this from my masters, the Arabs, following reason, while you are led by the bridle of authority. For what other word can we use to designate authority if not "bridle"? The [Latins] are led like stupid animals by a bridle, not knowing where they are being taken or why, knowing only that they must follow, that they are tied. In this way authority leads many of you, like so many chained captives, into peril. Because of this, some people have usurped the title of authority, as if it authorized them to write: in this way they do not blush to pass off the false as true in the eyes of bestial men. (Adelard of Bath 11)

This diatribe, presented as a letter to a nephew who (to Adelard's chagrin) had gone off to study theology at Laon, presents a sharp contrast between Arab and Latin approaches to knowledge. Adelard associates the Arabs, his "masters," with *ratio* (reason), while the Latins uncomprehendingly follow *auctoritas* (authority). Adelard was not the only European intellectual of the twelfth century to couch the debate in these starkly oppositional terms. His Arab "master," Petrus Alfonsi, tried to prove the truth of Christianity in the face of the rival claims of Judaism and Islam through arguments based on scientific and logical *ratio* and scriptural *auctoritas*. He subsequently lambasted French students of astronomy who preferred the inferior authority of Macrobius to Petrus's own knowledge of Arabic science, based on *experimentum*.[1] Englishman Daniel of Morley, like so many European youths of his generation, went to Paris to study around 1175. But Daniel didn't like what he saw there: pompous professors hiding their ignorance behind opaque verbiage and ponderous silences. Daniel hurried off to Toledo, capital of the *quadrivium*, which he calls the *doctrina Arabum*; there, he says, he studied with the "best philosophers in the world" (Daniel of Morley, preface §1–2).

These are, of course, polemical statements: the three authors denigrate Latin learning and, in particular, the teaching dispensed in the schools of northern France. There is no doubt a certain element of jealousy and frustration behind these accusations: a teacher like Peter Abelard attracted throngs to his Parisian classes in logic and theology, while Petrus Alfonsi complained that his students were few, unpunctual, and not particularly bright. One could also point out that these authors, despite their shrill invocations of reason, willingly submit to the "bridle" of their much-revered Arab authorities in realms such as astrology, geomancy, etc. (see Petrus Alfonsi, *Epistola*). Clearly the stridency of their arguments shows that in the twelfth century they faced an uphill battle in their efforts to include Arabic science in the curriculum of Europe's schools.

These efforts were of course successful in the long run: Greco-Arabic science and philosophy, translated into Latin in the Iberian peninsula (and to a lesser extent in Sicily), arrived massively in Europe in the twelfth and thirteenth centuries and completely revolutionized teaching and research. The impact of this transmission of texts and ideas was tremendous: the new Arabic texts were championed by a significant segment of the emerging clerical elite, though some looked on in alarm at the growing vogue for the new Arabic texts (see Tolan, "Reading God's Will in the Stars"). This is a story well-known and often told; there is no need to insist on this here.[2] Yet what does bear emphasizing is that there was a widespread acknowledgement of this cultural and intellectual debt, even if this acknowledgement was sometimes accompanied by uneasiness due to the fact that these thinkers whose works were translated were pagans, Jews and Muslims.

Hermann of Carinthia composed his *De essentiis* in 1143. He dedicates the work to his friend and fellow scholar Robert of Ketton, to whom he says:

> You remember, I think, that while we went forth from our inner sanctuaries into the public festival of Minerva, the multitude of people milling around were gazing at us with open mouths, not valuing us so much as individuals as admiring the trappings and decorations which long vigils and our most earnest labour had acquired for us from the depths of the treasuries of the Arabs. At that time I began to have a very deep sense of pity concerning those men who were so impressed by these outward appearances: How much they would value the undergarments, if it were lawful for them to look at them! (Hermann of Carinthia 70)

In this metaphor (if one of rather poor taste, by twenty-first-century standards), Hermann and Robert have, through devotion and study, been able to contemplate the goddess of wisdom in her underwear. The general public, ignorant of Arabic, is awed by the mere baubles that they display from Minerva's finery; this inspires pity in Hermann and indeed in the goddess herself, who finally bids her devotee to expose to the Latin public her undergarments – which, Hermann explains, are the basic principles of astronomy. This passage expresses clearly both the enthusiasm of the new adepts of Arabic science and the disdain they felt for those unable to read Arabic and hence contemplate the goddess of wisdom.

Not all were so enthusiastic. Peter the Venerable, abbot of Cluny, was ambivalent about the impact of this Arabic learning on Christian Europeans. He addressed his *Contra sectam siue haeresim Saracenorum* (1156), a polemical treatise against Islam, to fictitious Arab readers whom he praises as "learned in worldly knowledge," "not only rational by nature, but logical in temperament and training" (§29). A rational people follows what he attempts to prove is an irrational religion. In his preface to his *Contra sectam*, Peter hopes that the tract might "cure the hidden cogitations of some of our people, thoughts by which they could be led into evil if they think that there is some piety in those impious people and think that some truth is to be found with the ministers of lies" (§20). In other words, if some Latin Christians admired Muslims and thought their religion legitimate, Peter meant to show how wrong they were. Peter does not say which Christians he had in mind, but it was most probably those in Spain with regular contact with Muslims, and in particular those who read and admired the philosophical and scientific works of Muslim thinkers. Peter provides an eloquent example of the unease that intellectual contact with Muslim texts and thinkers could provoke in some Christian Europeans.

There was of course a paradox here: some of the same authors who praised the Arabs for their erudition and for their unflinching devotion to reason portrayed Islam as an irrational cult based on violence and lechery. A number of thirteenth- and fourteenth-century European authors well-versed in Arabic philosophy (Ramon Martí, Roger Bacon, Ramon Llull, Riccoldo da Montecroce) affirmed (rather disingenuously) that Arab philosophers were *not* in fact Muslims, that they rejected Muhammad's teaching in secret but professed it in public for fear of persecution (see Tolan, "Saracen Philosophers Secretly Deride Islam"). In this way the prominence of Avicenna and other Arab thinkers was frankly acknowledged at the same time that their religious difference, which potentially called into question the universality of Christian truth, was defused. Dante has no problem admitting a few chosen Muslims into the "castle of light" in the first circle of hell, a special and rather pleasant corner of the underworld fixed up for "virtuous heathens," including many prominent figures of Greek and Roman antiquity. Next to Greece and Rome's martial heroes the poet places "il Saladino," Saladin. More to our point, he sees Aristotle flanked by all the prominent philosophers and scientists, including Avicenna, placed between Hippocrates and Galen, and Averroes "who produced the Great Commentary" (Dante, *Inferno* IV: 129 and 143). These Arab thinkers are clearly, for Dante, very much a part of his own cultural and intellectual baggage, not members of a foreign "civilization."

I am emphasizing the importance of Arab learning and culture in the realms of science and philosophy, but of course the impact of Arab culture was profound elsewhere, particularly in literature, as María Rosa Menocal makes clear in her work, as do other contributors to this volume. In material culture as well: here the most numerous and eloquent witnesses are the thousands of dry and dull documents in the archives of Pisa, Venice, Genoa, Barcelona, and the Cairo Geniza, testifying to the extensive trade throughout the Mediterranean, bringing to Europe from the East spices, sugar, gold, glass, ceramics, silk, etc. (see Goitein, *A Mediterranean Society*). The Muslim East became, in the European imagination, a land of fabulous wealth, as we see in the works of European geographers, in the narration of travels real and imagined, in literature from the *chansons de geste* to the *romanceros*. Economically and culturally, Latin Europe is painfully aware of being the *parent pauvre* to the Muslim East.

Yet others, starting in the fourteenth century, sought to deny this common heritage. It is here we see the beginning of what Bulliet calls the "long and willful determination to deny their kinship," which will turn this common history into a "forgotten past." Petrarch, passionate partisan of crusading, rails against the influence of Arab thought in Latin Europe. In his *Rerum senilium*, Petrarch affirms that the Greeks established the bases of medicine and that the Arabs should be "banished" from the science. Averroes is a "rabid dog who barks against Christ," infecting with his "poison" unsuspecting Christian readers. "I hate the whole race" of Arabs, he says.[3] Various European medical writers in the fifteenth and sixteenth centuries echoed Petrarch's shrill condemnation of Arabic medicine, though others defended this heritage. Avicenna's *Canon* remained the basic textbook in most European medical schools until the eighteenth century (Siraisi 70–3).

Various Humanists studied Arabic and expressed their admiration for the great Arab thinkers: the most prominent examples are Marsilio Ficino and Pico della Mirandola. Pico, having read the Qur'an in Latin, learned Arabic so he could read the original. In his *Oration on the Dignity of Man*, he admiringly cites Muhammad as having proclaimed that he who is distant from divine law falls into bestiality.[4] But in an age when the Ottomans were conquering much of Europe, few displayed such open-mindedness. In many disciplines, Humanists enamored of antiquity tried to "purge" their sciences of "medieval" and particularly Arabic accretions. Cartographers revered Ptolemy as a supreme authority: as a result, fifteenth-century Humanist maps are often less accurate than the portolans of the previous century (Zumthor, *La mesure du Monde* 334). It became possible to deny the affinity between Arab and Latin cultures, to imagine "Islam" as a foreign civilization hostile to Europe.

I will not try here to trace the complex history of the development, over the following centuries, of the concept of "Western Civilization," defined over and against either a group of rival civilizations or simply against the rest of the world, seen as civilized or not. To the limited extent that there was a unified sense of European identity, that identity was based on the twin heritages of Greco-Latin antiquity and Christianity, with on occasion the addition of other elements (such as the supposed Germanic love of liberty). By the Enlightenment, the break seems to be complete: Montesquieu's Persian, Voltaire's or Lessing's Saladin, and Boulainvillier's Muhammad are presented as idealized mirrors of European society precisely because they are not European, but quintessentially other. The Persian and Arabic models that inspire Goethe's *West-östlicher Divan* are decidedly and refreshingly exotic, as are the Arab societies portrayed by the Orientalist writers and painters of the nineteenth and twentieth centuries.

Yet at the same time as the Romantics brushed a portrait of an exotic and enticing Orient, a number of European scholars revived the study of medieval Arabic learning and emphasized Europe's intellectual and cultural debt to Arab culture: in Spain, among others, Juan Andres, José Antonio Banqueri, and José

Antonio Conde; north of the Pyrenees, Sylvestre Sacy, Reinhardt Dozy, Ignaz Goldziher, Theodor Nöldeke, and others. In the history of science, significant ground was broken by Charles Homer Haskins and George Sarton in the first half of the twentieth century, work carried forward by scholars such as Marie-Thérèse d'Alverny, Danielle Jacquart, and Charles Burnett, among many others.

If these scholars contributed to the deconstruction, stone by stone, of the myth of Westernness, some attempted to erect new ideological structures of dubious solidity, overstating the centrality of the influence of Arab institutions on medieval Europe. Georges Makdisi, in *The Rise of Colleges* (1981) and *The Rise of Humanism* (1990), compares the development of educational institutions in the Middle Ages, in the Muslim world and in Latin Europe. He concludes that the schools of the Arab world, in particular madrasas, provided models that were imitated or reproduced in Europe, as the basis of Europe's new universities. Yet as Michael Chamberlain has shown for medieval Damascus and Jonathan Berkey for Mamluk Cairo, madrasas in fact bear little resemblance to European universities: they have no set curricula, no exams, and no diplomas. Students sought knowledge and prestige from renowned masters, not diplomas from institutions.[5] In his zeal to vindicate the long-denied importance of Arab influence on European culture, Makdisi overstates his case, making claims that do not bear up to close scrutiny.

In Spain and elsewhere, one notes the increasing number of "feel-good" events where Arab culture is celebrated, where the Spain of three religions is presented as a "lost paradise" – to borrow the title of a concert of medieval Iberian music by Jordi Savalls. In Europe, the role of medieval Arab culture in the construction of European cultures and identities has become a subject of cultural and political polemic, with some brandishing the cultural indebtedness of Europe to the Arab world as a proud legacy for Arab immigrants in Europe, others shrilly denying the very idea that European culture could owe anything to the Muslim Middle Ages.[6]

This brings us to the heart of our problem: if we are to deconstruct Westernness, with what (if anything) do we try to replace it? With a new, broader, and more inclusive construct? Richard Bulliet's paradigm of "Islamo-Christian Civilization" is, from the outset, an anti-Huntington argument. The centuries of economic, cultural and intellectual exchanges in the Mediterranean world form the bases of a common civilization. These exchanges are not between "Islam" and the "West," but between Catalans and Tunisians, Sicilians and Bougiotes, Venetians and Turks, Castilians and Granadans, Byzantines and Egyptians, etc. These exchanges are deep and constant at every level: economic, intellectual, artistic, culinary, sexual, diplomatic, etc. The reality of Islamo-Christian civilization, affirms Bulliet, "renders Huntington's 'Clash of Civilizations' nonsensical" (11).

This is more than just playing with words and it does not necessitate being blind to the depth and virulence of conflict. The wars of religion bloodied Europe for centuries; yet no one speaks of Protestant and Catholic Europe as separate "civilizations." A European country such as France has been, at one time or another, at war with each of its neighbours; yet no one affirms that the French are incompatible with "European" or "Western" civilization. To lump together the Ottoman siege of Vienna, the French conquest of Algeria, and the terrorist attacks of September 11th, 2001 under the rubric of a "clash of civilizations" is clearly nonsensical: it in no way helps us understand any of these events, hiding as it does real and specific historical causes under a smokescreen of supposed innate and perpetual hostility.

Bulliet's notion of "Islamo-Christian Civilization" is heuristic for a number of reasons. First of all, it restores the medieval sense of a shared intellectual and cultural inheritance that we have seen in thinkers from Petrus Alfonsi to Dante: the linguistically and religiously hybrid societies that ringed the Mediterranean saw themselves as heirs to the twin traditions of revealed scripture and Hellenistic science and philosophy. Second, it opens all sorts of interesting vistas onto the comparative history of societies and institutions. Bulliet compares the struggles between Abbasid Caliphs and their ulamas with those between European kings and emperors and churchmen: while the Caliphs succeeded more readily in affirming their power over the ulamas, the latter retained a broad legal authority and avoided a separation between religious and lay law. In Europe, bishops and popes fought more adamantly and more successfully to retain their privileges, but were increasingly excluded from power as kings asserted a monopoly over law and coercion. In Europe, popular Christian movements from the Beguines in the twelfth century to the Protestants in the sixteenth and seventeenth centuries were often brutally repressed in an effort to enforce orthodoxy and Christian unity. In Muslim lands, doctrinal variation and spiritual movements such as the Sufis did not provoke the same kind of systematic repression. These trends contributed to the clear distinction of Church and State in modern Europe and the lack of a comparable distinction in Muslim polities. I cite this as simply one example of a vista briefly sketched by Bulliet, showing the potential intellectual fruits of his notion of "Islamo-Christian Civilization."

There is another, perhaps more potent argument to compel us to write this history: if we don't do it, somebody else will. Any attempts to banish or eradicate myth-making are doomed to failure. After all, what is it that we medievalists (historians, philologists, paleographers, etc.) do, other than try to reconstruct plausible and representations of an irretrievable past, representations meant to stimulate, provoke, fascinate our students and readers? María Rosa Menocal acknowledges that, in her *Arabic Role in Medieval Literary History*, she indulges in myth-making, presenting "a myth that has several advantages" over the myth of Westernness (16): it allows for a richer and more complex understanding of medieval literary history and hence a fuller appreciation of the mixed roots of European cultures.

The same claims can be made for Bulliet's vision of Islamo-Christian Civilization: it opens new horizons to comparative cultural history and it provides a comprehensible and compelling model to oppose to the monolithic vision of Huntington and his ilk.

All well and good, one might say. Yet many observers realized how blatantly absurd Huntington's ideas were without Bulliet's help. The very idea of opposed monolithic "civilizations" is simplistic: a Sicilian has as much or more in common with his near neighbour in Tunisia as he does with a Swede or a Canadian. Huntington's thesis is based on a historical fallacy: "during most of human existence, contacts between civilizations were intermittent or non-existent" (21). To anyone with an even modest knowledge of medieval history, such an assertion is laughable: that a tenured professor at Harvard can make such an assertion, and that it is at the heart of his much-acclaimed thesis of the "Clash of Civilizations," is troubling to say the least. If Bulliet provides a clear demonstration of the inanity of Huntington's claims, so much the better.

Yet if we can happily toss "Western" and "Islamic" "Civilizations" into the dustbin of history, do we really need something called "Islamo-Christian Civilization" to replace it? After all, we can raise all the same objections to "Islamo-Christian Civilization" that we did to "Western Civilization": it is absurd to say that an Indian or Indonesian Muslim is part of the same "civilization" as an Irish Catholic or Mississippi Baptist, whereas his Hindu or Buddhist neighbour is part of a foreign civilization. Shouldn't we simply dispense with the idea of "civilization," which tries to steam-roll cultures into a falsified uniformity, in the face of all the richness and complexities of cultures as they appear to historians, linguists, anthropologists and others?

Specialists of the Mediterranean world, in any period, are aware of the weaknesses of the very notion of "civilization." Phoenician painting and sculpture, for instance, bear clear traces of strong influences from Egypt and Mesopotamia, yet these elements are transformed into something completely new, both in their forms and their uses (see Fontan and Le Meaux, *La Méditerranée des Phéniciens*). Peregrine Horden and Nicholas Purcell present cultural consequences of the Mediterranean world's paradoxical geography: it is highly fractured by rough mountainous terrain, yet unified by seafaring. This means that zones close to each other can live in relative isolation, while sea trade is essential for the livelihood and even survival of these communities (Horden and Purcell, *The Corrupting Sea*). A broad category such as "civilization" hides both the enormous diversity within the category and the profound links to those in a supposedly distinct category.

Latin writers from Petrus Alfonsi to Dante did not see themselves as part of a "Western" civilization distinct from "Islam." Tenth-century philosopher Al-Fârâbi saw himself as heir and continuator to the "great human legacy" that transcended cultural, linguistic and religious divisions. For historian of philosophy Alain de Libera, this is the heritage we should all claim, and forget "Europe of the ancient ramparts."[7] Let us indeed keep our Pythagoras, Plato, and Aristotle – but also our Avicenna, Fârâbi, and Averroës.

NOTES

1   See Tolan, *Petrus Alfonsi and his Medieval Readers*; on Adelard's knowledge of Arabic texts and his relation with Petrus Alfonsi, see Burnett, "Adelard of Bath and the Arabs."
2   The fundamental bibliographical reference is now R. Rashed, ed., *Histoire des sciences arabes*; on the acknowledgement of Latin debt to Arab science, see José Martínez Gázquez, *La Ignorancia y negligencia de los latinos*.
3   Petrarch, *Lettres de la viellesse (Rerum senilium)* 2:140–1, 4:158–9, 390–1. See Gabrieli, "Petrarca e gli Arabi"; Bisaha, "Petrarch's Vision of the Muslim and Byzantine East."
4   Giovanni Pico della Mirandola, *On the Dignity of Man*; Bisaha, *Creating East and West*, 166–73; Piemontese, "Il Corano latino di Ficino"; Valcke, *Pic de la Mirandole*.
5   Chamberlain, *Knowledge and Social Practice in Medieval Damascus* 69–90; Berkey, *The Transmission of Knowledge in Medieval Cairo* 44–94.
6   See the polemical book by Gouguenheim, *Aristote au Mont-Saint-Michel*, and the debate it has sparked in *Le Monde*: Droit, "Et si l'Europe ne devait pas ses savoirs à l'islam?"; Loiseau and Martinez-Gros, "Une démonstration suspecte"; Tolan, "Aristophane."
7   Alain de Libera, quoted in Birnbaum, "Polémique sur les 'racines' de l'Europe."

5 Reflections on Muslim Hebraism: Codex Vindobonensis Palatinus and al-Biqaʿi

WALID A. SALEH

This article is an attempt to reflect on the position of the Bible in the Islamic religious imagination. It builds on the insights gained from my study of al-Biqaʿi's encounter with the Bible, but focuses primarily on the woefully forgotten Codex Vindobonensis (Vienna MS. A. F. 58). I will argue that the main characteristic of the treatment of the Bible within Islamic religious scholarship was ambiguity, and that it was a creative ambiguity. In the process, I will have occasion to raise several concerns about the academic study of Islam, our work as scholars, and our relationship with past scholarship. The Codex Vindobonensis and the career of al-Biqaʿi were, ironically, contemporaneous, though they occurred at opposite ends of the Muslim world. One reflects the struggles of the minority Muslim community in Christian Spain during the fifteenth century, the other the encounter by a Muslim scholar with the Bible in Mamluk Cairo.[1] The aim of this article is to highlight the possibilities that these two neglected works can open, especially regarding the as-yet only partially documented intellectual life of Moriscos. I will also address fundamental questions raised by the Codex Vindobonensis: In what way is the vanished community of the Moriscos part of the story of the Bible in Islam? What can a narrative that includes their outlook contribute to the story of the Bible in Islam?

For Islam, the Bible is an unavoidable and insurmountable presence; it is an essential part of Islamic history. Yet it is also like a mirage: it shines brightly, only to move farther away when we approach it. Our vocabulary does not help us sometimes, for if by "the Bible in Islam" we mean "biblical material in the Islamic religious tradition," then we find the Bible everywhere. Biblical material is part of the Qur'an, part of the hadith, and part of religious literature in general. But that is not what I mean by Bible here. What I am in search of is the Bible as a book and an Islamic relationship with it as a codex, a physical book; thus a mediated knowledge of the Bible, though it might be an important component of the Islamic tradition, is not enough for my purpose here. I want a reader, a Muslim reader in this case, with a Bible in hand. The customary scholarly assumption is that this was a rare occurrence during the Middle Ages. This position is, however, becoming more untenable the more we understand about the heritage of medieval Muslims.

The opportunities for such an encounter were more readily available than we have so far been willing to admit, just as medieval Muslims are proving to have been more curious about the Bible than we might assume. Jewish communities and Christian communities were fully entrenched in the large metropolitan Muslim cities and soon official Arabic translations of the Bible for cultic use were common in the Middle East. Jews and Christians in Arab lands were fully Arabized. There was always more than one vulgate of the Bible in Arabic. One can speak not just of the possibility of encountering the Bible, but of the impossibility of not encountering the Bible. The question of the Bible in Islam is thus for me the question of the relationship of the Islamic religious tradition with non-Islamic scriptures. How does a religious tradition that enshrines scripture as central deal with the scripture of other traditions when read by its members?

A complicating factor in any attempt to study the Bible in Islam is that a history of the Arabic Bible is still lacking. The Arabic Bible has an illustrious history and rather unfortunate luck with scholarship. But this is about to change: we are witnessing an increased interest in the Arabic Bible and its history that transcends sectarian histories and the history of polemics, and therefore we are seeing a serious attention to the history of its translation. Yet without a basic outline of such a history, a meaningful generalization about its relationship to other topics will remain tentative. The great task of studying the Arabic Bible is, however, unavoidable; we will soon have to study all the manuscripts of Arabic Bibles and establish a history of their translation. The outline of this history that we have so far is insufficient. We are certain of one thing: there were more translations in existence than we have been told, and we need to document them carefully.

This article, however, is not about a Bible manuscript, but rather about a polemical treatise, Codex Vindobonensis. This manuscript has been known for a while, yet ironically has also fallen by the wayside. It has been known insofar as it was intensely studied in the nineteenth century and during the early twentieth century, but neglected in that it failed to change the general narrative about the Bible in Islam as it should have. My attempt at repositioning this manuscript as an important witness of what I am calling the Bible in Islam is also an attempt to come to grips with the accumulated scholarship in our field, and to raise certain questions about the manner in which we prepare ourselves for the task of studying Islam and of writing a history of its religious outlook across the ages.

The manuscript is Vienna MS. A. F. 58, first described by Fluegel in his catalogue of the Vienna collection in 1867. As such, the manuscript was both available and documented, and soon Goldziher was relying on Fluegel's description to characterize it. Eventually, a dissertation on parts of the manuscript and an edition were done.[2] So how did it manage to disappear from the narrative?[3] And in what way can we revisit a work that on first encounter appears to have been already studied, if not exhaustively?

Let me first describe the manuscript and its content. This is an Andalusian or Iberian manuscript, an Islamic manuscript that was written by Muslims in Christian Spain for the benefit of the Muslim community. The manuscript as it stands now is made up of one complete work which the scribe of the manuscript copied and another work of his which was in the process of being formulated; the second work exhibits characteristics of being a first draft. We thus have in Vienna MS. A. F. 58 two separate works.

The first work is entitled *Ta'yid al-Millah* (*Vindication of the Community*). The second is *al-Mujadalah ma' al-yahud wa-al-nasara* (*An Argumentation with the Jews and the Christians*, although in reality it is mostly a polemical work against Christian dogma). What has happened so far is that since the second work is incomplete and appears incoherent, most scholars have tended to study the first part only, which is a coherent composition. This is where I want to depart from the usual approach to the manuscript. I want to study the manuscript as it has survived, paying attention to it as a self-enclosed work, an artifact, and a coherent attempt by the scribe/author to defend his faith. In this sense, both parts of the manuscript should be approached together and must be seen as an attempt by the scribe/author to supply his community with a manual for self-defence in a predominantly Christian and Jewish environment.

What is fundamentally important about this work is, first of all, its uniqueness. It is a work written by a defeated, besieged and disappearing Muslim community. This is not the usual triumphalist rhetoric that we are accustomed to reading in Islamic polemical treatises. As such, it is an essential addition to the corpus. I am therefore deeply interested in its setting, its resigned tone, and especially the relationship to the Bible that it fashions, which on closer inspection is revealed as one of subservience: here we find an Islamic defence of the Qur'an that has to forgo the Qur'an to defend it. It has to face the Bible square on.

Goldziher referred to the manuscript when he reviewed the work of Steinschneider without being able to inspect the manuscript. Asín Palacios was the first to study the content of the first part of our manuscript, having discovered another witness in Madrid. Two Israeli scholars, Zucker and Strauss, studied the same title in the thirties and the forties. The first part of the manuscript was eventually edited by Kassin in 1969. This is the last time we find a scholar working with this manuscript. Unfortunately, the editor emphatically espoused the notion that the original writer of the first part was a convert to Islam from Judaism. The underlying assumption was clearly that such an extensive knowledge of the Bible must be indicative of a previous conversion, since a Muslim could not have such a detailed knowledge of the Hebrew Bible. This view was first advanced by Fluegel, and was accepted at face value by Goldziher but rejected by Asín Palacios, who offered the most exhaustive analysis of the matter. The issue was, in a way, a red herring and wasted an opportunity to place the work in the context of the larger narrative. The identity of the author, Jewish convert or not, became for scholars the most interesting aspect of this manuscript. We can see here how our preconceived knowledge of "typical" Muslim dealings with the Bible tends to affect our conclusions. The evidence from the manuscript makes it clear that the author was too profoundly aware of the wider Islamic world to have been a convert. But the issue of the conversion is, even if true, inconsequential to our assessment of the manuscript. We are, moreover, never told why a learned Jewish scholar would have converted to Islam in Christian Iberia and then manage to speak of *inqita'* (disconnection), a term to which I will turn later in this article, and why he would show anxiety about his Arabic language in terms that are indicative of a besieged community.

Let me now describe the framing of the Codex Vindobonensis Vienna MS. A. F. 58. By emphasizing the framing, I hope largely to avoid the issue of authorship. The scribe/author of the Vienna manuscript was the leader of his community in the city of Betroula (I have yet to finalize my views on which city this is), and he transcribed and authored this manuscript in 1404 as a guide to his community. He relied on an older native Morisco work, the *Ta'yid al-Millah* (*Vindication of the Community*), which had been written forty years earlier in the city of Huesca in 1361. This information we know because of the work of Asín Palacios, who found another copy of *Ta'yid al-Millah* in Madrid with the original colophon. The scribe/author of Vienna MS. A. F. 58 then added a larger part consisting of polemical arguments against Christian dogma, relying heavily on the works of Ibn Rushd and Aristotle to attack Christian theology.

The Codex Vindobonensis is thus a composite work, based squarely on native Morisco tradition, with no direct connection to the Islamic East. These Muslims were, so to speak, on their own, fending for themselves. The intensity of feeling is evident in the introduction, the conclusion and the colophon. The two authors agonize over their corrupt Arabic, and feel the need to justify their imperfect command of the language. They beg the reader for indulgence and express their hope and wish that, when and if the work should ever be read by the larger Muslim community out there in the East, its members will excuse the author his failings. Thus we perceive a multitude of anxieties in this text, which reveals that the Muslims of Christian Spain were no longer sure of how good a Muslim community they were.

The manuscript starts with a benediction that is decidedly submissive: it submits to the mystery of the fact that humans are distinct communities, each with a *shar'* (legal tradition) and *minhaj* (a way of life). The writer then declares his faith in the one God, and in Muhammad's prophecy. Muhammad came with a legal tradition that abrogated all and every code before him. Each element of this introduction is already familiar to us, but that these are the only elements in the introduction is a clear indication of the environment in which it was written: there is no recourse to vindications by history, no sign of God's benevolence to the Muslims as a political entity. Humanity here appears to be disunited, and in this case Muslims are not the rulers.

The *Amma ba'd* paragraph of the introduction (where the author justifies himself and gives his reasons for writing the book) is of such importance that I will offer a translation here:

> When I noticed the transformation and change of the age (*taghayyur al-zaman*), the corruption of its people (*fasad ahlih*), the disappearance of knowledge (*irtifa' al-'ilm*), especially in the land of disbelief (*shirk*) where we find ourselves, cut off from our community (*fi ard al-shirk allati nahnu fiha 'an ahl millatina munqati'in*) and disinvested of knowledge; then I saw that if Jews meet in their gatherings and at meetings they attack our prophet by falsities and slander, denying his law and his prophecy, claiming that God did not send a prophet but to them and no legal law or Scripture but to them. (Vienna MS. A. F. 58, fol. 1; Kassin, 303 Arabic text)

The author then lists a few of the accusations against Muhammad and his message. He next decides to pray to God to give him the strength to battle these falsehoods. In order to refute them, the author decided to read the Torah, the Psalms and the Nevi'im books (*kutub al-anbiya'*) and extracted material from them to respond to these accusations. He calls his book *Ta'yid al-Millah* (*Vindication of the Community*).

The author then explains to the reader that he decided to use only the Bible in his refutations not because such material is not available in the Qur'an, but rather because it is forbidden to Muslims to argue with non-Muslims using the Qur'an for the fear that their opponents might curse the Qur'an. God has forbidden Muslims to do so lest Muslims inadvertently cause the Jews to transgress. Instead, argumentation (*al-mujadalah*) should be carried out with the aid of what the opponents already know, such as their Torah, which God sent down to Moses — who, the author pointedly remarks, is also a prophet of the Muslims. Anyone who wishes to argue with them, then, has to use the arguments that the author supplies here. Indeed, he adds that this approach is a safeguard for the sanctity of the Qur'an, which should not be touched by defiled people; one is unable to argue using the Qur'an, since non-Muslims deny it and pretend not to know it. The author is keen to admit that one can, of course, make use of the Qur'an, which certainly has much to say about the perfidy of the Jews – as proof of the point, the author lists a series of Qur'anic verses to this effect – but in this case, he will refrain from such an approach. Readers should not think that the author is incapable of such a work, but rather that the arguments of the Muslims are all the more cogent when one uses source texts that one's opponents agree from the start are authoritative. This safeguarding of the Qur'an is not unusual: Muslim polemicists historically did see the value of using the Bible alone to argue with the Jews and the Christians. But their justification was one of principled logic. Here the argument is distinctly subservient: the Qur'an has no authority, for otherwise it would have been used.

Let us analyse some of the salient issues of this introduction. First, the author is facing a state of dwindling Islamic knowledge and expertise among the Muslims of Christian Spain. They are hardly in a position to have access to such knowledge; they are living in apocalyptic times (*irtifaʿ al-ʿilm*, the disappearance of knowledge, is one of the signs of the end of the world, as is *fasad al-zaman*, the corruption of times).[4] Far more important is that Muslims are in a state of *inqitaʿ*, a disjunction or a disconnection, from the *ummah*, the larger Muslim autonomous communities. I am not aware of any analysis of this term in scholarship. It may be of fundamental importance to pay close attention to this word as a technical term denoting dislocation, as well as disorientation. It is a term that reflects the ultimate horror of an endangered community which professes to belong to an *ummah*, which was perceived as a continuum both in the physical connectivity that linked its members and in its reach to Muhammad through generational continuity, extending through a chain of inheritance stretching across each successive generation all the way back to Muhammad, its *wasl* (the opposite of *inqitaʿ*); *wasl* to each other, and *wasl* with the past. In a fundamental sense, these separated Muslims here are not an *ummah* – a terrifying admission that they are now disjointed on a very basic level. This situation was so acutely disturbing that they reverted to a pre-Medina situation – to the time when Muslims were a mere collection of individuals with no political structure or clout; the author denies Muslims the authority to argue with the Jews using the Qur'an for fear of them cursing it, just as the Qur'an told the Muslims not to attack the gods of the Meccans lest the Meccans curse the God of Muhammad, at a time when Muslims were in no position to impose public deference towards the Qur'an and Muhammad.

The treatise for the most part consists of extensive discussions of biblical material that shows the perfidy of the Jews, their killing of prophets, their disobedience, and the punishment God inflicted on them. Moreover, the author interprets many of the biblical verses to refer to the Muslims and Muhammad. These quotations reflect the extensive knowledge the author had of the Bible, a knowledge that is at once intimate and detailed. It also shows that the Muslims of Spain certainly had access to Arabic copies of the Bible.

Having finished with copying this text, the author tells the reader that it should be studied and scrutinized (*yajtahid fi darsihi wa-al-taf'in fi ma'anih*), and that it should not be doubted, and that even if the Jews were to deny any of it, one should not lose faith. And then he adds this conclusion:

> And I apologize (*mu'tadhir*) to those who read the book and find grammatical mistakes (*lahn*). They should not blame me, since I quoted what I found in the Torah and other books and did not aim to fix the language or misquote it (*tazyin* or *tahrif*). And if they find in my own words also mistakes, then they should know that I am not up to the challenge. I am not fit to this task in the first place (*idh lastu miman ya'luh li-dhalik*); what prompted me was the fact that we are in a sick age which has sick understanding (*anna al-dahr kalil wa-al-fahm 'alil*) and the signs of knowledge are but traces (*wa-rasm al-'ilm daris*) in our country (*thaghr*), thus I wrote this book as an aid for argumentation (*munazarah*).

He finally finishes this conclusion with a prayer:

> May God have mercy on me and bring me out of this land of *shirk* to the land of the Muslims. He only can heal the brokenness of our fate (*yajbur al-kasr*) and turn misery into happiness (*yubaddil al-'usra bi-al-yusr*), and if God insists on piling on us misery, may he double the reward. (Vienna MS. A. F. 58, fol. 30b; Kassin, 434 Arabic text)

These were the words of the author from the original work, copied by the scribe/author in Betroula, on the tenth day of *Jumada al-awwal*, which corresponds to October 20 of the year 808 A.H. (1405 C.E.; the Christian year is not given, but the month is). He then informs the reader that he was also the leader of the Muslim community there (*al-imam bi-jama'at al-muslimin*), and finally that the original was a bad exemplar (*intusikh min umm saqimah*). Clearly, the scribe/author was a learned man, but the exemplar was corrupted and he attempted to fix the text. He gives his name as al-Raqli (or al-Raqili as Kassin transcribes it).

The framing of the work and the heavy editorial interventions of al-Raqli make it hard to draw a clear distinction between author and scribe here, since the original work is hugely modified, as the edition of Kassin makes clear. We are thus talking here about a living tradition of polemical Morisco efforts, which is building on groundwork that had already been established and which takes considerable liberty with the material to adapt it to the circumstances of the Muslims in the scribe's own town.

The colophon, moreover, exhibits additional signs of communal distress. We see more vocabulary that describes the condition of *inqita'*. We have the *kasr* (a term used to describe broken bones), a lame state of existence; where Muslims are living is a *thaghr*, a frontier land, suggesting that they are continuously aware of their precarious position. Yet this land is more than a frontier: it is also the land of *shirk* (disbelief). There is great despair conveyed in the realization that this ordeal is not going away but, on the contrary, is actually going to worsen, as well as a sense of resignation that the only compensation for the patience of this Muslim community will be a reward in the hereafter. Finally, there is great anxiety about *lahn* (grammatical mistakes). The very language is now slipping away from them, and the leader of the community is keenly aware of this linguistic alienation. The original anonymous author was unfit for the task, and he admits to that, while the scribe/author – a *faqih*, or jurisprudent – is eager to fix the language of the work, but is still hesitant.

Yet Vienna MS. A. F. 58 is still more than what we have so far described. It has an extensive new work, a new *Mujadalah* (*Disputation*) with the Christians, which appears after their theological doctrines. The two parts of this manuscript leave no doubt that the scribe/author has a clear program, consisting of an attempt to make the community immune to all its attackers. In this second part, he informs the readers that, in replying, he uses the Hebrew Bible and the Gospels, as well as the arguments of a certain judge (whose name he gives as Abu al-'Abbas Ahmad al-Lakhmi al-Sharqi), an indication that Muslim intellectuals in Christian Spain were kept rather busy defending their faith. In addition to these sources, the author/scribe relies on books of philosophy and logic, and it soon becomes clear that it is the works of Ibn Rushd that he has in mind. Indeed, the work is more a theological disputation than a refutation of the Gospels or the Torah. It is an answer to the aggressive Christian proselytizing that took place among the Muslims.

Far more indicative of the richness of this document is that we find in this section a large number of Latin/Spanish words written in Arabic script; indeed, it is clear that the Muslim community was, if not fully bilingual, then more probably monolingual with a passive knowledge of Arabic. In fact, the scribe has to transcribe the concepts into Latin/Spanish first, Arabic being apparently insufficient. He consistently refers to God as "Dios." The insistence on referring to Ibn Rushd (who, he tells the reader, is called "the Commentator" by the Christians) is evidence of the anxiety of the Spanish Muslim community caused by the use of a Muslim philosopher against them. Could it be that the use of Averroës by Christians in Spain was common knowledge among the Muslims and, as such, became an issue in the reception of the author later on among Muslims in general?

The second part of the manuscript leaves the impression of a work in progress. Thus the scribe/author thought he had finished his work at folio 49b, only to change his mind and continue adding more material for the benefit of the reader (Vienna MS. A. F. 58, fol. 49b). This part of the manuscript is deeply philosophical at times, if not arcane, but strikes a more popular tone at others, providing a medley of stories and arguments to provide solace to the believers. Remarkably, the work reviews some of the classical arguments used by the Muslim apologists and rejects them, offering new ones instead. This work is in no sense "popular," if by that term we mean "unreflective," especially since it is keenly aware of the use of the works of Ibn Rushd.

At a certain point, the author denies that victory (or, as he calls it, *bi-al-sayf*) is a sign of the righteous religion – the Christian opponents appear to be arguing that since, in every battle, Muslims are losing to the Christians, they must be the ones with the wrong faith. Instead, the author declares that true religion is based on real righteousness, and he quotes Aristotle to support his argument (fol. 50a). The manuscript halts all of a sudden, in the midst of a sentence. The manuscript has clear indications that it was at some point read by a Christian learned reader who knew Arabic and who made Latin comments and notes in its margins. Did it belong to an inquisitor?

It should be clear why I would prefer to assess the manuscript as a whole. The first part is a defence of Islam against the Jews, using scriptural arguments; the second is an attack on Christian doctrines using Ibn Rushd, Aristotle and other works of philosophy. It is imperative that we study the work as a whole, as a document of a besieged community attempting to come to grips with a very difficult situation. Moreover, the first part of the manuscript, though a clearly defined work, is modified all the same: thus, this manuscript fits in with a general picture of Morisco literature as a literary tradition that did not care about authorship as much as about continuing the connection of the community to the past.

The situation of al-Biqa'i and his encounter with the Bible could not have been more different. Here the issue was not the validity of Islam, or the prophecy of Muhammad; indeed, the issue was not about winning arguments against Christians or Jews at all. It was instead about the position of Muslims vis-à-vis the Bible. How do Muslims respond to the Bible as scripture? Here the Muslim scholar al-Biqa'i, though on safe grounds, had to answer the question of the relevance of a different scripture to his religious outlook. The Bible on its own is potent enough – present enough. The debate was an internal Islamic debate waged among the Muslims themselves, and was no less bitter for that. Muslims, it appears, do not have a *position* towards the Bible so much as a relationship. This relationship was always taut precisely because it was ambivalent. One could embrace and reject the Bible at the same moment, and both positions could occur at the same time. The Bible was a shadow of the Qur'an, always accompanying it, and always impossible to ignore.

This brings me back to the remark with which I began in the opening pages of this article. How do we acknowledge scholarly work that was done, but subsequently forgotten? This article builds on the work of previous scholars, attempting to turn our attention to our failures to build on this earlier scholarship. Where this article differs from the previous scholarship is in regard to the assessment of the significance of this manuscript. This article is thus a plea to reposition as central in the retelling of the story of the Bible in Islam a manuscript that reflects the voice of a besieged community, a manuscript that sheds a dramatic light on the customary attitude of Muslims towards the Bible. This manuscript needs to be studied more extensively and in conjunction with other polemical works. It is remarkable that this manuscript and its significance left no trace in the general history of the Bible in Islam. The legacy of studying Islam is now almost two hundred years old, and we as scholars have failed to keep our members informed of the basic outline of this scholarship. We are in a critical moment of our history as a discipline, in urgent need both of taking measure of what has already been done, and of pointing the way to the future.

I came across the manuscript described here while reading the catalogue of the Vienna collection. Only much later did I realize that it had already been studied and, in a way, dismissed. It is conceivable that I might have failed to notice the articles on this work, especially the non-English European scholarship. Here we are facing another dire situation: the issue of languages in our field. We should make clear to our students that part of an academic career in Islamic and Arabic studies is also a life devoted to the learning of languages. The consequence of not facing up to this situation is that we will otherwise produce parochial scholarship, fully unaware of its own history.

Let us then go back to the issue of the Bible in Islam, the Bible as a codex, a book to be read. We now have a far richer picture of this encounter by simply readmitting and repositioning one manuscript; but we should keep expanding the larger picture, learning more about the grand narrative, by binding all the pieces together. It is instructive that almost at the exact time our Morisco Muslim was busy defending Islam by using the Bible – where the issue of *tahrif* (scriptural falsification, the standard accusation of the Muslims levelled against the Jews and the Christians) is very minor (indeed, almost absent), thus submitting to the premise that the Bible is divine – another Muslim, al-Biqa'i, was simultaneously busy in Cairo appropriating the Bible as a religious text to be used by the Muslims to explain the Qur'an and defending its fundamental textual integrity.[5] The study of the history of the Bible in Islam is thus remarkably flawed: not so much because we are not aware of what is available (Goldziher as well as Steinschneider were both aware of al-Biqa'i and the Vienna manuscript), but because we have too often failed to build on that earlier work. When the history of the Bible in Islam has been written, it has too often been simply a history of polemical works seen merely as polemical works, not as cultural works that reveal far more than a polemical mindset.

NOTES

1 I have already studied al-Biqa'i's encounter with the Bible extensively; see *In Defense of the Bible*.
2 For the literature on this manuscript see the dissertation of Leon Jacob Kassin, "A Study of a Fourteenth-Century Polemical Treatise ADVERSUS JUDAEOS."
3 Hava Lazarus-Yafeh, in her *Intertwined Worlds*, dismisses the treatise as "popular," hence unworthy of our attention.
4 For a discussion of apocalyptic signs in Islam, see my essay "The Female as a Locus of Apocalyptic Anxiety in Medieval Sunni Islam."
5 See Saleh, "A Fifteenth-Century Muslim Hebraist."

6 "Mixing the East with the West": Cosmopolitan Philology in Richard Burton's Translations from Camões

PAULO LEMOS HORTA

"The original device of mixing the East with the West," ventures Richard Burton in his commentary on Camões, lends *The Lusiads* "a new and peculiar position" within the European epic. Perhaps the winter the Renaissance Portuguese poet spent on Hormuz Island, Burton speculates, afforded Camões "the glance of genius at Persian literature" and gave his *Lusiads* "a gorgeousness of tint unknown to the severer Epic schools." For Burton, Camões's sojourn on the Persian Gulf Island could help explain the epic's at-times "uniquely un-European style" and the "charm" and "perfect sweetness" of "that reflection of Eastern literature upon Western thought" (R. Burton, *Camoens* 1:102–3). In Camões's courtly love poetry Burton admires a chivalric quality that he finds indebted to the Middle East, and in his Homeric and Virgilian epic he praises the interpolation of figures and devices from the non-Western traditions. Burton's treatment of Camões is distinctive in its philological attention to the circulation between East and West of words and concepts of love and beauty, hospitality and etiquette, pagan gods, and the supernatural. The cosmopolitanism of Burton's philological practice did not signal an innocence of imperial design, but rather allowed Burton to articulate a complex engagement with the Portuguese experience of empire as a counterpoint for that of Britain in his own times. Burton did not see in the Portuguese imperial experience merely the cautionary tale of imperial decline observed by many of his English contemporaries. In the cosmopolitan travel and sensibility of the early Portuguese explorers, and in particular of Camões, Burton saw a positive model for the possible reform and reinvigoration of what he felt to be an ailing British imperial enterprise.

An explorer, anthropologist, and translator famous in Victorian England for his quest for the source of the Nile, his pilgrimage to Mecca and Medina, and his translations of the *1001 Nights* and the *Kama Sutra*, Burton is most familiar to contemporary scholars as one of Said's principal examples in *Orientalism* (194–7).

As a consequence, even the most nuanced scholarship on Burton's interest in Camões assumes it was motivated by the quest for exoticism often attributed to his *1001 Nights* and *Kama Sutra* (Myers 242). Burton's engagement with Camões, in six volumes published in his lifetime and a further four previously presumed lost,[1] reveals less a strict Orientalist than a Mediterraneanist with an eye for cross-cultural influences, parallels, and affinities. At his death Burton left unpublished, beyond the Elegies, Octaves, Eclogues, Triumphs and Roundels of Camões, manuscript translations of Ariosto's *Orlando Furioso*, Basile's *Muse Napolitane* (from the Neapolitan) and a tale from Tassoni's *La Secchia Rapita*.[2] In light of these newly catalogued manuscripts, it becomes evident that the literary translations from Romance languages rivaled those from Middle or Far Eastern languages. Burton's writing included literary translations from the Portuguese and several travelogues and monographs dealing with the aftermath of Portuguese imperialism in Goa and Brazil.[3] These works form part of the forgotten Lusophone and Mediterranean corpus of this "Orientalist" figure familiar from the scholarship inspired by Said. While it is tempting to follow current practice and read Burton's translations from Romance languages strictly as a function of his Orientalism, this study reveals his attentiveness to the interplay and intermingling of East and West in his literary translations from the Portuguese.

While Burton's proficiency in Arabic began at university and his Indian vernacular languages were acquired with the goal of advancement in the British East India Company, Burton's fluency in a half-dozen continental vernaculars and dialects was developed during an itinerant childhood in France and Italy as the child of a retired lieutenant colonel trying to stretch a modest pension in Tours, Blois, Pau, Pisa, and Naples. Scholarship has overlooked the nuances of this early itinerant identity and fluency in Romance languages and cultures, which enabled Burton to pick up Portuguese quickly in the 1840s and to return to Italian and Neapolitan as well as Portuguese in his literary translations made in Trieste in the 1880s. Burton's notes on his continental upbringing, edited by his widow Isabel, carefully differentiate the degrees of isolation of the English communities he experienced during his childhood – from the apparent self-sufficiency of the English at Tours, to the less organized and cohesive communities in Blois, Pisa, and Naples, to Siena where the English did not seek each other out for "almost all" were "fugitives from justice, social or criminal" (I. Burton 1:39). Dane Kennedy's study of Burton, *The Highly Civilized Man*, prefers to extrapolate from Burton's note on Tours a sharp division between the English and the locals (and self and "other") and to downplay the many cultural opportunities for the young Burton on the continent that have been documented by trade biographies.[4] Burton himself emphasized the transformative effect of the experience of childhood and youthful travel in writing about himself and in explaining his affinity for the

Portuguese poet. In his view, Camões was distinguished among poets, as he was himself among translators, by the cognitive breakthroughs afforded by long travel and sojourns in the East in youth, which would have made each more capable of cultural immersion and internalizing Eastern aesthetic forms and ideas. This shared experience would have qualified Camões and Burton to mediate between East and West in their poetry, translation, and commentary.

If modern philology pertains to the study of the textual communication between civilizations, Burton can be considered an imperialist precursor of this philological curiosity about the communication between civilizations. His conviction that philology could reveal traces of cross-cultural influence in *The Lusiads* differentiates his practice of philology from the medieval historicism of the Pre-Raphaelites, whom he otherwise admired. Burton's correspondence on Camões and the *1001 Nights* with John Payne, a peripheral member of the Pre-Raphaelite circle, demonstrates the cosmopolitan intentions of his philological concern with rendering Camões in archaic English. Much as Burton translated from Italian, Sanskrit, Portuguese and Arabic, Payne translated from Persian, Arabic, and French, and in their correspondence both men moved seamlessly between the overlapping Mediterranean and Middle Eastern worlds of Camões and the *1001 Nights*. Burton and Payne had a high regard for Pre-Raphaelite and Decadent aesthetics, were aware of the instrumental role of Rossetti and Swinburne in popularizing Edward FitzGerald's version of Omar Khayyam's *Rubaiyat*, and craved a similar reception for their respective translations from Persian and Arabic. Yet they differed in their assessments of how to follow Rossetti's advice. In Payne's estimation, the fact that "Camões, like all his peers, Portuguese & Spanish, is often singularly obscure," should not prevent his sonnets from being rendered "plainer" in good medieval English.[5]

Burton sought not to place Camões in the register of Spenser or Sidney, but to capture the worldview of the Portuguese poet that he saw as shaped by his formative experience of travel in the Persian Gulf and India. He thought it necessary to think alongside the metre and alliterative and assonant rhythm of the original and to preserve its moral inscape and ethnological value. Burton complained that "the music of the Neo-Latin tongue waxes harsh or slow in our rude Northern Runic" (*Camoens* 1:187). He wanted to educate the English ear — most distant to him from the courtly love tradition indebted to the Middle East — in the musicality of other languages, rhythms, and metres alien to Anglo-Saxon speech. Burton claimed as the guiding principle for his version of Camões' lyric poetry Rossetti's assessment of the responsibility of the translator to shun "any special grace of his own idiom and epoch" — any contemporary cadence, rhyme, or turn of a stanza (Rossetti 353). Rossetti's goal of finding in English (say, in the vocabulary of Spenser) the counterpart of Italian medievalism was at once reconstructive and normative, as George Steiner has observed, for it aspired "to make of the old manner a modern ideal" (Steiner 353). Burton likewise sought to make of the old and "obscure" manner of the lyric and epic poetry of Camões an ideal to guide his modern contemporaries, governed by its articulation of a worldview of chivalric virtue, courtly love, and the curiosity of explorers.

Epic

"None but a traveler can do justice to a traveler," proclaims Burton's preface to his 1880 translation of *The Lusiads*. Burton's portrait of Camões as a voyager provides the key to his view of the Portuguese poet as a fellow cosmopolite:

> A wayfarer and voyager from his youth ... a moralist, a humourist, a satirist, and, consequently, no favourite with King Demos; a reverent and religious spirit after his own fashion (somewhat "Renaissance," poetic, and Pagan), by no means after the fashion of others; an outspoken, truth-telling, lucre-despising writer ... a type of the chivalrous age. (Camoens, *Lusiads* 1:xi–xii)

A shared experience binds the translator to the poet he addresses as the "companion," "consoler," and "talisman" to his travels (*Lusiads* 1:xv). In this portrait the transformative experience of youthful travel functions as a prefix to distinguish the virtues that follow: Camões is the archetypal traveller-mystic, traveller-patriot, and traveller-moralist. In affirming his credentials for translating Camões, Burton makes the strong claim that, beyond geographic accuracy, travel affords the translator as it did the poet the ability to inhabit a cosmography informed by East and West.[6] Burton feels better qualified as a traveller to do justice to the mingling of Eastern and Western learning reflected in the Portuguese Renaissance cosmography famously expounded by Tethys in Canto X of *The Lusiads*. The *Erdkunde* of Camões, Burton insists, must be understood with reference to the changes to the map of Ptolemy "introduced by the Moslem and the early European, especially the Portuguese explorers who traveled with the Periplus and the Pelusian in hand" (*Camoens* 1:374–5). Burton's commentary on Camões's cosmography details how the Ptolemeic system was adopted "by the Arab philosophers, who garnished it with marvelous details" and includes a table systematically illustrating the variances introduced to the system in "medieval and Moslem astronomy" (*Camoens* 1:373). Burton seeks to improve on previous commentaries on *The Lusiads* by being more attentive to the non-European influences on the cosmography of Camões as a product of the epoch of Portuguese exploration and of the poet's own travels in the Persian Gulf and India.

With this accent on travel as a cognitive as well as an imaginative act, Burton claims *The Lusiads* to be an epic that speaks universally to *Reiselust* rather than an account of the discovery of a particular route to Asia that would appeal primarily to the English as the imperial successors to the Portuguese in India. *The Lusiads* promises to tell that tale of "seas never navigated before" ["mares nunca de antes navegados"], and the epic takes up the story of da Gama's expedition *in medias res*, at the point the Portuguese arguably were sailing seas never braved by Europeans before. Burton views *The Lusiads* as the epic of exploration,

> that poetry-passion of the Unknown; whose joy of mere motion lightens all sorrows and disappointments; which aids, by commune with Nature, the proper study of Mankind; which enlarges the mental view as the hill-head broadens the horizon; which made Julian a saint, Khizr a prophet, and Odin a God. (*Lusiads* 1:xv)

In Camões's interest in da Gama's exploration, Burton spies his own sense of travel as a distinctive realm of experience and knowledge. Hence, to translate *The Lusiads* is the "perfection of a traveler's study" (*Lusiads* 1:xi). The phrase captures well the cognitive and imaginative education Burton believed travel affords youthful travellers such as Camões and himself, and which he believed eludes the "learned" Orientalist who ventures East only after his schooling and specialization (*Lusiads* 1:xiii). In this view, travel in one's youth grants not only the potential for specialized knowledge about a particular destination, but a more fundamental capacity to inhabit and move among foreign imaginative terrains. In Burton's interpretation, *The Lusiads* becomes less an epic of discovery than an epic of exploration and the explorer's delight in the "mere motion" of constant travel and the cognitive breakthroughs and self-fashioning it affords.

Burton's claim that Camões was able to inhabit and draw from Middle Eastern and Hindu mythology casts in a new light the riddle of the intervention of pagan gods in *The Lusiads* that has puzzled critics for the half millennium since its first publication. In the twentieth stanza of the first Canto, the gods gather on Mount Olympus to "decide the future of the Orient" ["sobre as cousas futuras do Oriente"]. Bacchus, fearful that the planned trek of the Portuguese to India might diminish the luster of legends pertaining to himself and other unspecified pagan gods there, decides to intervene by taking human shape and spreading hatred against the Portuguese among the Muslim peoples of Africa. Venus, zealous to defend her devoted Portuguese, counters with rumours of their virtues and good intentions along the African Coast. The differing welcomes, ranging from bellicose to loving, that da Gama's expedition finds among distinct "Moorish" and Ethiopian lands are explained therefore as a function of the intervention of pagan gods. In *The Lusiads,* mythological beings not only debate and observe the progress of the Portuguese in their quest for a route to India, but they interact directly with men (as the giant Adamastor, the Genius of the Cape of Good Hope, does in cursing da Gama) and manifest themselves in human shape, as Tethys and the sea nymphs do in rewarding the Portuguese on the "Island of Love" for their discovery of a route to India. Since Bartholameu Ferreira, the initial censor of the text for the Inquisition, readers of *The Lusiads* have wrestled with the riddle posed by the intervention of pagan gods in a narrative of an expedition whose stated goal was the conversion of the "pagan" peoples of the East to Catholicism (Cochrane 117–18).

Burton's affinity for Camões's deployment of pagan mythology in *The Lusiads* is a product of German Romantic reclamations of the poem. Neoclassical Europe had seen a decline in the poem's fortunes, and provided a hermeneutic framework that encouraged the interpretation of what exceeded classical authority and criteria in *The Lusiads* as flawed. The *Short Survey of European Vernacular Literature* by Rapin, leading theorist of *classicisme*, tested Camões's epic with reference to Aristotelian rules and found it wanting "proportion in its design, justice in its philosophy, exactness in its expression" (quoted in Pierce 100). *Classicisme* provided a context for Voltaire – in his 1733 *Essay on Epic Poetry* – both to recognize Camões for "opening up an entirely new course" in contrast to poets who "weakly and timidly followed in the tracks of the ancients" and to condemn the "conflict" of pagan and Christian mythology for "disfigur[ing] the entire work in the eyes of sensible readers" (quoted in Cochrane 116). Romantic ideas of experience and imagination encouraged Schlegel to champion Camões's own experience as a voyager and his recourse to classical mythology in his work. In this manner, the device of the deployment of pagan mythology that had seemed quaint was reclaimed as new. Burton's variation on the Romantic reclamation of the poem is to attribute what is alien to classical models and criteria – and what makes *The Lusiads* original – to Camões's internalization of Islamic and Hindu cultural models and references. Burton sees this mixture of miracle and myth as an invitation by Camões, the traveller to India, to excavate from underneath Portuguese Catholicism the Mediterranean pantheistic faith Burton credits with enabling European Renaissance humanism in the arts and sciences (*Scinde* 172).

The originality of Camões's approach to classical mythology, for Burton, rested on his cosmopolitan ability to spy a kinship between the Mediterranean pantheism that informed the European Renaissance and the "pagan" pantheism da Gama encounters in India. To the assertion of a previous English translator of *The Lusiads* that "the monstrous idols of Hinduism bear no physical resemblances to the classic gods," Burton rejoins that as a traveller to India, "Camões knew better" that the "original gods traveled from Egypt by two main roads, Eastward to India, Westward to Greece" (*Camoens* 2:639). Burton's counterintuitive reading of *The Lusiads* as sympathetic to pagan gods of West and East, at the expense of the poem's professed narrative of Christian evangelization, is stated most boldly in a previously unknown original manuscript poem, "The Translator's Farewell to his Author":

> The Gods of Greece and Hind were quick again,
> The grey and grimly Nazarene despite,
> Poseidon, Proteus, harem and anew
> Venus and Cupid clear the ~~heavenly~~ blue
> Gallantest Manhood in full glory scene
> With gracious Womanhood, came hand in hand
> Like gods of Heaven in their gait and mien
> The Gods of Earth, a daring dainty-band ...[7]

Burton attributes to Camões the championing of the "Gods of Greece and Hind" and an almost pagan treatment of explorers as gods among men in the manner of the warriors of ancient epics in East and West. This poem's dismissal of "grey and grimly" Christianity explains the cursory ease with which, in his commentary on *The Lusiads*, Burton portrays the epic's proselytizing claims – and the moralizing stanzas that round off each canto – as concessions to convention and to the pressures of ecclesiastical censorship.

Burton suggests that Camões articulated a somewhat "pagan," "poetic," and "Renaissance" worldview that he felt best described explorers whose exploits he likened to the feats of the gods and warriors of classical epic poetry in East and West. In terms of philology, this task of capturing this Renaissance worldview entailed unearthing within the Portuguese language the submerged traditions of West and East that the explorers embodied and encountered in their route to India. In Burton's preface, the praise of *The Lusiads* for echoing "the true heroic ring" of "old ballads" (*Lusiads* 1:xiv) recalls his anthropological conviction that early poetry is the perfect expositor of a people.[8] While Burton's own philological anthropology sought to extrapolate from a people's earliest poetic expression its truest traits, Burton argued that the language of *The Lusiads* sought to capture the moment of the feats of navigation and discovery which Camões celebrates in his poem and which contrasted with the imminent imperial decline of his late years. Burton casts the author of *The Lusiads* as a philological archaeologist of his own language, keen to import into fifteenth-century Portuguese not only Greek and Latinate words but also the scientific terms, "colloquialisms," and "Orientalisms" of the language of navigation and exploration (*Camoens* 1:191). Burton's counterintuitive, "pagan" reading of *The Lusiads* requires him to correct English and Portuguese accounts of da Gama and of Camões that attributed to both an antipathy towards Islam and an evangelical zeal. Burton interprets the incorporation in *The Lusiads* of various Portuguese words of Arabic origin – *Algoz, Algema, Arraial, Alarido, Almadia* – as part of an attentiveness to the nuances and distinctions among the Muslim peoples da Gama encountered along his route to India.

These philological intimations of vestiges of Arabic in Camões's Portuguese encourage Burton to read into the poem perhaps more sympathy towards Islam than Camões intends, particularly with respect to instances of cross-cultural misunderstanding, such as (in the first Canto) the hostility that da Gama's expedition encounters among the *"Mouros"* (Camões's generic term for Muslims) of Mozambique. The poem notes that the islanders initially mistake the Portuguese for uncultured Turks before recognizing and resenting them as Christian Europeans, yet for Burton Camões may have intuited that the natives refused to relinquish their original perception of the foreigners as Turks and merely pretended to acknowledge their stated identity as European. Burton takes this as evidence that Camões was aware of the national rivalries among Muslims that would explain the hostility of the Mozambique islanders towards the Portuguese in terms of their antipathy to Turks. His commentary notes that Camões would have known better than to trust chronicles of da Gama's journey that insisted on the importance of its evangelical mission and its alleged successes – such as the apparent discovery of Catholic worship among the Hindus. From the vantage point of this philologically informed reading of the poem, Camões's relationship to Muslim and Hindu mythology was governed less by a strict antagonism than by a syncretism of Eastern and Western influences.

Burton's notes speculate on possible Hindu and Muslim antecedents for the episodes of pagan intervention in *The Lusiads* that Voltaire and the neoclassicists had found implausible: Bacchus's intervention on behalf of the pagan gods of the East, the curse of Adamastor, and the welcome Venus offers the explorers on the Island of Love after their discovery of a route to India. Bacchus constitutes a special case in the reception of *The Lusiads* in world letters, since his role as adversary to the Portuguese and their Christian mission to India has inspired a tradition of commentary identifying him as an allegorical figure for Islam. In the theory of one critic, Camões casts Bacchus as the enemy of Christianity because he believed Bacchus had been worshipped by the pre-Islamic Arabs of the time of Alexander the Great as an alternative to heaven. Burton rejected the hypothesis of the Dionysian figure of Bacchus as an allegory for "teetotal" Islam in the poem as "peculiarly unhappy" (*Camoens* 2:568). He posited instead that Camões intimated a kinship between Bacchus and Krishna. Burton prefers a "tradition" that derives Bacchus from "Mount Meru, the Olympus of Hinduism," and speculates that in India Camões "may have been told of Krishna, the popular Avatar (incarnation) and his Nymphs; a strange mixture of Bacchus and the Gospel of Infancy" (*Camoens* 2:567). Burton proposes the theory that the historical model for the "wine-god" was "some Syrian or Assyrian soldier-conqueror who, before the days of Semiramis (B.C.2017–1965?), marched Eastward, plundered Western India" and introduced viticulture to the subcontinent (*Camoens* 2:567). In this view, Bacchus's sympathy for the unnamed gods of India is attributable to Camões's knowledge of the kinship between the Greek wine-god and Krishna.

In speculating that Camões was curious about and sympathetic to the affinity between Bacchus and Krishna, Burton produces his own Romantic misreading of the uniqueness of *The Lusiads* as an epic poem. Burton took a common Romantic perception that Bacchus and Venus symbolized in the poem the clash of pagan and Christian cultures and opened up the possibility that for Camões the figure of Bacchus bridged the polytheism of India and Greece. Burton implicitly attributes to Camões some of his own affinity for Bacchus's concern for the fate of pagan deities in India threatened by da Gama's mission of evangelization. This perhaps constitutes reading the poem against itself, akin to Blake's proclamation of Satan as the true hero of *Paradise Lost*. Burton strikes a Romantic chord similar to Blake's in likening the role of Bacchus in *The Lusiads* to that of Satan in *Paradise Lost* – in Burton's gloss, "being doomed to fight, and to fight without hope" (*Camoens* 2:568). Modern scholarship has ascertained that the most demonstrable trace of the influence of Camões on Milton pertains to the deployment of Oriental imagery for the figure of Satan in a manner reminiscent of Bacchus in *The Lusiads* (Sims). Burton's hypothesis regarding Camões's awareness of the kinship between Bacchus and Krishna would add a further dimension to the observed parallels of Oriental imagery that accompany Camões's Bacchus and Milton's Satan. Likewise, this hypothesis might strengthen the evidence of modern critics who seek to recuperate Bacchus in *The Lusiads* as the sympathetic "Lord of India" in the framework of Camões's appropriation of Greek mythology (Alves 102–3). Given the poem's genealogy of Lusus as the companion or offspring of Bacchus, Burton's commentary opens up the intriguing possibility that Camões intended Bacchus in his affinity with Krishna as a figure of the parallels between Greek and Hindu gods that Lusus, as the embodiment of Portugal, ignores at its own peril. In this framework, Bacchus would stand in for the buried Mediterranean and pagan pre-history of Renaissance Portugal that the epic's ostensibly Catholic narrative seeks to erase.

In the episode of the curse of the Portuguese by Adamastor, the Genius of the Cape of Good Hope, a geographical marker of the divide between "West" and "East," Burton spies the imprint of Islamic folklore that would mediate between the mythologies of Greece and India. Disturbed from his slumber, the Genius of the Cape tells his story and foretells the failure of the Portuguese imperial enterprise. Key to the circulation of *The Lusiads* as a work of world literature, this episode also figures prominently in debates on the imperial discourses of *The Lusiads*. In light of an early tradition of commentary that – reading the poem in light of the *reconquista* – tends to identify all of the enemies of the Portuguese explorers in the epic with figurations of Islam, Faria e Sousa devotes nineteen pages of his 1639 commentary to prove that the giant was the prophet Muhammad. Burton finds Faria e Sousa's gloss of Adamastor as Muhammad – and the accompanying claims that the prophet Muhammad would have been baptized, travelled to Cordova, and died an atheist — "a stupendous monument to ignorance and fanaticism" (*Camoens* 1:87). Burton starts from the quite different assumption that the figure from Greek myth as appropriated by Camões in India after his sojourn in the Persian Gulf may have acquired traits associated with Islamic folklore. In his treatment of Adamastor, Burton is curious about the provenance of the giant in Greek mythology and in modern European letters (notably in Rabelais) and attentive to the possible echoes of other mythological creatures. Perhaps the coincidence that the Portuguese word *gênio* signifies both genius and jinni suggested a philological parallel which Burton would explore in a later note to the *1001 Nights* and which affords him the chance in his commentary to link the Genius of the Cape with the *Nights*' jinni.[9] The connection would appear particularly apt since the jinn, disturbed from their peaceful and invisible abodes, often respond with curses in the *1001 Nights* as in the tale of the "Merchant and the Jinni."

For Burton, the distinctive trait of Adamastor that exceeds his classical models and might be specific to Camões's familiarity with the lore of the jinn is the cloud-like nature of his appearance, which has puzzled critics from Voltaire to the present day. Burton is interested in the manner of Adamastor's appearance out of thin air high above the mast, like the condensation of dark clouds that blot out the night sky. Voltaire had found this scene incongruous, mocking the image of a phantom rising from the sea depths, its head touching the heavens, winds, tempests, and thunder raging around it. Burton counters that in appearing in the form of a "black vapour" that "towers high in the sky," the Genius of the Cape is "like the Jinn in the *Thousand and One Nights*" (*Camoens* 1:87). A different philological association and cultural contextualization make believable for him a scene that Voltaire found unpersuasive. Burton's insistence that the Genius Adamastor, like the Cape of Good Hope itself, mediated between East and West would prove pivotal to the genesis of the first American translation of *The Lusiads* by the Pulitzer-prize-winning poet Leonard Bacon in 1950. Bacon was inspired to translate Camões's epic upon encountering in John Fiske's *The Discovery of America* (1902) eight lines from the episode of Adamastor prefaced by Fiske's observation that Camões "represents the Genius of the Cape as appearing to the storm-tossed mariners in cloud-like shape, like the Jinni that the Fisherman of the Arabian tale released from a casket" (quoted in Monteiro 151n). Punning on the perceived association between jinni and demon, Bacon would recall "my *demon* told me there and then that some day, if only because of those eight blazing and sonorous lines, I would translate the epic" (quoted in Monteiro 150). Though neoclassicists and many later critics assumed Camões had only classical models in mind and that his Adamastor could be judged according to classical criteria, the first American translation of *The Lusiads* points to an alternative genealogy for the currency of this episode, founded upon the supposition that the figure of Adamastor was indebted to the jinn of the *1001 Nights* as suggested by Burton.

In the significant episode of the Island of Love that follows da Gama's discovery of a route to India, which accounts for almost one-fifth of the poem, Burton ventures that Camões may be appropriating Hindu mythology and presenting it to his Portuguese readers under the guise of Greek mythology. In this episode, Venus rewards the Portuguese explorers for the discovery of India with an amorous reception on an imaginary Island of Love in which da Gama is paired with his former adversary, Tethys, and his men with immortal nymphs. This episode has figured prominently in aesthetic and political critiques of the poem. In the wake of neoclassicism, Voltaire found the episode unseemly, and likened the reception given da Gama's men on the island to the welcome granted sailors in the brothels of Amsterdam (Pierce 118). In his postcolonial reading, Quint would interpret the episode as an imperial fantasy of miscegenation and the warm reception to be granted colonists by native women. Burton answered Voltaire's objections by noting episodes comparable to the Island of Love in the writing of Homer, Virgil, Dante, Tasso, Ariosto, Spenser, and Milton (*Camoens* 2:652–3). And he insists on the resonance in this episode of not only classical precedents and Renaissance parallels but also possibly a Hindu source, venturing that perhaps Camões as a cosmopolitan traveller may have derived the episode of the immortal brides with "a marriage and a marriage-feast" from Hindu mythology, for the "Gandharbas ('celestial musicians') become the wives of distinguished mortals, and Gandharba-lagan (nymph-espousals) is the Sanskrit term for such unions, which are legal although dispensing with clerical aid" (*Camoens* 2:652–3).

Here again Burton deploys an imagined cross-cultural resonance to buttress his counter-intuitive case for Camões's allegiance to Dionysian values that run counter to the poem's stated goal and da Gama's ostensible mission of vanquishing pagan values and propagating Christian ones. There is a rich tradition dating to the Spanish commentary of Faria e Sousa in 1639 that attempts to reconcile the presence of Venus and the Island of Love with the ostensibly Christian motive of da Gama's journey.[10] For Burton to insist on the relevance of a Hindu context was to affirm what he termed the pagan quality of Camões's faith and to refute the reconciliation of the episode with a Christian cosmography. It is in line rather with modern readings of the poem that stress the disconnect between its narrative of Christian patriotism and the *reconquista* and the "pagan" and Dionysian narrative of da Gama's voyage protected by Venus (to whom the Portuguese offer homage). In the modern line of commentary associated with the work of Antonio José Saraiva, the "ultimate sense" of the poem cannot be straightforward and bellicose given the "unhinging of the very mythological plot" from the outset when "the voyagers place themselves under the lovely sign of Venus" (quoted in Alves 99). Hélio Alves notes the Dionysian quality of the Island of Love: "the

Island of Venus is openly and exclusively Dionysian: that is, Venus the enemy of Bacchus rewards the explorers with the values of Bacchus" (Alves 103). The apparent struggle between Venus and Bacchus overlooks their common manifestation of Dionysian values. This reading would account for the disproportionate space devoted to the romantic episode of Ignes de Castro within the historical recitation of the battles of the *reconquista* and, more generally, the presence of invocations of Venus and sensual love in an epic of "arms and men."

Lyric

The matter-of-fact manner with which Burton asserts the debt of whole genres of European lyric poetry to Arabic and Persian literary traditions in his commentary on Camões's lyrics contrasts with the challenge faced by modern philologists like María Rosa Menocal and others to persuade specialists in national languages and literatures of the debt of Dante to Arabic astronomical sources or that of Boccaccio to the encyclopedic texts associated with the tri-religious tradition of Andalusia.[11] Burton admires in the lyric poetry of Camões the "quaint mixture" of chivalric traditions of East and West. For him, Camões belonged to the "more brilliant and buoyant age" of European courtly love poetry that preserved "the peculiarities derived from Provençal poetry and from the Sicilian Saracens who represented the Badawi chivalry of the Desert" (*Lyricks* 2:437). If English was the most removed from the rhymes, rhythms and "amorous terms" of this tradition of "all the modern tongues," Burton still hears in the sixteenth-century Portuguese of Camões's lyric poetry a trace of the chivalric realm of the *1001 Nights* tales, in which men were "never a day out of love" (*Lyricks* 2:437). Burton resituates the cartography and cosmography of Camões's concerns in his lyric poetry with reference to the poet's sojourns in the Persian Gulf and India. He observes the mediation of Camões's neo-Platonic sonnets (which he labels "Amorous Metaphysical" and "Sufistical") by the Sufism he likely encountered on Hormuz Island and in India, and champions the "masculine realism" of the autobiographical poems of nature and love in the tradition of the troubadours. He speculates that the Portuguese poet might have been familiar with the poetry of Hafiz that was championed by the Shah of Hormuz Island where Camões sojourned, and spies in the "mysteries" of Camões's neo-Platonic sonnets "echoes of Hafiz and the Sufis, who borrowed from Plato a doctrine probably learned during his thirteen years in Egypt" (*Lyricks* 2:440). The passing reference to the Egyptian provenance of Platonism suggests a broader Middle Eastern influence on all Renaissance neo-Platonism, rather than a unique claim on behalf of Camões.

Burton admires most the "autobiographical portion" of Camões's lyrics, which ranges from the "storm and stress of youth" to the loss and "nostalgia" of age, passing through all the phases of the poet's loves and "chequered career" – his "'four banishments,' his three campaigns, his many imprisonments, and his way-farings to the outer East" (*Lyricks* 2:443). These autobiographical lyrics of love, exile and travel best reflect for Burton the virtues of the courtly love tradition that he identifies with the chivalry of Provençal and "Sicilian Saracen" bards. For Burton, it was Camões's experience of travel – including travel to the East that figures in the lyric poetry composed or set in India – that set his work apart from the common European troubadour tradition. In this view, the lyric poetry, like the epic, demonstrates the practical knowledge of the traveller to be superior to the romance of the Orientalist writing of those who have not ventured East. Burton contrasts Camões's travel-inspired lyric poetry favourably to the "Nile-Sonnets" of poets who had not seen the river such as Shelley, Leigh Hunt, and Keats: "What has the Nile to do with Atlas or with the 'Desert's ice-girl pinnacles?' What means 'old hushed Egypt and its sands?'" (*Lyricks* 2:445). Only the "long travel" that "doubtless" completed Camões's education as a poet of nature "absolutely distinguishes him from his brother bards," allowing him to paint "the scene as a spectator" rather than "from the depths of their self-consciousness." Only pro-longed travel could instill in Camões a "bracing, healthy, masculine realism" and hence a gift for "simple, sensuous and impassioned" verse (*Lyricks* 2:445). Read-ing the Portuguese poet via the lens of the German Romantics and his own inves-tigations of sexuality, Burton has in mind an exemplary masculinity that balances masculine and feminine traits. For Burton, Camões illustrates Goethe's axiom that "the highest type of man must always contain something of the feminine," and he represents Burton's ideal of masculinity as defined by sympathy and "all that soft-ness and gentleness of spirit which characterize the noblest forms of humanity" (*Camoens* 1:46). Burton favourably contrasts what he terms the bracing, healthy, sensuous and impassioned realism of the autobiographic lyrics of Camões to the poetry of his own day, which he felt was marked by "strained introvision and vivisection" and "over-coloured brilliancy" (*Lyricks* 2:445).

Burton's concern with recuperating Camões's sympathetic interest in elements of Indian culture and stress on the masculine qualities of his lyric poetry dovetail in his manuscript translation of the roundel addressed to a "Bárbara Escrava."[12] While there is a tradition of interpreting the absent lover, to whom much of the lyric composed in Goa is addressed, as "indistinguishable from Portugal" (Myers 233), Burton prefers to focus on instances in which lovers absent or present in the lyric can be traced to real-life models. In the case of this roundel, which seeks to refute the charge that the dark lady is a barbarian and demonstrate the quality of her beauty, the originality of Burton's interpretation rests in suggesting that she is not an African slave, as previous commentators had held, but rather an Indian servant and mistress of Camões. In contrast to the grand terminology of the sonnets, Burton translates this poem in "simple, sensuous and impassioned" language:

Aquela cativa	That fair captive Mary
Que me tem cativo	Who captivated my spirit
Porque nela vivo	For I live in her light
Já não quer que viva	My life would deny
Eu nunca vi rosa	I ne'er saw a rose
Em suaves molhos.	Fragranced, pray
Que para meus olhos	In vision sway
Fôsse mais fermosa.	That lovelier glows.

The poem seeks to disabuse "the vain herd" ["o povo vão"] of the conviction "that [only] blond is fair" ["Que os louros são belos"] and insists that the captive "Right strange may appear / But Barbarous – no!" ["Bem parece estranha / Mas Bárbara não"]. Burton's reading of the roundel captures the underlying regressive politics of his at-times positive valuation of other cultures, for in his hierarchy of cultures, an Indian captive could capture Camões's imagination more easily than an African. For Burton, it would be more characteristic for Camões to have sought to prove the civilization of a woman who belonged to a culture which he perceived to have parallels with Greek civilization, and from which he likely borrowed certain mythological devices – such as the Hindu idea of celestial brides for *The Lusiads*.[13]

Burton emerges from the corpus of his writing on Camões, as choices like this attest, less the cultural relativist of the portrait recently offered by Dane Kennedy than the committed imperialist beholden to cultural hierarchies, however idiosyncratic, counterintuitive, and sometimes contradictory. In its emphasis on the cognitive breakthroughs afforded by the enabling experience of youthful travel, Burton's cosmopolitan practice of philology speaks less to relativism than to a desire for a reinvigorated imperialism. In translating Camões archaically, Burton seeks to recapture the ancient and lost virtues that he positively associates with the enterprises of chivalry and exploration. In holding up Portuguese *conquistadores* as a class to be emulated by their British successors, Burton advances the romance of an imperialism innocent of its contemporary flaws and sins, concerned with the dizzying possibilities opened up by exploration, discovery, and first cultural contacts. Burton privileges an idyllic image of the Portuguese *conquistadores* of Camões as a class braving forbidden and blank spaces on maps as a foundational imperial dream of conquest that could never quite be undermined by conditions on the ground and the poverty of its realization. Likewise, Burton projects a romance of British imperialism that cannot falter along with the failure of a particular British imperial enterprise or policy. In his commentary on *The Lusiads*, as in his other writing, this romance of empire coexists with a scathing critique of particular British campaigns, mistakes in battle, and the ignorance of senior diplomats and colonial administrators (Burton's superiors) regarding the peoples and customs they lorded over. Camões serves this discourse of imperialism by providing Burton with an opportunity to make of the old manner a new ideal – the chance to reconnect with the truer values of pagan and chivalric codes of honour preserved in the epic and courtly poetry of East and West. Burton's emphasis on the virtues of a "masculine realism" perfected by "long travel" points to the cosmopolitan agency he claims on behalf of the explorer poet and the explorer translator who follows in his footsteps. For him, the mixture of East and West is less something to be recognized by the traveller-poet than to be achieved and co-created by him.

In his translation of and commentary on Camões, Burton practices a speculative philology based on a cosmopolitanism enabled and perfected by travel, not the discipline of academic scholarship. It remains to be seen whether the resonances of non-western models in Adamastor, Bacchus and the Island of Love suggested by Burton can be corroborated by modern comparative philology. Burton sails outside the ports of the German philological tradition and the methods of the modern research university identified with that tradition. His self-consciously idiosyncratic method is evident in the characteristic phrasing of his philological notes, in which he declares he *prefers* to hear in a known word new and distinct cross-cultural echoes and associations. To what he perceives to be the paucity of the register of strictly academic philology, he contrasts the traveller's ear for the pronunciation, rhythm and musicality of words and their moral inscape and ethnological value. The traveller's practical knowledge would remain elusive to the academically trained philologist who travels belatedly to the East. In this regard, the philological practice of Burton's versions of Camões in the 1880s remains consistent with his earliest travelogues of the 1850s, which ridiculed the figure of the professional Orientalist freshly arrived on the subcontinent (*Scinde* 2:7). Burton's translations from Camões also complement his earlier critique of imitative rather than experiential Orientalism by positing that in contrast to the Keats and Shelley of the Nile sonnets, the poet who travelled in his youth could inhabit foreign forms and ideals. Burton fits awkwardly within the citationary mode of Orientalism that principally concerns Said (*Orientalism* 196), since it is in contrast to the scholar and poet's penchant for imitation and projection regarding Eastern matters that Burton champions the knowledge of the "practical" Orientalism or, more precisely, the Mediterraneanism he admires in Camões and seeks himself to practice.

Burton's Camões thus speaks to the neglected influence of this parallel philological tradition, a tradition in its scope at once Orientalist and Mediterraneanist. If Payne and Burton both sought to emulate the success of Edward FitzGerald's *Rubaiyat* with their translations from Persian and Arabic, it should be recalled that FitzGerald translated copiously from Calderón as Payne did from Villon and Burton from Camões. The regard for the mixture of East and West in Burton's work on Camões speaks less to the exceptionality of Burton than (as demonstrated by his correspondence with Payne) to the constant intermingling of Mediterranean and Middle and Far East in the work of self-taught rather than academic translators. At times, this parallel philological tradition would inform its mainstream counterpart: Burton's cosmopolitan philology in his work on Camões would influence a key text of imperial philology, *Hobson-Jobson: A Glossary of Anglo-Indian Terms and Phrases*, co-edited by Henry Yule and A.C. Burnell (1886). Burton's proof copy of his commentary is bookended by letters to him from Yule that are glued onto its front and back covers. Henry Yule would write to Burton to thank him for the "good many points" that he cribbed from the commentary for his glossary and to reassure Burton that he found not more than one "slip" in his "Geographical Comments."[14] These notes confirm that Yule and Burnell inherited from Burton, and English from Portuguese, more than the words credited to Burton in their glossary, and that Burton's attention to Portuguese as a conduit for non-western words and concepts to English did not go unnoticed by influential contemporary philologists. Burton's correspondence with Yule, as with Payne, speaks to the palimpsest quality of the imperial philologies, Portuguese and English, which would bridge the Mediterranean and "Oriental" worlds. *Hobson-Jobson* would in turn influence not only imperial but postcolonial letters, proving a key text for Salman Rushdie, who would contribute an introduction to the reissue of this favourite text and acknowledge it as central to his reclaiming of Anglo-Indian vocabulary in *Midnight's Children* and *The Moor's Last Sigh* (Rushdie 81–3).

If some of the cross-cultural affinities noted by Burton the amateur philologist are corroborated by modern scholarship, then a broadening of our conception of the influences working upon Camões as a Mediterranean Renaissance author becomes possible. Burton's careful parsing of literary from historiographic evidence in regard to the episode of da Gama mistaking Hindu for Catholic worship provides an example of an avenue of inquiry that has recently been taken up by modern scholarship on Camões as post-imperial author. Burton credits Camões with recognizing (unlike his historical sources) that the apparent Catholic ritual observed in India was Hindu or pagan. Burton contradicts Portuguese chronicles that attest to da Gama's claim that he witnessed Catholic worship in India by speculating that da Gama's expedition mistook cries of "Krishna" for "Christi!," the belief in the Hindu triad of Brahma, Vishnu, and Shiva for a belief in the Holy Trinity, and the adoration of Gauri, "the white Goddess," for worship of the Virgin Mary. Burton faults the Portuguese chroniclers for not probing "what conclusions might have been drawn from the likeness" (*Camoens* 2:420), namely the parallels that he, and in his view Camões, perceived between pantheism in India and the classical pantheism that still animated Portuguese Renaissance

Catholicism. Burton's comparative analysis of this episode in *The Lusiads* and its historical sources would provide Michael Murrin with the subject and sources for an essay that acknowledges Burton's commentary (cited sixteen times) as a point of departure, "First Encounter: the Christian-Hindu Confusion When the Portuguese Reached India." The avenues of inquiry opened up for modern scholars by Burton's version of Camões point to the further attention that may be merited to his overlooked translations from Italian and Neapolitan as well as to the writings of other nineteenth-century translators who bridged Middle Eastern and Mediterranean interests such as FitzGerald (who translated Khayyam alongside Calderón de la Barca) and Payne (who translated the *Nights* alongside Villon).

NOTES

This paper is indebted in a variety of ways to the Henry E. Huntington Library in San Marino, California: a Fletcher Jones Foundation Fellowship allowed me to discover the treasure trove of materials deposited there pertaining to Burton's translations from Camões; Alan Jutzi, Avery Chief Curator, Rare Books, generously granted and facilitated countless requests pertaining to the Burton Library (formerly held by the Royal Anthropological Institute); and Sue Hodson, Curator, Literary Manuscripts, afforded me access to the Richard Francis Burton papers (formerly the Edwards Metcalf collection) which, thanks to Gayle Richardson's excellent finding aid, I can now cite properly.

1 The published editions by Burton are Camoens, *Os Lusiadas* (*The Lusiads*); Burton, *Camoens: his life and his Lusiads: a commentary*; and Camoens, *The Lyricks*. Works in manuscript are *Camoens: The Elegies: Vol. VII*, A.MS.S. ([ca. 1885?]), RFB 79; *Camoens: Octaves and Eclogues: Vol. VIII*, A.MS.S. ([ca. 1885?]), RFB 80; *Camoens: Eclogues viii … Triumphs: Vol. IX*, A.MS. ([ca. 1885?]), RFB 81; *Camoens: Roundels: Vol. X*, A.MS. ([ca. 1885?]), RFB 82. Sir Richard Francis Burton Papers, Henry E. Huntington Library, San Marino, California.

2 See Richard Francis Burton, translator, Lodovico Ariosto, *Roland the Rageful: vulgarly known as Orlando Furioso* (autograph and typescript manuscripts, RFB 15–22); Basile's *The Neapolitan Muses* (autograph manuscripts, RFB 101 [1–2]); and Alessandro Tassoni's *The Original Tale of a Tub* from the *Secchia Rapita* (original title crossed out, *The Rape of the Bucket — Imitated from the Italian of Alessandro Tassoni*, autograph manuscript, RFB 133). Sir Richard Francis Burton Papers, Henry E. Huntington Library, San Marino, California.

3 See *The Uruguay*; *Iraçéma* (in collaboration with his wife, Isabel); *Goa, and the Blue Mountains, or, Six Months of Sick Leave*; *From London to Rio de Janeiro*; *Explorations of the Highlands of the Brazil*.

4 See Mary Lovell, "A Gipsy Childhood, 1821–40," in *A Rage to Live* 1–15; and Fawn Brodie, "The Impact of France," in *The Devil Drives* 32–9.

5 John Payne, letter to Sir Richard Francis Burton, A.L.S. (1882, Oct. 4), London. RFB 802. Sir Richard Francis Burton Papers, Henry E. Huntington Library, San Marino, California.

6 Burton believes the coincidence that his own wanderings from Goa to the Persian Gulf "have unconsciously formed a running and realistic commentary upon *The Lusiads*" lends him insight into the "small" but "telling" matters of the epic's ethnology and topography (*Lusiads* 1:xii, xiii).

7 This autograph poem has escaped the notice of previous authors, collectors, and curators of Burton, in part perhaps because the Richard Francis Burton papers, deposited by Edwards Huntington Metcalf at the Huntington Library in 1992 and bequeathed to the library by his estate in 2002, were only properly catalogued in 2008. Written on loose leaves, it has escaped notice and remains unlisted and uncatalogued in Gayle Richardson's excellent finding aid of July 2008. This find attests to what may remain unknown about Burton's Mediterranean corpus.

8 See especially "On the Prose-Rhyme and the Poetry of the Nights," in Burton, *Nights* 10:265.

9 For Burton's suggested affinities between genie and jinn and parallels between the Muslim jinn and the Hindu Rakshasa see Burton, *Nights* 1:n12 and 3:n259.

10 In Faria e Sousa's Catholic exegesis, which escaped the censorship of the Spanish but not the Portuguese Inquisition, Venus was a symbol of Divine Love corresponding to her spiritual aspect as Urania. This influential line of interpretation would be followed by Duperron in his commentary and by Mickle in his 1776 version.

11 On this last point, see Menocal, *The Arabic Role in Medieval Literary History* 137–54.

12 *Camoens: Roundels: Vol. X*, A.MS. ([ca. 1885?]), unnumbered roundel, RFB 82. Sir Richard Francis Burton Papers, Henry E. Huntington Library, San Marino, California.

13 Nineteenth-century philologists tended to share the assumption that Sanskrit was the mother of the Indo-European languages and hence that Sanskrit culture was the mother of all cultures. Burton partly agreed, differing in his insistence on a common Egyptian or Assyrian provenance to the languages and mythology of both classical Greece and India.

14 Respectively Yule to Burton, ALS 1/11/ 81 and ALS 15/ 7/ 85, pasted into the translator's proof copy of *Camoens: His Life and His Lusiads*; Burton Library, 79 b, Henry E. Huntington Library, San Marino, California. Burton in turn cites Yule in his commentary, for instance, 2:533.

7 Reading Backward: The *1001 Nights* and Philological Practice

KARLA MALLETTE

Nothing could be more philologically correct than to begin a discussion of philology with a survey of the changing semantic range of the word. The practice of philology, of course, has a long and checkered history, and one could gather a bouquet of definitions of the word, from Seneca's famous denunciation of philology as cheapened philosophy (*quae philosophia fuit facta philologia est*) to Giulio Bertoni's fascist-era declaration that "the object of philology is a reality to be conquered" (13). I won't go all the way back to the origins of the word – to the Greeks, for whom *philologia* meant both love of argument and reasoning and love of learning and literature: love of the word, that is, both spoken and written. Nor will I dwell on the Romans, for whom the word began to acquire the connotations that are most familiar to us: in post-Augustine usage, *philologia* meant love of reason, learning, and literature, but also explanation or interpretation of the writings of others. And I pass over the long history of the word through the Middle Ages and the early modern period, although my favourite definition of the word comes from a seventeenth-century author. He is Henry Cockeram, and his definition is "love of much babbling" (*OED* s.v. "philology"). In the nineteenth century things got interesting, as philologists claimed for themselves the task of reconstructing the tongues and texts of antiquity and the Middle Ages as distant touchstones for contemporary political and religious formations. They articulated a *philologie engagée* in which philological readings, assisted by modern technologies like stemmatic criticism or the insights of historical linguistics, functioned as archaeologies of modern communities defined in large part by their relation to ancient or medieval texts. Finally, some of the most dynamic and interesting twentieth- and early twenty-first-century philological works are multi-dimensional studies. The object of their analysis is texts from the distant past, but at the same time, they scrutinize the accretions of textual criticism that ancient and medieval texts have acquired through the centuries – looking back, for instance, at the *engaged philology* of the nineteenth century. It's this meta-philological scholarship that I take as my point of departure in this essay. Philology is a strategy of reading backward, attentive to the historicity not only of the text but also of the subsequent readings of the text, the encrustations of scholarship between the moment of the text's composition and the present.[1]

In this essay I will present a series of connected meditations that constitute less a cumulative argument than a series of narrative frames. I will consider first two methodologies proposed over the last two centuries for reconstructing the medieval (or classical) text that is the object of the philological inquiry. Then I will talk about one particularly thorny manuscript tradition in particular: the curious story of the reception and transmission of the text best known in the English-speaking world as the *Arabian Nights*. Finally, I'll peek inside this last frame to view the ripples that spread when Scheherazade spoke in that text. My aim is to sketch a framework for a broader consideration of the central problems posed by philological readings of medieval Mediterranean textual history, and in particular the complexity – it is considerable, but I believe that the philologist can no longer consider it a *fatal* complexity – of a comparative Romance-Arabic philology.

I.

In 1928 Joseph Bédier published an article that was nothing less than a manifesto attacking the method of textual criticism, at the time accepted as industry standard, known as the "Lachmannian method." I take this startling and innovative essay as a point of departure for my discussion of one of the central activities of the philological enterprise: the reconstruction of pre-modern texts. "La Tradition manuscrite du *Lai de l'ombre*: Réflexions sur l'art d'éditer les anciens textes" takes the form of a conversion narrative. Bédier apologizes on the opening page for the necessity to speak of his own life, excusing himself by explaining that he has had a lifelong engagement with the *Lai de l'Ombre*. In this article, he will present the conclusions of that work. His awareness of the complexity and corruption of the manuscript tradition of the *Lai* brought him to the point of despair when he came to believe that the Lachmannian critical method (applied by his teacher Gaston Paris to the manuscript history of the *Lai* in an article critical of Bédier's work on the text) could not clarify the convolutions of the manuscript tradition. This experience has taught him that the modern edition should not mediate between variant manuscript versions as the Lachmannian edition claimed to do; rather the textual critic ought to reproduce a single manuscript in its particularity and peculiarity – leaving intact, that is, its medieval alterity.

To make sense of Bédier's argument, we have to read backward to the model of textual criticism that he was attacking. The "Lachmannian method" – typically evoked today in quotation marks because it didn't really begin with Lachmann and because Lachmann himself didn't consistently practice it – describes a strategy pioneered during the nineteenth century for reconstructing a literary text produced in a manuscript environment. The vicissitudes (or the felicities) of non-mechanical reproduction generate variance. Because of scribal error and scribal intervention, no two copies of the same manuscript are identical. How should the modern scholar negotiate manuscript variance in order to reconstitute the text that is the object of the philological investigation? In the Lachmannian model of textual criticism, the scholar begins by constructing a *stemma codicum*: that is, a plausible history of textual transmission, the family tree or genealogy of the text as it has come down to us in its surviving manuscript copies. The textual critic identifies and removes variants that entered the tradition through scribal innovation, and systematically reconstructs an Ur-text – the oldest and purest version of the text.

Bédier attacked the Lachmannian method in part by arguing that, far from improving our understanding of the text, it detonated a hermeneutic circle and obfuscated the medieval text. He pointed out that the textual critic reconstitutes the text by referring to the authority of medieval usage in general. But it's the manuscript itself that is the authority in this matter: the manuscript teaches us the rules of medieval usage. Lachmannian method requires the scholar to sift manuscript variants, produce a *stemma codicum* to chart a manuscript genealogy that can account for variant readings, cancel those readings introduced through scribal error, make judgment calls where interpolation is suspected but cannot be positively identified, and use his own understanding of linguistic and literary history to propose plausible readings where the text has been mangled beyond hope of reconstruction. At each of these junctures, however, the scholar's intellectual arrogance might steer him wrong. Bédier mockingly lists the technical vocabulary that is the Lachmannian editor's armor, shining proofs of the scientific validity of the philological reading: "faute," "bonne leçon," "'leçon moins bonne,' ou 'suspecte,' ou 'altérée,' ou 'refaite' ..." How can the modern textual critic question the authority of the text on medieval literary or linguistic usage? To do so is to beg the question: to step into the vertiginous eye of the hermeneutic circle (Bédier 22–3).

Therefore Bédier advocated a modern edition that did not seek to reconstruct a lost text, but rather faithfully reproduced a single manuscript witness to the tradition. This did not mean that the editor relinquished all intellectual control over the edition, of course. Editorial expertise guided the scholar in selecting the manuscript to be reproduced: the editor should base the edition on the medieval manuscript that his scholarship reveals to be exemplary. Nor did it suggest that Bédier had relinquished the grand promise of the positivism of the Romantic era – the notion that current scientific scholarship granted the textual critic a substantially more accurate understanding of textual history than the methodologies that predated it. Rather, in the closing lines of the article, Bédier insists that if textual critics will only follow his method, the past will speak for itself, truthfully and accurately, *for the first time* (Bédier 71). Defenders of the Lachmannian model, after Bédier's attack, have argued that while it can be abused – the editor can make bad calls – in most cases it serves as a superb standard for producing the critical edition. Unlike a Bédierist edition, it accounts for the diversity of textual witnesses while not allowing manuscript diversity to threaten the intelligibility of the text.

Of course, Karl Lachmann was not the first nineteenth-century scholar to propose an innovative approach to textual editing. During the opening decades of the century, Angelo Mai, a Jesuit and Orientalist, pioneered another technology for unlocking the secrets of the pre-modern manuscript. He developed a method for reading the earlier and nearly eradicated script on medieval palimpsests, which he used in 1814 to reveal a Ciceronian text previously thought lost. Giacomo Leopardi wrote one of his most ardent canzoni in praise of Mai, who (in Leopardi's words) "awakened our fathers from their tombs" ["svegliar dalle tombe i nostri padri" (15)]. More recent historians of philology – in particular Helmut Müller-Sievers and Sebastiano Timpanaro – have looked on Mai's activities with a more critical eye.[2] The technique that Mai used to expose the *scriptura ima*, the lower or earlier hand – bathing the manuscript pages in a noxious chemical bath – brought hidden script to light, but only temporarily, long enough for the philologist to transcribe it. After that not only the earlier writing but also the subsequent hand would be destroyed. And because he typically disassembled manuscripts in order to submit them to this process, Mai sometimes damaged other works as well, or at least made it impossible for subsequent scholars to reconstruct their collation.

There is something ghastly but also enormously suggestive about Mai's contribution to the history of textual criticism. Müller-Sievers in particular has pointed out the parallels between Mai's method and contemporary Romantic notions of artistic method. The philologist read the text by achieving a spontaneous and temporary union with the manuscript; once this moment passed, no one would read it again. Add the chemical bath in which he submerged the manuscript – really a form of latter-day alchemy – and the image of the fathers in their tombs rising again, and a portrait emerges of Angelo Mai as the Dr Frankenstein of the Ambrosiana Library. That is, more than a Romantic artist, Mai resembles – in fact, he was – a *scientist* of the Romantic era.

And it is his scientism that links Mai to Lachmann and Bédier. The three scholars were intoxicated by positivism. They shared a profound faith in the new technologies they used to reveal the secrets of pre-modern texts, methods that would allow the dead to speak again. It's true that their scientism sometimes lulled their skepticism to sleep. Their faith in their own capacity to decipher the manuscript revealed by the chemical bath or the stemma codicum might occasionally blind them to the limitations of their methods: that is the vulnerability of philology. Nonetheless, in each case their methods had demonstrable advantages over those they replaced. Mai *did* resurrect the voices of literary paternity, which he understood to be the voices of Latin and Greek antiquity. It's interesting to note that his training in Orientalism – Mai had studied Hebrew, Aramaic, Syriac, and Amharic – was forgotten as soon as he discovered his technique for coaxing the earlier, classical Latin hand forth from the medieval manuscript page. Lachmannian and Bédierist textual criticism, however, engaged in an emphatic and sincere dialogue with evolving scientific models, and so they possess a veneer of the inductive methods of which Angelo Mai was wholly innocent. Speaking very broadly, the Lachmannian method is particularly good at representing the fluid multiplicity – the polygenesis – of medieval literatures. The Bédierist method honours the historical conditions of the successive incarnations of the literary work.

II.

It might be possible to find a better text to compare the relative strengths of the various models of textual criticism during the modern period than the *1001 Nights*. But one would be hard pressed to find one more engaging, more central to both popular culture and intellectual history and, in all honesty, more fun. The *1001 Nights* is among the most famous examples of a framed narrative in world literature. In framed narratives, stories are captured within stories, when a character in one tale begins relating another. The frame story typically has a hermeneutic function: it serves as a key to interpreting the stories within the frame. Edgar Allan Poe – in his extraordinary and outrageously mendacious essay, "The Philosophy of Composition" – describes such literary devices thus: "it has the force of a frame to a picture. It has an indisputable moral power in keeping concentrated the attention" (Poe 14:204).[3] So does the tale of Scheherazade in the case of the *1001 Nights*. The story of the valiant vizier's daughter become sultaness, who saves her city by enmeshing the murderous sultan in a net of tales, insinuates itself into the fabric of the stories within the frame. They are seen by modern readers (and modern writers) as celebrations of the capacity of narrative to vanquish abuses of power in the sphere of politics or of psychology. Scheherazade has been canonized as the patron saint of literary invention in successive generations of Western works that riff on the *Nights*, from novels to movies and even to translations of the *Nights*, which in a couple of noteworthy cases depart from the text so radically as to constitute independent literary works themselves.

The *Nights*, that is, is itself enmeshed in the Western tradition in a meta-literary frame. We see it irresistibly within the context of the European and, later, American riffs on the text. Furthermore, recent philological research has shown that the work as it has become known in the West, a motley crew of fantastic tales from the most various sources, is largely the product of Western Orientalists (and Arab philologists living in the West). For this reason – because the *Nights*, a framed tale, has itself been captured within an interpretive frame which has become perversely difficult to separate from the text itself – the work suggests a series of hermeneutic questions that scholarship has only recently begun to address: Where do we draw the line between the provinces of the pre-modern author and the modern textual critic, particularly in the case of a work whose proximity to the oral tradition makes it peculiarly fluid and therefore peculiarly vulnerable to modern manipulation? Is it possible to filter the Western interventions out of the text and to see it as a work of Arabic literature, in the context of the Arabic literary tradition? If not, can the Western imitations provide an interpretive lens for the text? Should they serve a hermeneutic function, or would that denature and destabilize the text? Is it possible to produce a coherent reading – using either the Lachmannian or the Bédierist method – of a text so radically contaminated (to use the technical philological term) by innovations and interpolations?

For the sake of narrative expedience, I won't discuss the Byzantine complications of the manuscript history of the *Nights*; rather, I refer the interested reader to the superb accounts of an extraordinarily convoluted history available elsewhere.[4] Suffice it to say that we possess, on the one hand, a single late-medieval manuscript that is both the oldest manuscript we have and the seed for all that the *Nights* has become in the West. On the other hand, I submit the *Nights* in the Western tradition: a groaning board of narrative drawn from a variety of sources, both Arab and Western. Because the *Nights* was received with irrational exuberance in the West while it remained a relatively obscure, primarily oral work in the Arab world, the Western versions of the *Nights* have exercised a gravitational influence on the *Nights* in the Arab world. Until quite recently, the Arabic editions of the *Nights* – those used by the scholars and philologists who studied the text – followed the contours of the text as it had emerged in the West. That is, they included Arabic versions of tales not associated with the *1001 Nights* until Western translators had drawn them into the framework of the text, as well as tales that had no written manuscript witness predating their translation into Western languages and that appear to have been considerably elaborated, if not invented outright, by the first "translator" of the text, Antoine Galland.

The decision to use this text as a foundation for scholarship implies a judgment about the polyvalence of the text that has sweeping implications. Such a reading assumes a robust Lachmannian understanding of the polygenesis of the text, its constitution across cultural boundaries. The frame story of the *Nights*, the story of Scheherazade, celebrates narrative as a means to correct aberrant governance – both political and psychological – and to achieve civic justice. The padded version of the text, which accepts Western interpolations as integral parts of the *1001 Nights* traditions, may be understood to support this thesis, if indeed it has a thematic unity at all. It is a vast, raucous, glorious celebration of the messy and exhilarating power of narrative. If the Lachmannian edition is a chorus, the singers who lend their voices to the *1001 Nights* are indeed an impressive and diverse crew. They come from the four corners of the world, and have been singing for a millennium with no sign of letting up.

There is a soloist in the *Nights* tradition, however, and she has recently begun to attract her share of scholarly attention. Scholars generally refer to her as the Galland manuscript; and she is the oldest version of the work we possess. In 1984, Muhsin Mahdi published an edition of this manuscript, a culmination of the work of successive generations – almost a century all told – of philological scholarship.[5] That edition in turn has been translated into a number of languages; it appeared in English translation in 1990. It's a gripping read; it's the translation that I would choose to read to my daughter, were I not afraid that it would give her nightmares. And it's substantially shorter than the more familiar versions of the *Nights*: it includes just nine of the twenty-one story cycles that appear in those expanded versions. Thus scholars can now, for the first time, attempt a Bédierist reading of the text, one that focuses on the nuances of an individual manuscript which can be (albeit not precisely) situated in a geographical and historical context. And such a reading challenges a number of the assumptions that inform Lachmannian readings of the work. It asks us to re-evaluate our assumption that the *Nights* was a work of popular literature *tout court*, suggesting the intervention of an authorial hand and the manipulation from a unifying perspective of the narratives it collects within its framework. It questions the notion that the *1001 Nights* celebrates the power of narrative, revealing that about the act of narration, in fact, the text is profoundly, disturbingly ambivalent. It challenges perceptions of the *Nights* as a work that transcends geographical or historical boundaries, setting the text in Abbasid Baghdad – or rather in memories of Abbasid Baghdad as they filtered through the centuries into the late medieval Arab imagination. Most emphatically, most unnervingly, it insinuates a nagging doubt into our celebration of Scheherazade as heroine and of narration as liberation. A Bédierist reading of the text suggests that Scheherazade herself may represent in compressed form the villains in one of the most shocking events in all of Arab history, an event that took place in Abbasid Baghdad: Harun al-Rashid's massacre of the Barmakid clan.

Readers of the *1001 Nights* will, of course, remember meeting the Abbasid caliph Harun al-Rashid – who ruled the Arab world from his sumptuous capital,

Baghdad, from 786 until 809 – in the pages of that work. Ja'far too is present, the bosom companion whom Harun ultimately murdered along with every other member of his Barmakid clan. Harun's massacre of the Barmakids is not mentioned in the *Nights*, yet the reader who knows that history cannot help remembering it when she encounters Harun and Ja'far in the pages of the text. Why did Harun execute Ja'far and his family? His motives remain murky to modern historians, although medieval Arab historians produced a story worthy of the *Nights* to explain it. Again, I won't go into the details of a complex and sordid tale: it's a soap opera that involves a substantial proportion of the women of both Harun's and Ja'far's extended clans as dramatis personae. In brief, what brought down the Barmakids was a palace intrigue, and in particular the perfidy of the women of the palace: Harun's sister (who was also Ja'far's wife), Harun's favourite wife, and an angry slave girl. According to the historians, conniving women poisoned Harun al-Rashid's mind and were the undoing of the Barmakids.[6]

Again, these palace intrigues are not mentioned in the *Nights*. Yet the reader who remembers that history cannot help reflecting upon it as she turns the pages of the text, because in the *1001 Nights* we do hear a feminine voice in the night that works a mysterious magic on the psyche of the ruler: the voice is Scheherazade's. She has the sultan's ear. And she uses her intimacy with the ruler of the state to manipulate his emotions and influence his governance. The stories she tells her murderous husband fall (to borrow Ramon Menéndez Pidal's description of Joseph Bédier's narrative voice [*La Chanson de Roland y el neotradicionalismo* 14])[7] somewhere between prophetic and menacing. Stories do save lives in the frame tale, and the frames within the frames: the story of the Merchant and the Demon, the Fisherman and the Demon, the Porter and the Three Ladies of Baghdad, the Hunchback. In the tales embedded within those interior frames, however, it's a different story. We meet a man who lies to his cousin in order to consummate his incestuous love for his sister. With the cousin's help the two inter themselves in a subterranean tomb and die in each other's arms; when their bodies are found, God's wrath has incinerated them. In another tale, a vicious queen lies to her husband about her lust for a repulsive slave. She turns her husband to stone from the waist down, but the king has his revenge on her when his ally, pretending to be her lover, murders her in their bed. In one of the most uncanny tales told in the *Nights*, the story of King Yunan and the sage Duban, the king – acting on the advice of an envious vizier – sentences to death the scholar who has cured him of leprosy. Duban promises the king a glimpse into a book that will answer any question he asks, but only after his own execution. The book that Duban gives to Yunan is blank, but its pages have been infused with poison; so as the scholar's reanimated head instructs the king to turn page after page, he poisons himself. The answer to the question that Yunan never asks is the narrative of Duban's vengeance and the king's death. It's true that the characters we meet in the *Nights* ransom their lives with tales; but in those tales, narrative has a striking rate of toxicity.

The *1001 Nights* is a spectacularly uncanny work of literature. Within a frame that celebrates as heroine a woman who whispers stories into the ear of a mad governor, it tells tale after tale illustrating the damage that narrative can do. Abbasid Baghdad makes a shrewd backdrop for the meta-literary drama that the text memorializes: the battle over the legitimacy of imaginative narrative. For it was in Abbasid Baghdad that imaginative narrative in Arabic had its Prague Spring, before Islamic scholars condemned it as immoral and irreligious.[8] William Granara has suggestively used Bakhtin's formulation of the *chronotope* to refer to modern Arab novelists' return to al-Andalus as a place that is also a historical era ("Nostalgia, Arab Nationalism, and the Andalusian Chronotope"). Granara argues that al-Andalus transcends its geo-temporal situation to represent the historical and potential capacity of Arabo-Islamic culture to interact fruitfully with bordering cultural systems. The manipulation of the historical figures Harun al-Rashid and his minister Ja'far in the *1001 Nights* suggests that for the medieval Arab imagination Abbasid Baghdad functioned as another such chronotope. David Pinault has shown that the embedded frame narrative "The Three Apples" riffs on historical accounts of the personalities of Harun al-Rashid and Ja'far (Pinault 86–99). Muhsin Mahdi has identified the episode, plucked from histories of Abbasid Baghdad, that inspired the King's Steward's tale from the Hunchback cycle ("From History to Fiction"). The *1001 Nights* circles round Abbasid Baghdad as it worries over themes of governance and passion and of narration, silence and death. It situates its interrogation of the splendors and dangers of imaginative narrative in a time and place associated with narrative opulence, political power, and the dangers provoked by political power ungoverned by reason.[9]

If Abbasid Baghdad encodes reflections on the potential and peril of imaginative narrative, the medieval Mediterranean has recently become for philologists a similar kind of chronotope. As in William Granara's reading contemporary Arab novelists use al-Andalus as a symbol of the possibility of negotiation between currently conflicting monotheisms, so do historians and literary historians use the medieval Mediterranean in general to historicize contemporary tensions between Christians and Muslims. Mediterranean history gives us a way to demonstrate the indebtedness of Euro-Christian culture to Islamic culture. Lines of cultural transmission and trade routes crisscrossed the medieval Mediterranean as well as cultural fault lines, interconfessional tensions that exploded into violence periodically during the era we study.

Given the robust quality of communication between cultures in the medieval Mediterranean, given the transmission of other sorts of cultural information between the Arabic and Latin-Romance cultural spheres, it may seem remarkable that the *1001 Nights* – gold mine of narrative material that it is – did not make the Mediterranean crossing before Antoine Galland's translation in the opening decades of the eighteenth century. Indeed, it is a little-known fact that the frame story did appear in European letters during the Middle Ages, as did one of the embedded tales from the *Nights*. The story of Shahrayar (Scheherazade is notable by her absence) appeared in the *Novelle* of Giovanni Sercambi (1348–1424), and Ludovico Ariosto retold it in canto XXVIII of the *Orlando Furioso* (1516). And we find a portion of the tale of King Yunan and the sage Duban in Bosone da Gubbio's *Avventuroso Ciciliano* (1311).[10]

The differences between the stories as they appear in the Arabic "original" (I am still reading outward from the early manuscript edited by Mahdi) and the Italian "translations" are instructive. Both Sercambi and Ariosto declaw the frame tale by stripping from it the figure of Scheherazade. A powerful man and his companion discover their wives' faithlessness; their despair leads them to wander like pals in a pre-modern buddy movie – so far, the Arabic and Italian tales follow identical paths. And the Italian heroes, like the Arab princes, will ultimately bed a woman whose faithlessness astonishes even them, cynical as they have become. But the Italians take a radically different moral from the experience. *Cosí fan tutte*, they say to themselves; a man's only rational response is to give as good as he gets. Sercambi – appreciably more misogynistic than Ariosto – returns his heroes to beat their wives and bed as many women as they like. Ariosto's protagonists give their wives license to play, as they themselves intend to do (Ariosto, it must be said, is as affable a writer as there is in world literature). There are no virgin brides, no murders, and no descent to the brink of anarchy and civic collapse; no Scheherazade arrives to save the day.

So, too, the version of the story of Yunan and Duban retold by Bosone da Gubbio is stripped of the elements that complicate it in the Arabic version. Indeed only one device remains: the book that poisons its reader as he turns the pages. Bosone inserts that motif into a relatively banal plot involving negotiations between two princes that degenerate slowly into war. There is no tension between a king – indecisive, easily dazzled and easily manipulated – and his learned, foreign minister. The poisoned book simply introduces a thrillingly sinister element into a mundane tale of diplomatic intrigue.

If we peer a bit deeper into the Yunan and Duban cycle as it appears in the oldest manuscript of the *1001 Nights*, however, it becomes evident that a sliver of the material present in that tale did penetrate more deeply into the literary traditions of the European languages. For there is a crossed wire between the story of Yunan and Duban and one of the most popular framed narratives of the European Middle Ages: the work known most frequently as "The Seven Sages of

Rome." That story, like the tale of Yunan and Duban, involves a king who hires a learned minister with an odd, foreign name to perform a personal service. In that tale, as in the tale of Yunan and Duban, the learned man's life will be threatened by envy and court intrigues. The name of the sage in the Arabic tale that inspired the European "Seven Sages" tradition was Sindbad (not to be confused with the sailor). And in the tale of Yunan and Duban as it appears in the *1001 Nights*, characters relate tales (one of many cases in the *Nights* of an embedded narrative itself framing embedded tales) that feature a king by the name of Sindbad. Furthermore, identical tales are embedded within the Yunan-Duban frame and the Sindbad frame in both its Arabic and European versions. David Pinault, noting this rash of parallels, has pointed out the obvious: the various traditions (the Arabic and Italian Yunan-Duban tales, the Arabic and European "Sindbad"-"Seven Sages" tradition) represent ramifications from a common stock of narrative material (Pinault 45).

One can draw a number of conclusions from these similarities, overlaps and coincidences. First, a comparison of the treatment of the narrative material in the Arabic and Romance orbits underscores the distinct historical resonance the tales had for diverse populations. None of the Italian versions of tales from the *Nights* – Sercambi's, Ariosto's, or Bosone's – reproduces the unique cocktail of themes that made the Arabic incarnations of the story so riveting. The tales are stripped of the plot elements that link narration and intellectual expertise to danger. They do not question the probity of the protagonist, as the Arabic tales implicitly challenge the judgment and the moral formation of the kings central to the narratives. Even the sprawling European tradition of tales inspired by the Arabic "Sindbad" – the work most frequently referred to as "The Seven Sages of Rome" – although it represents the king and his courtiers, as the Arabic version did, does not linger on the psychological tensions in the royal court. It plays up different aspects of the tale, making it in some versions a simple repository for misogynistic material, in others a bureaucratic procedural and royal tell-all that peeks behind the curtains to show us how aristocrats and their philosophical hired hands *really* live.

The refiguring of the *1001 Nights* and the "Sindbad" in the European languages demonstrates the malleability of narrative formations as they passed between the shores of the medieval Mediterranean. It suggests the manifest complexity of the literary communications that most literary histories refer to using the (deceptively simple) shorthand terms "influence" or "translation." Europeans transformed the narrative raw material that they imported from the Arabic to suit their own purposes; thus did the Arabic "Sindbad" become the wildly popular European "Seven Sages of Rome." At the same time, the textual history that I have traced shows that imported literary products must communicate with a local sensibility in order to find an audience. The reworking of the tales native to the *Nights* that we find in Sercambi, Ariosto and Bosone failed to grip a European audience because the Europeans, unlike the Arabs, could not read backward from the uncanny tales of narration and death to the sinister narratives of palace intrigues in Baghdad. It isn't true that the *Nights* was not known in Europe before Galland's translation; rather, before the beginning of the eighteenth century, Europeans lacked an interpretive lens that might make the material compelling to a hometown audience.

Second, the elaboration of the material from the *Nights* in diverse European frame tale traditions demonstrates how complex the literary history of the medieval Mediterranean is and how prickly the task of producing a rigorous Bédierist reading of that history must be. The Mahdi-edited manuscript of the *Nights* – though it provides a snapshot of the work's historical development at a given moment in time – still communicates both with its textual prehistory and with the genealogy of literary offspring it spawned. And in order to produce a thorough account of that unique, historically bounded manuscript of the *Nights*, our critical narrative must embrace its prequels and sequels.

In brief, it is difficult to know where to stop telling the story of the *Nights*. Should the philologist aim for a latter-day New Criticism, and limit her reading to the structures and images found in the text itself? Sumptuous as those are in the case of the *Nights*, by contemporary critical standards a reading that resists historicism altogether risks being condemned (with justice) as irresponsible. We must situate textual history within a broader historical context. The medieval literary historian knows that the point where a text ends and begins cannot always be precisely determined, however. The *Nights*, which bleeds into the "Seven Sages" tradition which itself has cognates in Syriac, Greek, Hebrew, Latin, and all the European vernaculars, is an extreme example of a literary-historical dilemma that we face each time we frame a reading of a text. But all medieval texts are situated within an intertextual web, and the historian must reconstruct its affiliations, both avowed and not. This understanding of the philologist's task – a labour of tracing story to story in a network of lines of transmission that crisscross the Mediterranean like a cobweb – makes the philologist herself into a bit of a Scheherazade, telling a tale that does not end because it obeys a moral imperative to account for a boundless multiplicity.

But in the real world, tales follow the fundamental rules of narrative: they have a beginning, a middle, and (sorry, Scheherazade) an end. The imposition of order on the untidy business of medieval literary history has been imaged in the past as an act of violence; most philologists remember Bernard Cerquiglini's denunciation of the philologist as Procrustes, the bandit of the Attic hills who trimmed his victims' bodies to fit his loathsome bed. In honour of the mother of all narratives, in honour of the text that memorializes both the narrative imperative and the anxiety that accompanies narration, we might propose an alternative, (slightly) less brutal image of the philologist as overeager editor: the sage Duban. In the tale as it appears in the *1001 Nights*, when Duban accepts his death as inevitable he presents a gift to the king: a book. He gives the king a mysterious powder and instructs him to press his severed head into the powder following his execution. When the king does so, Duban's reanimated head interprets the meaning of the book as the king leafs through its (blank) pages. The circumstances of Duban's death may gall a modern reader. We do not want Duban to go gentle into that cruel night; we want a deus ex machina to pluck him from danger. By the unforgiving logic of the fairy tale, however, Duban accepts his demise and orchestrates his revenge from a murky and impossible moment between life and death.

The philologist must not die in order to narrate, of course; narration is not always and only vengeance: the facts do not really fit (and thank God for that). Yet the philological reading, a bit like Duban's narration of the book without text, begins with a brutal schism (in the case of philology, the separation of the text from the textual and cultural network that generated it) and an arcane scientific transformation (the technologies of reading – from stemmata to chemical baths – that assist the philologist). Like Duban, the philologist narrates from an ambiguous and historically uncanny moment. Though we work assiduously to correct for the distance between ourselves and the text – to project ourselves into the past by emptying our critical narratives of anachronisms and inaccuracies – the disconnect between us and the text of necessity colours our readings. And any number of contingencies – above all, the historical narratives we use to interpret the text – distort the stories we make it tell.

This is the vulnerability of the philological method; this is what opens it up to appropriations like the *philologies engagées* that I mentioned at the beginning of this essay.[11] It makes the philological reading susceptible to *innovations* (and I mean that word both in the bad sense that it acquires in Lachmannian textual criticism and in the Bédierist recuperation of it as a synonym for the luxuriant variance of the medieval text). Yet philological method has means to correct for errant readings over time, as the philological reading offers itself for falsification by subsequent generations of scholars.

Few historical notions about the shape of medieval literary history have been vigorously debated without resolution for as long as the "Arabic thesis." The earliest systematic statements of the "Arabic thesis" – the proposition that medieval Romance poets not only knew but to some degree imitated the poetry of the Arabs – date to the dawn of the great century of philological research into the medieval origins of the European literary traditions. Giovanni Maria Barbieri's *Dell'origine della poesia rimata* (*On the Origin of Rhymed Poetry*) appeared in 1790. Juan Andres's *Dell'origine, de' progressi, e dello stato attuale d'ogni letteratura* (*On the Origin, the Progress, and the Contemporary State of Every Literature*) was published, in various volumes and editions, between 1783 and 1812. The subsequent history of the "Arabic thesis" is a narrative as familiar as the frame tale of the *1001 Nights* or the palace intrigues of Harun al-Rashid's Baghdad, and I need not rehearse the details here. I will rather select a single intervention in the long interrogation of literary communications in the medieval Mediterranean in order to demonstrate the extent to which the philologist communicates with contemporaneity as well as with the past, the degree to which the distant and the present become fused into a single indissoluble substance in the successful philological reading.

María Rosa Menocal's first book, *The Arabic Role in Medieval Literary History*, marked a watershed for scholarship on the effects that Muslim-Christian relations had on medieval literature. As in the case of any influential scholarly work, a number of factors contributed to the book's success. The book took fruitful advantage of the advances that philologists and historians had made in understanding the complexity of medieval literary culture. From the perspective of institutional literary history, this was a *counterintuitive* complexity; Menocal's courage in arguing her perception of the indebtedness of European literary traditions to the Arabs granted her reading a moral weight to balance the mass of philological and historical evidence she marshaled to support her thesis.

Scholars who have written on the question of Arabic-Romance literary communications in the wake of the publication of *The Arabic Role* have typically acknowledged the service Menocal performed by culling the evidence of literary communications and by stating her argument with elegance and force. However, appreciations of the book have not generally called attention to the peculiar difficulty of making the case that book made less than a decade after the publication of Edward Said's *Orientalism*. Medieval literary scholarship did not immediately take notice of Said's book (as specialists in modern literary traditions must do, given its prominence). Yet Menocal's argument explicitly challenged the Manichean reading of medieval literary history in *Orientalism*, and it did so on two fronts. Without denying the virulence of anti-Muslim polemic during the Middle Ages, Menocal demonstrated the existence of an opposing instinct in the Christian communities of the Iberian peninsula: she showed us Christians translating works of Islamic philosophy and evidence of Christian imitation of Arabic poetics. And she traced a genealogy of philological scholarship acknowledging the record of cultural communications between Muslims and Christians – even traversing the great century of Orientalist polemic, the century that Said read with penetrating intelligence, the nineteenth.[12]

The contemporary relevance of investigations of the interconnectedness of Islamic and Christian cultural history is another story that I need not tell; it is achingly familiar. Without the sense of urgency that current events grant our scholarship, without the interventions of previous scholars, it is doubtful that we would question the standard perceptions of medieval literary history and seek the sorts of connections that I have begun to trace in this essay. In medieval Iberia, a long history of conquest and counter-conquest meant that Muslims and Christians lived in each other's laps for centuries, and the scholar must be persistent indeed to believe that Arabic letters had no influence on Spanish literary history. In Italy, however, Arab settlement was limited to a region of modern national territory perceived as peripheral – Sicily and the southern portions of the peninsula. And scholars have generally assumed that the Latin heritage and the adjacent Romance languages, along with the native genius of the Italian authors themselves, are sufficient to account for literary developments. Yet no region was more open to the circuits of trade that linked the Christian territories of the northern Mediterranean to the Muslim territories on the southern and eastern shores than the Italian peninsula. And the late Middle Ages, which saw the formation and flourishing of the European narrative traditions I have been describing – the "Seven Sages" and Sercambi's and Bosone's versions of tales from the *1001 Nights* – was also the century of the mercantile renaissance in southern Europe. Did the merchants of Genoa and Venice bring the raw materials that formed these narratives into port, along with Egyptian cotton and Levantine spices? The history of philology teaches us that the scholar will pose such a question, formulate a provisional response, and seek the evidence that will prove or disprove her hypothesis only when a harmonic convergence of factors smiles upon the enterprise, among them the evidence collated by previous historians and philologists; a sense of relevance to the contemporary zeitgeist; and an insight, an intuitive guess about the shape of literary history, what Leo Spitzer called the "inner click" (6–7).[13]

Giorgio Pasquali, in a work published in 1934, defined the philologist this way:

> The best editor of a Latin author transmitted in medieval or postmedieval manuscripts will be the one who knows – as well as his author's language and times, as well as his own language and times – so too the Middle Ages and Humanism. A critic of this sort is an ideal that no one can incarnate perfectly in himself, but toward which everyone has the duty to try to come as near as possible. (Pasquali 123)

I close with this definition, which evokes so effectively the task of the metaphilologist: not to know *in toto* the textual history of the last two millennia, but simply to desire to know it. If this really were a framed narrative rather than a scholarly presentation, I would back out of my frames one by one, providing a resolution of each of the stories I have started: European manipulations of Arabic tales; interpretations of the narrative frame of the *1001 Nights*; the contributions of Angelo Mai, Karl Lachmann and Joseph Bédier to the science of

interpreting the pre-modern text; the philological lens. I won't do that, for the simple reason that there is no end to the story I'm telling. Whereas the literary writer can invent an ending and work backward from there, scholarship must be what Umberto Eco called – in a distant and more utopian critical moment – an *open text*. At the least it must open itself up to falsification by subsequent scholarship, which may prove it historically inaccurate or (more fatal still) simply uninteresting or irrelevant to the present. That means that philology is not only about the past; it's also heavily invested in futurity. A bit like Scheherazade's tales in the eighteenth-century European versions of the *Arabian Nights*, the story the philologist begins never quite ends.

NOTES

1 For a fuller discussion of the millennial history of philosophy – and some of the other topics touched upon in this essay – see my *European Modernity and the Arab Mediterranean*.

2 See Müller-Sievers, "Reading Evidence: Textual Criticism as Science in the Nineteenth Century" and Timpanaro, "Angelo Mai."

3 Poe is talking here not about frames per se but rather about the setting for the action described in the literary work; the sentiment he expresses is nonetheless appropriate.

4 The authoritative work on the manuscript history of the *Nights* is Muhsin Mahdi, *The Thousand and One Nights*. See in addition Dwight Reynolds, "*A Thousand and One Nights*: A History of the Text and Its Reception"; Grotzfeld, "The Manuscript Tradition of the Arabian Nights"; Mahdi, "The Sources of Galland's *Nuits*"; and Robert Irwin, *The Arabian Nights: A Companion*.

5 New manuscripts of the *Nights* predating Galland's translation have recently been discovered, one in a French library and the other currently in England; scholarship on these manuscripts is likely to transform our understanding of the text as a work of Arabic literature.

6 For al-Tabari's version of Abbasa's and the maid's betrayal, see *The Early 'Abbasi Empire* 2: 247.

7 Ramon Menéndez Pidal's discussion of Joseph Bédier's intervention in theories of manuscript editing in *La Chanson de Roland y el neotradicionalismo* is, of course, salient to the current discussion. Menéndez critiqued Bédier's isolation of the *Chanson de Roland* from the transnational tradition which generated it, and insists that it should be read in continuity with the Spanish epics that (like the *Roland*) commemorated battles between Christian and Muslim armies in the Iberian peninsula.

8 On imaginative narrative in 'Abbasid Baghdad see H.T. Norris, "Fables and Legends." On the complexity of medieval Arab views toward storytelling, see Bonebakker, "Some Medieval Views," and Reynolds, "Popular Prose in the Post-Classical Period" 252–4.

9 On women and power in the caliphal family in Abbasid Baghdad as reflected in the historical accounts of the downfall of the Barmakids, see Tayeb el-Hibri, *Reinterpreting Islamic Historiography* 42–4. For an overview of historical explanations of Harun al-Rashid's massacre of the Barmakids, see Hugh Kennedy, *The Early Abbasid Caliphate* 127–9.

10 Sercambi retells the *1001 Nights* frame tale in novella 84 of Renier's edition (294–9). For Bosone da Gubbio's retelling of the tale of Yunan and Duban, see *L'Avventuroso Ciciliano* (1834) 264–6.

11 I have borrowed this recurring phrase – "the vulnerability of philology" – from Karl Uitti's useful essay "Philology" in *The Johns Hopkins Guide to Literary Theory and Criticism*.

12 Menocal, with exemplary restraint, refers explicitly to Said's *Orientalism* only in two footnotes (notes 12 and 13, 21–2).

13 In the same essay – relevant to the current argument – Spitzer critiques the claims of scientism attached to literary scholarship during the nineteenth century, calling Romance philology (with palpable affection) a "sham science" (4).

PART TWO

The Cosmopolitan Frontier:
Andalusi Case Studies

8 Andalusi "Exceptionalism"

ROSS BRANN

Al-Andalus (conventionally called "Muslim Spain" or "Islamic Spain") is now commonly identified and celebrated as the site of an extraordinary, extended moment of complex social interaction and cultural ferment, creativity and transfer among Iberian Muslims, Christians, and Jews. Yet modern scholars such as Américo Castro and María Rosa Menocal, to name only two of the most prominent proponents of this particular approach, were not the first to cast al-Andalus in an uncommonly positive light. Philip Hitti, arguably speaking as a committed Arab nationalist, paints a mesmerizing picture of tenth-century Muslim Cordoba in *A History of the Arabs*. Reading Hitti, one cannot help but notice the pride a Lebanese Maronite takes in the cultural scene of a capital of *Arabo-Islamic* Spain compared with two great cities of western Christendom:

> Cordoba took its place as the most cultured city in Europe and, with Constantinople and Baghdad, as one of the three cultural centers of the world. With its one hundred and thirteen thousand homes, twenty-one suburbs, seventy libraries and numerous bookshops, mosques, and palaces, it acquired international fame and inspired awe and admiration in the hearts of travelers. It enjoyed miles of paved streets illuminated by lights from the bordering houses, whereas seven hundred years after this time there was not so much as one public lamp in London, and in Paris, centuries subsequently, whoever stepped over his threshold on a rainy day stepped up to his ankles in mud. (Hitti 526)

Early modern Jewish historiography was equally enamored of Iberia in the High Middle Ages. Heinrich Graetz, one of the pillars of the *Wissenschaft des Judentums*, in nineteenth-century Germany defined the Jews' ties to medieval Iberia and commemorated their cultural accomplishments, doubtlessly thinking of his own attachment to Germany and its high culture:

> While the history of the Jews in Byzantium, Italy, and France possesses interest for
> special students, that of their brethren in the Pyrenean peninsula rises to the height
> of universal importance. The Jewish inhabitants of this happy peninsula [Iberia]
> contributed by their hearty interest to the greatness of the country, which they
> loved as only a fatherland can be loved, and in so doing achieved world-wide reputa-
> tion … When Judaism had come to a standstill in the East, and had grown weak with
> age, it acquired new vigor in Spain, and extended its fruitful influence over a wide
> sphere. Spain seemed to be destined by Providence to become a new center for the
> members of the dispersed race, where their spirit could revive, and to which they
> could point with pride. (Graetz 3:41–2)

Following the cue of the great German Jewish bibliographer Moritz Steinschneider, Graetz concluded: "Jewish Spain became the home of civilization and of
spiritual activity – a fragrant garden of joyous, gay poetry as well as the seat of
earnest research and clear thought" (Gerber 85–92). No less a scholar than S.D.
Goitein, the incomparable student of the documentary Cairo Genizah, referred
to the literary cultural production of the Jews of Iberia as "the Spanish miracle"
(Goitein 5:425).

Representations of al-Andalus as a uniquely enlightened, inspired and still-
inspiring space also abound in modern scholarship on the history of ideas. For
our purposes, three illustrations will suffice. Oliver Leaman's study of Moses
Maimonides frames the twelfth-century rabbinic philosopher's Andalusi cultural
background as extraordinary for its time:

> Spain, *al-Andalus*, was a repository of considerable intellectual effort, with skillfully
> constructed libraries, observatories, and circles of scholars quite consciously setting
> themselves up in opposition to the traditional fount of both Islam and early Islamic
> theoretical thought in the east of the empire. This opposition was not in terms of
> opposition to the principles of Islam, but rather an assertion of the specific climatic,
> intellectual, and political virtues of the West (*al-fada'il al-Andalus*). (Leaman 5)

In *Arab-Islamic Philosophy: A Contemporary Critique*, Mohammad ʿAbid al-Jabiri, a
contemporary Moroccan thinker, offers his own historically minded assessment
of the unique intellectual venture of Andalusi Islam. Chapter 5, entitled "The
Andalusian Resurgence," asserts that "intellectual activity [in the Maghreb and
al-Andalus] met with a different fate than in the East" because of "the absence
of a pre-Islamic heritage" and because Andalusis "had remained independent
from, and ideologically in conflict with, the Abbasid caliphate and likewise with
the Fatimids subsequently creating a constant cultural competition" (al-Jabiri
63–119). For his part, William Gallois identifies the social basis of the cultural

distinctiveness of al-Andalus. Addressing Todorov's *The Conquest of America: The Question of the Other*, Gallois asserts that "from his vantage point in Early Modern Spain Todorov need not have looked far for an ideal encounter between selves and others, for he would have found such a meeting in cosmopolitan Umayyad al-Andalus" (Gallois 75). To put it another way: Leaman and others have come to posit an Andalusi intellectual and social exceptionalism within pre-modern Islam, despite their awareness of the constant movement of scholars, traders, and pilgrims across the different Muslim polities, East and West – or rather, precisely on account of the continuous exchange of ideas and competition within the cultural unity of Islamdom these various movements signify.

Aside from the unique place al-Andalus and Sefarad have come to occupy in modern historiography and the history of thought, the idea of a multicultural and/or intellectually vibrant Iberia has inspired the modern *literary* imagination. Writers in various European languages and Hebrew – as well as authors writing in Arabic, as William Granara has shown (Granara, "*Extensio Animae*"), and in other languages in which Islamic culture is conducted, as Yaseen Noorani has demonstrated (Noorani, "The Lost Garden of Al-Andalus") – have come to depict al-Andalus variously as a place of great socio-cultural accomplishment and socio-political tolerance, as a "multicultural garden" (said of Cordoba in particular) and as a "paradise lost" (Granada). Clearly, medieval Iberia occupies a special place in the historical and literary imagination of scholars and writers who are inclined to find it appealing for reasons having to do with their own time, place, and cultural condition.[1] Al-Andalus and Sefarad have long since come to constitute *tropes of culture* – fertilized and constructed by the interface of history and memory, the literary imagination, and geographical desire.

The trope of Andalusi/Sefardi exceptionalism is of course highly contested. In the field of Islamic studies, for instance – apart from outstanding work being done by members of the Spanish academy, as well as select American historians of Arabic literature and social, religious and legal historians of Islam – al-Andalus is still frequently neglected or consigned to a marginal position on account of its arguably peculiar socio-political and socio-religious history or its place on the far western frontier of Islamdom and Christendom. Similarly, a few prominent historians of the Jews have assailed a scholarly fixation on what they call the "Sephardi mystique" (Marcus), an approach to Jewish historiography valorizing the cultural achievement of the Jews of Iberia and supposedly inflating its actual role and place in Jewish history (Schorsch).

One of the early and solitary cautionary voices advocating a sober assessment of the place of al-Andalus and its cultural production in the history of Arabo-Islamic letters belongs to the great Hungarian Islamicist Ignáz Goldziher. Although Goldziher specifically set out to dispel the view that al-Andalus ever attained cultural superiority over the Muslim East, he framed the contested subject in 1876 almost as though he were party to the current debate on the significance of al-Andalus in the history of civilization:

> There is a widespread opinion, both in historical works and with the educated peo-
> ple, that the medieval Spanish Arabs were above the general cultural level of the
> Muslims; that their civilization was superior to that of all the other Muslim peoples;
> that scholarship was more cultivated by them than by other Muslim groups; that their
> philosophical erudition mitigated Muslim intolerance and fanaticism; that they were
> more sensitive and susceptible to the beautiful in both life and art than their Eastern
> kinsmen – in a word, that from the viewpoint of humanism Andalusian Islam is the
> most pleasing phenomenon of Muslim cultural history, one in which civilized man
> delights more than in Eastern Islam. It is remarkable that this prejudice has not only
> misled the conceptions of European scholars but has falsified the views of many
> medieval Arab scholars as well …
>
> [I]t is undoubtedly true and undeniable that the Spanish Arabs had great and last-
> ing merits in improving civilization in the Europe of the ninth century. It is true that
> these merits are, even in recent times, ridiculously exaggerated above their correct
> level by careless and superficial enthusiasts. (Goldziher 1:370–1)

The temporal staying power and geographic diffusion of this trope of Andalusi exceptionalism – its enduring appeal for two of the religious communities of al-Andalus as well as for scholars and writers in modern times – invites us to interrogate how Iberian and Maghribi Muslims and Jews themselves depicted and remembered the place and its culture. Because the trope is a form of representation, as Derek Gregory observes, it "draws attention to the different ways in which the world is made present, re-presented, discursively constructed … working through grids of power" (Gregory 104). Accordingly, we are obliged to inquire *under what circumstances, in what form, and for which purposes* Muslim and Jewish literary and religious intellectuals established, developed and nourished al-Andalus and Sefarad as tropes of Muslim and Jewish culture.[2] Such a comparative perspective is instructive, since both communities had longstanding economic, cultural and intellectual ties to and rivalries with other regional centers in North Africa and the Muslim East and even more significant *religious* orientations and connections to their respective holy places in Palestine and the Hijaz. From a comparative per-spective, it is also significant that Andalusi Muslims and Jews shared a discursive tradition for inscribing their reflections on al-Andalus and Sefarad in Arabic and in its Hebrew and Judeo-Arabic sub-cultural literary adaptation.

For historians and literary historians of al-Andalus, the Andalusis' sense of cultural competition with the Muslim East and the difficulties they encountered in pacifying, controlling, and absorbing Berber elements in Andalusi society before and after al-Andalus was incorporated into the Almoravid and Almohad kingdoms have much to do with Andalusi cultural and historical self-definition.[3] From the twelfth century onward,[4] Andalusi identity and the legacy of al-Andalus became inextricably intertwined with North Africa, as Andalusi exiles and Maghribi scholars interested in al-Andalus preserved and transmitted Andalusi traditions and offered their own reflections upon them, mediated by the socio-political and religious concerns of their own time and place and their temporal and geographical distance from the remembered and imagined wholeness of the past.[5] During these later centuries, writing Andalusi social and literary history inclined to freezing a vision of the past so as to preserve, cultivate and transmit the idea of al-Andalus whole into the present.

Of the trope's predominant forms of expression the one most often discussed is the Andalusis' nostalgic longing. The elegiac-nostalgic paradigm originated during the eleventh century, when fresh memories of the Umayyad glory days and their still-visible wreckage aggravated the immediacy of loss. Over two centuries of interrelated historical shocks catalyzed genuine angst and nostalgia for the wholeness of a past remembered and then increasingly imagined, and the Andalusis' melancholic longing found expression in a highly stylized literary form rooted in the classical and neo-classical poetic motif *al-hanin ila al-awtan* (longing for one's homeland) and the traditional Arabic poetic genre *ritha' al-mudun* (city elegies; see Decter, "A Myrtle in the Forest"; Garulo; Enderwitz; Arazi; Elinson). The dissolution of Umayyad rule into *fitna* (political turbulence, discord and instability), the disintegration of the once-powerful and -unified Muslim state into competing and contending *muluk al-tawa'if*, and subsequently the incremental contraction of these Muslim mini-polities and their loss of territory to the Christian kingdoms (and loss of sovereignty to the Almoravids and Almohads) beginning at the end of the eleventh century and proceeding down to the end of the fifteenth were unprecedented historical traumas in western Islam.

Under these circumstances the "city elegies," a traditional Arabic literary response to catastrophe with ancient Near Eastern antecedents (Ferris Jr.), served as a poetic response to the historical experience, inscribing memories of displacement, hope for collective recuperation, desperate pleas for assistance and intervention (addressed to the Maghribis and Ottomans), and more specifically subjective representations of home, homelessness and homesickness.[6] In approximate chronological order of composition, the best-known of these "city elegies" are by Ibn Zaydun and Ibn Shuhayd regarding the collapse of Umayyad Cordoba; Ibn Hazm shedding tears at the ruins at Madinat al-zahra'; Ibn al-Labbana on the Almoravid conquest of Seville; Ibn 'Abdun on the fall of Aftasid Badajoz to the same conquerors, and subsequently regarding the territories lost to the Christian kingdoms; elegies by Ibn Umayra al-Makhzumi and Ibn Khafaja on the loss of Valencia (another of Ibn Khafaja's lyrics on the city's temporary recovery is discussed below); poetic appeals to the Hafsids of Tunisia to come to the defence of al-Andalus by Ibn al-'Abbar and Hazim al-Qartajanni; Abu al-Baqa' al-Rundi on Castile's capture of Seville; another dirge on the fall of Seville attributed to Abu Musa b. Harun; the Nasrid king Yusuf III on the loss of Antequera; and two anonymous elegies on the downfall of Nasrid Granada.

Even as eleventh-century Andalusi literary intellectuals were drawn to voicing conventional expressions of nostalgia, important scholars in this group such as Ibn Hazm and Sa'id al-Andalusi were also at work articulating the idea that al-Andalus had been and continued to be the repository of great learning and culture despite and even as a consequence of its fractured polity. Indeed, the *ta'ifa* courts' intense competition in patronizing the arts and sciences marked the period as culturally ambitious and uncommonly productive. From the twelfth century on, Ibn Bassam and Ibn Sa'id would endeavour to immortalize Umayyad rule as singularly prosperous, just, a bulwark of orthodox piety and sponsor of every manner of scholarship and the arts – in sum, as a model Islamic polity (Safran 185–6).

For all the attention the nostalgic sensibility has received, the endurance of the trope's turn in the Arabic (and Hebrew) elegy should not be isolated from other expressions of Andalusi (and Sefardi) exceptionalism. Rather, the trope's persuasive power rests not only on the ritualized remembrance of experienced and imagined loss, but also and more particularly on the community's recollection of *exactly what was lost*. That is, the palpably wrenching yearning for formerly Andalusi cities and towns, their institutions, outstanding poets and scholars, and for the vanished or diminished religious and communal life evoked in the elegies and documented in the Arabic historiographical tradition is dependent upon a prior construction of al-Andalus (and Sefarad) as (1) a lush and fertile territory capable of sustaining a culturally productive community and (2) the site of cutting edge Arabo-Islamic (and Judeo-Arabic) cultural production.[7] Indeed, we might say that the elegiac voice and the representation of agricultural richness, affluence, and cultural productivity flow from the reciprocal relationship between the textual genres in which they find expression – that literary celebration of *fada'il al-Andalus* (the excellence of al-Andalus) represents the flip side of the communal elegy. Or, to put it another way, textual riffs on *mafakhir al-Andalus* (the glories of al-Andalus) provide the substance informing and justifying the Andalusis' deep sense of loss and longing from the eleventh century onward. To fully address the trope of Andalusi exceptionalism, we must examine the intersection of the trope's spatial, temporal, and conceptual modalities and its varied incarnations in different literary forms, keeping in mind questions of historical periodization and the trope's social agency.

We can trace the textual origins of the idea of al-Andalus as a culturally distinct, ambitious and brilliant place to the historical moment in which a fully defined Andalusi *religious and political identity* was articulated and promulgated: that is, to the tenth century, when al-Andalus came of age as a formally independent Islamic polity with universal pretensions in conscious (albeit somewhat symbolic) opposition to the Abbasid caliphate in Baghdad and the Fatimid caliphate in Egypt. As Maribel Fierro observes: "Along with belonging to a universal religious community, they [Andalusi elites] had a distinct, but not static, Andalusi identity that separated them from other Muslims ... This Andalusi identity is generally considered to have been promoted especially by the Cordoban Umayyad caliphs, beginning with 'Abd al-Rahman al-Nasir, as it helped them strengthen their rule" (Fierro, *'Abd al-Rahman III* 7).[8] The Umayyads' formal adoption of Maliki orthodoxy with its implicit lines of Islamic continuity going back to the time of the Prophet Muhammad in Medina served to define Andalusi identity in the tenth century (Fierro, *'Abd al-Rahman III* 134–5).[9] Such legitimacy-conferring gestures evident in court historiography were also reinforced by the production and dissemination of Arabic panegyrics addressed to the caliphs (Stetkevych, "The Poetics of Ceremony"), the performance of rituals of allegiance to them as heads of the universal community of Muslims, and the Umayyads' monumental building projects, especially the iconic congregational Mosque of Cordoba described by al-Razi (*apud* al-Maqqari) as "the largest in the world" (al-Maqqari, *Nafh al-tib min ghusn al-andalus al-ratib* 4:460).

Let us now turn to a few depictions of al-Andalus that begin with references to its agricultural richness, which constitute the initial sign of the trope of Andalusi exceptionalism. An oft-cited, apparently early reference to al-Andalus's perfect clime and verdant land is attributed to the important tenth-century Umayyad chronicler Ahmad ibn Muhammad ibn Musa al-Razi (d. 955) as transmitted by al-Maqqari:

> The land of al-Andalus is the western extreme of the fourth clime. In the opinion of the knowledgeable it is a land abundant in lowlands with good soil, fertile agricultural settlements, flowing with plentiful rivers and abundant fresh springs. Venomous beasts are rare. It is temperate in climate, weather and breezes. Its spring, fall, winter and summer are relatively temperate and well-balanced such that no season generates excess ... Its fruits are ripe, at most times not wanting. (al-Maqqari, *Nafh al-tib min ghusn al-andalus al-ratib* 1:129–30)[10]

This tradition is said to have established the framework for descriptions of al-Andalus by later Muslim geographers and historians such as Ibn al-Khatib, who amplifies the picture of a marvelously fertile landscape and depicts a divinely blessed country whose people's material prosperity, cultural productivity and intellectual character set them apart:

> God, may He be exalted, has endowed the country of al-Andalus with fertile land and abundant irrigation, sweet foods and swift animals, bountiful fruits, plentiful waters, extensive dwellings, clothing of excellent quality, fine utensils; plenty of weapons, and pure air. He has endowed its people with whiteness in complexion, superior intellect, an aptitude for crafts, verve for the sciences, penetrating discernment, cultural refinement mostly lacking in other lands. (al-Maqqari, *Nafh al-tib min ghusn al-andalus al-ratib* 1:125–6; trans. mine)[11]

For the reader uncertain about the constructed nature of al-Razi's Andalusi landscape, one need only recall its pre-Islamic parallel in Isidore of Seville's (d. 636) eulogistic prose poem prologue to the *History of the Kings of the Goths*, establishing the genre of "Laudes Hispanae" ("Praise of Spain") that would inspire other Christian writers down to the Renaissance:

> Of all lands which stretch from the West to the Indies, you are the most beautiful, O Spain, sacred and ever-blessed mother of leaders and of nations. By right you are now queen of all the provinces, from whom not only the West but also the East obtains its light. You are the glory and ornament of the world, the most illustrious part of the earth, in which the glorious fecundity of the Getic people rejoices much and abundantly flourishes.
>
> Deservedly did indulgent nature enrich you with the abundance of all growing things. You are opulent in berries, flowing with grapes, rich in the harvest. You are clothed in grain, you are shaded by olive trees, you are covered with the vine. You are flowery in your fields, leafy on your mountains, full of fishes on your shores. You are situated in the most pleasant region in the world; you are neither burned with the warm heat of the sun, nor are you consumed by icy cold, but girded with the temperate zone of heaven, you are nourished by favorable west winds. For you produce everything fertile that fields bear, everything precious that mines bear, everything beautiful and useful that animals bear. Nor must you be considered inferior in those streams which the distinguished fame of illustrious herds ennobles ... (Van Liere 524; Isidore of Seville 1–2)[12]

The motif of al-Andalus's agricultural bounty and extraordinary beauty also found a conventional poetic outlet in the production of Andalusi Arabic "nature poetry." Abu al-Walid al-Himyari of eleventh-century Seville even assembled a collection of such poems (*Al-Badi' fi wasf al-rabi'*) "to prove the superiority of his country in that sphere" (al-Nowaihi 5). Although not a new theme in Arabic verse, the Andalusi poets cultivated this subject as a segment in the polythematic *qasida* and as a semi-independent genre. A few poems, such as the following lyric by Ibn Khafaja, explicitly consider the divinely bestowed richness of the Andalusi landscape even as it suggests poetically a possibly ominous future:

> O people of al-Andalus! God grant you abundance:
>> water and shade and rivers and trees.
> No Garden of Paradise but your homes;
>> if I had a choice I would take you.
> After this do not fear to enter Hell;
>> after Paradise you will not enter the Fire.
>
> (Ibn Khafaja 364 ["Ya ahla andalusin"])[13]

The *Risala fi fadl al-andalus wa-dhikr rijaliha* (*Treatise on the Merit of al-Andalus and Remembrance of its Men [of Letters]*) by Ibn Hazm (d. 1064) was apparently the earliest literary effort specifically and entirely devoted to highlighting Andalusi cultural achievement (Ibn Hazm 3:171–188).[14] According to the text preserved by al-Maqqari, Ibn Hazm composed the treatise in response to a formal request from Ibn Rabib al-Tamimi al-Qayrawani, a companion with whom Ibn Hazm had discussed a mutual disappointment. The two scholars lamented that no work had set forth the history of al-Andalus detailing the prominent achievements and virtues of its scholars and its rulers' exploits.[15] Ibn Hazm's tract itself closely follows this agenda, transmitting Islamic traditions *about* al-Andalus, foregrounding in considerable detail Andalusi religious scholarship in all the Islamic sciences before turning to sketches of the Andalusi contribution to Arabic grammar, rhetoric and lexicography, poetry, historiography, medicine, philosophy and metaphysics, and in each case measuring al-Andalus against its Eastern rival.[16]

For both historical and literary historical reasons, it is no accident that the first *literary* efforts to capture the cultural glory of al-Andalus date from the eleventh century.[17] Regarding their *hasab wa-nasab* (lineage or descent), Andalusi Muslims were always mindful, sometimes to the point of preoccupation, of what the Easterners thought of their literary cultural production (Fierro, *La heterodoxia* 78; 83 n. 26). The foremost Andalusi historians Ibn Hayyan (d. 1076) and Ibn al-Khatib (d. 1375; *Mufakharat malaqa wa-sala*) and the literary-cultural historian Ibn Bassam (twelfth century) devote considerable space to praising Andalusi cultural achievement, implicitly or explicitly placing it on a par with their Eastern rivals.[18] For their part, Andalusi Arabic literary historians devoted themselves to continuous cultivation of the *zajal* and *muwashshah*. These distinctively Andalusi strophic forms, their unique thematic repertoire, introduction into Arabic literature of new personae and voices, and the *muwashshah*'s unorthodox linguistic mix of the classical and vernacular represented a living Andalusi tradition that transcended temporal and geographic boundaries. Ibn Dihya, a thirteenth-century Andalusi in Baghdad, asserted that "the *muwashshah* is the cream of poetry and its choicest pearl; it is the genre in which the people of the West excelled over those of the East" (Rosen, "The Muwashshah" 166).

Whether we read it as pride of place, provincialism, apologetic and defensive, or as authorizing a culturally powerful Andalusi identity in counterpoint to political weakness, by the time Ibn Hazm first sketched Andalusi scholarly and cultural achievements the *fada'il* genre had already become an established literary vehicle for showcasing the singular cultural or religious merits of places across the Islamic world. The genre's appearance and increasing popularity during the tenth and eleventh centuries signifies an impulse to localize identity – arguably in reaction to the troubling and contested tripartite confessional division of the polity of Islam – even as it draws upon a longstanding Arabic rhetorical predilection for juxtaposing competing claims and voices. So too, as Manuela Marin keenly observes, if the Andalusis came to be widely regarded as a militarily inferior and effete people subject to Maghribi or Christian rule from the turn of the twelfth century on, it became essential for them and their heirs to invest themselves mightily in the trope of their literary and cultural predominance in counterpoint to the new socio-political situation (M. Marin, "Historical Images of al-Andalus and Andalusians" 421).

The Jews of al-Andalus shared an idyllic construction of the Iberian landscape with their neighbours, as seen in a mid-tenth-century Hebrew letter nearly contemporary with al-Razi.[19] Commissioned by Hasdai ibn Shaprut, the Jewish physician-courtier-diplomat of 'Abd al-Rahman al-Nasir and official leader of the Jews of al-Andalus, his court secretary Menahem ibn Saruq composed the well-known text that initiated the Andalusi Jew's famous correspondence with the king of the Crimean Khazars:

> I, Hasdai, son of Isaac, may his memory be blessed, son of Ezra, may his memory be blessed, *belonging to the exiled Jews of Jerusalem, in Spain* ... We, indeed, who are of the remnant of the captive Israelites, servants of my lord the King, are dwelling peacefully in the land of our sojourning, for our God has not forsaken us, nor has His shadow departed from us. The name of our land in which we dwell is called in the sacred tongue Sefarad, but in the language of the Arabs, the indwellers of the land, al-Andalus ...
>
> The land is rich, abounding in rivers, springs and aqueducts; a land of corn, oil and wine, of fruits and all manner of delicacies; it has pleasure-gardens and orchards, fruitful trees of every kind, including the leaves of the tree upon which the silkworm feeds, of which we have great abundance. In the mountains and woods

of our country cochineal is gathered in great quantity. There are also found among us mountains covered by crocus and with veins of silver, gold, copper, iron, tin, lead sulfur, porphyry, marble, and crystal. Merchants congregate in it, and traffickers from the ends of the earth, from Egypt and adjacent countries, bringing spices, precious stones, splendid wares for kings and princes, and all the desirable things of Egypt. Our king has collected very large treasures of silver, gold, precious things and valuables such as no king has ever collected. (Kokovtzov 10; trans. Kobler 1:98 ff.)[20]

Ibn Shaprut echoes al-Razi and Isidore regarding the lushness of the land, but goes farther in linking its agricultural richness, abundance of natural resources and its commercial prosperity to his principal concern, the status and security of its community of Jews ("We, indeed, who are of the remnant of the captive Israelites, servants of my lord the King, are dwelling peacefully in the land of our sojourning"). He furthermore emphasizes the aristocratic, Jerusalemite origins of his community and the role Providence plays in safeguarding its wellbeing. It fell to later Andalusi Jewish intellectuals, notably the twelfth-century literary intellectual Moses ibn 'Ezra', to connect explicitly the motifs of land and nobility to the matter of the Jews' extraordinary cultural production.

The competitive inflection of the trope resonated among Andalusi Jews as well. Their political-religious and cultural rivalry with the Muslim East for pre-eminence in the Jewish world finds a place as a motif in Hebrew poetry. In one ninety-five verse *qasida* ("*Tehillat el*"), the usually irascible and rarely unctuous eleventh-century poet Solomon ibn Gabirol offers an unnamed patron – almost certainly his erstwhile benefactor, the irrepressible Samuel ibn Naghrila (the Nagid), to whom a cluster of Ibn Gabirol's poems are addressed – the entire conventional catalogue of generalized praise. However, in an unusual passage midway through the lyric, the poet temporarily departs from rehearsing conventional *madih* themes. He envisions the reception of the Nagid's wisdom by the Jewish communities of the Muslim East, in particular ascribing to the Easterners consciousness of Samuel's rabbinic and intellectual acumen and accomplishment as belonging to *Sefarad*:

His responsa are read throughout Iraq
    and expounded by communal authorities.
In the councils of the heads of Nehardea and Sura
    the great towns of (rabbinic) jurisprudence
They elevate his responsa above the rest
    and inscribe them in scrolls with golden ink.
People say: "The Sefardim have discovered
    the wonders of concealed knowledge;

They behold the truth, their Master overpowers
>   while we envision delusion.
Compared to them we dress in tatters
>   while they're attired in finest apparel.
Their dignity resembles the lions';
>   compared to them we are like ewe lambs.
Wisdom's full-grown shoots are picked clean for them
>   while we pick unripe ears of corn.
The eyes of their blind and their deaf ears are opened up
>   while our ears merely tingle.
The Master delights them and their joys abound;
>   they delight in divulging his praises.
In his presence it's as though Rav Hayya never existed,
>   inadequately equipped to answer him with words."

>   (Ibn Gabirol 46–47, vv. 43–51)

Such verses clearly exceed the patron's expectation that the poem enthusiastically promote his incomparable virtues. Indeed, the acclaim the lyric heaps upon the patron succeeds in elevating the entire community over its counterpart in the East, whose leaders' day has come and gone.[21]

Moses ibn 'Ezra's (d. after 1138) *Kitab al-muhadara wal-mudhakara* (*The Book of Conversation and Discussion*) was written during the latter years of the author's protracted exile from Granada in Christian Spain three generations after Samuel the Nagid and the height of Jewish socio-political influence in the *ta'ifa* kingdoms. The work's fifth chapter, entitled "Shufuf jaliyyat al-Andalus fi sha'ni l-shi'r wa-l-khutab wal-nathr" ("The clear superiority of the Jewish community of al-Andalus in matters of poetry, rhetorical discourse and prose") is clearly patterned after the Arabic *fada'il* and *mafakhir* literature (Ibn 'Ezra' 54–88). Ibn 'Ezra' departs from Ibn Shaprut's approach and places far more emphasis on the aristocratic lineage, gift for cultural production, cultural accomplishments and inheritance than on the richness and security of the country for its Jews.

> There is no doubt that the people of Jerusalem from whose exile community we hail were more learned in classical literary language and in transmission of rabbinic knowledge than the communities of other places and towns [*kanat a'lama bi-fasihi l-lugha wa-naql 'ilmi l-shari'a min sa'iri l-bilad wal-qura*]. (Ibn 'Ezra' 54 [29a])

As Ibn 'Ezra' goes on to explain, the Jews of al-Andalus excelled across the entire classical Jewish and Arabic cultural curricula on account of their lineage – in rabbinics, grammar, scriptural exegesis, philosophy, science, and above all in poetry. Why no reference to the specific virtues conferred by place? The late eleventh and early- to mid-twelfth centuries were even more devastating for the Jews of al-Andalus than for the Muslims, especially compared to the Umayyad caliphate at its zenith. Although he laments his own exile from Granada in a stirring cycle of lyrical complaints – Ibn 'Ezra' will never return to al-Andalus – Ibn 'Ezra's Arabic prose writings, and the Hebrew texts from later twelfth-century authors originating or writing in the Christian kingdoms but still enamored of the Andalusi Jews' Judeo-Arabic heritage (Judah al-Harizi's imaginative rhymed prose and Abraham ibn Daud's historiography), had no choice but to privilege lineage and learning over place and its political economy. At least their cultural identity was portable, as long as they nurtured its aesthetic, literary and scientific values in Arabic and in Arabic-to-Hebrew translation.[22]

As for the Andalusi Jews' sense of loss and thus nostalgia, the abrupt demise of their community as Almohad rule spread across al-Andalus in the mid-twelfth century was of course remembered as another lamented chapter in the Jews' exile. The moment occasioned an often-imitated dirge by Abraham ibn 'Ezra' after the fashion of Arabic city elegies in which the poet bundles his literary response to the tribulations of Seville, Cordoba, Jaén, and Almeria together with reaction to the concurrent ordeals suffered by the Maghribi communities Dar'a, Sijilmassa, Tlemçen, Ceuta, Meknes and Fez. Elsewhere I have offered a reading of Ibn 'Ezra's lyric alongside al-Rundi's aforementioned Arabic elegy and shown how the former spiritualizes the Andalusi and Maghribi Jews' sense of home and homelessness and crosses the boundaries formally separating Arabic-style Hebrew social poetry and Hebrew liturgical verse (Brann, "Constructions of Exile"). In style it stands apart from more traditional and numerous Andalusi Hebrew liturgical gestures lamenting the interminable exile of catholic Israel as well as liturgical poems bemoaning specifically Andalusi disasters such as Isaac ibn Ghiyath of Lucena's dirge on the events of 1066 Granada.

Al-Andalus was both *a place with a socio-political and cultural history* and *an idea whose own history stands in dialectical relation with the history of the place itself.* For its producers and consumers, the particulars of our trope – the richness of the land, the community's love of learning, and its erudition, cultural sophistication and noble lineage, all inscribed in the social, intellectual and literary history of al-Andalus – defined Andalusi identity. It constructed and defined an idealized and transcendent Andalusi identity in relation to its own storied past, with respect to al-Andalus's complex association with the Maghrib and the Berbers, in terms of its cultural competition with the Muslim East, and finally, from the twelfth century onward, its uneasy relationship with the Christian north. In Robert Edwards's words, we might say this trope endeavours "to rediscover and enact the values that are presumed to have governed the original order" (Edwards 25). In reaching back to that originally remembered and then increasingly imagined past, the trope authorizes an intellectually and aesthetically vibrant and powerful identity for the Andalusis and their heirs, rooted in an alluring vision of the country and projecting an unmistakable sense of Andalusi exceptionalism.

NOTES

1 Thus, for instance, Gil Anidjar reconsiders "what is meant today by al-Andalus as a literary and cultural object of Arab Jewish letters" (Anidjar 3).

2 In a project devoted to these questions, I am concerned with identifying the stable and unstable elements in representations of al-Andalus and Sefarad respectively: that is, in tracing the history of the trope and in examining its shifting contours and significance and its social agency for the architects of Andalusi Muslim and Jewish culture and subsequently for the guardians of its legacy beyond its borders, especially in the Maghrib and, for the Jews, in the Christian Iberian kingdoms to the north. I am also interested in how differently majority and minority communities textualized their attachment to the country and defined its heritage. Many of these lines of inquiry are examined in my *Andalusi Moorings: Al-Andalus and Sefarad as Tropes of Muslim and Jewish Culture* (forthcoming).

3 For a discussion of the ways in which Andalusi Jewish identity was established in opposition to Muslims and Islam, see Esperanza Alfonso, *Islamic Culture through Jewish Eyes*.

4 The twelfth century was also critical in framing another, very different variation of the trope in response to the religious revivalism of the Almoravids and Almohads – the construction of the Andalusi elite as insufficiently pious and unduly materialistic and hedonistic.

5 According to Aziz al-Azmeh, the work of al-Maqqari, a seventeenth-century Moroccan scholar writing more than a century after Nasrid Granada fell to the Catholic monarchs, "is a vast celebration of the excellences of by-gone al-Andalus … an Andalus of the imagination, one that is constructed not from vision but from nostalgia" (al-Azmeh 260). However, in *Andalusi Moorings* I argue that nostalgia itself is variable and historically contingent: that is, the nostalgia expressed during the eleventh century differs from that of the twelfth, thirteenth, and thereafter. See Alexander E. Ellison, *Looking Back at al-Andalus: The Poetics of Loss and Nostalgia in Medieval Arabic and Hebrew Literature* (Leiden: E.J. Brill, 2009).

6 Here I differentiate lyrics addressing the collective sense of loss and longing from the occasional personal poems composed by poets such as Ibn 'Ammar, al-Mu'tamid, and Moses ibn 'Ezra', who experienced exile and composed lyrical complaints on the theme.

7 Comments and occasional passages about the merits of al-Andalus are thus embedded in Arabic literary texts of every genre; one finds them in Ibn Rushd, Ibn Battuta,

and Ibn Khaldun, for whom "the Spaniards are found to have a sharpness of intellect, a nimbleness of body, and a receptivity for instruction such as no one else has"
(Ibn Khaldun, *Al-Muqaddimah* 1:400; Ibn Khaldun, *The Muqaddimah* 1:179). Even as
imaginative a text as al-Saraqusti's *al-Maqamat al-luzumiyya* (#41, the *Maqama* of the
Berbers) captures the trope brilliantly when the narrator Ibn Tammam (who appears
in this *maqama* as an Arab from the East) reflects on al-Andalus from the vantage
of Tangier. Ibn Jubayr's famous *Rihla* stresses the unique rightness of Islam in the
maghrib ["la islama ila bi-biladi l-maghrib"] (*Rihla* 87; see Ross Brann, "Inscribing the
Mediterranean Journey: Two Paradigmatic Twelfth-Century Texts from Iberia," in *The
Medieval Mediterranean and the Origins of the West*, ed. Sharon Kinoshita and Brian Catlos
(forthcoming, Palgrave). In "Representing and Remembering," Justin Stearns identifies three themes with which al-Andalus is integrated into general Islamic historiography. Two of these themes (the third views al-Andalus as a place of *'aja'ib* [wonders
or marvels]) accentuate its distinctive role in the religious imagination: al-Andalus as a
"land of *jihad*" and as the site of eschatological events.

8 For my purposes here I do not address the historians' question of the social reality as
posed by Guichard: that is, whether social cleavage between Berbers and Arabs continued unabated into the eleventh century, or whether the distinct Andalusi identity
the Umayyads sponsored widely took hold in the tenth. See Wasserstein 164–5.

9 The historiographic traditions about the *tabi'un*, the pious warriors who were "followers of the [Prophet's] Companions" and were among the early settlers in al-Andalus,
serve a similar purpose. See Makki 179 ff.

10 I have slightly altered the translation of Jonathan P. Decter (Decter, "A Myrtle in the
Forest" 137).

11 For another example of this tradition, see 'Abd al-Wahid al-Marrakushi 115.

12 Isidore's historiography posits a continuous narrative connecting Roman Hispania
to the Visigothic kingdom of his era. His admiring readers would later extend this un-
interrupted narrative through the rise of the Catholic monarchs down to the modern
period. The prosperity of the land is also referenced in the *Chronicle of 754* as attract-
ing the attention of the Muslim invaders in 711 (Wolf 133).

13 See also *"Inna li-l-jannati fi-l-andalus"* (*Diwan ibn Khafajah* 136 [#88]). For additional
illustrations, see Lévi Provençal 61–2, and Terés 292–5.

14 The thirteenth chapter of Sa'id al-Andalusi's (d. 1070) *Tabaqat al-umam* (*Categories of
the Nations*) accentuates the Andalusi contribution to scientific study.

15 Indeed, Ibn Rabib places the responsibility squarely upon the Andalusis themselves.

16 Nearly two hundred years later, and in response to very different socio-religious and
political circumstances than Ibn Hazm confronted, two thirteenth-century authors
resumed the Andalusi iteration of this Arabic literary tradition. Ibn Sa'id al-Maghribi's
contribution takes the form of an addendum to Ibn Hazm, picking up where his
predecessor left off, while Isma'il ibn Muhammad al-Shaqundi's (d. 1231 or 1232)

Risala fi fadl al-Andalus (*Treatise on the Merit of al-Andalus*, in al-Maqqari, *Nafh al-tib min ghusn al-andalus al-ratib* 4:149–211) represents an independent essay on the theme that is regarded as the more artistically accomplished *adab* work on the subject. The four texts drawn from al-Maqqari were published together and introduced by Salah al-Din al-Munajjad as *Fada'il al-andalus wa-ahliha.*

17 Maya Shatzmiller likewise traces to the eleventh century the earliest textual expressions of *mafakhir al-barbar* (glories of the Berbers) and *mahasin ahl al-maghrib* (good qualities of the people of the west) – echoes of Berber resistance to Arabic acculturation (Shatzmiller 31).

18 For another collection of Andalusi texts on this score see E. García Gómez, *Andalucia contra Berberia.*

19 For my purposes here I note that Ibn Shaprut and the Andalusi Jews regarded "Sefarad" as equivalent to al-Andalus. Obviously "Sefarad" came to connote the mental and geographic space occupied by Iberian Jews in the Christian kingdoms following the Almohad invasion of the mid-twelfth century (see Decter, *Iberian Jewish Literature* 5–6). As late as the fourth decade of the twelfth century, Moses ibn 'Ezra', an exile from Almoravid Granada living in the Christian north, asserts: "Sefarad is al-Andalus in the language of the Arabs."

20 By contrast, "Afudat nezer le-shevet moshlim" (Schirmann and Fleischer 1:6–8), one of two panegyrics accompanying the epistle commissioned by Ibn Shaprut and composed by Ibn Saruq, portrays catholic Israel ["*knesset yisra'el*"] as subjugated. See Esperanza Alfonso, "Constructions of Exile in Medieval Hebrew Literature" [Hebrew] and "The Uses of Exile in Poetic Discourse."

21 Esperanza Alfonso cites the following lyric by Ibn Hazm as a parallel:

> I am the sun that in heart's sky shines.
>> My only defect is to have risen in the West.
> Had I risen in the East,
>> What a plunder of the renown I now lack would it be!
> My soul is in love with Iraq's distant islands
>> But what a small wonder it is that a lover longs for his beloved.
>>> (Alfonso, *Islamic Culture through Jewish Eyes* 40)

However, while also resting on the opposition of West to East, it actually strikes the reader as an admission of the centrality of the East over the West (ll. 1–3; transmitted in al-Maqqari, *Nafh al-tib min ghusn al-andalus al-ratib* 2:81).

22 The construction of Andalusi-Sefaradi exceptionalism in Moses ibn 'Ezra', Abraham ibn 'Ezra', al-Harizi's *Tahkemoni*, and Abraham ibn Daud's *Sefer ha-Qabbalah* is studied in my forthcoming *Andalusi Moorings.*

9 The Convivencia Wars: Decoding Historiography's Polemic with Philology*

RYAN SZPIECH

"Our Romanticism is contradicted by our Enlightenment, our inner by our outer."

Richard Tarnas, *Cosmos and Psyche*

The quincentenary remembrance of Columbus's first voyage, of the expulsion of Iberian Jews, and of the conquest of Muslim Granada produced a barrage of texts meditating on the nature of medieval Iberian multiculturalism, specifically as it might reflect the *convivencia* (coexistence or cohabitation) of disparate groups. The concept of convivencia, while falling from favour among many academics, has (in historian Jonathan Ray's words) "been embraced and distorted by an ever-widening group of academics, journalists, and politicians" (1).[1] Despite the spread of this popularity and the persistently positive spin that the concept has come to acquire in current usage, not everyone can agree that convivencia equates with harmony. In 2005, historian Olivia Remie Constable posed the vexing question, "Is convivencia dangerous?"[2] As she explained, convivencia, or any form of cultural intermingling, was viewed with skepticism by many in medieval Iberia for its "potential to foster actual harm: whether physical, economic, social or sexual." It is, more importantly, dangerous as a modern concept, "since it can tempt us to read the Middle Ages through a murky – though often rosy – lens of biased historical memory and deterministic modern values." While convivencia may indeed be dangerous because it is too simple a model, it may equally be so because it is too complex: it may be dangerous for modern Iberianists, historians and literary critics alike, because it represents a conundrum that cannot be solved, an irreducible set of contradictions that can, judging by the manifold and contradictory spirit in which it has been employed, be easily evoked and yet not so easily explained. John Boswell adroitly captures this difficulty in *The Royal Treasure* when he observes, "The question of convivencia, the living together of the various Iberian religious and ethnic groups, is intensely complicated, and the task of a scholar trying to understand and describe this symbiosis is rather like that of a man attempting to reconstruct a broken and crumpled spider's web" (12).

Because of this complexity and fragility, convivencia has generated for over half a century and continues to generate a vast array of widely divergent and fractious interpretations. Convivencia, ironically, has become a source of modern scholarly conflict and an inspiration for ongoing polemic. As Maya Soifer comments, "many scholars today treat it like a once sought-after guest who has overstayed her welcome" ("Beyond Convivencia" 20). One is hard-pressed to find another critical term that has exerted such a long-term impact in Ibero-medieval studies or spurred such a polarized mix of zealous devotion and fierce opposition across disciplines. Yet a closer consideration of the scholarly arguments over the term *convivencia* and what it is used to describe suggests that the debate over medieval Iberian tolerance and intolerance, rather than deriving from the actual difficulty of "reconstructing" that "crumpled web" – difficult though that certainly is – is in fact the product of unsettled rivalries generated by the shared disciplinary history of philology, historiography, and literary criticism, methodological rivalries that at their core have very little to do with medieval Iberia. The overall argument I wish to proffer here – that the ongoing debate over convivencia can best be explained as opposed reactions to the conflict of method in the human sciences in the wake of the linguistic turn – consists of three parts: first, that the comparatist method followed by Américo Castro and other literary historians of his generation (most notably, Erich Auerbach) derived ultimately from an early Romantic concept of history, itself an expression of an earlier model proposed by Giambattista Vico, of the intimate connection between philology and philosophy; second, that the collapse of this model has created a methodological rift between interpretive and empirical arguments both within and across Humanist disciplines such as philology and historiography; and third, that this division has produced a profound conflict of method between a predominant focus on hermeneutics in North America and on scientific philology in Spain. The disagreement over the meaning of convivencia is principally a symptom of this methodological division. By better understanding the rivalries generated by this division and their impact on the various disciplines implicated in the study of medieval Iberia, we may be able to frame the discussion in new terms that do not reduce the question of interaction between the faiths of medieval Iberia to a facile one simply of tolerance or intolerance, but instead emphasize the importance of methodology in determining the outcome of historical and philological research.[3]

The Epistemological Origins of Convivencia

Before considering Américo Castro's connection with other Romance philologists such as Erich Auerbach and his engagement with the interpretive insights of early

Romanticism, it is necessary to trace the emergence of his terminology out of a vocabulary of scientific linguistics.[4] The term *convivencia*, "living-together-ness" as it has been awkwardly translated, has been associated with competition from its early scholarly use. The grandfather of modern Spanish philology, Ramón Menéndez Pidal, adapted the term (the use of which can be found in Spanish at least as early as the seventeenth century)[5] in his massive history of the language, *Orígenes del español* (1926), using it to describe the coexistence of phonetic variants among regional versions of medieval Romance in Iberia, the "convivencia of many norms that struggle among themselves with equal strength" (555).[6] For example, the word for "old," from late Latin *vetulus*, existed as *biello* in Aragonese, *bieyu* in Leonese, and *viejo* in Castilian; river, *río*, varied within dialects, alternating with *rido* and *rigo*; and so on. Pidal provides scores of examples of such variation, driving home the point that on the local level of the evolution of languages, convivencia was not a static concept describing a balance of forces, but a dynamic one, associated from the very beginning with competition.[7]

> Within the disconcerting variety of forms that the documents present we should not see a jumble of chance, but rather a silent battle of tendencies [un sordo combate de tendencias] that, although slowly and obscurely, surely brings a victory and a defeat. (*Orígenes* 556)

Various scholars have highlighted the pseudo-scientific overtones of Pidal's language. Linguist José Portolés attributes Pidal's notion of evolution to nineteenth-century German linguist August Schleicher (45–8). Responding to Portolés, Thomas Glick has shown how such notions of competition were directly informed by Pidal's own understanding of evolution not only as it had been distilled in Schleicher's linguistic trees, but even more significantly through evolutionist concepts such as Darwin's theory of competitive selection and the notions, received from early evolutionary biologist Jean-Baptiste Lamarck, of the "will to develop" and of "inherited changes" ("Darwin" 36–9).[8] The competition that Pidal describes is that of the survival of Castilian as the fittest of many variations among the languages of Iberia, and the "will" he attributes to Castilian expresses a belief in competitive adaptation arising out of an evolutionary need to take precedence over other dialects. Convivencia, in Pidal's formulation, denoted conflict, competition, and victory.

This is, to be sure, not the meaning that has persisted. The word was made famous not by Pidal in his linguistic history but by his student, Américo Castro, who applied the term to describe not the competition of linguistic variants but the social coexistence of peoples, specifically of medieval Jews, Christians, and Muslims in the Iberian Peninsula. First in 1948 in his work *España en su historia*, and through subsequent revisions in 1954 and 1962 in *La realidad histórica en españa*, Castro developed his notion of religious syncretism and symbiosis, which he proposed as essential for understanding Spanish history. As is now well-known, the charged and far-reaching nature of his terminology and arguments provoked bitter polemics among his contemporaries, most notably Claudio Sánchez-Albornoz and Eugenio Asensio.[9] Rejecting Pidal's scientific, philological notion of progress, conflict, and evolution, Castro gave the term "convivencia" a more nuanced, metaphorical sense to indicate cultural interpenetration, interdependence, and coexistence. It was his synchronic model – read in a positive, presentist light – that has caught on so famously.

The Polemic over Convivencia

Reversals such as the one the evaluation of convivencia has undergone, especially in so short a span, are themselves dangerous because they threaten to obscure the origins of ideas and make them comprehensible only within the terms of one interpretive model. Such paired extreme images abound in the histories of medieval Iberia, and ramify from the ill-conceived original debate between tolerance and intolerance. Some familiar examples include the lachrymose and neo-lachrymose schools of Jewish historiography with their emphasis on persecution,[10] or other views recasting multiculturalism as a panacea for modern woes in the context of postcolonial immigration, soaring unemployment, and the Bush-era "war on terror."

There has been more recently a critical effort to reassess the legacy of Castro's terminology and propose alternative models without vituperation, such as Constable's timely remarks on the question, Brian Catlos's wry renaming of convivencia as "conveniencia" ("convenience" or "agreement"), or María Rosa Menocal's insistence that convivencia is most fruitfully understood as inherently paradoxical and not exclusive of violence and reconquest – a point that David Nirenberg has defended with extensive evidence.[11] Others, like Mark Meyerson, have explored "the economic foundations of convivencia" (*Muslims of Valencia* 271), showing how complex social relationships created interdependence apart from categories of religious or cultural difference. In an effort to rethink the question of the influence of modern bias on our understanding of medieval attitudes, Ray has noted – in terms very similar to those of Constable cited above – that cultural openness was "seen as a primary challenge to Jewish religious piety, social cohesion, and political autonomy" (12). Equally balanced in their assessment are Jewish-studies scholars Esperanza Alfonso (*Islamic Culture through Jewish Eyes*) and Jonathan Elukin (*Living Together, Living Apart*) who emphasize that within the nineteenth-century positivist "Science of Judaism" in Germany (*Wissenschaft des Judentums*), the notion of a Sephardic Golden Age provided a model of successful integration for modern Ashkenazi Jews, reifying the early modern Jewish myth of tolerance under Islam and suffering under Christianity.

Parallel to the many balanced and valid criticisms of convivencia, a more vehement polemical attack on the term can be seen in both popular and scholarly writing.[12] Within Spain, numerous academics – including Serafín Fanjul, professor of Arabic at the Universidad Autónoma in Madrid and member of Spain's Royal Academy of History – have lodged vociferous criticism of the concept of convivencia. Although Fanjul criticizes all extreme views including those that represent medieval Íberia as completely intolerant, he devotes more energy to demonstrating that "the splendid [exquisita] convivencia of the three cultures is … imaginary" (*La quimera* 22), arguing that "this panorama of … tolerance … cooperation, and jubilant friendship among communities breaks down soon after we begin reading original texts" (28). He even goes so far as to claim that Islamic al-Andalus was "a regime more like South African apartheid, *mutatis mutandis*, than the idyllic Arcadia invented by Castro" (29). Equally acerbic in his assessment is distinguished medievalist Miguel Ángel Ladero Quesada, who in the foreword to Fanjul's *Al-Andalus contra España* called Fanjul's book "the only adequate way to respond to the ocean of falsities denounced in the book and to the limitless capacity for confabulation, prejudice, and self-delusion, of … biased ignorance or mental laziness observable among those who elaborate and proffer" such ideas (xi). These comments suggest that, far from being a closed chapter in twentieth-century Iberian Studies, the polemic over convivencia is alive and well and continues to adduce new observations to support its arguments.

In all fairness, the tone of these arguments does not exemplify mainstream voices in the academy. Yet one can detect a more muted opposition to one-sided presentations of convivencia, in large measure corrective of earlier trends, even among more balanced writers. Consuelo López Morillas, scholar of *Aljamiado* literature, explains in her overview of scholarship on Al-Andalus in North America that that the celebrations of 1992 ushered in "a bias towards themes of intercultural and interconfessional contact" (242). She includes within this bias a more general criticism of the concept of convivencia, specifically as it has come under scrutiny within studies of religious polemics:

> Al-Andalus is often hailed as a model of tolerance, or at least of toleration, but that idealized view … is belied by the many varieties of polemic that have recently come under study…. All these reveal, as one scholar has put it, that so-called convivencia was a precarious affair. Such investigations as these can only lead to a more nuanced and less cliché-ridden understanding of the true relations among the major religious confessions in medieval Spain. (243–4)

Arabist Manuela Marín is more emphatic in her conclusions: "The myth of the Spain of Three Cultures, a title used as an element of propaganda, is so far from the historical reality that it cannot but generate new elements of confusion in a debate already perverted in many aspects" (Marín and Pérez, "L'Espagne" 23).[13] Hispano-Arabic lexicographer Federico Corriente also criticizes what he calls the "myth of the three cultures," which he claims was invented during the late Franco era, and instead proposes a three-religion/two-culture model that dissolves "Sephardic culture" as another "contemporary myth." We should avoid

> fabricating for Spain three medieval cultures, Christian, Islamic, and Jewish. There were only two … both "practiced" by one people with the aim of eliminating the other, despite circumstantial situations of delicate and short-lived convivencia. This is the only historical truth that should prevail, even though we all would have liked that the past and present were otherwise. (46–7)[14]

In chorus with these arguments, Eduardo Manzano Moreno, medieval historian and director of the humanities centre at the Consejo Superior de Investigaciones Científicas, denounces the modern ideological motivations he sees behind an overly Romantic vision of Islam:

> If in place of defending the existence of values shared between Islam and Christendom, we project onto the past the ideas of "tolerance" and "convivencia" as intimately linked to peninsular Islam and in opposition to secular Hispanic provincialism [cerrilismo hispáno], we do nothing more than make an ahistorical and equally idealistic transposition of a series of contemporary concepts which have their justification in a history that is never described or interpreted but simply depicted [plasmada]. (37)[15]

Against "the heap of lyrical nonsense that continues to be written about Al-Andalus with great frequency" (37), he praises the perceived trend in peninsular Arabism since the 1970s of establishing connections with other disciplines like history "without giving up scientific rigor."[16] Hebraist María Fuencisla García Casar criticizes what she calls Castro's "original but quixotic intuitions" and "dangerous deformations which are in no way beneficial," instead praising Castro's critics Eugenio Asensio and José Maravall for "balance," "detachment," and "historical rigor." "Their unbiased reading is in all ways obligatory if we desire that future studies on Spanish Judaism … do not continue to be based on supposition, vacuous dialectic, and trite but profitable topics [manidos pero rentables tópicos]" (81). In the face of such perceived scholarly misguidedness, Corriente displays the same overweening *gravitas* with regard to detached historiography, stating that "the mission of the historian is to transmit faithfully the facts and give them their correct interpretation, never altering them with a moral or ideological goal" (47). As Ladero Quesada emphasizes, "one must stop the falsifications of History" (Fanjul, *Al-Andalus* xiv).

What unites the historian and the philologist for these critics is their shared attention to objective facts and intention to avoid bias. Corriente explains his position clearly:

> There is a hierarchy of interests in research in which the establishing of facts takes precedence over the listing of opinions given about them ... For those of us who like scientific rigor, we find ourselves more easily trying to confirm the reality of things and preventing their oblivion than gathering and valuing what opinions may have been given about them with greater or lesser accuracy. (39)

Given the shared histories of the disciplines of philology and historiography, histories which we will here examine more closely, it is not surprising that these examples share a very clear pairing of the two disciplines as somehow converging at their most elevated and disinterested state in the love of hard facts. In order to understand better the significance of this opposition in Spanish scholarship between "lyrical nonsense" and "scientific rigor" on the one hand or between convivencia and "the supposed scientific truth" (Castro's words), on the other, it is necessary to situate the debate in a wider historical context and to identify the specific origins of this parting of ways that has had such a profound and determinative effect on Iberian medieval studies, both in Spain and in North America.

Castro, Auerbach, Vico, and Figural History

The "hierarchy of interests" between facts and opinions within Iberian medieval studies of which Corriente speaks is only part of a wider conflict between empirical and interpretive criticism within all of the disciplines that were born out of philology. The distilling of the anti-convivencia polemic into an unspoken companionship between philology and history on the grounds of their shared scientific objectivity automatically recalls the words of Castro's contemporary and one of the twentieth century's greatest Romance scholars, Erich Auerbach, who wrote at the end of his life, in his very last work (*Literary Language and Its Public in Late Latin Antiquity and in the Middle Ages*), "My purpose is always to write history" (20). One can only imagine how, *mutatis mutandis*, the historians and philologists of today with a pronounced love for scientific rigor would find ample cause to attack such a statement.

In explaining how it could be that a philologist's primary cause was not text editing and the cataloging of manuscripts, but something as vast and as nebulous as "to write history," Auerbach invokes the well-known words of another historian-philologist hybrid, Giambattista Vico, who (he says) viewed history and philology together as one discipline. Vico's ideas were of primary importance for

Auerbach's understanding of literary history; and because of the wider context in which the rhetoric of the convivencia debate must be understood, its connection to Auerbach's Vichian thought is in no way coincidental.[17] Not only was Auerbach trained in the German tradition of Romance philology that evolved from the second half of the nineteenth century until the rise of National Socialism, the same tradition had a determinative influence on the philological discipline in which Castro himself was trained.[18] More importantly, both Auerbach's invocation of Vico and Castro's promulgation of convivencia can also be understood as reactions against the limits of that tradition. As a result, there is a direct intersection of terms and concepts in Auerbach's and Castro's definition of historiography and, correspondingly, the criticism of the ideas of Castro and his later proponents closely resembles, both temporally and conceptually, the critical reaction against Auerbach and his notion of literary history. The parallels between the two thinkers and their reception are so marked that an examination of Auerbach's Vichian thought can lead to a better understanding of the latter as well as provide insight into the origins of the internecine wrangling of modern Iberianist scholarship. The verbal wars over convivencia are by no means meaningful in a limited or local context only, but are in fact part of a wider, more universal epistemological divide within the intellectual history of the West.

As is well known, Vico distinguishes between what he calls the true (*verum*) and the certain (*certum*); and he associates the former, understood as absolute truth, with "philosophy" and the latter, understood as the certainties subject to historical change, with "philology." As Vico's famous (if overemphasized) remark, *verum ipsum factum* – that which is true is the same as that which is made – has been understood, the task of the scholar is to seek the true in a human context, in human things, not in nature or metaphysics.[19] In short, the universally true must be approached only as it is manifested within the locally certain, an insight that Isaiah Berlin has described as "a sense of knowing which is basic to all humane studies" (*Three Critics* 116).[20] Auerbach saw Vico's concept as a stronghold within which to protect the *Geisteswissenschaften* from the incursion of excessively linear, mechanistic, or scientific methodology. Philology, the study of human language, is comparable (as Auerbach sees it) to history, precisely because the stuff of its conclusions is the human, the *certum,* and it is only possible to approach the *verum* spread across history by observing the patterns of individual certainties. Auerbach explains that

> the truth sought by philosophy is inseparable from philology, which investigates the *certa* both singly and in their systematic context … [T]his philological philosophy or philosophical philology is concerned with only one thing – mankind … [S]uch is the conception of philology that I have learned from Vico. (*Literary Language* 16)

As a result, rather than (as Corriente urges) "faithfully transmitting facts and giving them their *correct* interpretation" (italics mine), Auerbach's history is not a chronological construction, in which the past is understood to be the sum of its individually measured and verified empirical parts. As he asserts, "it is patently impossible to establish a synthesis by assembling all the particulars" (*Literary Language* 18). Rather, his historiography is "vertical": a conceptual history that is extra-chronological, built not around the ordering of data but around the prominence of repetitions. This historiography is exegetical, not scientific; circular and paradoxical, not linear and logical. Because for Vico (and for Auerbach) one can only fully understand what one has made, history, like philology, is not based on measurement but on interpretation. As Auerbach explains, "Strict scientific methods are not applicable to historical phenomena or to any other phenomena that cannot be subjected to the special conditions required by scientific experimentation" (8). History is, literally, *figural*: built around the operative narrative concepts of proleptic prefiguration and analeptic fulfillment, just as the Hebrew Bible is understood, in Christian exegesis, to foreshadow and be fulfilled by the New Testament on a figural level of interpretation. In his exposition of figural reading – which he is careful to distinguish from allegorical reading, in which signifiers are read plainly as non-literal or metaphorical – Auerbach insists that the connection of two events in history through "prefiguration" and "fulfillment" both preserves the literal historicity of facts and events from being transformed into allegories or metaphors, and at the same time insists that such historicity is never transparent but must always be received and explained within an interpretive framework (*Scenes* 54). Although itself not based in fact but in interpretation, figural "omni-temporality" (to borrow one of Auerbach's terms; *Mimesis* 544),[21] free of strict causal and chronological ties but still defined in its warp and weft by the perceived interconnectedness between events, is the only proper way, he suggests, to access the human past. Auerbach insists that "history, with all its concrete force, remains forever a figure, cloaked and needful of interpretation ... [T]he history of no epoch ever has the practical self-sufficiency which ... resides in the accomplished fact" ("Figura" 58–9).

For this anti-empirical position, Auerbach was attacked by his fellow philologists, precisely because they believed his history was not historical enough (Nichols, "Philology in Auerbach's Drama" 66). René Wellek criticized what he saw as Auerbach's "reliance on intuition and interpretation," his "disregard for generic boundaries dividing fiction from non-fiction," and his attempt "to discard the whole conceptual structure of modern scholarship in favor of what he calls 'philology,' textual interpretation, close reading, combined with something which can at best be described as personal insight, artistic imagination" ("Auerbach's Special Realism" 305). At the same time, Dutch philologist Joseph Engels dismisses

Auerbach and other interpretive philologists like Leo Spitzer and Ernst Robert Curtius as aesthetic, literary critics who wrongfully subordinate the study of language to that of literature. Following the Danish linguist Otto Jespersen, he rejects the term "philology" altogether, advocating instead linguistics as a positivist science separated from literary study (Engels 22–4), a view put forth only a few years earlier by René Wellek (*Theory* 38).[22]

According to Stephen Nichols, this clash of philological titans resulted from the emergence at the end of the eighteenth century of two divergent notions of language: the classicist vision of (in E.R. Curtius's words) "the universal concept of Antiquity, which unites philology and history" (519) and the vision of comparative grammarians, in which language was to be studied for itself (Nichols, "Philology and Its Discontents" 122–3). Out of this division, a crisis between language as systematic object (linguistics) and language as culture (philology) was precipitated by Romantic ideas of creativity.[23] Nichols calls the debate between philology and linguistics "the issue at the heart of philology's discontent" (123), a conflict of identity built on the clash of subjective, interpretive criticism, and objective, empirical science, or as Jan Ziolkowski puts it (with tongue in cheek), between "*thinking* about what we are doing and *knowing* what we are doing" (9; italics his).[24] We can easily see the traces of this clash not only in the modern division between academic units of linguistics and literature, but also within medieval studies in the truculent debate between those who approach philology as synchronic – i.e., as textual criticism and manuscript scholarship – and those who see philology as diachronic, i.e., as the study of the evolution of culture within language. Philology survives in its erstwhile hybrid state of hard science blended with hermeneutic sensibility in both classical and medieval studies; but in the latter there is a more troubled divide among those who edit manuscripts and those who read them, a divide, as Nichols and Hans Gumbrecht name it, between "fundamentalist philology" and "essentialist philology" (Gumbrecht, "A Philological Invention" 32–3).[25]

Because both Auerbach and Américo Castro were trained in the former and moved steadily towards the latter throughout their careers, their views on both philology and historiography are extremely similar and bear the marks of this profound shift in focus. In fact, on the subject of history, Auerbach's words are almost indistinguishable from those of Castro, who himself reflected obsessively on the task of the historian in all of his works after *España en su historia*, principally in the 1950s (the same years when Auerbach finished *Literary Language*). Beginning with his essay "Ensayo de historiología" in 1950, he presents a theory of history very similar to Auerbach's figuralism in which he rejects all pretensions to scientific methodology. He developed his historiographical theory in the 1954 version of *La realidad histórica en España* (chapter 2, although much material was subsequently removed from the final version in 1962),[26] and presented the most precise version of this theory in his essay "Descripción, Narración, Historiografía" (in *Dos ensayos*, from 1956), where he states: "The human past … is made present in us like a link between a possibility and its realization" (22). Like Auerbach, Castro rejects all possibility of scientific objectivity in history, stating in his 1959 work *Los españoles, cómo llegaron a serlo*, "the pretension of arriving at the rigorous truth of what happened in the past is illusory" (253).[27] Even more directly, he states: "Historiography cannot shelter itself beneath a science that covers it like a roof of fixed and univocal concepts … No history is scientific" (241). It is logical that "those … who like scientific rigor" (as Corriente says) would find Castro's historiography problematic.

This vision of historiography as essentially poetic rather than scientific, expressed in almost equal terms by Auerbach and Castro in the very same years, is itself a polemical response to a contrary model: the model of history as antiquarianism or science rather than narrative. The aim of historiography to rise above what Hayden White calls historiographical "emplotment" (*Metahistory* 5–11) by cleaving as closely as possible to facts is based on an implicit valuation of things above ideas, of data as a substitute for interpretation and as a way to ensure objectivity and impartiality. In this view, history becomes not a narrative but a result, the sum of its measurable parts rather than a deliberately constructed interweaving of possibilities. The history of this model of historiography reveals that the separation of history writing from narrative and criticism was achieved only through a series of decisive divisions within the human sciences over the last two centuries. Thus, this fissure between hermeneutics and empiricism by which philology was divided and parceled out to its modern heirs, linguistics and literature, did not run through philology only, but also through its problematic Doppelgänger, history; and so historiography too, in its modern sense invented at the same time that philology came into being as an academic subject, has evolved into its current state of valuing objective, archival research over mere interpretive narrative.[28] The resulting "hierarchy of interests" forms part of the essential framework of human sciences as they are distributed across academic disciplines today, and the debate over convivencia is caught in the middle of this methodological bifurcation.

History and Philology between *Bildung* and *Wissenschaft*

Although it is generally accepted that the valuing of empirical exactness in historiography has its origins in Germany in the nineteenth-century Romantic reconception of Enlightenment models of scientific history, it must be stressed that in its Romantic beginning, this "empiricism" did not exclude interpretive narrative. Following Vico's first proposal for a "New Science" centred on human action, a new, holistic, organic representation of the past emerged in Romantic historicism, represented by the oft-misconstrued recommendation of Leopold von Ranke (a founding father of primary-source-based history) to write history "wie es eigentlich gewesen [ist]," *as it essentially was* (*Geschichten* 7). This early nineteenth-century historiography, patent in the foundational histories of Ranke and Michelet, sought to blend the text criticism developed in classical philology and the erudition of legal scholars with narration and interpretation of a universal world history (Breisach 229).[29] History is, in Ranke's words, a "holy hieroglyph,"[30] interpretation of which required not the objectivity of a scientific method but the Romantic hermeneutic of empathy and identification with one's object of study.[31] This Romantic notion of "sympathy" – which implies a complete, inner identification with the world of the past through what Wilhelm Dilthey, the transmitter of the Romantic tradition, later called an inner experience (*Erlebnis*) of empathy (*Einfühlung*)[32] – was based on a dialectical opposition between self and other. This opposition derived from the Hegelian effort to reconcile the idealism of Kant and especially Fichte with the realism of Spinoza through an organic and holistic notion of the animated universe.[33]

The quintessential expression of the Romantic reconciliation of idealism and realism within a holistic organicism is the cultural ideal of *Bildung*, the notion of self-realization of the individual through education and aesthetic cultivation. *Bildung*, as the highest ideal of German Romanticism, was the form given to a belief in harmony between inner consciousness and outer manifestation, between idealism and realism, and in this sense the cultivation of the individual towards self-realization was a consciously social act. In practical terms, the ideals of early Romanticism (*Frühromantik*) were manifest most significantly in the realization of a new ideal of university learning, marking a new constellation of areas of academic work, especially in Prussian universities like University of Berlin, founded under the neo-Humanist guiding hand of Wilhelm von Humboldt in 1810.

In these new disciplines, the Romantic realm of *Bildung* – of personal cultivation and aesthetic judgment – intersected with neoclassical *Wissenschaft* – science and research, understood in a pre-positivist, neo-Humanist sense.[34] Humboldt's concept of *Bildung durch Wissenschaft*, self-cultivation through research, found its most apposite application in classical philology. Pioneered by figures such as Friedrich August Wolf and his pupils, the development of classical philology as a new academic *Altertumswissenschaft*, a science of antiquity, with its epicenter at the University of Berlin, came to embody the ideal of *Bildung* and the holistic vision of academic work.[35] Wolf's vision of philology's intersection with history, elaborated further by his pupil August Böckh, was to have a decisive influence on the growth of both disciplines, above all through those influential figures who attended Böckh's lectures, including August Droysen, Jakob Burckhardt (who also studied under Ranke), Friedrich Nietzsche, and Wilhelm Dilthey.[36] Many of the disciplines established at this time following the model of Wolf and Böckh – source-based historiography with Ranke, comparative grammar and Indo-European linguistics with Friedrich Schlegel and Franz Bopp, German philology with the Grimm brothers, and later Romance philology with Friedrich Diez – not coincidentally shared a Romantic vision of language as simultaneously the stuff of both neo-Humanist *Wissenschaft* and Romantic *Bildung*, a meeting point of exteriority and interiority. Such a view, later developed in the herme-neutical thought of Dilthey at the turn of the twentieth century and manifest in Spain, in altered form, in the early educational reforms of Krausism, can be epitomized by Schlegel's dictum, "It is equally deadly to the spirit [gleich tödlich für den Geist] to have a system and not to have one. One must ... combine the two" (Athenäumsfragment no. 53, in *Kritische* 2:173).

This Romantic synthesis was, in practice, short-lived. In the wake of the revolutions of 1848, the mixed ideals of Romantic historiography and philology were no longer tenable within the same paradoxical conception. There was, especially among the Neogrammarian philologists later in the century, both a sharp criticism of *Bildung* as overly subjective and a concomitant tendency towards a new *Wissenschaft* of science and positivism.[37] Likewise in historiography, poetic and teleological narratives of the past – of history understood as a *Geisteswissenschaft* – quickly became, when stripped of Romantic or Christian or Idealist bias, a renewed devotion to historical and linguistic study as a *Naturwissenschaft*: a natural science, although different from the Enlightenment mechanical view that early Romantic thinkers sought to transform and to transcend.

The bifurcation between *Bildung* and *Wissenschaft* in nineteenth- and early twentieth-century human sciences such as philology and historiography formed part of an essential schism of method that eventually developed into our modern divisions between linguistics and literature, or our active ones in medieval studies between "real" scholarship and mere criticism. It was the same division between Rankean historicism and liberal positivism that relegated *Bildung* either to cultural historians such as Jakob Burckhardt and Johan Huizinga or to narrative histories designed as nationalist and racist propaganda.[38] It was the same division that prompted Nietzsche, himself a philologist unhappily divided across philology's split purposes, to lambaste the philological tradition from which he emerged and, like Burckhardt, to define himself in opposition to it.[39] The harsh criticism weathered by Burckhardt for his cultural histories and Nietzsche for his efforts to *épater les philologues* with unconventional classicism evinces the degree to which *Bildung* became detached from scholarship both in historiography and in philology. In this context we can understand the lament by philosopher Karl Jaspers in 1923 and again in 1946 that "the university is impoverished when there is only philology and no more philosophy, only technical practice and no more theory, endless facts and no ideas" (48; translation, Ringer 257).[40]

The duality of science and metaphor is present at the very heart of all of the human sciences founded at this time, and the schism produced by the loss of this Romantic ideal is still very much with us today in our disciplinary and methodological squabbles, even though the modern university has evolved far from the Humboldtian or Krausist blueprints. Following Nietzsche's lead, and in opposition to Saussure's reification of the *Bildung/Wissenschaft* divide as a divide between synchronic and diachronic sign systems, between objective *langue* and subjective *parole*, the general postmodern and poststructural aversion to any form of *grand récit* (including narratives of collective identity – liberal or conservative – in post-Francoist Spain, and defenses of closed cultural canons in contemporary North America) has driven deeper the wedge between philological science and criticism.[41] This divide between empiricism and evaluation is not only limited to the conflict between linguistics and literature, but has also prompted critics like Edward Said to lament that Near Eastern Studies now suffers from a "retrogressive position when compared with the other human sciences, [a] general methodological and ideological backwardness, [a] comparative insularity" (*Orientalism* 261), and medievalists like Lee Patterson, in the same vein, to denounce the "barriers that divide medieval studies from the rest of the human sciences" (104). While medieval Romance philology has allowed some new pockets for generalization by occasionally sharing space with cultural and gender studies, Arabic or Near Eastern philology – especially in Europe – has put up a firm opposition to the incursions of non-specialists like Castro and his proponents.[42]

This resistance is largely in keeping with the tradition of western Arabic philology since its inception. Despite the well-demonstrated connection between the formation of philology and the emergence of modern Orientalism – comparative Indo-European philology emerged under the structure of a classicist model, which itself was structured in part on a model of biblical Hebrew studies[43] – there was at first a notable division between Indo-European philology, interested in establishing the ancient foundations of European languages, and "Semitic" philology, which consisted principally of the study of biblical Hebrew and initially gave little attention to the study of Arabic.[44] The two most important pioneers of academic study of Arabic in the nineteenth century, Antoine-Isaac Silvestre de Sacy (1758–1838) and Edward Lane (1801–76), did not share the ideals of German Romanticism, even though many of the key figures of Indo-European philology studied with Silvestre.[45] The upshot of this lack of commitment to neo-Humanist notions of *Bildung* within Arabic studies sets it firmly apart from other subdivisions of philology such as classical, Indo-European, German, and Romance. When Silvestre's student Ernest Renan (1823–92) began to enlarge the curriculum of his teacher, the paradoxes of Romanticism began to give way to a pronounced dualism between opposed methods of research.[46] The decidedly vocational and practical approach to Arabic by Silvestre de Sacy and the critical agnosticism of his pupil Renan had the effect of situating Arabic philology at a distance from the purely Humanist ideals that guided other branches of philology while at the same time infusing Arabism with a dominant empiricist vision of textual study as an exact science. In Spain, by contrast – although the patriarch of Arabic studies in the Peninsula, Francisco Codera, studied under one of Silvestre's Spanish students, Pascual de Gayangos (1809–97), and had pursued studies in natural science before turning to Arabic (Monroe, *Islam* 128–33) – Arabic studies were quickly linked to cultural and religious studies (one can think of the musical interests of Julián de Ribera or the religious comparativism of Miguel Asín Palacios)[47] and eventually to nationalist historiography rather than the Arabic language in itself.[48] The scientific tradition that peninsular Arabists have cultivated for the last few decades can be seen as a deliberate attempt to distance themselves from the focus of their past tradition and associate more closely with the ideals of Arabic studies beyond the Peninsula.

The issue, however, is not one confined to Arabic philology, but also reflects a more general trend in the evolution of peninsular academic culture in the twentieth century. In Spain, the attacks against German idealism as the "foreign secularism" of Krausism and its educational reforms through the Institución Libre de la Enseñanza (which directly impacted Castro early in his career) came not from positivists but from conservative Catholic nationalists such as philologist Marcelino Menéndez y Pelayo (1856–1912). Such attacks, to be sure, formed part of Spain's own larger ideological divide that, in political form, came to a decisive climax in the Spanish Civil War. Not surprisingly, peninsular academic "science" since the transition to democracy after the death of Franco in 1975 has aimed to distance itself from *both* of "the two Spains" of its past, progressive/idealist and conservative/nationalist. We can thus equally sympathize with the condemnation by historian Carlos Carrete Parrondo of "pseudoscientific propagandists" who "confuse historical reality with extreme sentimentalism [and for whom] interpretive calm is lacking and nineteenth-century impulse abounds" (146). The embracing of "science" as an alternative to both reformist idealism and religious nationalism has led in historiography to a decisive local focus and in Arabic studies to the final emergence of an explicitly scientific philology as an independent discipline, similar to that cultivated elsewhere in the West (Manzano Moreno 25).[49]

Contextualizing Convivencia

When we take these various factors into account, it is not surprising that Auerbach – who, like his contemporary Curtius, sought to rise above the horrors of nationalism through his philology – would find his closest affinity with Vico, a pre-nineteenth-century proto-Romantic model whose history was in no sense riven by this essentialist-fundamentalist divide or co-opted to the projects of racism or nationalism. It is not surprising either that the contemporary anti-nationalist vision articulated by Castro would be based on a theory of figural historiography very similar to that espoused by Auerbach. Nor is it surprising that both Auerbach and Castro wrote their unifying, anti-positivist poetic historiographies during the same period, both from an exile produced by the excesses of nationalism that had its roots in the projects of nineteenth-century philology (an exile that, for both men, ended in the United States). Finally, it is not surprising that Spanish Arabist philology – still within living memory of Francoism and its own conflicted identity as a part of western Orientalism – is now very much on guard against interpretive or poetic histories that use philology as a technique for *Bildung*, whether national or individual; and that consequently it hews very close to the righteous rigors of philology as a fundamentalist science of post-Romantic *Wissenschaft*.[50]

Given that Castro posed such ideas as a Romance philologist, it is also not surprising that Castro's ideas have had their deepest impact and have found their most steadfast defenders in North America, where the ideological preference for comparative criticism in the humanities is closely tied to the same Germanic tradition of Romantic hermeneutics from which Castro drew many of his fundamental insights.[51] At the very moment when Spanish Arabists, in attitude and in method, made a firm break with previous Arabic philology insofar as it was linked to nationalist or religious ideology, philological studies in North America have moved in the opposite direction. The influx into the North American academy in the second half of the twentieth century of French poststructuralism and postcolonialism and German hermeneutics and neo-Marxism, alongside the comparatist ideas brought by exiled European philologists such as Auerbach, Wellek, de Man, and Spitzer, has brought about a preponderate theoretical concern with exclusion and impurity. This dual focus has produced a general opposition to closed canons, a fascination with subalternity and the conceptually marginal as the manifestation of the postmodern law of supplementarity, and a penchant for hybridity and other perceived manifestations of intermixing of racial and national identities. It has also provided a commitment to the perspective of the individual reader – as a region of marginality vis-à-vis the public and the state – through meditation on the subjective reception, transformation, and subversion of historical tradition. Such tendencies have contributed to the cultural preference for interdisciplinary and interpretive criticism over a focus on single national or linguistic traditions or the punctilious work of material philology.[52]

The different circumstances under which the history of totalitarianism was weathered have, not surprisingly, provoked different methodological responses in the academy in general and in Iberian medieval studies in particular. In the same sense that convivencia has represented an attractive, albeit simplistic, model for some medievalists faced with what were perceived as dangerous tendencies towards uniform models of Eurocentric westernness, so it has come to represent for other philologists and historians a dangerous imprecision that runs the risk of resurrecting the ideologies of nationalism and propagandistic historiography. This divergence, however, can be traced to the same source: the epistemological rupture upon which the human sciences as such were founded. Ironically, both the embracing and the rejection of convivencia – and both hermeneutic and scientific philology more generally – can be understood as articulations of local cultural identity in response to the thorny by-products of the decay of Romanticism.

The opposed uses of the concept of convivencia by Menéndez Pidal and Castro are only reflections of the wider epistemological split in both philology and historiography between empirical linguistics and poetic metaphor. As such, convivencia, which has "consistently failed on empirical grounds" (Soifer 31), can serve as a sort of litmus test concerning how the various human sciences view their object of study in different cultural settings. In both historiography and literary criticism, it forces the decision to view the Middle Ages, in Brian Stock's words, as either "an objectified period or a subjective state of mind" (542). It seems dangerous because, in the wake of the linguistic turn, it is unstable, representing an active fault line in the rupture between *Bildung* and *Wissenschaft* as it manifested itself in a rupture between interpretive philology and scientific linguistics, between literary and social histories, or between figural readings of coexisting opposites and scientific models of competitive evolution. In this precarious position, convivencia is indeed dangerous precisely when it is forced from being a term of figural, nonlinear history or even of *mythopoesis* into being only an empirical term of analysis, a tool of scientific historiography or reified critical periodization.[53] This danger, moreover, cuts both ways. We risk not only the local danger of misunderstanding caused by the careless mixing of metaphors, but a broader danger, on a disciplinary level, of reducing our representation and understanding of manifold and contradictory historical circumstances to the rigid terms of one philological or historiographical model. Those critics who have taken pains to expose "the Spain of three cultures" as a modern historiographical myth have at the same time left little room for reflection on the critical question of how an absolute embrace of scientific method with the deliberate goal of detaching scholarship from ideology itself serves as a counter-myth of identity with equal potential for ideological distortion.[54]

In the face of this divide, no totalizing synthesis can or should claim precedence. Contrasting visions of the past must not be taken as mutually exclusive, but as coexisting alternative approaches to an inexhaustibly rich and ultimately unreachable past, approaches judged to be no more or less valuable (or "true") by virtue of being empirical or interpretive, descriptive or evaluative, literal or metaphorical. It is only through the coexistence of competing, opposed, but mutually correcting historiographical and philological models that critics can effectively protect each other from the occluding blinders we unwittingly wear by relying too heavily on any one master narrative of the past. As Fanjul himself reminds us, "scientists end up identifying, to a greater or lesser extent, with their object of study" (*Al-Andalus* xxix). If this is so, then any vision of history premised on the priority of only one epistemological model is always at risk of decaying into a consuming dualism in which scholarship ends up being overspecialized and hermetic at best, divisive and hegemonic at worst. Anything less than convivencia among scholars, itself viewed simultaneously as both balanced coexistence and progressive competition, will most certainly engender not only its own polemics and ideologies – as it already has – but also its own crusades, its own inquisitions, its own reconquests, and ultimately, the impoverishment resulting from expulsion, exile, and oblivion.

NOTES

* This research is part of a collaborative project entitled "The Intellectual and Material Legacies of Late Medieval Sephardic Judaism: An Interdisciplinary Approach," directed by Dr Esperanza Alfonso (CSIC). I wish to thank the European Research Council for its support of this project with a four-year Starting Grant and to thank Dr Alfonso for her ongoing coordination as Principal Investigator of the project. I also wish to thank Murray Baumgarten, David Wacks, Catherine Brown, and Edward Casey for their helpful criticism of previous drafts of this essay.

1 Examples supporting Ray's point abound: the term has been adopted for things as disparate as the titles for a music ensemble and performance festival in France, a bookstore in Brazil, a conservative Christian radio station in Mexico, an ecumenical church in Texas, and a civil liberties lobbying group in Catalonia, to cite just a few of the odd examples of its wide dissemination. Likewise, scholarship has seen a proliferation of collections of essays treating the subject of "contact" between Islam, Judaism, and Christianity, such as *Convivencia* (eds. Mann, Glick, and Dodds); *Chrétiens, musulmans et juifs dans l'Espagne médiévale* (ed. Barkaï); *Creencias y culturas* (eds. Meyuhas Ginio and Carrete Parrondo); and *Christians, Muslims, and Jews in Medieval and Early Modern Spain* (eds. Meyerson and English).

2 Professor Constable read her paper at the Fortieth International Congress on Medieval Studies (2005) in Kalamazoo, Michigan. I am grateful to her for sharing her paper with me and granting me permission to cite the text.

3 I here follow the illuminating observations of Monroe in "Américo Castro" and, above all, Martínez Montávez in "Lectura de Américo Castro," which are among the very few attempts to offer an analytical explanation of the extreme reactions to the work of Castro and his disciples.

4 The origins of the notion of *convivencia* have now been carefully laid out by Glick ("Convivencia" 1–2; *Islamic and Christian Spain*, on which, see n.7 below), and summarized by various scholars, including Novikoff (18–21), Akasoy, "Convivencia and Its Discontents" and Wolf, "Convivencia in Medieval Spain."

5 De la Puente, *Tomo primero de la convivencia de las dos monarquias catolicas* (1612). The Latin "conviventia," the shared food of a (monastic) community, can be found as early as the tenth century (Gysseling and Koch 294).

6 Unless otherwise noted, all translations in this essay are mine.

7 In his *Islamic and Christian Spain*, Glick has traced the early use of the term in Pidal's *Orígenes del español* (281, 293–6). It is possible to see this usage even earlier than Glick has claimed. Pidal employed the word in 1921 in *El Cid en la historia* (30–1) to mean "coexistence," a sense Julián Ribera had already used in 1912 to discuss medieval Iberia (*Discursos* 54).

8 Cerquiglini has observed a similar influence of theories of evolution, especially in the theories of Joseph Bédier, who "introduced neo-Lamarckian thought into philology" (69).

9 Sánchez-Albornoz mounted his attack in *España: un enigma histórico* in 1956. The first of Asensio's various attacks came with "Américo Castro historiador" in 1966, followed by numerous later additions. This conflict has now been amply reconstructed by various scholars including Glick, *Islamic and Christian Spain* 6–13 and Gómez-Martínez, *Américo Castro*, among others. The specific debt of both Castro and Sánchez-Albornoz to Peninsular Arabic studies has been traced by López García in "Enigmas de al-Andalus."

10 See Mark Cohen, "The Neo-Lachrymose Conception" and the response by Stillman, "Myth, Counter-Myth and Distortion."

11 Novikoff has presented a detailed overview of the criticism and defense of the notion of tolerance in medieval Iberia ("Between Tolerance and Intolerance"), and much of the important scholarship relevant to the debate can be found cited there. Catlos first proposed this notion in his article "Cristians, musulmans i jueus" and has since repeated the notion (*The Victors* 407). Menocal, who has avoided using the word almost completely in any of her books, commented in her "Visions of Al-Andalus" that "the conceptual error that has plagued all sides of the study of [medieval Iberia] is the assumption that these phenomena, reconquest and convivencia, are thoroughgoing and thus mutually exclusive" (14). Nirenberg presented his views most completely in *Communities of Violence*, in which he observes, "*convivencia* was predicated upon violence; it was not its peaceful antithesis. Violence drew its meaning from

coexistence, not in opposition to it" (245). The compatibility of these views has gone little remarked by critics.

12 It is easy to write off certain popular critics of convivencia as mere conservative reactionaries or uninformed editorialists, such as the journalist Cesar Vidal, whose many publications include the 2004 polemical history, *España frente al Islam*, in which he proposes to meet "the challenges that Islam presents for free, peaceful, and democratic *convivencia* in Spain" with stricter immigration quotas. Another example from among the fourth estate, though less reactionary, is the *New York Times* critic Edward Rothstein, "Was the Islam of Old Spain Truly Tolerant?" (2 September 2003). The popular press has served as a forum for numerous salvos from academics as well; see, for example, Joseph Pérez, "Chrétiens, Juifs et Musulmans."

13 In "Arabistas en España" Marín also observes, "in the origins of academic Arabism there is a firm desire to extract from the history of Al-Andalus the Romanticism and exoticism with which it has been so much viewed both inside and outside Spain. This exoticism has been renewed and transformed to take on some peculiar forms today, which are no less false for being new (such as the myth of the Spain of the three cultures)" (389).

14 In the face of such pronouncements, Ridao (e.g., in his *El País* article, "El oscurantismo reverenciado") has argued that the debate over "multiculturalism" depends on a clarification of what is actually being meant by the word "culture." See also Juan Goytisolo's similar concurring remarks in "Convivencia con el Islam."

15 In a similar vein, Durán Velasco observes, "If there had not been a *Reconquista* and al-Andalus had survived until today, the country would have been just as monocultural and monoreligious as it was after the decrees of expulsions of the moriscos by Felipe III. Three cultures? No way. [De tres culturas nada]" (168).

16 Rodríguez Magda complains that "the supposedly pacific convivencia of three cultures and religions postulated by Castro has become an uncritical cliché repeated ad nauseam" (*Inexistente* 38) and condemns "all of those who, far from rigor, use pseudo-historical rhetoric as a projectile weapon" (24). Madariaga, who shares her complaints, notes with approval that Spanish Arabists have recently "reconsidered with a critical spirit some of the mythical aspects of the society of al-Andalus and analysed this historical past with scientific rigor, free of ideological passions and interferences" ("En torno" 82–3).

17 Auerbach wrote pieces explicitly devoted to Vico on no fewer than thirteen occasions (Wellek, "Auerbach and Vico" 85–6n1). He noted his debt to Vico in his introduction to *Literary Language*, stating that Vico's conception of philology "in a very specific way … has complemented and molded, in my thinking and in my work, the ideas deriving from German historicism" (7). On this connection, see also Bahti, "Vico, Auerbach."

18 Araya, *El pensamiento*, divides Castro's work into two periods before and after 1938, noting the traditional philological cast of his first period of work (27–8). Portolés

discusses in some detail Castro's early "positivist" phase as a scientific philologist beginning at the Centro de Estudios Históricos in Madrid under the influence of Menéndez Pidal, when he translated the *Einführung* of the Neogrammarian philologist Meyer-Lübke (*Medio siglo* 97–103). For a general overview of the conflict between Romance philology and linguistic studies, see Malkiel, "Filología española."

19 While Vico actually only expresses this phrase as such in an early work, *De antiquissima Italorum sapientia* (*On the Most Ancient Wisdom of the Italians*), it is one of the guiding principles of his later versions of the *New Science*. On Vico's concepts of *verum* and *factum*, see Berlin, "The Philosophical Ideas" 34–8 and "Vico's Theory of Knowledge," both in *Three Critics*; "Vico's Concept of Knowledge" in *Against the Current*; and Morrison, "Vico's Principle."

20 Significantly, Berlin locates Vico at the heart of what he has named the Counter Enlightenment, the beginning of an anti-rationalist and anti-empirical thread that, he argues, culminated in the emergence of various lines of anti-empirical thinking cumulatively referred to as "Romanticism" ("Vico and Herder," in *Three Critics* 8–12). In this sense, we can appreciate Croce's assertion that Vico "was neither more nor less than the nineteenth century in embryo" (*La filosofia* 257).

21 See Uhlig in "Auerbach's 'Hidden'(?) Theory" 42–34 and 257n33.

22 This summary of the criticism of Auerbach is drawn largely from Nichols, "Philology in Auerbach's Drama." In espousing this view, Engels was only repeating a view put forth nearly a century earlier when linguist August Schleicher proposed enforcing a firm division between the aesthetic bias of philology and the scientific rigor of the newly emerging science of linguistics. As he stated, "the method of linguistics is totally different from those of all the historical sciences, and essentially joins ranks with the methods of the other natural sciences" (from *Die Sprachen Europas* [1850], cited in Amsterdamska 45). On the question of Schleicher's blending of biological and Hegelian ideas, see Arbuckle, "Schleicher" and Amsterdamska's critique in *Schools* 44–50 and 277n.31.

23 As Anthony Grafton remarks, "in the late eighteenth century … scholars throughout Europe were desperately trying to drive two very different horses in a single yoke: the historical method that tried to situate every text in a unique context and the comparative method that tried to find in every text a normal stage in the uniform development of all societies and cultures" ("'Man muß'" 423).

24 On the history of philology, see Cerquiglini, *In Praise of the Variant* and Helsloot, *Een korte geschiedenis van de rede*; Gumbrecht, "'Un Souffle d'Allemagne'"; Amsterdamska, *Schools*. For consideration of the issue in a specifically Spanish context, see Gerli, "Inventing the Spanish Middle Ages"; Hess, "'Castilian Hegemony'"; and Brown, "The Relics."

25 Endorsing the former, Old French philologist Mary Speer states that a philologist's work is "empirical, properly focused on the concrete realities of one or more manuscript traditions and therefore skeptical – in an informed way – to theories of any

kind … their primary allegiance is to the text" (cited in Nichols, "Philology and its Discontents" 115). In essentialist philology, on the other hand, which focuses on the "manuscript matrix" (Nichols's term) rather than just the manuscript, the concern is with the hermeneutics of signifiers, not only their materiality. Brian Stock summarizes the conflict thus: "The good editor still wishes in part to emulate the Enlightenment goal that history, in revealing the perversities of the past, will free him from them. But he is also tainted by historicism. His re-creation of context, if only in the apparatus, may be interpreted as a minor tributary of relativism, and his search for origins and analogies implies a characteristically Romantic conception of the organic unity of the age" (542). It is not insignificant that this conflict within Medieval Studies is represented *in nuce* in one of its most venerable journals, *Speculum*, whose title can be deconstructed alternately as both a mirror dispassionately reflecting its historical object (*Wissenschaft*) and as a *speculum puerorum* serving as a subjective interlocutor for teaching wisdom and interpretive judgment (*Bildung*).

26 For example, he removes all mention of Fichte and greatly reduces discussion of Dilthey in the 1962 edition. Compare e.g. 40–68 in the 1954 edition with 80–111 in the 1962 text.

27 The text from 1959 was entitled *Origen, ser y existir de los españoles*, which was republished in expanded form as *Los españoles: Cómo llegaron a serlo* in 1965.

28 In the words of Michel de Certeau, "by distinguishing between two discourses – the one scientific, the other fictive – according to its own criteria, historiography credits itself with having a special relationship to the 'real' … Debates about the reliability of literature as opposed to history illustrate this division" (201). On the question of the historiography of historiography and its relationship to philology in the late eighteenth and early nineteenth centuries, see Muhlack, "Historie und Philologie"; Gildenhard, "Philologia Perennis?"; and Gadamer, *Truth and Method* 174–97. For a critique of Gadamer's theory, see Gjesdal, "Hermeneutics and Philology."

29 It is no coincidence that Michelet was primarily responsible for recuperating Vico from oblivion, translating the *New Science* in 1827 and even stating in his *History of France*, "Vico was my only master" (cited in Gossman, *Between History and Literature* 162–70).

30 "God dwells and lives and can be known in all of history … the connectedness of history in the large … stands there like a holy hieroglyph… . May we, for our part, decipher this holy hieroglyph!" (*The Secret* 241–2).

31 In Spain, the same universalizing and still-empirical tendency is embodied by Rafael Altamira (1866–1951), who infused Peninsular historiography and pedagogy with a commitment to a holistic vision of civilization and sought to apply that vision in the service of national reform. For a discussion of Altamira, see Boyd, *Historia Patria* 135–46, and the bibliography cited there.

32 In his unpublished text *We Philologists*, Nietzsche observes that "Experience [*Erlebnis*] is certainly an essential prerequisite for a philologist" (113). Nietzsche's use of

the word "Erlebnis" instantly evokes the contemporary thought of Dilthey on the essential role of *Erlebnis* within interpretation in the human sciences. On the history of the word "Erlebnis" in hermeneutics, see Gadamer, *Truth and Method* 60–70. Not only was this term of vital importance for Castro and his concept of "vividura" (on Castro and Dilthey, see Gómez-Martínez, *Américo Castro* 120–5); Leo Spitzer, in his lecture on "Linguistics and Literary History," a lecture he was invited to give by Castro at Princeton, calls for all literary reading to be *inductive* rather than *deductive*, arguing "Methode ist Erlebnis" ("Method Is Experience"; 1). On the polemic that developed between Castro and Spitzer, see Gómez-Martínez 74–7.

33 Beiser, *The Romantic Imperative*, explores this "marriage of opposites" in his chapters "The Paradox of Romantic Metaphysics" and "Kant and the *Naturphilosophen*" 131–70. For an exploration of the concept of alterity in early Romanticism, see Gossman, *Between History and Literature* 259 and 283; and Gumbrecht, "'Un Souffle d'Allemagne'" 4–10. Gadamer urges a privileging of *Erfahrung*, meaning "experience" in a wider, more transcendent sense, over Dilthey's *Erlebnis*, which he sees as contaminated by the concepts of scientific method. See *Truth and Method* 346–62.

34 On the question of *Bildung* and *Wissenschaft*, see the foundational documents anthologized by Ernst Anrich; the discussion by Beiser, *The Romantic Imperative* 88–105; Hofstetter, *The Romantic Idea*, especially 104–7; Schelsky, *Einsamkeit* 63–9; Ringer, *The Decline* 83–90 and 102–13. On the growth of science and specialization, see Turner, "The Growth of Professorial Research"; for a general consideration of the history of Prussian universities, in addition to Hofstetter's brief history, see T. Ziolkowski, *German Romanticism* 218–305.

35 Grafton has shown that Wolf's philological *Altertumswissenschaft* was centered on a fundamentally historical method (417), and this vision had a deep methodological impact on Karl Lachmann, the father of modern text editing (Lachmann in fact succeeded Wolf at Berlin in 1825 after Wolf's death the previous year). Lachmann's comment that "the establishment of a text according to tradition [nach Überlieferung] is a strictly historical undertaking" (*Kleinere Schriften* 2:252) reflects this context. See also Marchand, *Down from Olympus* 16–24.

36 On Böckh's comprehensive notion of philology as the study of culture that combined history, classical philology, and philosophy in a striving toward self-realization through *Bildung*, see Gossman, *Between History and Literature* 277–8 and Amsterdamska, *Schools* 67. It was, not coincidentally, what Stock calls "broad philological training in the tradition of Boeckh" that led Auerbach to develop "a distinctive aesthetic historicism" (531).

37 Gossmann observes, "where the neohumanists saw [classical philology] as a total inner education or formation of the individual ("*Bildung*"), the [neogrammarian] philologists saw it as an exercise in critical method and an accumulation of reliable information ("*Wissenschaft*")" (*Basel* 161). On this divide, see also Reill, "Philology" 28.

38 Jarausch and Ringer, among many others, have both charted the decay of Romantic ideals of nation and identity within the late nineteenth-century rise of nationalism and militarism in Prussia. Recently, the essays contained in *Out of Arcadia* (edited by Gildenhard and Ruehl) have explored connections between that decay and classical philology.

39 Burckhardt, who was fiercely opposed to dry, punctilious scholarship and was instead committed to an early Romantic concept of *Bildung* that he believed had been lost, deliberately stated, in the introduction to his *Cultural History of Greece*, "We are 'unscholarly' [unwissenschaftlich] and have no method; at least we do not follow that of others." He even states that he, like his reader, is a *Nichtphilologe*, a non-philologist, who is *jeder humanistisch Gebildete*, ["any Humanistically educated layperson" (both quoted in Gossman, *Basel* 308)]. It is in these terms that we can understand Burckhardt's words to Nietzsche in a letter from 1882 – nearly the same words that Auerbach spoke of himself seventy years after – stating, "Fundamentally, of course, you are always teaching history" (quoted in White, *Metahistory* 331–2). On Nietzsche's relationship to philology, see Whitman, "Nietzsche." On his relation to historiography, see Brobjer, "Nietzsche's View."

40 Similarly, Heidegger remarked in 1929 in "What Is Metaphysics?": "Only if science exists on the basis of metaphysics can it advance further in its essential task, which is not to amass and classify bits of knowledge but to disclose in ever-renewed fashion the entire region of truth in nature and history" (*Basic Writings* 111). It is in this vein that Gadamer, his prodigal student, could insist thirty years after that "the hermeneutic phenomenon … is not concerned primarily with amassing verified knowledge, such as would satisfy the methodological ideal of science – yet it too is concerned with knowledge and with truth … [T]he human sciences are connected to modes of experience that lie outside science: with the experiences of philosophy, of art, and of history itself. These are all modes of experience in which a truth is communicated that cannot be verified by the methodological means proper to science" (xxi–xxii).

41 On the development of modern linguistics see Amsterdamska, *Schools*; Lehmann, "Philology to Linguistics"; and Henkel, *The Language of Criticism*, who also provides a critique of perceived misapplications of linguistic ideas by literary theorists. Against the traditional view that Saussure was deeply influenced by German Romantic philosophy and linguistic thought, see Aarsleff, *From Locke to Saussure*. For a penetrating criticism of Aarsleff, see Hacking, "Locke, Leibniz, Language." For an overview of the implications of the "linguistic turn" in historiography, see Toews, "Intellectual History"; Clark, *History, Theory, Text*; and Iggers, *Historiography*.

42 This resistance has alternated between cold silence and outright attack. On the silence over Castro's work in Spain, see Subirats, "Américo Castro Secuestrado" and his "Nota Preliminar" in *Américo Castro y la revisión de la memoria (El Islam en España)*; Juan

Goytisolo, "Américo Castro en la España actual" in the same collection; and Martínez Montávez, "Lectura de Américo Castro" 21–5. One example of resistance from outside Spain is the Arabist-only stance of Allen Jones of Cambridge in regard to the study of Arabic *muwashshahas* and their final *kharjas* (Jones, "Sunbeams" and "Eppur si Muove"). Monroe, "Pedir peras" offers one of various ripostes to Jones. For a recent reconsideration of the debate, see Mallette, "Misunderstood."

43 See Grafton, "'Man muß'" 419–23, for a discussion of Wolf's debt to Eichhorn's *Einleitung*.

44 August Schlözer proposed the term "semite" in a racial sense to describe descendants of Shem in the Bible ("Von den Chaldäern" 161). Renan, in his *Histoire générale et système comparé des langues sémitiques* (finished in 1847 and published in 1855), makes specific reference to this and rejects the notion of a racial grouping. He is, in a sense, the first to develop the notion in a linguistic context, setting out (as he states) to do for "semitic" languages what Bopp did for Indo-European. See Said, *Orientalism* 139–41.

45 Amsterdamska observes that the differences between Silvestre de Sacy and Bopp correspond to a difference between a view of philology conceived as *Bildung* in Germany and professional training in France (71). For a recent exploration of the intersection of early Orientalism and the discourse of historiography, see Freitag, "The Critique" and Ganim, *Medievalism*.

46 When Renan made statements in his work *The Future of Science* such as "The founders of the modern mind are philologists" and "Philology is the exact science of things of the mind [des choses de l'esprit]," his language shows traces of a Romantic understanding of education; but his belief in philology as a "lay science" ("science laïque") stands in marked contrast to the pantheistic, undeniably spiritual outlook of *Frühromantik* in Germany. On what Gossman calls Renan's "sclerotic dualism" (Gossman, *Between History and Literature* 193–4), see Said, *Orientalism* 130–48; and his essay "Islam, Philology, and French Culture" in *The World* 268–89.

47 Arabist García Gómez calls Francisco Codera the "root" of Spanish Arabism, from which grew the "trunk" in his student Julián Ribera, and the "delicate flower" in their disciple, Miguel Asín Palacios ("Primer centenario" 208). "As may be expected from the character of his work," Monroe concludes, "Asín's ideas have found less than sympathy among Islamic Scholars" (*Islam* 194).

48 As Manzano Moreno observes, this is evident in the general dearth of any complete grammar or dictionary of Arabic in Spanish before the last quarter of the twentieth century, and the fact that the primary tools for studying the Arabic of Al-Andalus — those of Dozy and Levi-Provençal — were until then by non-Spaniards (24–5). For the abundant historiography of Peninsular Arabism, see the bibliography provided by Penelas, "Hispano-Arabic Studies" 238–9; Fück, *Die arabischen Studien* 265–9; Monroe, *Islam*; Manzanares de Cirre, *Arabistas españoles*; López García, "Arabismo y

orientalismo" and "30 años de arabismo"; Martínez Montávez, "Sobre el aún 'desconocido' arabismo"; Míkel de Epalza, "Les études arabes"; Manula Marín, "Arabistas
en España"; Ridao, "L'arabisme"; and Viguera's introduction to the new edition of
Francisco Codera's *Decadencia y desaparición de los almorávides en España.*

49 Ironically, the epicenter of scientific research is the Consejo Superior de Investigaciones Científicas, the inheritor of the educational reforms of Krausism in the Junta
de Ampliación de Estudios e Investigaciones Científicas – which was itself a creation
of the Krausist Institución Libre de la Enseñanza and the final fruit of the seeds
sown by Castro's professor, Giner de los Ríos. On the commitment to "science" in
Peninsular Arabism, see Martínez Montávez, "Lectura de Américo Castro" 26–30.
For a penetrating consideration of science within the academic debate over "las dos
Españas" in historiography, see the epilogue in *Historia de la historiografía española* by
José Andrés-Gallego, "El problema" 297–338. For a discussion of the new "local-
ism" of Peninsular historiography, see Marín Gelabert, *Los historiadores españoles,*
11–33. For an overview of Spanish medievalist historiography, see Mitre Fernández,
"La historiografía."

50 Marín observes that in Spain, "Arabists had to fight, from the first moment, to construct for themselves an academic [científica] reputation, as much in Spain as outside
it" ("Arabistas en España" 390). On the conservative ideological shift in Arabism
brought on by the civil war, see Monroe, "Américo Castro" 355.

51 The unique character of Spanish Romanticism is due in part to the conservative
resistance against foreign Romantic ideas, the eventual waning of Krausist Idealism and educational reform, and the trauma of the Spanish Civil War, among other
things (see Shaw, "The Anti-Romantic Reaction"). The rise of a manifestly "scientific" philological tradition in Spain can be seen as a simultaneous rejection of both
Krausist idealism and its heirs and the conservative religious nationalism that attacked
and dismantled it. On Krausism and the Institución, see De Puelles Benítez, *Educación
e ideología* 166–88 and 283–96. For the conservative criticism of the Institución, see
Díaz, "La Institución Libre." On Castro's link to Romanticism and the Institución,
see Marichal, "Américo Castro."

52 Two clear examples among many are the article by Amer, "Integrating Multiculturalism"; and Nichols's endorsement of what he calls the "manuscript matrix" ("Introduction" 9).

53 Glick's proposal to attribute the debate over *convivencia* to an "inadequate theoretical
grasp of the relationship between social relations and cultural interchange, between
social distance and cultural distance" ("Convivencia" 7) intimates the underlying
divide in methodology, but does not provide an acceptable explanation because it
attributes the methodological debate over "history" and "criticism" to an inherent
division in the "reality" of medieval Iberia between society and culture, rather than
understanding this division itself to be a product of modern scholarly methodologies.

54 As Umberto Eco pointedly observes, "Frequently, to be really 'scientific' means not pretending to be more 'scientific' than the situation allows. In the human sciences one often finds an 'ideological fallacy' common to many scientific approaches, which consists in believing that one's own approach is not ideological because it succeeds in being 'objective' and 'neutral.' For my own part, I share the same skeptical opinion that all inquiry is 'motivated.' Theoretical research is a form of social practice" (29).

10 "In One of My Body's Gardens": Hearts in Transformation in Late Medieval Iberian Passion Devotions[1]

CYNTHIA ROBINSON

In *Shards of Love: Exile and the Origins of the Lyric* (73–90), María Rosa Menocal explores an often-cited lyric by the late twelfth-century Andalusi poet, Muhyi al-Din Ibn 'Arabi, the most influential Sufi mystic produced by Iberian Islam. The lines on which she focuses her attention will be familiar to many readers: "My heart can take on any form; a meadow for gazelles, a cloister for monks …" The poet goes on to transform his heart into sacred ground for idols, a "Ka'ba for the circling pilgrim, the tables of a Torah, the scrolls of a Qur'an." Placing Ibn 'Arabi's lyric beside Ramon Llull's *Llibre de contemplació en Deu*, Menocal offers close readings of both, turning away from an overly simplistic comparatist reading of textual content (syncretism; religious tolerance; an over-idealized *convivencia* imagined as idyllic) and towards the apparent conundrum posed by Ibn 'Arabi's and Llull's choice of "secular" or "profane" love lyrics as an appropriate vehicle for the exaltation and performance of transformative union with the Divine Beloved.

In the pages that follow I will argue that, just as they spoke to Ibn 'Arabi and Ramon Llull, for many Iberian Christians throughout the fifteenth century the topoi of hearts, lovers and the beloved in transformation provided a solution to one of the most complex problems of late medieval devotions: how to imagine and how to confront – despite the worshipper's reluctance to do so[2] – the suffering human body of Christ Crucified. Though for most of Christian Europe throughout the later Middle Ages the heart was a locus of visualization designed to lead to somatic union with the suffering Saviour (Bennett; Bestul; Haug; Johannes de Caulibus), in Iberia the heart serves other purposes and is conceived of in a different manner: it is the proper place for the veneration of an image of Christ Crucified which is almost never exteriorized in the form of graphic visual production intended for individual or private devotions.

Indeed, until the final decades of the fifteenth century, religious art in Christian Castile – in sharp contrast to visual culture elsewhere in Europe – is curiously devoid of any reference to the more humiliating aspects of Christ's Passion. The rest of Christian Europe is deeply engaged in devotions to Christ's humanity and death during the thirteenth and fourteenth centuries, a current which comes to full fruition in the fifteenth (for bibliography see Robinson, "Preaching to the Converted"). But in Castile, Christ's body and Passion are sublimated into a highly abstract and symbolic discourse that concentrates on theophany, divinity and revelation. And though visual culture sees considerable stylistic transformations (Silva Maroto; Pereda, *Las imágenes de la discordia*; Robinson, "Preaching to the Converted"), the thematic concerns of Castilian devotions continue to hold sway through the fifteenth century. Only as that century draws to a close, in response to ecclesiastical and royal pressures for orthodoxy and the purge of nonbelievers from Iberian society, does the suffering body of Christ – often accompanied by heavily indulgenced prayers – become increasingly present in Castilian liturgy, devotions and (from the 1480s forward) religious imagery.

This strikingly different visual panorama is also reflected in the textual topography of Castile's devotional landscape. Even at moments when Castilian Christians had no choice but to engage the Passion, preferences were not for the classic texts of Passion devotions which by the late fourteenth century had spread to all corners of Europe (Bestul; Robinson, "Preaching to the Converted"). Rather, Castilian worshippers chose excerpts from a "homegrown" version of Christ's life, the *Vida de Jesucrist*, a multi-volume work written around the turn of the fifteenth century by Catalan Franciscan Françesc Eiximenis and translated into Castilian as the *Vida de Cristo* by Gonzalo de Ocaña, a Jeronymite Friar, in collaboration with a Cistercian prior, in the 1430s (Robinson, "Preaching to the Converted"). Volumes VIII–X were frequently transmitted separately as a treatise on Christ's Infancy and Passion (e.g., BNE Ms. 14924, 18772 from the library of the Marqués de Santillana); and extensive passages concerning Christ's infancy, public works and Passion are interpolated into Castilian translations of the *Flos Sanctorum* (BNE Mss. 780 and 12688). In terms of "imported" texts, among the most popular were not the widely disseminated *Meditationes Vitae Christi* (hereafter *MVC*; Johannes de Caulibus, introduction; Frank), but rather less narrative, more evocative texts, such as the *Stimulus Amoris*. This work was authored during the late thirteenth or early fourteenth century by Jacopus Mediolanensis – though medieval inventories frequently attribute it to St Bonaventure – and translated into Castilian by the mid-fifteenth century as the *Estímulo del Amor de Jesucristo*. It was known by several titles to a Latin-literate readership, including *Incendium amoris* and *De triplici via*; at least one manuscript in the Biblioteca Nacional de España (hereafter, BNE) identifies it as *Transformatio in Christum*. And its interest and importance will become clear in the pages that follow.[3] Also important was the *De instructione vel doctrina cordis*, most often attributed to either Hugh of St Cher or Gérard of Liège, dating to the thirteenth century, and translated into Castilian probably during the middle decades of the fifteenth century as the *Enseñamiento del corazón* (e.g., BNE Ms. 9209).

Although the *Doctrina Cordis*, the *Stimulus Amoris* and Eiximenis's *Vida de Jesucrist* address the Passion, unlike their European counterparts none of these texts dwells on wounds, blood, lacerations or humiliations. Indeed, although the *Vida de Jesucrist* is in large part narrative, its primary intent was to convince and convert infidels rather than to bring its readers closer to mystical union with Christ through a detailed evocation of his humanity (Robinson, "Preaching to the Converted"). Moreover, in the context of specific meditations on Christ Crucified Eiximenis presents Christ's body as a highly unstable entity, one that refuses to be defined or described and that slips beneath a chain of metaphorical evocations rather than exhibit its shameful weaknesses to the eyes of those who would probably rather not consider them too closely anyway.

In effect, Eiximenis converts Christ's body into an empty space, frequently conceived as architectural. The body's presence is an absence whose outer configurations are in continual transformation, and within which transformations are likewise wrought. This conception of Christ's body is linked to a general process of interiorization (as opposed to the exteriorization through narrative ordering and visualization that typifies other European Passion texts) which, together with the interest in the heart as the locus of transformation and union with the divine, is evident in Castilian devotional culture during the first three-quarters of the fifteenth century and beyond.

In order to probe further the differences between the Iberian approach to meditation on the theme of the crucified Christ and that prevalent in the rest of Christian Europe, the first section of this essay will be devoted to comparison of passages from Eiximenis's meditations to a roughly contemporary series of prayers frequently attributed to St Bridget of Sweden (though this attribution is now disputed; Bartlett and Bestul 85–117). Following this, I will propose that the particularities of Eiximenis's meditations are due at least in part to a cultural climate in which members of the three confessional communities lived side by side, but conversions and reversions were frequent and beliefs and confessional expression were profoundly affected by constant contact with other religious communities.

In the third and final section, I will consider the idea that, in the meditations of many Castilians and for most of the fifteenth century, the Virgin's Passion to a great extent replaced her Son's. Although several recent studies have explored Iberian manifestations of the cult of the Virgin throughout the later Middle Ages, highlighting in particular her relationship to themes of conquest and conversion (Pereda, *Las imágenes de la discordia*; Remensnyder), the only extensive examination to date of Passion texts which concede to her a starring role has been undertaken by Jessica Boon. The texts examined by Boon date largely to the Golden Age; the evidence I will present demonstrates the existence of this devotional trend in Castile throughout the final centuries of the Middle Ages. Castile does first come to the Passion through Christ's mother. However, she – rather than provide a conduit for the abject emotions engendered by the awful spectacle of Christ's torture, humiliation and death (as is often the case) – offers to Castilian devotees not only the chance to suffer and grieve (thus to experience the Passion with *her* rather than with *him*) but also to transcend the baseness of the physical violence done to her Son and to reach the heights of mystical ecstasy. Her heart – examined by the fire of the Passion and emerging unscathed – rather than His body becomes the preferred locus of devotion; and the image of Christ Crucified is placed securely under lock and key, deep within its recesses.

St Bridget of Sweden, one of the most widely venerated of late medieval secular holy women, was a pious widow, a pilgrim to Santiago de Compostela, Jerusalem and Rome, and the receiver of a number of divine *Revelations* (Birgitta of Sweden; Morris et al.). Her writings, along with the monastic order she founded, influenced devotional life and practice throughout much of Christian Europe during the fifteenth century. Among the texts frequently attributed to her are fifteen prayers directed to Jesus and focused on the bitter sorrows, sufferings and humiliations of his Passion, in which the devotee seeks to share. All begin with some variation of "O, Ihesu"; hence the name by which they were popularly known, the "Fifteen Oe's":

> O Ihesu abyssus profundissime misericordia rogo te propter profunditatem vulnerum tuorum que transierunt carnem tuam medullam ossium ac visceru[m] tuorum ut me submersu[m] in peccatis emergas et abscondas in foraminibus vulnerum tuorum a facie ire tue donec pertranseat furor tuus domine. Amen. (Bodleian Library, Ms. e Mus. 226 10v)

> [O Jesus, deepest abyss of mercy, I beg you – because of the depth of your wounds, which passed through your flesh, the marrow of your bones and your organs – to extract me, submerged in sins, and hide me in the openings of your wounds from the face of your anger until your fury has passed, Lord. Amen.]

St Bridget's Christ has organs, bones and marrow, which have been brutally penetrated by the wounds which forge a path for her (and for those who pray her prayers) to the interior of that body. The "Oe's" (whether or not they are St Bridget's) constitute one of the most widely circulated sequences of prayers on the Passion of the later Middle Ages, particularly in Northern Europe, though they are not attested in Castile. Fray Alfonso Pecha – St Bridget's confessor and her invaluable assistant in getting her *Revelations* recorded, vetted for heretical content and finally distributed – was a native of Guadalajara and brother of the founder of the Jeronymite order, Pedro Fernández Pecha. It is therefore noteworthy that only one copy of excerpts from those *Revelations* exists in the BNE (Ms. 4444); and it comes not from a Castilian but an Aragonese convent. If Castilians had wanted Bridget's prayers, they could very easily have obtained them; the conclusion must be that they did not.

However, Eiximenis's meditations occur frequently in Castilian devotional compendia, and though originally composed in Catalan they constitute the first generation of Castilian Passion devotions. They studiously avoid direct confrontation with the violated body of Christ through narrative, description or suggestions of visualization, and are never transmitted together with images. They appear in manuscripts designed to serve purposes ranging from sermon preaching to individualized or personal reading and meditation (Robinson, "Preaching to the Converted"). The quotations used in the present essay are taken from a manual (BNE Ms. 8744) which dates to the 1450s and is designed to aid its users in preaching and pastoral care. Eiximenis's meditations, entitled "How the Christian should think about Christ Crucified" ["Como deve el cristiano penssar en Cristo Cruçificado"], appear twice. The first iteration is fashioned into a sermon or treatise on the Holy Sacraments (ff. 282r–323v), excerpted and interspersed with the anonymous compiler/author's own comments; the second is cited completely under the proper title (ff. 323v–350v). On neither occasion, however, are the meditations attributed to Eiximenis. I have chosen to cite them from the Sermon on the Sacraments in BNE Ms. 8744 because of the implications of their incorporation into a manual of vernacular compilation designed for maximum dissemination in oral form.

In sharp contrast to more widely distributed treatises on the most sacred of the Seven Holy Sacraments, which encourage those in attendance to envision specific moments from Christ's Passion as the Mass is said (see, e.g., William Durandus, though there are many others [Pozo Coll, "La devoción" and "Un gesto litúrgico"; Durandus]), these meditations on the mysteries contained in the sacrament are divided into two unequal parts. The first, and shorter, is devoted to Christ's Passion; the second, much longer part (where extensive quotations from Eiximenis's passion meditations are found) is a treatment of the ecstasy and union offered to those who reverently consider and then take part in the sacrament. The treatise on the sacrament opens by stating its dual purpose:

> Venit hermanos et vet las obras maravillosas de dios. Et singularmente eneste muy
> exçelente sacramento del preçioso cuerpo et muy sanctissima sangre de nro señor ihu
> xpo. Los misterios del qual son tan altos y maravillosos que non es lengua humanal

nin angelical que perfectamente los pueda esplicar nin declarar … Por lo qual digo que en este sancto sacramento primeramente se contiene misterio de profundo dolor et compassion. Lo segundo aquí es contenido misterio de infinito amor, suavidat et dulzor … (BNE Ms. 8744, ff. 282r–v)

[Come, brothers, and see the marvelous works of God. And especially in this most excellent sacrament of the precious body and the most holy blood of our Lord Jesus Christ. The mysteries of which are so high and marvelous that no tongue, whether human or angelic, can perfectly explain or declare them. For which I say that in this holy sacrament is contained first a mystery of profound pain and compassion. Second, here is contained a mystery of infinite love, gentleness and sweetness …]

The specific enumeration of Christ's pains and sufferings during the Passion is limited to a litany-like evocation of about ten lines of text; the section closes a few folios later with a rather terse "Et hoc sufficit quantum ad primum" (f. 288r). Devotees are never instructed to envision the particulars of Christ's Passion, but rather to

aver en si diligente memoria et conpassion dolorosa de aqueste piadoso señor por nos muerto et passionado. (BNE Ms. 8744, ff. 282v–283r)

[have within themselves the memory and painful compassion of this pious Lord, tormented and killed by us.]

Rather than the specific pains and sufferings endured by Christ during the passion, in this section Eiximenis – along with his Castilian translators and transmitters – prefers that his readers first consider who is this man from whose sufferings they, who also caused them, have so richly benefited. Rather than a human body that bleeds and suffers, Eiximenis presents a Saviour whose divinity is manifested in his infinite spatial dimensions, incomprehensible to the human mind:[4]

Pues que podre yo dezir de aquel que es mas alto que el çielo y mas profundo que el abismo al qual el çielo y la tierra nin todas las cosas enellos contenidos non pueden comprender … E final mente padesçio de muy viles el muy exçelente et muy santo dios el que es infinita sapiençia de muy crueles *el que es abismo de piedat* et de muy vil corrupçion el que es perdurable resplandor … Lo segundo digo que este sancto ssacramento contiene en si misterio et *abismo de infinito amor, suavidat et dulzor* … (My emphasis; ff. 285v–288r)

[What then can I say about Him who is higher than the sky and deeper than the abyss, who cannot be comprehended by the sky or by the earth or by all the things contained in them … And finally, he – most excellent and most holy God – suffered at the hands of the vilest of people, he who is infinite wisdom (subject to) their cruelty, *he who is the abyss of mercy*, (victim of) the vilest of corruptions, he who is everlasting brightness … And, second, I say [to you] that this holy sacrament contains in itself a mystery and *abyss of infinite love, gentleness and sweetness* …]

Eiximenis, like the author of the "Oe's," addresses Christ as the "abyss of mercy"; but unlike the Swedish saint (or the anonymous English male monastic), he also avoids all direct contact with his Saviour's lacerated body. Instead, throughout these passages, Christ's body is continually in transformation, at once present in the devotee's consciousness and impossible to localize or pin down. And these traits are further heightened as Eiximenis (and his Castilian readers) pass from the Passion to the Sacrament's second mystery, that of "the abyss of love, gentleness and sweetness":

Et la profundidad deste misterio digo ser tan grande en este ssacramento que asi como la lengua de nigund ome mortal non lo puede fablar nin asi mesmo *coraçon penssar* nin entendimiento comprender. (My emphasis; ff. 288 r–v)

[And the depth of this mystery, I say to you, is so great in this sacrament that, just as no tongue of mortal man may tell of it, so there is no *heart that may conceive of it*, nor understanding that may know it.]

Again, the "abyss" is released from all direct relationship to Christ's human body; rather than scaled to elicit human empathy and somatic identification, its dimensions are unfathomable both to human understanding and to human hearts, although it is in the heart that all the memory and joy of the Sacrament of which humans are capable take place. The same body is then transformed into a cauldron of divine love in which Christ's lovers are transformed and from which they emerge burning:

Ca los sanctos martires … primeramente fervieron enla ssoberana caldera del amor divinal, la qual caldera es preçioso cuerpo del nro salvador. Et de aqui salieron asi fervientes … (f. 291v)

[For the saintly martyrs … first boiled in the noblest cauldron of divine love, which cauldron is the precious body of our Saviour. And from it, they came out burning …]

From a cauldron, Christ's body is transformed yet again into a vessel that contains divine treasures, pleasures, delights and riches:

[P]orque dentro deste preçioso cuerpo son ençerrados todos los thesoros de dios padre. Et incluso todo los plazeres et deleytes del çielo. Et ascondidas todas las rriquezas de paraíso. (f. 292r)

[(F)or within this precious body are enclosed all of the treasures of God the Father, even all the pleasures and delights of Heaven. And hidden all of the riches of paradise.]

It then becomes a lofty tabernacle, a rich cell and a beautiful palace, all the while producing the "excessive heat" necessary for transformation of all those who enter:

Et por ende quien podria creer nin penssar que quien entrar en tan alto tabernaculo et tan rica çella et en tan hermoso palaçio pueda de aqui salir sin alteraçion noctable et sin exçesivo calor. (ff. 292r–v)

[Thus who could believe or think that whoever enters into such a high tabernacle and such a rich cell and such a beautiful palace might be able to leave it unchanged and without excessive heat.]

Finally, it extends to the hearts of men as a ladder by which they may effect their ascent to "divine heights,"[5] while yet remaining a fountain, the source of all beauty, delight, love and honour:

Por que nactura humana et por esta carne et cuerpo de dios ome vesible ffaga escalera al coraçon del ome para ssobir ala divinal alteza. Por la qual ssobida vea en este preçioso cuerpo la fuente de todas las hermosuras, de deleytes, amores et onores … (f. 292v)

[For out of this human nature and flesh and body of God as Man Visible let there be made a ladder for man's heart so that it may climb up to the divine heights. Through which ascent let him see in this precious body the fount of all beauties, delights, loves and honors …]

For Eiximenis and his readers, Christ's body – rather than composed of sinews, bones, organs and blood – is a vessel devoid of all human content, ready to be transformed an infinite number of times, just as it transforms all those who enter it. And Christ's followers are told to direct their attention to their hearts in order to conceive of this inconceivable body – though not, as is frequently the case in northern texts on the Passion (Haug), in order to visualize the Saviour's sufferings with the "eyes of their hearts."

Todo ome debe ençender et fazer arder su coraçon enel amor divinal. Et mayor mente en aquel abismo et fornaz de amor infinito, el qual esta ençerrado dentro dela arca del testamento. Conviene ssaber dentro del preçioso cuerpo de nro señor ihu xpo. (f. 291v)

[All men must ignite and make their hearts burn with divine love, particularly in that abyss and furnace of infinite love, which is enclosed inside the ark of the testament. That is, within the precious body of Our Lord Jesus Christ.]

Both José Miguel Puerta (Puerta 744–807) and Michael Sells have provocatively explored Sufi notions of transformation and union as expressed particularly by Ibn 'Arabi, himself heavily impacted by the school of illuminist mysticism established by eastern mystic al-Suhrawardi. For Ibn 'Arabi, transformation – though it involved, as for the European Christian writers and images discussed above, the mimetic identification of lover with divine beloved – was not based in the visual but rather in the erasure of any stable image of the divine that might exist in the devotee's imagination (which for Ibn 'Arabi was equivalent to the heart, or *qalb*; Puerta, 750). This erasure was achieved by drowning any existing mental image of divinity, much as Eiximenis chose to do almost two centuries later, in a "fugue-like" cascade of metaphors. All of this occurs in the heart: a site not of visualization but rather of veiling, containing, and continual and simultaneous evocation and obliteration. These processes are necessary because no one image or symbol is sufficient to the task of evoking the divine; rather "each new term reveals something and veils something. There is always an obscurity, an undefined term, a new paradox … It is the moving image rather than any particular frame that is significant" (Sells 63–4).

In order to avoid the heresy of "binding" (*taqyid*) the Divine into fixed categories and forms, within the ever-changing heart (the root *q-l-b* also implies change and transformation; López Baralt, "Simbología mística musulmana" 50 and *A zaga de tu huella* 81–184; Sells 92) the truth (*al-haqq*) "manifests itself to itself through innumerable forms or images but is confined to none. *The forms of its manifestation are continually changing*" (Sells 83; emphasis mine). Much like the souls of Christ's lovers who, emerging from the divine cauldron that Eiximenis makes of his body, are transformed and changed, within the system constructed by Ibn 'Arabi the individual must also be in a state of constant change in order to reflect "the True/the Real." Thus, just as for the viewers of Christian images examined by Jill Bennett and Michael Camille, union with the divine involves mimesis; but the process here is conceptual and unstable rather than somatic and stable:

When the same images are no longer seen as fixed, mutually exclusive, but rather as perpetually changing forms of manifestation, they become transparent and revelatory … once an attribute has been brought into relationship with the identity of the divinity, it can no longer be the identity, and must be replaced by a new, transcendent identity … (Sells 93–4)

Ibn 'Arabi places images of lover and beloved into a continuum of continual transformation through their relationship with a classic repertoire of garden and desert metaphors in the mystical poetic compositions that make up his *Tarjuman al-Ashwaq* (*Translator of Desires*):

Full moon above a branch
       Whose are these fingertips that touch me?
Whose the mellifluous voice I hear?
       They belong to two with full breasts, each in her tent of silk,
safe from all imperfection, safe from time.
       Full moons above branches,
With their beauties, their pleasures and their jewels.
       In one of my body's gardens
there is a dove perched on the branch of a bân tree.
       They die of love, they melt with passion,
When that which ravishes me assails them …

              (Ibn 'Arabi, *Tarjuman al-Ashwaq* 176–7)

The lover's body, in an eternally metamorphosing mimesis of his beloved, has become an indeterminate series of (literal or metaphorical) gardens inhabitable by the Divine Beloved: full-breasted beauties in silk tents, who transform into a striking dual variation on a classic topos ("moons above a branch") and then into a solitary "dove perched on the branch of a *ban* tree" (Robinson, "Trees of Love, Trees of Knowledge" and "Les Lieux de la lyrique"). For Ibn 'Arabi, "the central mystical event is passing from duality to non-duality" (Sells 66), and he wants his language in some way to reflect this event – just as, it would seem, did Eiximenis.

The ecstatic scenes evoked by Ibn 'Arabi in the lyric quoted above take place in "one of his body's gardens," certainly to be understood in the context of Ibn 'Arabi's poetics as his heart. Though I have not found a translation into Castilian of this particular lyric – penned in a notary hand on a bill of sale for a herd of goats and a vineyard that dropped from between the folios of a fourteenth-century breviary from, say, the cathedral of Palencia – I am able to offer what I consider to be the next best thing. Among the late medieval European Passion texts translated into Castilian and present in libraries prior to the end of the fifteenth century is *De instructione vel doctrina cordis et anime*, circulated in Castilian as the *Enseñamiento del corazón* (mentioned above).[6] Probably composed in the thirteenth century by either Hugh of St Cher or Gérard of Liège, it was also well-distributed in northern Europe and has captured the attention of scholars because of the "homey" house-cleaning analogy offered by the author in the earlier chapters of the treatise, which instruct readers in the preparation of their hearts for the arrival of the Bridegroom (Renevey). What has not received comment from scholars, however, and would certainly have captured Castilians' attention, are the ecstatic depictions of union with the Bridegroom from the Song of Songs which characterize the final chapters of the work, devoted to the *via unitiva*. Already in the introduction readers are made aware that their ultimate ecstasy will be fueled not by images but by words: "Ca las palabras de dios son asi como unas uvas que estan llenas de gran abastança de vino" ["For the words of God are like grapes full of a great supply of wine" (BNE Ms. 9202, f. 2r)]. Once they are crushed and fermented, their juices will be sent to the "wine-cellar of the heart" ["la bodega del coraçon"] where the "truth of celestial teachings" ["la verdat del enseñamiento celestial"] will "give you to drink and make you drunk" ["para te abebrar et enbriagar"].

Though meditation on the Passion is mentioned early in the treatise as part of the process of the "cleaning of the heart" ["alimpamiento del Corazon" – i.e., the *via purgativa* (BNM Ms. 9209, ff. 13v-14r)], it is soon converted into the joyous wedding feast with her Bridegroom which awaits the loving soul (e.g., BNE Ms. 9209, f. 38r). Though the current of mystical thought known as "Bridal Mysticism" was widespread throughout northern Europe (Hamburger) and its reception through the translation of the *Doctrina cordis* can in no way be claimed to be unique to Castile, I believe that the other particularities of the Castilian panorama discussed in this essay warrant the special consideration I give to it in the Castilian context.

For Ibn 'Arabi (and for the Shadhili school of Andalusi Sufis), the devotee's heart was a receptacle (Asín Palacios; Puerta 750–2; Sells); for Castilians who read the *Enseñamiento del corazón* it was a wine-cellar, and Christ's crucified body, just as for Eiximenis, was conceived as an architectural space that could be entered, one whose "walls were broken" and whose "door was opened" when His side was pierced by the lance (BNM Ms. 9209, f. 84r; this is the only graphic mention made of any moment of the Passion in the entire treatise). Christ's body is also compared to the "arc of the testament," and it is through this architectural mimesis rather than through the contemplation of a graphic image of His suffering that the devotee's heart is prepared for union with the Bridegroom.

As they approach the moment of mystical, celestial union, readers are advised that – although few actually do it ("pocos son los que piensan con su coraçon"; BNE Ms. 9209, f. 89v) – they should strive to think *with* rather than *in* their hearts. This prepares them to raise up their hearts, which will then – in the first of a series of lengthy paraphrases of the Song of Songs that drive this ecstatic portrait of mystical union (Saint Bernard's commentaries are invoked) – "run to the aroma of the celestial balms and enter into the garden of divine delights" ["correr al olor delos ungüentos çelestiales et entrar enel huerto delos deleytes"]. Just as for Ibn 'Arabi, for the Castilian translator and readers of the *Enseñamiento del corazón* the seat of true knowledge and understanding is the heart, and it is only with the eyes of the heart that the soul may see its beloved:

> … la entençion es ojo del coraçon. Et con aqueste ojo deve ver el alma a ihu xpo su amado por que el sea despertado et movido amayor ternura de amor çerca dello. Segund aquello que dize el refran. El tu açercamiento sea simple et amoroso et tal que faga amoroso al tu amigo. (BNE Ms. 9209, f. 93r)

> [… understanding is the eye of the heart. And with this eye the soul should see Jesus Christ, her beloved, so that she may be awakened and moved to greater tenderness of love for him. Just as the saying goes: Let your approach be simple and loving, and such that it awakens the love of your beloved.]

Though, as in northern Passion texts, readers are instructed to contemplate with the "eyes of their hearts," what is evoked is not a narrative vision of the suffering and humiliations of the Passion but rather the image of the Beloved. No description is undertaken and no particulars are given; the emphasis is on the reciprocity of the loving relationship into which the soul enters with the Beloved prior to the ecstatic final chapters of the treatise. Further exploration of the implications of a Castilian readership for this treatise, as well as the imagining of a multi-confessional dialogue concerning mystical ecstasy, must be left for a lengthier study. But it is possible to affirm, in the context of this discussion, that the election to translate the *Doctrina cordis* rather than the *MVC* was no accident.

As mentioned earlier, Eiximenis clearly intends for his readers' experience of the crucified Christ – for all intents and purposes a "disembodied" Christ – to take place *inside* their hearts. And it is equally clear that he does not, like his European contemporaries, link this process to vision or to visualization. Rather, his crucified Christ is to be *remembered*, not *seen*. Several fifteenth-century Castilian devotional miscellanies contain suggestive parallel versions of an anecdote in which a Christian is taken captive by an infidel ruler during battle. The Christian affirms that he bears Christ Crucified in his heart and refuses to back down before the sovereign's insistence that he recant. In a fit of rage, the infidel king orders him killed and his heart opened. There the image is found, just as the Christian described it, and all those present are so impressed that they immediately convert to Christianity (BNE Ms. 8744, f. 186). Though the origins of this anecdote are possibly found in the legend of St Ignatius (Constanza de Castilla 4–5, n. 10; Lightfoot 1, 38), its embellishment and diffusion in this context are worthy of note: while clearly resonating with the devotional concerns regarding interiority exhibited by Eiximenis's meditations, it also fulfills the objective of hiding the holy image from the eyes of the infidel.

It is, moreover, reminiscent of Ibn 'Arabi's attitude towards images and devotion, some of the specifics of which are expounded in the *Futuhat al- Makkiyya*:

> When the *shari'a* of Muhammad arrived and images were banned, he enclosed Jesus's truth and folded Jesus's *shari'a* within his own. Our *shari'a* dictates that we worship him as though we could see him; and if we embody him in our imaginations, which is the meaning of *taswir* (representation; depiction), it is prohibited that he should appear in a sensory sense, or in a physical likeness. This particular *shari'a*, however, which is "Worship God as though you could see him," was not uttered by Muhammad in any way, shape or form. Rather, it was pronounced by Gabriel, peace be upon him, and it was he who manifested himself to Mary as a comely man on the occasion of Jesus' conception, may peace be upon him … (Ibn 'Arabi, *Al-Futuhat al-makkiya* I, 337–8)

Ibn 'Arabi's interpretation of the well-known and widely circulated "Gabriel *hadith*" ("man should worship God as though he could see him"; al-Nawawi, hadith no. 2, *An Anthology of the Sayings of the Prophet Muhammad* 28–33) emphasizes images of interiority and "folding within." Indeed, for Ibn 'Arabi, "embodiment [of God] within the imagination" is the very definition of *taswir* (representation, or depiction), though with the stipulation that the Divine should never appear in a physical or human likeness and must always be constituted within the heart of "the complete human" (*al-insan al-kamil*; Sells 66).

The same *hadith* is "performed" in a *muwashshaha* by late-thirteenth-century mystic al-Shushtari in which the poet uses the iconic topoi of the Arabic *khamriyya* (wine song) and *ghazal* (love lyric). Al-Shushtari traces the melding of earthly lover into divine beloved during a *majlis* in a garden experienced through the senses of both; indeed, they are indistinguishable. The lover's transformation is urged along by the beloved:

Refrain:

> My beloved has no equal, and he has no guardian who keeps vigil over him!
> He came near to me, and he whose presence cannot be hidden was there!

Fifth and Sixth Couplets:

> It is because of him that I hear, through him that I see; my soul is before him!
> I am all alone with my beloved; I am annihilated, far from all existence!
> Thanks to him my drink is sweet, and through him I gather roses.

He manifested himself before me, and I saw him, he who is far above the excellence
of my heart!
He called me and I went to him; he ordered me to look into his mirror,
And I saw his face, like a new moon!
He received me and greeted me, saying, "Change! Transform yourself, my brother, and
live here with me!" (Al-Shushtari 39–40; Spanish translation 213–15)

Much like the image of the crucified Christ which Eiximenis's meditations always
stop just short of evoking, or the blurry allusion to an abstract Beloved glimpsed
by the eyes of the soul's heart in the *Enseñamiento del Coraçon*, for Ibn 'Arabi and
al-Shushtari this and other related *hadith*s provide the basis for the establishment
of a particular relation between *tanzih* (abstraction, non-similitude) and *tashbih*
(similitude, likeness; Puerta 784–91). Moreover, al-Shushtari pushes Ibn 'Arabi's
"heart that takes on every form" (Sells 90) a step further: the lover's heart is, in
the end, unable to contain the excellence of the divine vision, so it manifests itself
before the eyes not of his heart but of his body. The oral performance of such
songs or compositions took place for centuries before audiences that, on occasion, must have included Christians.

Although it is impossible to explain the specific interchanges that resulted in
the transmission of the contents of the "Gabriel *hadith*" to a Christian milieu, it
is worthy of note that Alfonso del Madrigal, "el Tostado," who was Archbishop
of Ávila during the middle decades of the fifteenth century, makes a statement to
the same effect in his exegesis of the Ten Commandments: "Man should worship
God as though he could see Him" (BNE Ms. 4202, f. 121r). The comment appears in the context of a discussion of the symbolic value of the Eucharist, which
el Tostado emphatically privileges above visual representations of Christ. Indeed,
he – like his contemporary, the Castilian Franciscan thinker Alonso de Espina –
denies all relationship between the image and Christ himself. Pereda has traced a
previously unstudied tradition of acerbic debate between Castilian church intellectuals concerning the role and meaning of images and image devotions, demonstrating that disagreements occurred not only between Christians and "infidels"
but were deeply rooted within the Christian community itself (Pereda, "El debate"
and *Las imágenes de la discordia*). Both el Tostado and the converso Archbishop of
Burgos, Pablo de Santa María (ca. 1351–1435), incidentally, were of the opinion
that veneration of any image of Christ (crucified or otherwise) was best reserved
for the interior of the devotee's heart (Pereda, *Las imágenes de la discordia*, 96).

St Bridget's *Revelations* contain accounts of several visions of the Crucifixion
and of the apocryphal moment in which Mary cradles her son's lifeless body in
her arms (an image which coalesced into the Pietà) conceded to her by the Mother
of God. The Virgin provides both St Bridget and her readers with a devotional
exemplum encouraging him or her to see her Son, wounded "from the top of

his head to the soles of his feet, all black and blue and marked with the red of his own blood," and to scrutinize "the bitter sight of the holes – in his feet, in his hands, and even in his glorious side":

> Praise be to you, my Lady, O Virgin Mary. With bitter sorrow you saw your Son hanging on the cross: from the top of his head to the soles of his feet, all black and blue and marked with the red of his own blood, and so cruelly dead. You also gazed at the bitter sight of the holes – in his feet, in his hands, and even in his glorious side. You gazed at his skin, all lacerated without any mercy … (Birgitta of Sweden 223)

For St Bridget's readers the site of identification, in addition to Christ's body, is the Virgin's eyes.

For Castilians, on the other hand, the site of identification and locus of devotion is displaced to the Virgin's interior. In his narration of the events of Christ's Passion (*Vida de Cristo*, Castilian translation of the *Vida de Jesucrist*, BNE Ms. 18772, ff. 82r–185r), Eiximenis evokes the wrenching emotions experienced by both Mother and Son on numerous occasions. These sufferings are mutual and mutually incremental: Christ's suffering is heightened as he witnesses his mother's, and the Mother's pains are aggravated as she perceives those of her Son. Moreover Eiximenis stipulates that these pains and suffering, ultimately inexpressible, are "inviscerados," "atravessados en sus entrañas" – that is, located deep within the interiors of both the Virgin and Christ, confined to a place which Castilian readers would almost certainly have identified as their hearts:

> Todos los dolores della tenia el inviscerados et atravessados en sus entrañas. Et asi el moria et padesçia por ella et ella por el … (BNE Ms. 8744, f. 283v)

> [All her sufferings he held lodged deep inside in his organs, pierced (by the sword). And thus he died and suffered for her and she for him.]

Although the *Stimulus Amoris*, Eiximenis's writings and other Iberian Passion texts make it clear that the Virgin has seen her son, both on the cross and on her lap, she would appear to have hidden the image away even from the devotee's sight, deep within her heart. Ibn ʿArabi would have approved.

There is, moreover, a tradition in Iberia – in complete opposition to elsewhere in Christian Europe – that highlights not only the stoicism of the Virgin but even her ecstasy in the face of the Passion. Part of this tradition comes from Eiximenis himself, but it is attested at least as early as the fourteenth century. This tradition would have coloured Castilians' reading and reception of imported texts concerned with the Virgin's experience of the Passion, which enjoyed much greater and much earlier success than did their Christological counterparts.[7] Many of these texts evidence a particular interest in the Virgin's heart, as is the case with a short chapter of the *Stimulus Amoris* dedicated to the Virgin's experience of the Passion:

> … çiertamente [estabas] en la cruz con el tu fijo porque alli fuiste cruçificada con el … Señora, el tu coraçon es atravesado con lança, coronado de espinas, escarneçido, vituperado … Acato y conssidero, Señora, el tu coracon y ya non veo coraçon … non fallo sino llagas y dolores ca toda eres transformada en ellos … (San Lorenzo del Escorial b-IV-8, *Estímulo del Amor de Jesucristo* [*Stimulus Amoris*; hereafter SLE] ff. 16–18)

> [… surely (you were) on the cross with your son, for you were crucified there with him … Lady, your heart is speared through with a lance, crowned with thorns, scorned and reviled … I contemplate and consider, O Lady, your heart, and I no longer see a heart … I find only wounds and pain for into them are you completely transformed …]

Here the Virgin's heart is transformed into a container for all of the pain and humiliation of her Son's passion. Indeed, she seems to witness the Passion for her devotees, in their stead, and thus to save them from the horror of direct confrontation with the awful spectacle.

Although these implications are not explicitly present in the *Stimulus Amoris* and were probably not even intended by the text's original author, other texts written in Castile assure us that a Castilian readership would have drawn just such conclusions. In a lengthy and unedited Castilian treatise of Marian lore (Robinson, "Trees of Love, Trees of Knowledge"), the Virgin's heart is a locus of stability. Offered as a model for the preparation of the contemplative's heart, it serves as a "mine" from which the reader may extract metals with which to fortify his or her own:

> *XL: de xpi conceptione et de diversis generibus cordium secundum diversa genera metallorum et de preparatione cordis:* Maria dicitur minera … (*Mariale sive in Laudibus BMV*; BNE Ms. 8952, f. 57v)

> [XL: On Christ's conception and on the different types of hearts according to the different types of metals, and on the preparation of the heart: Mary is called a mine …]

She is then compared to the jeweled (or, here, "golden") city of *Apocalypse* XXI, for her heart is forged of that most noble of metals, gold (f. 59v). Elsewhere, in a passage reminiscent of Eiximenis's cauldron, it is stated that her heart – because it was of gold – was the only one that emerged unscathed (read: unchanged, untransformed) from the fires of the Passion by which it was examined: it burned, but, like the "mulier amicta sole," was not consumed. Her heart's wounds were inflicted by words heard rather than sights seen; each is a thorn that attempts, unsuccessfully, to puncture her heart, and then morphs into the stars of her crown. In chapter LXIX, her heart is compared to onyx, the densest of all precious stones, into which her tears also metamorphose before they hit the ground (ff. 101v–103r). In other chapters, as she stands beside her Son's cross, the Virgin is raptured and made drunk with ecstasy (ff. 85r–86v).

This fixation on Mary's heart, melded with earlier interpretations that assert her ecstasy during the Passion, characterizes a uniquely Castilian liturgical piece, the *Officium Transfixionis* of the Blessed Virgin (SLE Ms. b-III-4, Castile; partial and corrupt text in BNM Ms. Res. 197, both late fifteenth century). Although it shares numerous hymns, versicles, antiphons and responsories with an earlier *Office of the Compassion of the Virgin*, preserved in a number of variants throughout libraries in Europe and frequently interspersed with the *Office of the Passion* (Hughes), the two are definitely different (Robinson, "El Retablo de Miraflores romanzado"). Indeed, the *Officium Transfixionis* appears to subvert several of the assertions made in the *Officium Compassionis* in order to render the Virgin, triumphant over her sufferings, in a state of ecstasy. The office opens with an evocation of Symeon's prediction of the *gladius passionis* that would pierce her heart as her Son hung on the cross:

> Et benedixit illis Symeon et dixit ad Mariam matrem eius … et tuam ipsius animam pertransiet gladius ut revelentur ex multis cordibus cogitationes … (*Officium Transfixionis BMV*; SLE b-II-4, Invitatorium [Luke II: 34])

> [And Simeon blessed them and said to Mary his mother … and a sword shall pierce your very soul so that the cogitations of many hearts may be revealed …]

A rare and early version of the *Office of the Compassion* is preserved in Castile; very different from better-known versions, it is frequently bound with a particularly Castilian "Salterio de la Virgen," or "Psalter of the Virgin" (Robinson, "El Retablo de Miraflores romanzado"). The *Hours of the Compassion of the Blessed Virgin Mary* are narrative in tone, and, combined with the *Hours of the Passion,* they take the reader (or participant) through the Passion step by step:

> **Antiph**. Crucifige clamitant hora terciarum illusus induitur veste purpurarum. Caput eius pungitur corona spinarum. Crucem portat humeris ad locum penarum …

> **Antiphona**. Videns virgo virginum hora terciarum. Caput punctum filii corona spinarum. Crucem ferre scapula ad locum penarum … (*Horae Compassio BMV*, Bodleian Ms. 62, f. 38v)

[**Antiph**. 'Crucify him,' they cried at the hour of Terce; he was mocked and dressed in cloth of purple, his head pierced by a crown of thorns. He bore the cross on his shoulders to the place of his sentence …

Antiphona. The Virgin, seeing her son's head pierced by a crown of thorns at the hour of Terce, bearing the cross on his shoulders to the place of his sentence …]

By comparison, the *Office of the Transfixion* is static, fixated on the moment at which the sword pierces the Virgin's heart. No narrative or descriptive details are given; rather, the Virgin remains "transfixed" beneath the Cross, until her own heart is transfixed just as was her Son's. Though she sees, neither she nor the narrator describes to us what she sees; rather, in a text which readers are almost certainly intended to juxtapose with Psalm 130 (Domine non est exaltatum cor meum; neque elati sunt oculi mei [Lord, my heart is not raised up, nor are my eyes exalted]), we are told that her eyes are "not darkened, but illuminated," because they have seen her Son "transfixed":

Non sunt obscurati sed illuminati beati occuli marie virginis qui[a] transfixum vide-runt beatum ihesum … (*Officium Transfixionis BMV*; SLE Ms. b-II-4)

[The blessed eyes of the Virgin Mary are not darkened but enlightened, for they have seen blessed Jesus pierced through.]

Similarly, the sword that pierces her heart, in addition to unutterable pain, brings her ecstatic joy.

The *Officium Transfixionis BMV* spatially alters the Passion in two important ways. It reduces the entire Passion to two moments: the Virgin's vigil beneath the cross and – through repetition of the hymn "Gaude celi curia," which portrays the Virgin holding her Son in her arms following his death and descent from the cross – the Pietà. And it displaces the experience of the Passion onto the Virgin, more specifically (through her refusal to give details) projecting the suffering of the Passion into her interior, her heart or her "*entrañas*." Given that this *Office* circulated in manuscripts intended for private reading as well as for liturgical performance (BNE Ms. Res. 197, mentioned above), we are probably justified in juxtaposing it with images, and particularly with images of the Pietà, which were the earliest and most prolifically produced personal devotional images to circulate in Castile (J. Molina; Robinson, "Preaching to the Converted" and "El Retablo de Miraflores romanzado"). Though Ibn 'Arabi would have had reservations about any exterior image of divinity (further complicated by the fact that, as Castilian Christian polemicists well knew, neither Jews nor Muslims believed the Passion actually happened), he might have approved of the Virgin's jealous guarding of some of the more disturbing images she remembered in the deepest recesses of her heart. He might also have agreed with the displacement of Passion devotions, and the majority of Castilian Christian devotions in general, onto the Virgin. He himself, particularly in the verses that compose his *Tarjuman al-Ashwaq*, frequently had recourse to Woman as a place-holder in the impossible (and forbidden) task of representing the divine:

> … the vision of Him found in Woman is the most perfect perception which the human being may have of Him … (Ibn 'Arabi, *Fusus al-Hikam* [*Bezels of Wisdom*] 217; *apud* Puerta 761)

Ibn 'Arabi was of the opinion that Woman was as close as human beings should get to a vision of the Divine in this life.

NOTES

1 I first met María Menocal when I was a second-year graduate student, on the eve of the publication of *The Arabic Role in Medieval Literary History: A Forgotten Heritage*, and have been inspired and challenged by her work ever since. I dedicate this paper – along with the bits and pieces of the past that my stubborn digging has unearthed – to Prof. Menocal.

2 With the possible exception of members of the Dominican order during the early fifteenth century and of certain members of the clergy during the mid-fifteenth century (Robinson, "El Retablo de Miraflores romanzado").

3 See BNE Ms. 7767, *Liber qui repertorium sive devotionarium nuncupatur continensin se quamplurimos libros diversorum tractatuum et divinarum scripturarum: valde memoriae commendabiles*, ff. 288–331v. Still bound in its original mudéjar binding, this fifteenth-century manuscript was copied by a notary at the behest of Fr. García de Entrena, prior of the Jeronymite convent of San Miguel de la Morcuera (near Madrid) for another Jeronymite establishment at La Estrella (in the province of Logroño, near Aragón). Thus the compendium would appear to have enjoyed a certain degree of success, at least among a Jeronymite public; we may therefore assume that the treatise was known by this name to an appreciable portion of its Latin-literate readership. See Robinson, forthcoming.

4 Many of the techniques that Eiximenis suggests his readers employ to meditate on Christ Crucified (particularly the emphasis on memory rather than visualization) are also used extensively by Ramon Llull, whose importance for Castilian devotional life during the later Middle Ages has, in my opinion, been greatly underestimated; these issues will be explored in much greater depth in the monograph currently in preparation.

5 The metaphor of the ladder occurs at least once more in these meditations, offering to devotees (just as in this case) an ascending path toward union with Christ. They kiss

his feet, his hands, and finally his mouth, though – significantly – no mention is made
of the five wounds.
6 Ed. Juan Varela de Salamanca, 1510.
7 On this tradition in Castilian devotions see Robinson, "Trees of Love, Trees
of Knowledge," "Preaching to the Converted," and "El Retablo de Miraflores
romanzado."

11 Arab Musical Influence on Medieval Europe: A Reassessment

DWIGHT REYNOLDS

María Rosa Menocal's *The Arabic Role in Medieval Literary History* posed a provocative central question: Why had Romance Philology refused to explore the possibilities of Arabic influence on European medieval literature despite abundant historical evidence that contact with Arabic literature, written and oral, had taken place in many different times, places, and manners throughout the Middle Ages? The critical issue was not then, nor is it now, whether any one specific genre, style, or theme was shaped, wholly or partially, by Arab influences, but rather why potential links to Arab culture were not being actively explored by western scholars. The answer in its simplest form is that western scholars had created a master narrative that presupposed a medieval world in which speakers of Latin/Romance had virtually no contact with speakers of Arabic, bilingualism was deemed to have been almost non-existent, and translation (though acknowledged to have existed) was portrayed as a limited, erudite activity that had no broader impact on the development of medieval Iberian culture. In the twenty-five years since the publication of Menocal's work, however, that master narrative has been disassembled in a multitude of ways, and a new generation of scholars has been trained to examine and evaluate contacts, influences, and even hybridization with more open minds.

The argument that Menocal posed regarding medieval literature over two decades ago can still be posed today in the field of music history. In the first half of the twentieth century, scholars such as Julián Ribera y Tarragó (*La música de las cantigas, La música andaluza medieval, Historia de la música árabe medieval, Music in Ancient Arabia and Spain*) and Henry George Farmer (*A History of Arabian Music, Historical Facts for the Arabian Musical Influence*) made wide-ranging arguments about Arab musical influence on Occitanian and Catalonian troubadours, the *Cantigas de Santa María* of Alfonso X, and the Gallego-Portuguese *cantigas de amigo*, arguments which were vigorously denied by scholars who refused to acknowledge any influence from – indeed often any contact with – Arab music whatsoever. In hindsight, it is clear that, in some ways, the Arabist arguments suffered from many of the same weaknesses as those of the "European nationalists." The architects of the "Arab hypothesis," like their opponents, saw cultural history primarily in terms of influence and transmission, and ignored the prodigious complexity of human culture. Independent developments, hybridization, creolization, cultural interactions, mutual influences, and many other nonlinear processes simply did not play a role in their vision of musical history. Indeed, some of the scholars who argued most fervently for Arab musical influence on medieval Europe saw Arab music itself as scarcely more than a vehicle for transmitting the earlier musical ideas of the Greeks, Byzantines, and Persians, parallel to the western portrayal of Arabo-Islamic culture as little more than the bearer of Greek thought to Europe. Musical traditions and knowledge were conceived of as essentially static, and musical history was therefore primarily a narrative of unidirectional transmission from the ancients to the Arabs, and then from the Arabs to western Europe.

In this essay I argue that both of these constructs break down under scrutiny and that at least one of the most cherished symbols of the "Arabist" narrative (Arab musical influence on the Occitan troubadours), can be rather clearly disproven. The "European nationalist" narrative which portrayed medieval Christian and Muslim communities as having little to no direct contact (which meant that there was therefore no historical context in which musical influence from Andalusian Spain could have taken place) is scarcely tenable with so much historical evidence to the contrary now available, while the "Arabist" narrative of unidirectional influences moving from Muslim Spain northward to the Christian Iberian kingdoms and further into France can now be shown to be equally simplistic. Instead, the image that emerges from the historical evidence is one of hybridization, multiple levels of interaction, and *complex genealogies*, processes that are demonstrated here through a series of examples, each of which resists characterization as simply "contact" or "influence." While this is not an attempt at a comprehensive survey, these examples should suffice to demonstrate some of the complexity of musical life in medieval Iberia. This complexity should, in fact, come as no surprise, for it is the very nature of human culture to develop in multiple, interactive ways. Master narratives of unidirectional influence are more often than not the product of political or ideological agendas rather than of careful analysis of historical evidence.

Arab Music: The Early Centuries

Abu Faraj al-Isbahani's tenth-century *Kitab al-Aghani* (*Book of Songs*) offers a pointillist but highly detailed account of the transformation of Arab music from a regional musical tradition found primarily in the Arabian Peninsula and parts of modern Palestine, Syria, and Iraq, to a complex, urban, and highly cosmopolitan tradition during the first three centuries after the advent of Islam. This is a historical narrative that has been recounted by Farmer (*A History of Arabian Music*), Ribera (*Historia de la música árabe medieval*), and Quettat (*La musique classique du Maghreb, La musique arabo-andalouse*), among others. Several major developments occurred within the first three Islamic centuries (seventh–ninth centuries C.E.), but perhaps the most notable and most influential of these was the rapid emergence of a class of urban professional singers and composers who gained fame – and notoriety – for their public performances and musical production.

The majority of the female singers whose biographies have been preserved in the "Books of Songs" were "slave-singers" (Ar. *qiyan* or *jawari*), many of whom received specialized training in music and poetry, particularly in the city of Medina, which had quickly emerged as the centre of the Arabo-Islamic musical world. These slave-singers were a critical social and cultural institution from the seventh to twelfth centuries C.E., but disappeared somewhat mysteriously (perhaps due to changing patterns of patronage) in the thirteenth and fourteenth centuries. Al-Isbahani also transmits information about free women who gained fame as singers and composers, and notes that a number of the more famous female slave-singers either purchased their own freedom or were manumitted by their owners in the latter portion of their lives. Some of these women went on to establish great "houses" where younger female singers were trained. While these women were slaves in the sense of not being able to choose their own fates (they were bought and sold, or given as gifts, at the whim of their owners), they were also trained professionals, extremely expensive, and highly valued, so many of them led lives far more luxurious than, for example, common household servants, poor urban-dwellers, or agricultural workers in the countryside, and not a few anecdotes portray the most famous of them as wielding significant social influence. To name but a few examples from among the most prominent female singers of the early Islamic centuries, 'Atika bint Shuhda (eighth century) was the daughter of a singer and lived as a freewoman in Basra; 'Arib (ninth century) is thought to have been the illegitimate daughter of the powerful vizier Ja'far al-Barmaki, was owned by two caliphs, manumitted by a third, and then continued to perform as a freewoman in the caliphal court; 'Azza al-Mayla' (seventh century) and Jamila (seventh century) both lived their lives as freewomen, but Badhl (ninth century), Hababa (seventh-eighth century), Sallamat al-Qass (seventh century) and countless others were trained, bought, and sold as slave-singers.

On the other hand, most of the male singers recorded by al-Isbahani were free men, rather than slaves, who pursued independent careers. It is noteworthy that a large number of them were mixed race or non-Arab: the singer Ibn Surayj was half-Turkish; al-Gharid was half-Berber; Ibn Misjah and Ma'bad were each half-African; Ibn Muhriz, Nashit, and Sa'ib Khathir were of Persian origin, though Malik ibn Abi Samh and Ibn Mish'ab were Muslim Arabs, and Hunayn ibn Balu' al-Hiri was a Christian Arab. (Al-Isbahani gives far less information about the ethnic origins of female singers.)

The emergence of this multiethnic, urban, highly cosmopolitan class of professional musicians is matched by accounts of various different musical influences on the Arab tradition, particularly from neighbouring Byzantium and Persia. The singer Nashit (seventh century), for example, was a Persian slave, later freed by his master, who is credited with bringing Persian melodies to Medina, but who in turn had to master Arab music in order to survive as a professional singer in the highly competitive musical life of that city (Farmer, *A History of Arabian Music* 55). Ibn Misjah was famed for having brought a number of foreign influences back with him to Medina after extensive travels:

> In Syria, he [Ibn Misjah] learned the melodies (*alhan*) of Byzantium and received instruction from the barbiton players (*barbatiyya*) and the theorists (*astukhusiyya*). He then turned to Persia, where he learned much of their song (*ghina'*), as well as the art of accompaniment. Returning to al-Hijaz, he chose the most advantageous of the modes (*nagham*) of these countries, and rejected what was disagreeable, for instance, the intervals (*nabarat*) and modes (*nagham*) which he found in the song (*ghina'*) of the Persians and Byzantines, *which were alien to the Arabian song*. And he sang [henceforth] according to this method and he was the first to demonstrate this [method] and after this the people followed him in this. (Farmer, *A History of Arabian Music* 69–70; emphasis in the original)

This image of a master singer creating a new style by bringing together elements of different traditions is an oft-repeated trope in Arabo-Islamic music history. In fact, Ibn Misjah's own student, Ibn Muhriz, is also credited with this same accomplishment by al-Isbahani (Farmer, *A History of Arabian Music* 70); Ibn Fadl Allah al-'Umari (10:385) tells us that Sulaym, a singer in the court of al-Hakam I of Cordoba combined the music of the Christians with the singing of Iraq at the turn of the ninth century C.E.; Ibn Hayyan (307–35) says that Ziryab created a new and distinctive style only a few decades later in the Cordoban court of 'Abd al-Rahman II (mid-ninth century) that became so popular that it was practiced by all singers in al-Andalus for several centuries thereafter; and Ahmad al-Tifashi tells us that Ibn Bajja (twelfth century) mixed the "the songs of the Christians with those of the East, thereby inventing a style found only in al-Andalus, toward which the temperament of its people inclined, so that they rejected all others" (Liu and Monroe 42). In none of these cases is it possible to know exactly which elements were being borrowed from the Byzantines, Persians, or Iberian

Christians, but there are several things that can be said about the resulting musical styles. In each case the "new style" was distinctive and separate from that of the culture(s) from which new ideas have been adopted; that is, borrowing Persian melodies did not result in something that resembled or could be mistaken for Persian music, but rather produced something new and quite distinct.

In part this was due to the fact that the Arab musical tradition was dominated by the aesthetics and structures of Arabic poetry. There are almost no historical accounts of performers singing in other languages for Arabic-speaking patrons or publics, a fact that accords with the general understanding that music among the Arabs was considered a vehicle for sung poetry, rather than being a completely independent art form (there is sparse evidence, for example, of performances of purely instrumental music other than as a prelude or interlude in the performance of sung poetry). And, in the case of the early Arab music portrayed in the "Book of Songs," it is clear that these "new styles" were not only subjugated to the rules of Arabic metre and poetry, but also to the structure of Arab rhythms, for although al-Isbahani carefully recorded the rhythms of all of the songs he discussed, there is almost no mention of rhythms from outside the Arab system. Thus, according to al-Isbahani, melodies and perhaps vocal techniques were at times adopted from other cultures, but only when they did not possess intervals or modes that were alien to Arab music, and even then they were performed to Arab rhythms and Arabic lyrics.

The term "Arab music" in reference to this period should therefore not be taken to mean that the singers and composers were necessarily of Arab origin, nor that there was an unchanging "Arab style" that had been transmitted from pre-Islamic times onwards. Rather, the term refers to a constantly evolving, highly cosmopolitan musical tradition, performed solely in Arabic, that accepted and adopted musical influences from both Byzantium and Persia (and possibly Africa as well), yet remained quite distinct from the traditions of those civilizations, and which subjugated outside influences to a core set of aesthetic ideas about song-forms, rhythms, and metres dictated by the primacy of Arabic poetry. It is in this sense that the term "Arab music" remains valid and it is this complex amalgam of traditions and influences, constantly changing and absorbing new material, but held together by a remarkably distinctive aesthetic, that Arabs brought with them to Spain when they conquered it in 711 C.E.

Arab Music in al-Andalus

Except, of course, that the "Arabs" did not conquer "Spain." Rather, two multilingual, multiethnic, complex societies came into contact and one successfully conquered the other. On the Iberian side was a society dominated and ruled by a tiny Germanic-speaking minority, the Visigoths, who may have numbered no more than 300,000 out of a total population of six million, and who were at the time of the invasion divided over the question of the royal succession. Next in status were the Ibero-Romans, a landed noble class with roots in the earlier Roman conquest and domination of the peninsula, followed by remnants of a number of other indigenous and invading peoples such as the Basques, Celts, and Suevi, and, at the very bottom of the social system, Jews who lived nearly as slaves in the final years of Visigothic rule. On the other side, the invading Muslim forces were equally diverse in origin and included Arabs, Egyptians, new converts from diverse groups in the Eastern Mediterranean, Berbers and other North Africans (and quite possibly a few descendants of the Vandals who had been chased out of Iberia by the invading Visigoths and who then settled in North Africa), and their ranks may well have included native speakers of Arabic, Aramaic, various Berber languages, Coptic, Germanic, Latin/Romance, and Byzantine Greek.

The new Islamic society, on its way to becoming an empire, was structured in a manner remarkably similar to that of Visigothic Iberia: the ruling class of Arab Muslims was few in number and was additionally divided into rival Northern and Southern tribal confederations; next came non-Arab converts to Islam of many different backgrounds, followed by Christians and Jews, who were recognized as "People of the Book," and then non-monotheists, whose presence was scarcely and only temporarily tolerated. In 711 this multiethnic, multilingual military force conquered the Iberian peninsula, and, like the Romans a few centuries earlier, brought a foreign language (Arabic rather than Latin), a foreign culture (Islamic rather than Roman), and a foreign religion (Islam rather than the Greco-Roman gods and later Christianity), and eventually brought a significant number of colonists (from North Africa and the Eastern Mediterranean rather than the Italian Peninsula) as well. Neither Roman nor Islamic culture was indigenous to the Iberian Peninsula, and both were promulgated by military conquest.

Most crucial to the argument made here, however, is that these two cosmopolitan societies also possessed a variety of different musical traditions rooted in diverse regional, urban, ethnic, linguistic, and sectarian communities, about many of which, unfortunately, we know extremely little.

From the first decades of Islamic rule in al-Andalus, during which political power was exercised by a series of short-term governors dispatched from Damascus, there is little to no evidence of musical life in this westernmost outpost of the new Islamic Empire. But by the end of the eighth century C.E., after only a few short decades of unified rule under the Umayyad Andalusian dynasty, it is clear that a vibrant musical culture had taken root and was being actively patronized by the Cordoban Emirs, particularly al-Hakam I and 'Abd al-Rahman II. The primary source for Andalusian music in this period until very recently was *The Scented*

Breeze from the Tender Branch of al-Andalus and Mention of its Vizier Lisan al-Din Ibn al-Khatib (*Nafh al-tib min ghusn al-Andalus al-ratib wa-dhikr waziriha Lisan al-Din ibn al-Khatib*), an historical compilation assembled by Ahmad al-Maqqari (d. 1632). In recent decades, however, two new sources have come to light that provide a far more detailed understanding of the formation of early Andalusian music: 1) the section of *Kitab al-Muqtabis* by the eleventh-century author Ibn Hayyan (d. 1076), published in 2003, from which al-Maqqari drew most of the materials for his biography of the famous ninth-century musician Ziryab; and, 2) a section of the fourteenth-century encyclopedic work *Masalik al-absar* (*The Paths of Perception*) by Ibn Fadl Allah al-'Umari (d. 1349), which contains the biographies of some eighteen hitherto-unknown Andalusian and North African musicians from this period.

The comparison of Ibn Hayyan's original biography of Ziryab to the highly selective summary transmitted centuries later by al-Maqqari shows that the latter author very deliberately created a legendary, almost superhuman, image of the singer Ziryab, an image that bears little resemblance to that held by his contemporaries or found in the earliest historical texts (Reynolds, "Al-Maqqari's Ziryab"). More significant to the present argument, however, are the biographies of singers transmitted by Ibn Fadl Allah al-'Umari, which provide the earliest evidence of musical hybridization and innovation in al-Andalus:

Sulaym, a client [*mawla*] of al-Mughira, son of al-Hakam: A man who was fortunate in his patrons and who rose until he saw the stars draw near ... He learned singing [*tarab*] from emissaries who came to [al-Hakam] from the Christians [*al-nasara*]. It was ordered that they be delayed and [Sulaym] was put in charge of them until their departure. He mastered their art and learned it thoroughly. Then al-Mughira, son of al-Hakam, brought him an Iraqi singing-girl who had been selected for him from the women's quarters ... She taught him [Iraqi] singing [*ghina'*] until he became proficient and he [then] combined the Iraqi singing with what he had gathered [from the Christians]. There occurred sessions between the two of them in the gathering [*majlis*] of al-Mughira more delicate than dawn breezes and more aromatic than fragrant trees ... (Ibn Fadl Allah 10:385)

From this same source we also learn of one Hisn ibn 'Abd ibn Ziyad, from North Africa ("the opposite shore") who came to Cordoba as a singer, but who apparently converted to Christianity and then fled northwards into Christian lands. There he remained for many years, but eventually returned to the sanctuary of Islam, "having earned nothing except some songs after many long years" in the North [*wa-raji'a ma kasaba illa al-ghina' ba'd tul al-sinin*], songs which he then proceeded to perform in al-Andalus (Ibn Fadl Allah 10:390–1). Sa'idah [Sa'iduh?] ibn Buraym, in contrast, was a Christian in Cordoba who converted to Islam, fell in love with Arab music, studied singing with teachers there and eventually became such a star that he travelled to the East and performed to acclaim in Cairo, Damascus and Baghdad. If we add to these biographies the already-famous accounts transmitted by al-Maqqari of Qalam ["Reed Pen"], the Basque slave-girl who was sent to Medina to be trained as a singer and was then purchased for the Emir 'Abd al-Rahman II, and of Mansur, the famous Jewish musician of the courts of al-Hakam I and 'Abd al-Rahman II, we have a portrait of a vibrant musical life in Cordoba that incorporated Christians, Muslims and Jews, as well as musical innovations and influences from a number of directions. The central element that held these diverse elements together, the very core of the tradition, was Arabic poetry.

Arabic Poetry and the Role of Rhyme

Arabic poetry was distinctive in this period in that it was composed not only in regular metres but also with obligatory mono-end rhyme such that every verse within a poem ended in the same syllable. Although certain ancient cultures possessed various types of metre, no other culture in the Mediterranean or Middle East used regular end-rhyme. It was not found in Sumerian, Babylonian, Akkadian, Ancient Egyptian, Hebrew, Greek, Latin, Persian, Aramaic, Berber or any other neighbouring language. Rhyme was not unknown in Latin, but it was used as an occasional embellishment *within* verses (much as assonance or alliteration is used in modern English poetry), and not as a structuring element. Indeed, Arabic was nearly alone in the world during this period in its use of regular end-rhyme. To the East, one must look as far afield as China to find anything remotely parallel (and Chinese end-rhyme is a very distinct phenomenon due to its tonal nature), while to the West, the frequent use of alliteration, assonance and half-rhyme in Irish Gaelic and Welsh may go as far back as the seventh and eighth centuries.

The use of end-rhyme as a structuring device (rather than an occasional embellishment) is critical to the development of precisely those poetic and musical traditions in which proponents of the "Arab hypothesis" see evidence of Arabic influence. In this context, the oft-cited passage by Alvarus of Cordoba, written circa 850, in which he complains that the Christian young men of that city were scarcely able to pen a letter in Latin competently but were all proficient in the composition of Arabic poetry, is of particular interest. The passage is normally cited as evidence of the increasing linguistic "arabization" of the Christian population of al-Andalus in the ninth century, for it appears that, at least in the capital, many Christian men were already more literate in Arabic than they were in Latin:

> Alas! Christians do not know their own law, and Latins do not use their own tongue, so that in all the college of Christ there will hardly be found one man in a thousand

who can send correct letters of greeting to a brother [in Latin]. And a manifold crowd without number will be found who give out learnedly long sentences of Chaldean [= Arabic] rhetoric … (*Corpus scriptorum Muzarabicorum* 1:314; cited in Zwartjes 7)

I would like to argue, however, that it is the phrases *following* this complaint which are the most important and that their significance seems to have escaped the notice of scholars. The passage is fraught with awkward phrasing (Roger Wright declared the final passages almost "unintelligible"), and it has been published and analysed in a variety of different, conflicting ways (see Zwartjes 7). Ironically, Alvarus's complaint about bad Latin is itself couched in rather bad Latin! However, it seems clear that he is struggling here to explain the structure of Arabic poetry to his northern Christian brethren, and he does so in a manner that I believe reveals that he had rather detailed knowledge of Arabic poetics. To demonstrate the difficulty in interpreting this passage, I quote here Gil's translation, followed by a translation by Karla Mallette which incorporates suggestions by Suzanne Akbari, Brian Stock and Jill Ross, all of whom I thank for their assistance:

So that from *the more sophisticated song of those people* they embellish their final clauses metrically and in more polished beauty with *the bond of a single letter*, according to the demands of that tongue, which closes all phrases and clauses with *riming vowels* and even, as is possible for them, the various expressions containing the letters of the whole alphabet are all metrically reduced to *one ending or to a similar letter*. (*Corpus scriptorum Muzarabicorum* 1:314–15)

They can even make poems, *every line ending with the same letter*, which *display greater beauty and more skill* in handling meter than the Gentiles [i.e., the Arabs] themselves possess. And as the idiom of that language requires, which *ends the hemistiches* [*commata et cola*] with all vowels [or "long vowels"], in rhythm – or rather, as befits them, in meter – the letters of all the alphabet are constrained, by means of a very great variety of diverse words [or "inflections" or "styles of speaking"], to *one ending or a similar letter*. (Karla Mallette, personal communication 2/25/08)

A number of the details in Alvarus's description are obscure and require more detailed study of other Latin and Arabic texts for elucidation: Why does he repurpose a term normally used to designate a certain kind of word division in Latin manuscripts, typically written "per cola et commata," to describe (apparently) the hemistichs of Arabic verse? What distinction is he making between "rhythm" and "meter"? Why does he describe rhyme at some points as a single letter and at others as being a vowel or long vowel? Some of the most confusing elements of this description seem to betray a rather detailed knowledge of the Arabic "science of rhymes" [*'ilm al-qawafi*], which analyzes rhyme primarily by the final consonant of a word which is termed the *rawiyy* or "binding letter" (from a verb that means, among other things, "to twist rope" and "to bind something on the back of a camel"), an interesting parallel to Alvarus's use of *constringo* (to bind fast, tie up). In addition, little importance in Arabic is placed on the preceding vowel, but the rules of rhyme dictate that any vowel occurring *after* the final consonant must remain constant in all of the rhyme words, although, by poetic license, the poet may choose to drop all of the case-endings from the words at the ends of the verses and rhyme solely on the final consonant, and occasionally, though it is considered a "weakness," the poet may use a different, though similar consonant (L for N, for example). It is thus not surprising that Alvarus might have difficulty expressing all of these possibilities clearly! In this case, knowing the Arabic system well may have greatly hindered his attempts to offer a simple description. In addition, it is possible that Alvarus's terminology regarding hemistichs shows that he is aware that the opening verse of an Arabic poem traditionally rhymed *both* at the end of the first hemistich (i.e., just before the medial caesura), and also at the end of the verse.

A full analysis of Alvarus's statements will have to await a future study, but for the moment, the critical observation is that Alvarus's addressees are apparently not familiar with the principle of end-rhyme, and Alvarus himself has difficulty expressing the concept. This would seem to be important evidence against the long-held claim of Romance philologists that rhymed poetry was a widespread, common phenomenon among speakers of Vulgar Latin/Romance, but one which, due to its popular nature, did not find its way into the written record until the late tenth century. If rhymed poetry were a common phenomenon in the spoken language of the Iberian populace, Alvarus could simply have compared Arabic poetry to the songs of the common folk, which he did not, and he presumably should also have had an easier time expressing the concept in Latin if such a tradition had existed.

Certainly no aspect of the overall debate regarding Arabic influence has engendered more discussion than the mid-twentieth-century discovery of the Romance *kharjas* at the end of a handful of some of the earliest Arabic *muwashshahs* (Stern). Some scholars have read these closing verses as fragments of larger Romance-language songs that were quoted at the end of the Arabic, and may even have indicated the melody to which they were to be sung; others have pointed out that these verses are in fact bilingual, and not solely in Romance, and if they were indeed snippets of songs from Iberian oral tradition, they would seem to indicate a very pervasive state of bilingualism; and finally, others have rejected the idea that these verses were ever part of independent Romance songs and argued that they were probably composed or at the very least heavily reworked by Arabic-speakers (see Zwartjes). The most powerful argument for this last interpretation is that the rhymes of the bilingual *kharjas* obey the Arabic, rather the Romance, rules for rhyming. Since there is an overlap between the two systems, many of the end-rhymes in the *kharjas* are acceptable in both Arabic and Romance, but no examples demonstrate patterns of Romance rhyme that conflict with the Arabic rules of rhyming, hence some amount of "reworking" the material seems to have been present (Zwartjes 158–79).

While the issue of metre, and to a slightly lesser extent rhyme, has been studied by scholars in some detail (see Heijkoop and Zwartjes), two key elements have not been given sufficient treatment, elements which are equally fundamental to the emergence of the *muwashshah* and *zajal* and are deeply intertwined: strophic structure and musical structure. Scholars arguing for the Arabic origin of the *muwashshah* and *zajal* have argued primarily from evidence of a variety of different multi-rhyme experiments in Arabic in the centuries previous to the appearance of those genres, and have been at pains to offer various explanations for the metrical irregularities found in these poems. But they have ignored a highly significant, indeed central, problem: Arabic did not possess strophic or stanzaic forms, and this was as much of a revolution as (and musically in fact a more significant one than) the shift from mono-end-rhyme odes to multiple-rhymed songs. To understand how radical a break strophic poetry was within the Arabic tradition, we must first examine the musical structure of Arabic courtly song as it existed in the early Islamic centuries.

The Musical Structure of Arabic Song from *Sawt* to *Muwashshah*

Al-Isbahani's *Book of Songs* provides a great deal of technical information about early Arabic songs, though not, of course, the melodies themselves, since there was no commonly used method of musical notation. The process of creating a song (*sawt*) is made clear through hundreds of examples cited in his work. The composer of a song (who was usually, though not always, a singer) selected a small number of verses (usually two to six) from a longer, pre-existing mono-end-rhyme poem, which might already have been centuries old at the time the song was composed (the use of verses by pre-Islamic poets as song lyrics, for example, remained common even in the tenth century). If the composer was not a gifted performer, the song might be taught to a singer, often a female slave-singer, who gave the song its debut performance. If that first performance took place before a famous or high-ranking person, al-Isbahani noted that historical information, along with the song's lyrics, melodic mode, and rhythm. If a later composer or singer reworked the song and created a new or improved version, which might be in a different melodic mode or rhythm, this information was recorded as well. In his fullest accounts of particular songs, al-Isbahani would therefore include the name of the poet along with a biography and possibly information about the history of the poet's tribe, followed by the name of the composer along with biographical information, the name of the singer and an account of his or her life (if this person were separate from the composer), an account of the debut performance (if this were memorable in any way), and information about other versions, as well as any particularly amusing or unusual anecdotes in any way connected to this song.

Though the melodies themselves have not survived, numerous passages indicate that the *sawt* was musically quite complex, that it was the repertory of highly trained professional singers, and that the performance of a *sawt* often involved elaborate improvisation and verbal artistry. Here is a brief anecdote that gives some indication of the musical complexity of a fine *sawt*. The original poem was composed by one Ibn Yasin, a little-known poet who was, however, a friend of the great composer Ishaq al-Mawsili. The music was composed by Ishaq in the rhythm "heavy light" [*khafif thaqil*] and al-Isbahani comments that "this song is one of Ishaq's eternal and most extraordinary compositions" [*wa-hadha al-sawt min awabid Ishaq wa-bada'i'ih*] (al-Isbahani 5:427). The song text uses only two verses from the original poem, and the theme is one of the most common in ancient Arabic poetry – the poet spies the traces of a campsite where his beloved once stayed and the fading traces of human habitation remind him of the ephemerality of life and love:

The traces and the remains have been abandoned by the people,
They have grown wild after the tribe's departure and are now a desert wasteland.

[*Al-tululu wa-l-dawarisu faraqatha al-awanisu
Awhashat ba'da ahliha fa-hiya qafrun basabisu.*]

Al-Isbahani then transmits the following account of the song's performance for the Caliph al-Wathiq as reported by Yazid ibn al-Muhallabi (note: Ma'bad was one of the greatest composer/singers of an earlier generation):

I was with [the Caliph] al-Wathiq and [the singing-girl] Saja, to whom Ishaq had given the song [to be sung] for the caliph, and [al-Wathiq] said to Mukhariq and 'Alluya [two other singers]: "By God if Ma'bad were alive today he would never be able to compose anything to compare to this song of Ishaq's!" They responded, "Yes, O Commander of the Faithful, it is good." [Al-Wathiq] grew angry and said to them, "Is that all you have to say?" Then he went to Ahmad ibn al-Makki and said, "God save me from these two fools! The first verse of this song is but four words ... Look and see whether there is any technique in the art of singing that Ishaq did not manage to put into these four words! He started [the song] out in *nashid* and then followed that with *basit*, in it he shouts and he coos, [in some places] he gives preponderance to the melody and [in others] he steals from it, and he did all of this in four words! Have you ever heard of anyone among the ancients or the moderns who has composed the like or is even capable of this?" (al-Isbahani 5:426–7)

Clearly the artistry described here was not accomplished in a single line of singing, but rather the four words appear to have been repeated a number of times, worked and reworked in the composition, perhaps first in free, unmeasured fashion similar to the modern Arabic *mawwal*, and then in measured music (this is the most common interpretation among scholars for the terms *nashid* and *basit*). At some points the singer cries out, singing at full volume (literally "shouting"), and at others he sings tenderly, cooing like a dove; at some points the composition forefronts the melody, perhaps in long melismatic phrases on a single syllable, and at other points the composer "steals from" the melody and forefronts the words instead, perhaps in a single-note *recitativo*. We cannot reconstruct the melodies or even the structures of these works, but from this and hundreds of other anecdotes we can derive an understanding of the courtly *sawt* of this era as a musically complex, highly professional form of singing.

Performances also involved intricate ornamentation and modulations, making them difficult for non-professionals to sing. The thirteenth-century Tunisian author Ahmad al-Tifashi, for example, wrote of hearing a female slave-singer improvise for two hours on a single verse of poetry and of hearing an Andalusian male singer embellish one verse with seventy-six *hazzat* (shakes or trills). Al-Tifashi also drew a distinction between "light" songs and "heavy" songs in the Andalusian repertory, noting that the "heavy" songs could only be performed by the most highly skilled of singers (Liu and Monroe 37). All of this evidence indicates a musical structure and style that was diametrically opposed to that of the *muwashshah* and *zajal*.

The most basic musical structure of the Andalusian strophic genres consists of two melodic units that alternate in step with the rhyme-scheme of the poem. The rhyme-scheme itself consists of two alternating sections: in one section the rhyme remains constant, and in the second section there is a new rhyme at each recurrence, such that a typical rhyme-scheme might be AAA BB CCC BB DDD BB, and so forth. In this case, the two melodies typically alternate in exactly the same pattern: xxx yy xxx yy xxx, etc. Ibn Sana' al-Mulk in his twelfth-century treatise on the structure of the *muwashshah* alludes to this melodic structure, and nearly all surviving *muwashshahs* display some close variant of this pattern (Reynolds, "Musical Aspects"). Thus, over the course of a five-strophe *muwashshah* (which Ibn Sana' al-Mulk claims was the norm), for example, one of the melodies would be repeated no fewer than fifteen times, and the second would be sung ten to twelve times, depending upon whether the song started with an opening *matla'* (opening verses of the recurring rhyme). Add to this the possibility of repeating the *matla'* as a refrain, a practice which appears to have been known at least in the medieval Jewish community (Monroe, "Maimonides on the Mozarabic Lyric"), and the second melody might recur as many as twenty times in a single song! This was a radical break from the aesthetics of the *sawt* tradition with its intricate ornamentation, verbal artistry, and improvisation. Even a cursory glance at the texts of a *sawt* of only two to six verses in length, and a *muwashshah* of some twenty-five or more verses, reveals that a tremendous shift has taken place, one in which the focus has moved from intricate musical interpretation of a very short text with a single rhyme to a rather straightforward musical interpretation of a lengthy text embellished with intricate rhymes.

The simplicity of the *muwashshah*'s musical structure (two alternating melodic units), the constant repetition of the tunes (ten to twenty or more times in a single song), and the relatively unelaborated singing style probably all contributed to its popularity. If the courtly *sawt* was a genre that could only be sung by highly trained professionals, here was a genre that nearly everyone could sing. Ibn Khaldun may have been indicating something along these lines when he wrote that *muwashshahs* "were appreciated by all the people, both elite and the masses, due to the ease of grasping them and the familiarity of their style" ["li-suhulat tanawulihi wa-qurb tariqatihi" (Ibn Khaldun 2:767)]. Strophic songs are to a great extent *designed* to be easily memorized and sung, and are a quintessentially popular form.

Thus the *muwashshah* and *zajal* genres represented several distinct breaks from the earlier Arabic poetic and song traditions. The issues of metre and rhyme have been dealt with extensively by scholars, but the dramatic and sudden appearance of the strophe along with the binary melodic structure, which together represent a far more radical and revolutionary development than those in metre or rhyme, have been for the most part ignored. The evidence presented above would appear to suggest that the *muwashshah* and *zajal* emerged as hybrid forms that brought together the Arabic concept of end-rhyme, the Romance concept of strophe, and a simple musical structure which may have been drawn from the folk music of any one of the many different peoples represented at that time in al-Andalus (Iberian, Arab, Berber, Germanic, Celtic, or Basque). Some scholars argue for a pre-existing Romance rhyme tradition, but even if this were the case, it would seem that, at the very least, the prestige of Arabic poetry in the early Middle Ages helped elevate rhyme from the level of "folk poetry" to that of high culture. Given the lack of musical notation from any of the possible source traditions in this time period, it is simply impossible to know the origins of the basic musical structure of the *muwashshah* and *zajal*. But it is precisely this distinctive musical structure that allows the "Arab hypothesis" to be put to the test in at least one case – that of the Occitan troubadours.

Muwashshah and Troubadour Repertories Compared

I originally approached the musical repertory of the Occitan troubadours with a somewhat peculiar aim in mind. Since there is no extant medieval musical notation for Arabo-Andalusian music, and if one assumed the "Arab hypothesis" to be correct (i.e., that Andalusian music had indeed deeply influenced the music of the troubadours), might it not be possible to "recuperate" some sense of medieval Andalusian music by studying the music of the troubadours? The results, however, were very surprising.

There are some 2,500 surviving Occitan troubadour lyrics, of which 246 songs (almost exactly ten per cent) have come down to us with musical notation preserved in four separate manuscripts using three different systems of notation. The interpretation of these early notational systems has been the subject of great scholarly debate, for while they give a fairly clear idea of pitch, the question of how long each note was held, and thus the overall rhythmic structure of the music, is much more difficult to determine (Aubrey). The challenge therefore was to determine, given the absence of notation from the Arab side and the gaps of what can be known for certain from the early Troubadour notations, if there were any aspect that could be reliably compared. Fortunately, the one structural element of which we can be rather certain from the Arab side is the close relationship between the rhyme scheme and the musical structure, and this same element can be examined without any difficulties in the Occitan materials, since it has nothing to do with the problematic issues of rhythm or the duration of notes.

When described in poetic terms, the parallels between the troubadour songs and Arabic *muwashshahs* are striking: they were both composed as songs (and are not poems set to music); they are both strophic and structured by complex patterns of end-rhymes; the earlier examples in both traditions use simpler rhyme-schemes and later examples develop increasingly intricate patterns of rhymes; there is a tremendous range and variety of different rhyme-schemes; both traditions use a semi-refrain in which the rhyme returns but with different words; and certain examples close with a distinct set of verses (*kharja/tornado*). Add to this the parallels in content such as the shared tropes of distance from the beloved, love as sickness, love as madness, the lover as vassal or servant to the beloved, the pleasure of the pains of love, hallucinating visions, nearness to death, etc., and the similarity in the *dramatis personae* of the "love worlds" in both bodies of poetry including the lover, the beloved, the watcher, the slanderer, and the messenger, and it is difficult indeed not to expect to find some sort of echo of the musical structure of the *muwashshah* in these songs.

In the Arabic *muwashshah*, as we have seen above, the melody changes when the rhyme does. This relationship, however, simply does not exist in the troubadour repertory – the melodic structure of the troubadour songs is entirely independent of their rhyme schemes. Melodies change in the middle of sequences of repeated rhymes and remain the same even when the rhyme changes. Rhyme and melody simply do not mirror each other, and in the corpus of 246 songs that possess musical notation there is not a single example where melody and rhyme changes are perfectly synchronized. This is an extraordinary and radical difference from the Arabic tradition. The two simply do not seem to be related.

The musical structure of the Arabic *muwashshah* is quite straightforward and highly repetitive. There is little possibility that a professional or skilled musician could have heard *muwashshahs* performed without walking away with a clear idea of the musical structure of this genre. Yet for all of the parallels in content and poetic structure, these two traditions are wildly divergent in their basic musical ideas. In one, the element of rhyme and melody are synchronized like clockwork and rarely if ever take separate paths, while in the other, the two elements are essentially unrelated and unfold completely separately from one another. This does not, of course, mean that the Occitan troubadours were never exposed to Arab music and poetry, but rather that when they composed their songs they did not choose to imitate the structure of the Arab *muwashshah* and *zajal*. They may well, however, have been imitating the more prestigious Arab *sawt* tradition, the courtly song that they would have been much more likely to have heard in the courts of Pedro I of Aragon or Alfonso VI of Castille and Leon (who married two different sisters of William IX of Aquitaine, dubbed "the first troubadour," *and* the daughter [or daughter-in-law] of King al-Mu'tamid of Seville), both of whom are believed to have been literate in Arabic. This comparison shows only that the musical structure of the medieval Andalusian *muwashshah* was not that used by the troubadours.

It is also important to note that this comparison of musical structures says nothing about possible Arabic *literary* influence on Occitan troubadour poetry (as noted above, the parallels are indeed striking), but it does strike at the heart of the most oft-repeated arguments for *musical* influence. On the other hand, already by the time of the thirteenth-century *Cantigas de Santa María* we are in a different world, a world in which very similar musical structures can be found in both Christian and Muslim Iberia and where much fruitful work remains to be done.

Conclusion

Iberia and the nascent Islamic Empire were highly complex, multilingual, multiethnic, multisectarian, cosmopolitan societies when they met. Early Arab music was an art form performed by professionals of many different backgrounds, which absorbed and reworked influences from several other cultures while maintaining a clear aesthetic core grounded in Arabic poetry that allowed diverse musical elements to be incorporated into the whole without losing its distinctiveness. The early historical evidence from al-Andalus shows a vibrant musical culture in which Christian, Jewish and Muslim singers performed before Muslim, Christian and Jewish patrons. There is evidence from even the earliest period of musicians who learned more than one song tradition, musicians who performed music from one community to patrons of another, musicians who actively combined different styles of music, and others who created innovative new styles entirely on their own. The song forms for which al-Andalus would later be famous appear to have combined the basic principles of Arabic rhyme with Romance strophic forms and briefly maintained a bilingual structure in the *kharja*, which, however, appears to have been regulated by the Arabic concept of rhyme for the short period of its existence. The melodic structure of these strophic forms was a radical departure from the courtly music of the period, though it may have borne some affinity with more popular song forms. Although there is a tremendous affinity between the poetic structure and the most common themes of Occitan troubadour songs and those of the Arabic *muwashshahs*, the one musical element that can be compared with some degree of certainty given the limitations of the extant documentation is not shared by these two repertories.

All of these elements – innovation, change, independent development, hybridization, bilingualism, demographic mixing, and multiple influences – argue against *both* the "European nationalist" version of Iberian music history (in which Christian music developed unsullied by "Moorish" influences) *and* the "Arab hypothesis" (in which musical influences flowed westward through al-Andalus from Muslim Arabs to Christian Spaniards in unidirectional transmission). Instead, the evidence points to complex genealogies and patterns of cross-fertilization that resist being captured in simple master narratives, but that, on the other hand, show the medieval musical world to be far more familiar and comparable to our own.

12 Sicilian Poets in Seville: Literary Affinities across Political Boundaries

WILLIAM GRANARA

I veri legami tra Spagna e Sicilia araba non appartengono dunque alla storia politica e militare, quanto a quella della civiltà e della cultura.

Francesco Gabrieli

[The true links between Arab Spain and Sicily, therefore, pertain not to political and military history, but rather to the history of civilization and of culture.]

Spain and Sicily: Like Mother and Daughter

In the winter of 1184, a severely damaged ship returning from Mecca floated miraculously to safety to the port city of Messina on the northeast coast of Sicily. On board was Ibn Jubayr, traveller-scholar and poet from the city of Granada, who survived the ordeal and lived to tell about it. His account of the storm at sea, the ship's wreckage, pilgrims bellowing in fear, and the anticipated anxiety of entering an unknown foreign country ruled by an enemy people would end on a positive note with the appearance of King William II, who personally came to the shore and offered the stranded and desperate pilgrims a helping hand. In a similar vein, Ibn Jubayr's later diary entries of his days in Sicily, replete with contradictory reports of cross-cultural conflict and coexistence, reveal much about the ways Sicily and Spain interacted throughout the Islamic periods of their history. Having survived the tumultuous landing, and given time to observe and reflect, Ibn Jubayr delivers his oft-quoted observation: "It suffices to say that Sicily is the daughter of al-Andalus in the splendor of its buildings, the abundance of its fertile lands, and the prosperity of life. It is blessed with all sorts of fruits and vegetation" (Ibn Jubayr 295–300).

It has been an age-old custom to pair Muslim Sicily with Muslim Spain, and there is much to justify the comparison. Arab travellers and geographers coming to Sicily from Spain submitted to the temptation to compare. Closer to our own time, Francesco Gabrieli (1904–96) suggests that the constructions of Muslim Spain and Sicily's modern "histories" are linked in the academic relationship between Reinhart Dozy and Michele Amari, as reflected in their pioneering works, *Histoire des Musulmans d'Espagne* (1861) and *Storia dei Musulmani di Sicilia* (1872).[1] Both lands are situated north of the Mediterranean divide, where Christianity had long ruled. Both were subjected to internal divisions running along fault lines that pitted indigenous populations against a foreign ruler – i.e., the Visigoths in Spain and the Byzantines in Sicily – that facilitated the successful penetration of invading Muslim armies and their subsequent establishment of kingdoms that rivaled the great powers of the world. Both lands were blessed with clement weather, fertile land (as attested to by Ibn Jubayr), and an abundance of natural resources. Both Spain and Sicily lay at the crossroads of the Mediterranean world; and both, in the Islamic period, came to preside over diverse populations of Arabs, Berbers, Spaniards and Sicilians, Jews, Greeks, and Slavs, who eventually made their way to the forefront of trade, agriculture, science, crafts, industry, philosophy and culture. Both Muslim Spain and Muslim Sicily were defined as Islamic "frontiers," actively involved throughout their history in a holy war against Christendom that defined the contours of their foreign and domestic policies. And lastly, both were constantly plagued by perennial internal challenges to their social cohesion in the form of tribal or sectarian rivalries, Arab-Berber tensions, and the constant monitoring by vigilante religious communities over what were regarded as deviations from the righteous path.

On the other hand, there is much that differentiated and separated the two countries. The Muslim armies conquered Spain in a stunningly short period of time (711–16), aided and abetted by disenfranchised local Christian and Jewish populations. And the conquest of Spain was initiated and completed during the Umayyad caliphate (661–750), when at least the semblance of universal Islamic unity and legitimate sovereignty were still intact. This Iberian conquest, although launched from North Africa, was still connected to the Islamic Conquest, and thus was a victory for all of Islamdom. Sicily, by contrast, took seventy long years to fall to Islam, with massive Byzantine and local Christian resistance, and the Sicilian jihad was conceived and executed by the autonomous Aghlabid ruling family of Ifriqiya (r. 800–909), which at the time was embroiled in nasty domestic political squabbles. The conquest of Sicily was as much a local Aghlabid victory as a universal Muslim one. Furthermore, the establishment and longevity of the Umayyad emirate in Cordoba (756–1031), culminating in 'Abd al-Rahman III's reclaiming the title of "caliphate" in 929, gave Muslim Spain a period of political stability and cultural particularism that was only briefly achieved in Palermo (960–1000) before the Norman conquest began. And, finally, the contributions of Andalusian Mozarabs and Jews to the linguistic, cultural and religious matrix that created a uniquely "Andalusian" identity was absent during Muslim rule in Sicily. There were no substantive numbers of Jewish cultural intermediaries in Sicily until they appeared at the Court of Frederick II at the beginning of the thirteenth century, and the number of Byzantine Greek functionaries working at the Kalbid court in tenth-century Palermo is impossible to quantify through the meager extant sources.[2]

Political Frontiers and Cultural Boundaries

Any historical and cultural affinities or parallels that lay, realistically or abstractly, between the Arabs of Spain and the Arabs of Sicily by the last decades of the eleventh century were intersected by a series of internal, geopolitical, and religious tensions that kept the two worlds apart. There was, however, more than a trickle of Sicilian Muslims from Sicily to Spain at the time of the Norman invasion of Sicily, c. 1050. The main topic of this study, most of them were poets who sought refuge at the courts of al-Mu'tamid Ibn 'Abbad of Seville and other petty kings of al-Andalus. Apart from this group, there had not been a steady flow in discernible patterns or in significant numbers of Andalusian and Sicilian Arab cross-traffic. The first century of Muslim Sicilian history (831–909) witnessed sporadic excursions by sea-borne Andalusian merchant adventurers who made half-hearted attempts to meddle in domestic Sicilian squabbles. And occasional commercial and academic journeys created a modest degree of linkage between the two peoples. The majority of the Muslim Sicilians at the time were still primarily involved in (physical) jihad, and their contacts with the rest of the Muslim world were largely limited to the motherland of Ifriqiya. By the middle of the eleventh century, however, Sicilian civil institutions and culture were in full bloom; ironically, this period coincided with the Norman conquest that had recently begun its final descent from the Italian mainland. Thus, Sicilian-Andalusian connections were disrupted – or prevented – by both internal and external boundaries that make the Sicilian poets' exodus to Seville in 1060 somewhat extraordinary.

The facile linkage of Islamic Spain and Sicily as two *frontiers*, from both European and eastern Muslim perspectives, calls for an investigation to reveal more complicated reasons for the Sicilian poets' emigration to Seville in the eleventh century. Recent frontier studies provide a wider lexicon to help unravel some of the complexities that divided and united peoples in the medieval world. Eduardo Moreno makes a distinction among *unstable*, *enclosing*, and *expanding* frontiers that may be useful for us in understanding the lines of connection and separation between Palermo and Seville during the heyday of the petty kings. He defines an *unstable frontier* as one "whose limits change constantly depending on political, military, or diplomatic factors." An *enclosing frontier* separates "two distinctive and well-defined political, economic, social or cultural areas." And an *expanding frontier* is a "frontier of potential colonization … whose main feature is the occupation of land by settlers" (Manzano Moreno, "The Creation of a Medieval Frontier" 35).

In a variety of ways and for a host of reasons, both Islamic Spain and Sicily may be viewed, at different times, as frontiers of each of these types. First, they are *unstable* frontiers on both "foreign" and "domestic" fronts. By the very nature of their rise through military conquest, both realms lived in a perpetual state of war with Christendom — offensively in the early, golden years of conquest, and defensively when the Christian Reconquest gained the upper hand. Neither the Iberian peninsula nor the island of Sicily was ever completely conquered, nor did military confrontations ever cease. Regions and towns passed from one hand to another, and the boundaries that divided Islam from Christianity were forever changing. Internally, tribal and ethnic rivalries and religious and political ideologies clashed constantly to destabilize both realms. By the first decades of the eleventh century, the demise of the Umayyad Caliphate and the rise of the petty kings in Spain, and the downfall of the Kalbid Court and the division of Muslim Sicily among three local petty warlords, carved up the Dar al-Islam in both territories into a patchwork of warring fiefdoms competing for economic advancement and political legitimacy. Adding pressures to the precarious coexistence among these rival Muslim princes was the ominous rise of religious fundamentalism. In the onslaught of Christian aggression, the culture of love, wine, music and chivalry patronized by the various courts and their gilded entourages was aggressively contested by the resurgent voices of an assertive Maliki *ulema*, long the protectors of the urban and rural poor and guardians of strict orthodoxy, who came to represent the truest expression of popular discontent and resistance. The muscle flexing of the religious reformers triangulated the already-problematic relations between Muslims and Christians on the one hand and among Muslims on the other. In Spain, al-Mu'tamid Ibn 'Abbad's squabbles with Alfonso VI, which (as we will see) came to a head in 1086, were confounded by his unholy alliance with the fundamentalist, Qur'an-brandishing Almohad warlord, Yusuf Ibn Tashufin, graphically illustrating such a political triangle.

Second, from a broader geo-political perspective, Spain and Sicily, particularly as they related to each other, were *enclosing* frontiers. The Umayyad emirate and later caliphate in Cordoba (756–1031) had long viewed the Aghlabid allegiance to the Abbasid caliphate in Baghdad — even if merely a nominal or symbolic allegiance — as a potential venue for Abbasid attacks on their Umayyad nemesis. Then the Fatimids' ascension to power in Ifriqiya in 909, with their Shi'ite ideology and broad appeal to the disenfranchised Berber tribes, threatened Umayyad hegemony over the western provinces of the Maghreb. As long as both Aghlabid and Fatimid North Africa continued to exercise hegemony over Sicily, the island remained a potential enemy to Muslim Spain. Furthermore, the Umayyad-Fatimid rivalry for supremacy over the western Mediterranean, by land and sea, was largely played out through a series of proxy wars among the Berber tribes across North Africa, making travel between Spain and Sicily particularly hazardous. In this hostile political climate, the life of an itinerant court poet (among others) was seriously jeopardized.

Third, Spain and Sicily remained *expanding* frontiers by virtue of their *colonizing* projects. As conquerors of peoples with different religious, linguistic, and cultural traditions, the Muslim settlers built their own variegated and layered infrastructures that expanded and cut across ethnic, religious, and social boundaries. Religious conversions, new political alliances and allegiances, and the rise of various professional and social categories (guilds) and groupings – from the military and political elite and nouveaux-riches to travelling merchants, mercenaries, domestic and public slaves of all kinds, client clans and families, bureaucrats, pirates, adventurers, and men and women living on the margins of society – assimilated and dissimulated into new Andalusian and Siculo-Muslim identities, creating among themselves flexible and porous boundaries through which unlikely or improbable linkages were formed. While hostilities may have existed at the highest echelons of the state, human (social and economic) and cultural contacts forced themselves into the collectivity of everyday life.

Muslim Sicilian Poets in Exile

In the year 1078, one of Muslim Sicily's premier poets, 'Abd al-Jabbar Ibn Hamdis (1055–1132), chose self-imposed exile and, seeking fame and fortune as a court poet, traversed the North African littoral and made his way to the court of al-Mu'tamid Ibn 'Abbad, prince of Seville and noted poet in his own right. Ibn Hamdis was born in Syracuse in 1055 to a family from the Arabian tribe of al-Azd who had come to Sicily six generations earlier. Born into the privileged life of the landed gentry, his childhood coincided with the political disintegration of Sicily. By the time he left Sicily, Palermo had already fallen to the armies of the Norman Count Roger I, and it was only a matter of time before the southwest province of Noto, including Ibn Hamdis's beloved Syracuse, would follow suit (1091).[3]

This was a time of large-scale emigration of Muslims, and the scant information we have identifies specific destinations that strongly suggest that Spain and Sicily were not closely connected. Muslims loyal to the Fatimid-Kalbid government, predominantly bureaucrats and military personal, fled to Cairo; Maliki jurists and scholars returned to the motherland of Ifriqiya; highly accomplished scholars of philosophy and linguistics headed to Baghdad and points east. And poets went to al-Andalus. Thus Sulayman ibn Muhammad al-Tarabanshi (Ibn al-Qatta' 29) went first to Ifriqiya and then al-Andalus to reside among the petty kings. The work of poet Abu Sa'id 'Uthman ibn 'Atiq (Ibn al-Qatta' 50) survives only in a fragment of four lines praising al-Mu'tasim ibn Samaduh, prince of Almeria and a rival and enemy of al-Mu'tamid. Abu al-Hasan 'Ali ibn 'Abd al-Jabbar, a.k.a. Ibn al-Kamuni, emigrated to Al-Andalus and composed an elegy to Sicily during the height of the island's civil strife:

> Our abode, when we inhabited it,
> > lived in the shade of a sweet and fertile life;
> Security wrapped its blanket over it, then its very mention
> > departed with those who departed,
> And those who failed to give thanks for the blessings bestowed on them
> > were given the bitter instead of the sweet.   (Ibn al-Qatta' 58)

The poet known as Abu al-'Arab, Mus'ab ibn Muhammad ibn Abi al-Furat al-Qurashi, was born in Sicily in 423/1034; he migrated during the Norman invasions and arrived at the court of al-Mu'tamid in 1074. Among only a handful of Sicilian poets whose poetry survives in significant quantity, his verses articulate the bitterness of forced exile as he extols his new patron with the stock phrases of courage and generosity:

> I seek a cure in a gentle beloved's phantom
> > who quenches my bitter thirst when we meet,
> A phantom who fears not caution during a visit
> > even when the phantom's spy is a vigilant eye.
> Is it of the essence of time that we return to our closeness,
> > or does it suffice that we be as we were?
> How many a night gives us pleasure,
> > nights which seem to give us endless gifts of munificence.
> He is a valiant prince who commands an army vast in number,
> > marching like a visitor into the lands of the enemy.
> As though the bright morning fades as it bedecks itself with clouds
> > and the eye of the sun is speckled with motes and ash.
> You would say he is a pitch black night amidst the light of day,
> > or a frothy ocean amidst a stretch of dry land.
> It is as though the havoc he wreaks disperses them astray,
> > and the poet dedicates his verses to him with the voice of swords.

I was rescued and my life is renewed;
>   for the safety of a young man after great fear brings new life.
The days have done great and kindly deeds,
>   such that my today and tomorrow compete for his kindness.[4]

>   (Ibn al-Qatta' 99)

Ibn Hamdis's difficult first days in Seville, after what must have been a grueling journey, were magically reversed in a single night, according to an anecdote from the seventeenth-century historian al-Maqarri's *Nafh al-Tib*. Alone and depressed in an inn on the outskirts of Seville, despairing of receiving an audience with al-Mu'tamid, Ibn Hamdis made the decision to pack his bags and depart the following day. Suddenly a young page appeared in the dark of night, leading a horse with one hand and holding a lantern in the other, and summoned the dejected poet to meet the sultan. When he arrived at the palace, al-Mu'tamid offered him a seat and then asked him to rise and look out a window. In the distance was a glass ironsmith's furnace with two doors; a woman was opening and closing them to stoke the flames. Al-Mu'tamid suddenly unleashed a line of poetry describing the fire, and challenged Ibn Hamdis to match it or best it. After three quick rounds of poetic sparring, al-Mu'tamid was sufficiently impressed and invited Ibn Hamdis to join his royal retinue (al-Maqqari, *Nafh al-tib min ghusn al-andalus al-ratib* 3:616).

The anecdote – a wonderful snapshot of medieval court life and of the tricks of the trade of an itinerant court poet – defines in many ways the relationship between the two men and perhaps between the two countries. It draws attention to the power and importance of patronage in the world of medieval poets. Above all, it reinforces what we already know to be *de rigeur* for an aspiring poet: that wherever he might go, he must bring the proverbial trunk of poetic knowledge and lore – that is, the *philology* of centuries of poetic text and intertextuality, of countless words and stock phrases, of rhetorical devices and images, of metres and rhymes; that the poet be always ready to draw from his verbal sheath a line or two or even a whole poem, on the spot, on any given subject or theme, with mastery of the traditions and artistic originality; that he rise to the challenge and respond to the demands of the moment, using these tools to create a poetic statement that compacts the *worldliness* of the Arab culture and politics of his time.

The 'Abbadid court of Seville (1023–91) was a logical sanctuary for Sicilian émigré poets for a number of reasons. Al-Mu'tamid, like his father al-Mu'tadid (r. 1042–69) before him, was an enthusiastic supporter of culture, and he surrounded himself with talented bards as much to bolster his legitimacy vis-à-vis his rival petty kings and local warlords as to enhance his own skills as a poet.

The 'Abbadid project to re-create a court culture in the image of their Umayyad forebears at Cordova, who flourished a century earlier, can be best read as both nostalgia for the glory days gone by and the realization that Arab grandeur and Islamic eclecticism were both precious commodities in threat of extinction. Al-Mu'tamid's famous apology to his father composed in verse, his joint compositions and exchange of epistolary poems with his minister and poet-mate Ibn 'Ammar (whom al-Mu'tamid had killed in 1184 over what he considered to be an act of betrayal), his patronage and friendship with the Andalusian poet Ibn Labbana (d. 1113), and his hospitality to the Sicilians Abu al-'Arab and Ibn Hamdis all construct an image of a shared high Arabic culture linking Spain and Sicily.[5]

The poetry composed during his thirteen-year stint in Seville reflects Ibn Hamdis's own artistic formation and sensibilities as a court poet on the one hand, and defines the parameters of a shared literary terrain between Spain and Sicily on the other.[6] I cite here three of his pieces, richly representative of the artistic bonds between him and his new patron, for discussion: the first is a panegyric (*madih*) to al-Mu'tamid; the second, also a panegyric of sorts, is more properly an occasional poem, a congratulatory ode on al-Mu'tamid's victory at the Battle of Zallaqa in 1086 against Alfonso VI of Castille; and the third is a poem of correspondence in which Ibn Hamdis conveys his sympathies for al-Mu'tamid's demise and imprisonment.

The panegyric (*Diwan* #110) is a short 28-line poem that contains the familiar features of Ibn Hamdis's "insignia" panegyric (*madih*) — that is, explicit references or subtle allusions to his native land and his emotional responses to separation from it. Several evocations of Sicily in this poem suggest that it was composed early in his Seville period, soon after his arrival in 1078. The mood is optimistic and the tone sincere. The opening lines address the physical features of the subject (*mamduh*) and quickly move to his military qualities. The mixing of religious and profane imagery is powerful: by asserting that "the true believer becomes more devout" (line 4), and then following up with the epithet of "defender of the faith" (line 5), the author adjusts the tone of the poem to resonate with his Muslim audience. This strategy allows Ibn Hamdis to explode freely in a barrage of classical *jahili* (pagan) images, with lions' claws and swords dripping, drunk with blood, exemplary of what Suzanne Stetkevych calls "the metaphorical (and ritually symbolic) equivalence of blood and wine in the Arabic tradition, as drinking wine is a metaphor for quenching one's thirst for blood vengeance" (Stetkevych, *The Poetics of Islamic Legitimacy* 131).

The punning use of the word "al-mu'tamid" — at once the *nom de guerre* of the patron and an active participle meaning "relying upon" or "deriving strength from" — constructs a chain of divine command whereby the faithful subjects, including the poet himself, rely upon al-Mu'tamid, who in turn relies upon God. This conjures the image of the legitimate Islamic ruler, crucial to the post-scriptural understanding of jihad. The interlacing of religious (Islamic) and pagan (*jahili*) motifs, politically and artistically, continues with pairing tyranny to disbelief (*kufr*) and the evocation of the Battle of Uhud, an early battle between the Prophet's army and his Meccan enemies that ended in a Muslim defeat due to poor coordination and disobedience. Its evocation here may be inspired by the simple fact that the word "Uhud" fits into the rhyme scheme of the poem. However, the battle's symbolism in Islamic history as a warning against disunity and poor planning in the face of the enemy adds a contemporary and local meaning to the poem in light of the petty kings' warring among themselves and their apparent failure to resist the Christian Reconquest.

The last lines shift the praise from the qualities of might to that of magnanimity.

You spin the wheels of generosity,
     and your justice lends support to every man in need.
People who hope flock to you, and with your very mention
     they inhale the aroma of your musk and find a cure in you.
You never disappointed one seeking your magnanimity,
     and you never turned away a man in exile [*sadd*].
I now have no distance in my distant wandering from my homeland;
     since I departed you rendered *Hims* a country for me.
As a substitute for my closest kin I was given your kin;
     may God not separate me from them in all eternity.
How many of my people in far away lands does the earth embrace?
     I could not see any of them because of my separation.
The death of my father did not compel me to travel from your abode,
     though the death of a father greatly distresses the son.
You did not obstruct my path to return to them;
     you made my separation [*sifad*] from them a blessing [*safad*].
This most tender loving care, whose sweetness abounds in my heart,
     cools the scorching heat of my sorrow.   (Ibn Hamdis 170–1)

The reference to al-Mu'tamid as the provider of shelter for one without a home takes the poem from the abstract to the concrete: from the poetics of panegyric to the reality of the poet's arrival at the court. Sicily is linked to Spain on both levels. The first-person voice of the panegyrist allows this last segment to construct a boast without any rupture or departure from the general theme (*gharad*) of the poem. In these six lines, Ibn Hamdis collapses all of his personal experiences of departure from his homeland, his separation from kin who are now far away, the loss of his father while in exile (see the Elegy to the Father, *Diwan* #330), and his welcome into the court of al-Mu'tamid, whose loving care cools the fires of the poet's grief, bringing the panegyric to its culmination. We see here Suzanne Stetkevych's "mythic concordance" (Stetkevych, *The Poetics of Islamic Legitimacy* 35) between poet and patron, a ritual exchange by which al-Mu'tamid is elevated to the eternal panoply of the aristocratic poet-warriors and legitimate heirs to Arabo-Islamic political legitimacy, while Ibn Hamdis is rewarded with a sanctuary from exile and, more importantly, a forum from which to espouse his own Sicilian cause.

Eight years after that fortuitous evening when Ibn Hamdis first met and locked poetic horns with al-Mu'tamid, the 'Abbadid kingdom faced its greatest challenge from the Castilian Alfonso VI at the battle of al-Zallaqa (a plain in the area of Badajoz in southwest Spain). The battle ended in a highly publicized victory for al-Mu'tamid, but one that presaged his disastrous demise five years later. For the occasion, Ibn Hamdis composed and performed a public congratulatory ode.

The Castilians' position of strength, despite the Muslim victory, is recorded in Arabic historiography. Alfonso, smarting over al-Mu'tamid's failure to pay his tribute tax, demanded that his pregnant wife occupy the royal palace at the Madinat al-Zahra' compound,[7] home to the Umayyad caliphate during the golden age of Andalusian Islam. He also demanded that she be allowed to give birth inside the Grand Mosque of Cordoba. In a clear case of religious and political ribbing, the Christians intended to trespass the sacred spaces of the Muslims. To force the Muslims to host the delivery of his child, who might well lord over them someday in the not too distant future, was Alfonso's way of rubbing salt in their wounds. Behind his public posturing and muscle-flexing bravura lay al-Mu'tamid's realization that he could not defeat the Castilians on his own. And so he appealed for help to the much-feared Yusuf Ibn Tashufin – Berber warlord and founder of the Almoravid dynasty (1061–1147) – asking him to cross the Straits of Gibraltar.

Why an enlightened and cultured prince of a kingdom that reveled in the patrimony of religious, intellectual, and cultural tolerance and florescence would submit himself to a desert warlord on a mission of religious fundamentalism and political and cultural repression remains a question for the history books. The fifteenth-century historian al-Himyari reminds us that the other petty kings of al-Andalus warned al-Mu'tamid against this alliance. Al-Mu'tamid's response to them has survived as one of the great one-liners in Christian-Muslim polemics: "Herding camels," he replied, "is better than raising pigs" ["*ra'i al-jimal khayrun min ra'i al-khanazir*"]: better to stay with Muslims – even in the desert – than to stay with Christians here (M. al-Himyari 83–95).

Al-Mu'tamid's political gamble and his appeal to the rhetoric of jihad succeeded in bringing a military victory and a brief respite from Muslim factionalism in al-Andalus. Ibn Hamdis, as official court poet, was called upon to extol his patron and the happy occasion of the victory he designed. The challenge this time was no less daunting, as the exiled poet from Syracuse now stood in poetic judgment before the throngs of giddy celebrants, including a severely wounded al-Mu'tamid (according to al-Himyari's account) as well as an ambitious Berber warlord on a mission to restore Islamic civilization to its scriptural foundations. To meet the seemingly contradictory demands required of the *philology* of an accomplished Arabic court-poetic performance and the *worldliness* of the inauspicious victory of Zallaqa, Ibn Hamdis chose to stand on firm, canonical literary ground, opting for the conventional paradigm of the tripartite *qasida* to launch his congratulatory ode.

The poem may be divided as follows: lines 1–10 form a wine song (*khamriyya*); lines 11–16 constitute a battle poem (*harbiyya*); and lines 17–46 constitute the praise (*madih*) proper, in which the poet injects an invective (*hija'*) in lines 27–36, and which he completes with a supplicatory ending (*du'a'*) in lines 45–6:

I clothed the dear little daughters of the vine
>with the embellishments the remains of abodes used to be clothed with;
I followed the path of al-Hakami in pursuing them;
>how could I deviate from [the path of] this wise man's theme?
For what is the superiority of the abandoned ruins over fresh wine,
>which exudes musk into the breath of fresh air?
The love of wine is renewed in every heart,
>since wine rubs away the rust of anxieties.
In the days of old, I longed for the pleasures
>[that awaited me] in the old castle.
If I thirsted, then my cup was returned to me,
>just as the full breast is returned to the weaned child.
I would not ask a muted ruin to speak,
>as though it possessed the signs of one who speaks.
But rather I would ask for melodies from a lute,
>which arouse pleasures in the bosom of a gazelle.
And many a slumber would come to my inebriated drinking companions
>in which I chased away their dreams with these melodies.
The drinking companion would awake, as the eye of early morning
>still has the [shimmering] residue of the dark night.
As though the early morning, face to face with its darkness,

were a combatant looking down in disdain at its opponent.
As though the East, between the one and the other,
        were a battle line, in which Zanj and Rum come face to face …
In the abode of Ibn 'Abbad we alighted,
        and we were regaled with munificence from one so resolute.
Such that kings would lower their eyes
        to pay homage to the aura of the greatest king …
Your monotheism dissuaded [Alfonso] of his [trinitarian] polytheism,
        snipping at the hands of a fear, raging with anger.
In early morning he came with crosses that led the infidels astray
        and he concocted the stratagems of a mongrel army.
It was as though they [appeared] like devils,
        but you hurled at them the fire of stars.
Infidels, [although] their battle coats are made of armor,
        the whiff of their odor gives them away… .
So pray to your God who is worshipped, and make a sacrifice
        to Him of their leaders, one after the other.
And celebrate with divine guidance, and prepare for the enemy
        the punishment of war, with the most painful of pains.

(Ibn Hamdis 435–8)

The choice of the wine song instead of the customary *atlal* for the opening segment underscores both the festive mood of the occasion and the bonds of male companionship, especially in the aftermath of a ferocious battle, the epitome of homo-social bonding. Such events were often celebrated poetically through themes and images of wine, women, and song. Also, the metaphoric symbiosis of wine and blood, once again, allows for an ambiguous blending of the connotations of "getting drunk" and "taking vengeance," making Ibn Hamdis's choice of opener most appropriate to the occasion. The frequent allusions to the classical theme of the abandoned ruins (*atlal*) are coupled with the evocation of the celebrated wine-song poet [al-Hakami] Abu Nuwas (750–810), who composed the famous poem mocking the obsession with the hackneyed "abandoned ruins" theme in favour of the vitality and currency of the wine song. Ibn Hamdis manoeuvres within this playful paradox to champion the cause of wine while manipulating the emotional effects of the *atlal*. In so doing, he conjures up images of his own youth, his own lost loves, whose real meanings lie deep within the subtext of the poem. Moreover, his preference for the wine song as opener of the poem assures for himself the role of drinking companion and personal confidant to al-Mu'tamid, while at the same time linking Muslim Sicily to Muslim Spain through their shared historical circumstances.

The second segment shifts the poem from the wine-song to the battle scene, where the poet employs pairs of binary images: sleep and wakefulness, darkness (night) and light (morning), Zanj (Arabs) and Rum (Christians). But this segment is completely overpowered by the theme of the desert crossing (*rahil*) with its familiar *topoi* of vast hostile terrains and sturdy but exhausted she-camels with bleeding hooves. The sequencing of these two segments, the first of which bears the dominant themes of the abandoned ruins (*atlal*) and the second those of the desert crossing (*rahil*), suggests that Ibn Hamdis was at least overtly following the conventions of the classical tripartite qasida to the letter as well as in spirit. What renders this seemingly traditional sequencing ironic, playful, subversive, and quite contemporary for that matter, is the poet's boast that he follows the path of the great poetic rebel, Abu Nuwas. In sneering at poetic conventions, Ibn Hamdis elevates himself to the level of master panegyrist in the Arab tradition. This sequencing also allows Ibn Hamdis to work his favourite theme of Sicily as "abandoned ruin" into the poem, even at the level of subtext (see line 5: "In the days of old, I longed for the pleasures of the old castle").

Having captured the audience's attention and aroused their poetic emotions with the familiar themes of the *atlal/rahil*, while remaining well within the literary horizons of expectation during this highly public performance, Ibn Hamdis proceeds to the third and major segment of the qasida: praise (*madih*). Here, clusters of imagery include all too familiar variations on the theme of the patron's magnanimity, perspicacity, and noble Arab lineage. Attributes of might and sacredness portray him as "defender of the faith."[8] He immediately proceeds with an account of the battle through a series of binary images, vacillating between the sacred and profane, of praise for al-Mu'tamid and invective against Alfonso. Ibn Hamdis ends with a return to the wine-song, bringing the poem full circle, perhaps one last reminder to the audience of the festive occasion which has brought them all together. And to give a religious sanctity to what has transpired, the poet offers a prayer asking God to continue His guidance and support.

Under Siege: Homeland, *Convivencia*, and La Dolce Vita

As the Christian Reconquest in both Spain and Sicily were making deeper inroads into the shrinking realms of high medieval Arabo-Islamic political and military sovereignty, as linguistic and cultural polyphony were chipping away at literary and cultural orthodoxy and giving way to exciting new forms of expression, and as religious fanaticism was gaining wide popular appeal over a tired *secular humanism*, out-of-touch in its overly intellectual preciosity, the petty kings and their loyal entourages retreated to their palatial halls and pleasure palaces to face their fears and nurse their wounds, seeking from their poets, in impeccably traditional verses,

reassurance of their noble heritage, divine right to rule, military prowess and superhuman magnanimity. On the outskirts of the great urban centers, emirs took
solace in their "country estates" (*munya*, *muntazah*), where, after a hard-fought
battle or a strenuous hunt, the emir presided over an evening of wine, women,
poetry and song. Architectural heirs to the classical Roman hunting lodges that
dotted both the Iberian and Syrian landscapes in late antiquity (Ruggles 37–8),
these pleasure palaces continued to exist as favoured refuges for Spanish and
Sicilian princes, Muslim and Christian alike,[9] where the memories of past glories,
fantasies of grandeur, and illusions of power were meticulously preserved.

Ibn Hamdis composed a short poem in which he offers a glimpse of one
such evening: in this scene, a company of imbibers is seated around a brook into
which the server places rounds of wine; each man takes a cup as he desires and
returns the empty one, which sails back to the server. The poet likens the brook
to a great river, the guests to cities along the river, and the cups of wine to ships
sailing between them (Ibn Hamdis 192; Monroe, *Hispano-Arabic Poetry* 204–5).
More than a celebration of nocturnal male bonding in intoxication, the poem
may be read as a highly romanticized metaphor for the world of the medieval
Islamic Mediterranean, where ships sailed on calm waters and men drank merrily
in sumptuous, paradisiacal gardens.[10] It was a world far away from the reality of
Christian-Muslim wars of (re)conquest, of petty rivalries and religious fanaticism,
but one tenaciously adhered to by a small group of like-minded men who shared
a certain vision.

Al-Mu'tamid's fame and glory following his success against Alfonso VI were
short-lived. Five years later, in 1091, Yusuf ibn Tashufin returned to Seville with a
vengeance and put a violent end to the 'Abbadid emirate, sentencing al-Mu'tamid
and his family to a prison in the Maghrebi city of Aghmat, just south of modern Marrakesh. Evocative of that first encounter thirteen years before in which
patron and poet engaged in poetic sparring, Ibn Hamdis and al-Mu'tamid were
fated to exchange verses one last time. Both the occasion and the relationship
between the two poets had been totally altered. From his prison cell, al-Mu'tamid
addressed his poem to his former panegyrist and loyal boon companion, pon-
dering his own fate, expressing his painful longings for a home, a homeland,
and even his paradise lost, and wondering if there would ever be a return – questions, feelings, and poetic themes all too familiar to the Sicilian exile. Al-Mu'tamid
asks:

> Would that I knew if I shall ever again spend a night
>> with a garden before me and a pool of water behind me?
> In a grove of olive trees, the heritage of nobility,
>> where doves coo and birds warble?

In its towering Zahir, where the fine soft rain refreshes it,
>   while Thurayya [the Pleiades] beckons to us and we to it?
While the Zahir glances at us with its *Sa'd al-su'ud* [its luckiest constellation],
>   both of them jealously, for the much devoted lover is ever jealous?

Ibn Hamdis's response qasida waxes philosophical, in a tone of political resignation articulated well within the classical idiom:

Our affairs run counter to the decrees [of Fate],
>   while Fate is at times just to man and at times unjust … .
It ennobles all captives that it be said: "Muhammad is a stranger,
>   captive in the lands of the West."
Brave men sighed because of its manacles in its captivity,
>   and some of them are broken by misfortune in it …
Until now no sturdy camels on whom the rider gallops at dawn
>   have ever alarmed the night-flying sand grouse.
Nor has a generous man ever rejoiced at the wealth
>   a poor man puts into his hands.
You have protected God's religion with the best of protections,
>   as though you were its heart, and it the thought.
>   (Monroe, *Hispano-Arabic Poetry* 200–3)

Conclusion: Between Philology and Worldliness

Edward Said, in a chapter entitled "The Return to Philology" published in his posthumous *Humanism and Democratic Criticism* (2004), offers a new reading of the binary of *philology* and *worldliness* (secularism, in other contexts), saying that "Philology, an undeservedly forgotten and musty-sounding but intellectually compelling discipline, needs to be restored, reinvigorated, and made relevant to the humanistic enterprise in today's United States" (Said, *Humanism and Democratic Criticism* 6). In this essay, I have evoked *philology* and *worldliness* as concepts to shape our understanding of how Spain and Sicily interacted, both poetically and politically, during their Islamic periods. Said defines *philology* as "a detailed, patient scrutiny of and a lifelong attentiveness to the words and rhetorics by which language is used by human beings who exist in history," and (secular) *worldliness* as "a mechanism that allows for the changing bases for humanistic praxis regarding values of human life that are now upon us in this century" (Said, *Humanism and Democratic Criticism* 61). These definitions capture the time and place of the exiled Sicilian poets and their Andalusian patrons where obstinate loyalties to cultural traditions were constantly challenged by a radically changing world.

Ibn Hamdis's destabilized, itinerant and unpredictable life and poetic production belong to an era of Andalusian Islamic civilization that was as much "secular" as it was religious. At the time, the rivalries, insults, skirmishes, and even ferocious battles between Muslims and Christians were offset by great moments of cultural eclecticism, by bouts of religious and political tolerance, of intellectual curiosity and artistic experimentation, all permitted to exist and flourish through a humane understanding of Islamic jihad. The emotive power of the farewell verses cited above rests upon the lived experience of knowing the life of luxurious gardens, of male bonding, of hard fighting, hard drinking, and hard loving, and losing it forever in a split second. And perhaps, in the public square of the royal palace on that morning when he delivered his congratulatory ode to al-Mu'tamid on his victory at the Battle of al-Zallaqa, Ibn Hamdis was all too aware that the destructive forces of the world he came to extol in his poetic recollections lay not with the Christian "other" but rather with the extremist "self"; that the sweet life and the world of poetry begin to unravel not in a holy war with the Christians but in a unholy process of disunity, intolerance, and repression. If this is the case, then it is understandable why the Zallaqa poem, on such a solemnly Muslim occasion, was grounded in the bedrock of the classical qasida, why the sequence of themes faithfully follows its tripartite paradigm, why al-Mu'tamid's attributes are those of the Arabian warrior of ancient times, and why the invective against the enemy is as much poetic humour as it is religious invective.

What joined Ibn Hamdis of Syracuse to the hip of al-Mu'tamid Ibn 'Abbad of Seville was less a historical or geographical conjunction between Sicily and Spain, or a religious zeal and ethnic consanguinity, than a shared *philology* and *worldliness* that informed the ways the two men chose to live life and respond to its challenges. They remained allied in their passionate attention to linguistic detail, the digestion of millions of words, images, stock phrases, metres, puns, half- and full verses, whole poems, diwans, and blind devotion to and persistence in the centuries-old canons of the philology of Arabic poetics. They reveled in their common cause to evoke, articulate, create, and inscribe the worldliness of late-eleventh-century Spain and Sicily, with all the successes and failures, victories and defeats, allegiances and betrayals, onto the sacred pages of Arabic literary history, revealing to us a way to understand how the disconnected worlds of these two men came together.

The echoes of al-Mu'tamid and Ibn Hamdis's relationship, in all its aesthetic and political dimensions, reverberate some nine hundred years later in Iraqi poet 'Abd al-Wahhab al-Bayati's (1926–99) poem in which he expresses his pan-Arab solidarity for his Moroccan compatriot, 'Abd al-Latif La'bi (b. 1942), poet and political activist, who was persecuted and imprisoned by a repressive government and then forced into exile and a life of wandering, a sentence meted out to many of the Arab world's intelligentsia in our own times. It was only natural that al-Bayati, like so many other contemporary Arab artists and intellectuals,[11] chose to tap into the symbolic universe of al-Andalus, in all its richly evocative historical and mythical significations, to poeticize their shared vision of culture and tolerance and their experience of coercion and displacement. The poem ends:

> I see you: while from exile to exile
> I carry the soil of the nation –
> The forbidden poems – the secret newspapers – the fire.
> I see you: crossing the market and
> The police, in their report, at the border stations,
> Feverishly cover with pins and wax the faces of the Atlas poor –
> The maps – the sacrifices – the tombs – the solemn vows.
> The Andalusian poet in the prisons of the new world
> Is dying in the prison cell of the last caliph of Cordoba.   (al-Bayati 144–5)

NOTES

1 Gabrieli, *Dal Mondo dell'Islam* 88–99. He writes of "the history of the two *Jaziras*, the island and the peninsula, of Europe, upon which Arabo-Muslim rule created lasting rule; of the two Mediterranean Latin lands for which the Arab adventure was not a passing incursion but a well-defined period of their history, one that distanced them temporarily from the Occident in spiritual terms and incorporated them in an altogether different civilization, an altogether different world" (91).

2 Gabrieli makes note of a further distinction between Spain and Sicily: the glaring absence of eminent Sicilian figures, works, and other historical landmarks that distinguish the two histories (Gabrieli, "Arabi di Sicilia e arabi di Spagna" 92–4).

3 For a more extended study of Ibn Hamdis's professional trajectory, see Granara, "Remaking Muslim Sicily."

4 The author wishes to thank Nicola Carpentieri from Harvard University for the preparation of this translation.

5 Arab historians report that Ibn Labbana, Abu al-'Arab and Ibn Hamdis are all buried in the same cemetery on the island of Majorca.

6 Gabrieli sees in Ibn Hamdis something of a high point in Spanish-Sicilian Arab unity: "Siculo-Andalusian cultural unity in the centuries of common Arab rule found its fulfillment and, as it were, its symbolic incarnation in the greatest poet of Muslim Sicily, Ibn Hamdis" (Gabrieli, *Dal Mondo dell'Islam* 109).

7 For an excellent study, see D. Fairchild Ruggles 53–85.

8 The interlacing of physical prowess and military might into the panegyrics at this time and place cast serious doubt on Cynthia Robinson's assertion that court tastes in the

petty kingdoms turned away from such attributes and toward heavenly pleasures (Robinson, "Seeing Paradise" 147).

9   The Norman princes of twelfth-century Sicily, from Roger II until William II, were particularly partial to these; see, for instance, 'Abd al-Rahman al-Buthayri's poem to Roger II (Amari 282–3).

10 Cynthia Robinson ("Seeing Paradise") persuasively argues for a metaphorical extension from the poetic to the architectural.

11 For longer studies on the theme of al-Andalus in modern Arabic culture, see Granara, "*Extensio Animae*" and "Nostalgia."

13 Vidal Benvenist's *Efer ve-Dinah* between Hebrew and Romance[1]

DAVID A. WACKS

In an article in the 2004 *Cambridge History of Spanish Literature* titled "Beginnings," María Rosa Menocal writes that "the Jews are as much (or as little) Spaniards as anyone else inside this volume – from Seneca to Alfonso el Sabio … This reflects the reality in the historical moment in which their culture flourished in Spain; their literature is in Hebrew, but that too is part of a Spanish tradition defined now as being multifaceted and encompassing languages that would later be rejected and exiled" (70–1). The fact that this idea – that Spanish Jews were, indeed, Spanish – needs to be made explicit in a contemporary literary history of Spain reflects the reality of the historical moment in which *our* culture has flourished. Indeed, the Hebrew poetry of Christian Iberia, and in particular that of poets active into the fifteenth century, has been long overlooked by both Hispanists and Hebraists (Targarona Borrás 251, 266).

This study of one Hispano-Hebrew author, Vidal Benvenist, is part of a larger project intended to situate the Hebrew-language literature of Christian Spain within Hispanic studies. Not surprisingly, we Hispanists tend to view the literature of medieval Iberia through the filter of vernacular Romance language and culture, especially literary practice. Also not surprisingly, it has been Hebraists (whether Spanish or not) who have been foremost among scholars of the Hebrew literature of medieval Spain (Millás Vallicrosa 197–207; Schirmann; Pagis, *Hebrew* and *Innovation*; Scheindlin, *Wine*; Brann). Most of these scholars, largely owing to the culture of specialization common in academia, are not necessarily professionally involved with the Romance literary traditions of medieval Iberia. The long centuries of Spain's official alienation from its Jewish history and the total lack of an openly Jewish population in Spain between the sixteenth and twentieth centuries have made it less likely that a critical voice stressing the Hispanic cultural setting of medieval Spanish Hebrew authors would emerge. In recent years, however, critics in Spain and abroad have begun to comment on the need to situate the Hebrew literature of Christian Spain within its vernacular setting (Doron, "Dios"; Scheindlin, "Secular" 35–6; Sáenz-Badillos, "Crossroad"; Targarona Borrás). Here I wish to examine what it meant for a native speaker of Romance to write in Hebrew in the Middle Ages.

Vidal Benvenist lived in Zaragoza at the end of the fourteenth century and the beginning of the fifteenth, during very difficult times for the Jewish community of Aragon. He belonged to a group of Jewish intellectuals, the so-called Circle of Poets that included, among others, Solomon da Piera and Solomon Bonafed (Schirmann, *New Hebrew Poems from the Genizah* 564; Huss 5–12; Targarona Borrás and Scheindlin; Scheindlin, "Secular" 26; Cole 305). At about the turn of the fifteenth century, Benvenist wrote a *mahberet*, the Hebrew term for the originally Arabic *maqama* genre of rhyming prose narrative interspersed with poetry (Arie; Blachère; Drory, "Maqama"; Hämeen-Anttila). Between the twelfth and fifteenth centuries, similar mixed narrative genres flourished in Hispano-Arabic (the *maqamat* of al-Saraqusti and the anonymous *Hadith Bayad wa-Riyad*) and in Romance (the anonymous *Aucassin et Nicolette*, Dante's *Vita nuova*) throughout Europe. In Spain, the Toledan scholar Judah al-Harizi popularized the genre in Hebrew beginning with his translation of al-Hariri's Arabic *maqamat*, and following this with his own original composition, *Tahkemoni*. Several other authors in Spain and elsewhere wrote *mahbarot* in the two centuries before Benvenist wrote *Efer ve-Dinah*, during which time many strayed considerably from the stylistic requirements demonstrated by the "classical" Arabic *maqamat* of al-Hariri (Peretz xv).[2]

We would do well to understand Benvenist's use of the term in light of contemporary Romance practice. Though printed editions have given it various titles such as *Melitsat Efer ve-Dinah* (*The Rhyming Prose Tale of Efer and Dinah*) and, more commonly, *Melitsah le-maskil* (*A Rhyming Prose Tale for the Scholar*), the title in the manuscripts is simply *Maase Dinah* (*The Deeds of Dinah*), or *Maase Dinah ve-Toldot Efer* (*The Deeds of Dinah and History of Efer*), after the first line of the composition (*Don Vidal Benvenist's Tale of Efer and Dinah* 3 n. 1). The term *maase* (lit. "deeds"), which had long been used to describe tales, eventually became associated with the European novella. There is a late thirteenth-century tale collection from southern France titled simply *Sefer ha-maasim* (*The Book of Tales*), which contains various types of narratives, about one quarter of which are Hebrew novellas.[3]

In addition to its identification of the term *maase* with European novella, *Efer ve-Dinah* adopts the practice common to the European romance narrative of naming the text after the lover protagonists. Benvenist's text is in fact unique in doing so among medieval Hebrew narratives. In Spain, such texts are represented by the French *Floire et Blancheflor* (an alternate version of which flourished in Spain since at least the thirteenth century) (Grieve 22; Infantes and Nieves 85–127); the (somewhat later) Castilian *Grisel y Mirabella* (ca. 1480) and *Grimalte y Gradissa* (ca. 1485) of Juan de Flores; and the Hispano-Arabic *Hadith Bayad wa-Riyad* (late thirteenth or perhaps early fourteenth century) (Nykl; Robinson, *Medieval Andalusian Courtly Culture*). It is possible that Benvenist understood his work not only as Hebrew *mahberet*, but also as European novella or romance. Unfortunately, Benvenist himself does not address the matter. What he does tell us is that his work is meant to be an enjoyable allegorical morality tale in which the arrogance and spiritual decadence of the protagonist lead him to ruin. The first stanza reads:

> Learn clear words and sayings of books,
> Behold the deeds of Dinah and the history of Efer.
> In it is a delightful lesson for the children of Time
> To read about the vanities of sin and the parables of mortality.
> In it you will find moral admonishments,
> A vision for those wise of heart and erudite.
>
> (*Don Vidal Benvenist's Tale of Efer and Dinah*, 151, vv. 1–3)[4]

Efer is a very wealthy and morally corrupt man of a certain age whose virtuous, long-suffering wife falls ill and passes away. Shortly thereafter, Efer falls desperately in love with the young and lovely Dinah. Her father, eager to benefit from his daughter's beauty, arranges for her to marry Efer, who has promised to provide a comfortable lifestyle for both Dinah and her father. After the wedding, Efer finds he is unable to perform his conjugal duty. Hoping to mask the truth of his impotence, he obtains an aphrodisiac, and by misadventure, administers himself a fatal overdose.

Hayyim Schirmann has described *Efer ve-Dinah* as a "curiosity" (Schirmann and Fleischer 610). It sits at the nexus of several different Hebrew and vernacular Romance textual genres and traditions of practice. Benvenist himself was a subject of the crown of Aragon and a native speaker of the Aragonese dialect of Iberian Romance.

In order to understand the various intellectual traditions upon which the work draws, an overview of the contemporary socio-cultural landscape is in order. Benvenist's work reflects the tensions and intersections of a unique cultural moment in Spain. The violent pogroms of 1391 that ravaged the Iberian Peninsula resulted in the deaths of thousands of Jews and the conversion of thousands more (Baer, *History* 2:95–116; N. Roth, *Conversos* 34; Marcó i Dachs 172–88; Hinojosa Montalvo 21–66; Doñate Sebastià and Magdalena Nom de Deu 41–4). Twenty-two years later, the Disputation of Tortosa occasioned another wave of conversions, including those of many of the religious leaders of the Jewish communities of the Crown of Aragon (N. Roth, *Conversos* 55–61). During this period of "terror" (Maccoby 83) in which the community lived with the constant threat of violence, several of Benvenist's family members and close associates converted (Schirmann, *Hebrew Poetry in Spain and Provence* 2:566), including his own teacher Shelomo da Piera (Baer, *History* 2:211; Targarona Borrás and Scheindlin 68–9).

We have eyewitness accounts of the violence. In a letter to the Jewish community of Avignon, Hasday Crescas, a prominent scholar and leader of Catalan and Aragonese Jewry, lamented – and greatly exaggerated (N. Roth, *Conversos* 34) – the events of 1391:

> And all the others [who were not killed] changed their religion. Only a few fled to the places of the nobles … a child might count them … but they were notables. And for our many sins there is not this day a single Israelite to be found in Barcelona. (Baer, *History* 2:105)

The future of the Jewish community in the Crown of Aragon seemed grim at best. In these apocalyptic times, the Zaragoza poets saw themselves as the guardians of the Hebrew poetic tradition, manning the literary ramparts of a community under siege. They took refuge in literary conservatism, cultivating the styles of the Hebrew poets of al-Andalus, turning their backs on innovation, and exhorting their peers to shun the vernacular as a literary language (Targarona Borrás 249). In a letter to fellow poet Astruc Rimokh, Da Piera chides his fellow poet for having written him a letter in the vernacular:

> The language of the Torah alone gives forth poems;
> > It rectifies the babbling of those of barbarous tongue
> I have been given the laws of poetry; what do I care for
> > the language of Yael or the dialect of the chief of Qenaz?
> The Hebrew language is my intimate; what do I care
> > for the language of the Arameans or the musings of Ashkenaz?
> I shall anoint the Holy Tongue as my priest
> > What could I possibly care for the babbling of the babblers?
> > > (Da Piera 89, no. 92, vv. 47–50)

In an environment so hostile to Jews, it was a predictably defensive, proto-nationalist move to proclaim the superiority of Hebrew over Romance. Da Piera and his peers were simply continuing a debate in which Jewish intellectuals of al-Andalus had championed the Hebrew language vis-à-vis Arabic (Allony; Brann, *The Compunctious Poet* 23–58; Drory, "Words"). In Christian Iberia, where the Romance vernaculars were gaining traction as literary languages, the debate continued. A generation before Da Piera and Benvenist wrote, the Castilian Samuel Ibn Sasson had similarly scolded his much better-known colleague, Shem Tov ben Isaac ibn Ardutiel ("Santob de Carrión" in Spanish), for composing verse in Castilian (Brann et al. 81; Díaz Esteban 69):

> Accept the gift of the language that is as close to you as a son, in which only the most learned can jest;
> Accept the poetry that encompasses cosmic wisdom, and cast aside the banner of *their* language.   (Ibn Sasson 76, no. 44, vv. 1–2)

During this time, the fortunes of Castile's Jewish community had declined considerably since the more liberal policies under Alfonso X "The Learned," and their literature began to reflect the values of the bourgeois, as opposed to courtly, patronage enjoyed by Hebrew writers in the fourteenth century (Brann et al. 77). By Da Piera and Benvenist's time, the situation had worsened, and the Hebrew poets of Zaragoza were rallying for the preservation of the legacy of Hebrew poetics during a period not of decline, but rather of "universal ruin" (Baer, *History* 2: 134).

The result, at least for Da Piera, is a sort of religious linguistic nationalism whose goal is "the defence of a world view and its symbols" (Barbour 2) against rival forces. Though it may be an anachronism to speak of "nationalism" in a time before the existence of nations per se, we can at least understand this proto-nationalism in terms of the active and programmatic formation of group identity, rather than political or territorial affiliation as in modern nationalisms (Armstrong 3). In any event, the goals of Da Piera's ideology coincide with that of modern linguistic nationalisms, to "derive unifying and energizing power from widely held images of the past in order to overcome ... fragmentation and loss of identity" (J. Fishman 9). James Monroe has noted a similar siege-mentality effect in the poetry of Nasrid Granada in the fifteenth century. The response of Granadan poets and artists to Christian political superiority and imminent annexation was to eschew Christian influences vigorously and turn to African and Eastern models that recalled the heyday of the Caliphate (Monroe, *Hispano-Arabic Poetry* 62–3).

Such literary proto-nationalism notwithstanding, this was a Jewish community that shared a common vernacular culture, language, and literature with their Christian neighbours, and their literary practice reflected this reality. Even without taking into account the Romance language production of Spanish Jewish authors that has been lost to us, it is clear even from the Hebrew, and particularly from *Efer ve-Dinah*, that these are authors working in the Romance world. The Zaragoza poets' jealous cultivation of Hebrew and condemnation of the vernacular did not ensure their isolation from the literary practice of the Romance world in which they lived, and Vidal Benvenist's *Efer ve-Dinah* bears witness to this.

A merely cursory look at Benvenist's choice of language (Hebrew) and style does not, however, place him next to his counterparts writing in Romance. Benvenist wrote in the type of clever rhyming prose typical of Spanish Hebrew authors, linguistically conservative and rich in biblical allusion. The setting and the characters bear biblical names, and we see none of the geographic and cultural specificity that one associates with the vernacular Romance prose fiction of the times, as for example in Boccaccio's *Decameron* or Don Juan Manuel's *Conde Lucanor*. Stylistically, then, *Efer ve-Dinah* does not seem to have much in common with its vernacular counterparts.

What is it, then, that places Benvenist's text within Hispano-Romance literary practice? We might start to answer this question by asking another: for what purpose and for what audience did Benvenist write? The introduction of Gershom Soncino to his edition of *Efer ve-Dinah* (Rimini 1523) describes it as a Purim entertainment for young people (Benvenist 201). Whether or not Benvenist intended *Efer ve-Dinah* to be performed during Purim, the fact that Soncino presents it as such suggests that readers and audiences understood the work as belonging to the tradition of Hebrew parodies practiced as part of the Purim celebration.

The Jewish festival of Purim commemorates Persian Jewry's narrow escape from destruction in the fourth century B.C.E. In addition to a public reading of the biblical Scroll of Esther, Purim celebrations have historically included the performance of original works. Vernacular versions of the Esther story had been read alongside the Hebrew since at least the ninth century (Abrahams 261), and in Spain, Rabbi Isaac ben Sheshet Perfet (Ribash) cites Nahmanides (Ramban) and other Catalan and Provençal rabbis reporting that such vernacular readings of Esther were widespread during their lifetimes (thirteenth-fourteenth centuries) (Perfet 2:551, § 388). He also chastises one of his peers for allowing vernacular readings of the Esther story to the women of his community (Perfet 2:551, § 388). In fifteenth-century Spain, Provence, and Italy, there were two traditional genres of such paraliturgical Purim literature. One was the performance of original, light-hearted versions of the Esther story in both Hebrew and Romance vernacular. Of these, the best-known are the fourteenth-century Provençal and Hebrew Esther poems (Silberstein; Einbinder, *No Place of Rest*; Davidson 32–4). Alongside the Esther narratives there is also a tradition of biblical and exegetical parody, such as the bacchic spoof of the Book of the Prophet Habakuk titled *Sefer Habakbuk Hanavi* (*The Book of the* Bakbuk, *or* Bottle, *of the Prophet*), or the Talmudic parody of Kalonymous ben Kalonymous, *Masehet Purim* (*The Tractate of Purim*). In the carnivalesque spirit of Purim, these texts celebrate the pleasures of this world: drunkenness, gluttony, and indulgence in general (Silberstein 34–6; Davidson 32–4).

On the surface, *Efer ve-Dinah* does seem to fit with the ludic spirit of this Purim paraliturgy. Like paraliturgical versions of the Esther story, it is a highly novelized morality tale, yet unlike them, it cannot be read as a retelling of Esther. The levity of the Purim holiday is deemed appropriate for the obligatory merry-making prescribed by the Talmud for a wedding celebration (Ketubot 8:2a), and so a literary parody of the public reading of the ketubah, or wedding contract, is a natural topic for a Purim entertainment.[5] This parody of the "performance" of Efer and Dinah's ketubah displays much of the same linguistic playfulness and irreverence as the other Purim parodies mentioned above. The text in parentheses may be understood as the whispered commentary of invited guests as they listen to the public reading of the traditional text of the ketubah. One can easily imagine a live Purim performance of the passage, with actors playing the parts of Efer, Dinah, the presiding rabbi, and witnesses, the audience as guests, and a narrator in the wings interpreting Benvenist's snarky narration. In this passage, Benvenist plays on the practice of translating each phrase of the Aramaic of the traditional ketubah into the vernacular as it is read aloud, for the benefit of guests unable to understand the original (N. Roth, *Daily* 44). But instead of translating, he inserts the voice of the narrator, who provides us with a blow-by-blow commentary on what is happening during the reading itself.

> Then one of the witnesses came beside him, and raised his voice, saying: "On the sixth, on Shabbat," (the noise of the groomsmen's drinking ceased) "on the ninth day of the month of Av," (the bridesmaids were fainting, they felt Dinah's pain in their own flesh) "Whereas [this man] Efer is the groom," (emanating profanity, radiating vanity, the desolation of his face terrifying the crowd) "He said to Dinah," (who was surrounded by her bridesmaids, all singing her praises) "you shall be my wife," (she appeared to be in mourning, like an oak tree with withered leaves) "and I will honor, maintain, and serve you," (he is like a filthy, abominable branch, considered [as ineffectual as] smoke and wind) "and to go into you as is the custom of all lands." (Don't put your trust in vanity, i.e., "Don't bank on it.") "And this is the dowry that the bride brings." (Horns and whistles[6] are heard.) (Benvenist 173, ll. 259–64)

Although such broad comedy would seem to place *Efer ve-Dinah* squarely in jocular Purim traditions of text and performance, Benvenist makes it clear that his moral message is deadly serious. In a lengthy excursus at the end of the tale (186–200, ll. 410–568), he explains that *Efer ve-Dinah* is not just the bawdy tale of the sexual arrogance of one old man; rather, it is an allegory for the human soul's struggle with the temptations of the material world, couched in the type of saucy prose favoured by young readers who would otherwise not pay attention to its moral content:[7]

> And now, wise and sage men, who fill your verses with knowledge and fear of God, take this parable to heart, and God will be with you. Listen attentively, come into the house of hidden meaning and enter into the chambers of its ornament, so that you might experience its hidden benefit and enjoy its exalted brilliance. I have not set down the words of this parable for my own good, my thoughts for any vain purpose. God forbid I should write foolishness within my precious words, my glory. Let my good name not depend on the surface meaning of my words, for there are useful teachings within my parable, hidden and occulted away. They are a medicine for the soul and an elixir for the body. [The apparent and the hidden] complement one another; if the words at first seem shoddy, soon their fragrance changes and their taste alters. Come to know their secret, and you will catch a different breeze. As the wise man said: do not trust in the surface meaning of ideas, in their form. Rather, focus on what is within them, for there is a difference between a word's form and what is buried in its bosom, between the shell of the nut and its meat. However, in order to entice young readers, who enjoy a good jest, and who are not motivated by moral teachings alone, and whose mouths run with the delights of vanity, after which men chase, I have said: I shall open my mouth and speak words of deception, as is their manner, as an offering to entice them, in order to fill their hearts with wisdom. I shall bind them and lead them with their own ropes and cords: those of vain desires, they who would make a mockery of love. (Benvenist 187–8, ll. 410–24)

According to these words, Benvenist's purpose is clear: he wants to speak to the youth "in their own language," much as current-day clergy strive to deliver their spiritual messages in music and other media popular among their younger congregants. As he goes on to explain, the allegory is to be understood as follows: Efer represents man's earthly existence, his deceased first wife represents the wise soul who guides us on the narrow path, and the beautiful young Dinah represents man's earthly desires and pleasures that ultimately lead to spiritual ruin (Schirmann and Fleischer 612–13; Huss 68–9). In explaining the allegory, Benvenist uses the well-worn metaphor of the shell (exoteric form) and meat (esoteric meaning) of the nut (Benvenist 187, l. 420), so common to both the Jewish and the Christian literature of his era (Laird 151–2), and famously so to readers of the Castilian *Libro de buen amor* (*Book of Good Love*) (Ruiz 14–15, st. 17–18), that appeared some seventy years before *Efer ve-Dinah*.[8]

The historical context suggests that, while perhaps inconsistent with the carnivalesque tone of traditional Purim literature, Benvenist's moral *gravitas* is sincere. These were, after all, disastrous times for the Jewish community, and Benvenist's peers used prophetic language to lament the calamities of 1391 and 1413 (Bernstein; C. Roth; Pagis, "Dirges"; van Bekkum). According to them, the *conversos* became rich but abandoned Hebrew poetry, Jewish religion, and brought disgrace to the community (Baer, *History* 2:134–7). Even before the catastrophe of 1391, Jewish sources stridently denounce those who abandoned the ancestral faith. The introduction to the 1354 *takkanot* (ordinances) of the union of Jewish communities of the Crown of Aragon has the following to say about the *conversos* from their community:

> Fire and sulphur and a scorching wind is the portion of their cup; to shoot the upright in the heart [the loyal Jews] they bend the bow and make ready according to their desire their arrows … Therefore, children of transgression [conversos] have become great and grown rich, and those who are borne from birth have changed their glory and that which they promised for shame. (ed. Baer, *Juden* 2:150; trans. N. Roth, *Conversos* 46–7)

The accusation that the *conversos* were selling out their community for personal gain was not unfounded. Long after the Disputation of Tortosa, Pedro de la Cavallería, a relative of Benvenist who converted in the second half of the fifteenth century, justifies the accusations made in the *takkanot* of 1354. In his testimony before a tribunal of the Inquisition, he quite frankly admits that money and status were powerful considerations in his decision to convert:

> … could I, as a Jew, ever have risen higher than a rabbinical post? But now, see, I am one of the chief councilors [jurado] of the city. For the sake of the little man who was hanged [Jesus], I am accorded every honor, and I issue orders and decrees to the whole city of Saragossa.
> … que pudia subir estando judio de rabi en suso? Agora so jurado en cap, y por un enforcadillo ahora me fazen tanta honra, y mando y viedo toda la ciudat de Çaragoça. (trans. Baer, *History* 2:277; ed. Baer, *Juden* 2:463)

In the face of such motivation, at least some of Spain's Jews saw themselves *entre la espada y la pared*, "between the sword and the wall": between the rewards of this world, or of the world to come; a difficult but virtuous life as a Jew, or a more comfortable but pernicious life as a *converso* (Marcó i Dachs 209).

In light of this predicament (and given his explicit moralistic reading of his own tale), it is altogether likely that although he is working in a parodic genre, Benvenist's message is dead serious and speaks to anxiety in the Zaragoza Jewish community over the deleterious effects of money on moral judgment. Schirmann suggests that *Efer ve-Dinah* may well have been based on actual stories of older men who were forced to dissolve marriages to younger women based on their impotence (Schirmann and Fleischer 613–14; Huss 48), meaning that Benvenist was addressing a social problem – and not simply a literary motif – familiar to his readers. This moralizing intention is consistent with the serious messages of much of the poetry of his peers Da Piera (Cole 300) and Bonafed (Cole 314) (though not perhaps in keeping with much of his own poetry). Yet even in answering Da Piera's poetic call to Hebrew arms, Benvenist does not hesitate to draw on some of the generic conventions and narrative materials of the vernacular literature held in such disdain by his fellow poets. Despite the professed conservatism of the Zaragoza poets, Hebrew literary practice was continuing to exist in dialogue with the literatures of the vernaculars spoken by Hebrew authors. In order to understand fully what is going in *Efer ve-Dinah*, we must read below the surface and beyond the Hebrew context, into the vernacular practices of the times.

A few examples are in order. According to Raymond Scheindlin, the Zaragoza poets' preference for conservative style and mannerism resonated with the literary tastes of the Castilian and Aragonese nobility in the fifteenth century. He maintains that their poetry espoused the values of courtly love as codified by Ibn Hazm in the eleventh century and Andreas Capellanus in the twelfth, values that inspired the lyrics of the troubadours and of the Italian poets, and that became the common currency of the discourse of poetic love in medieval Europe (Scheindlin, "Secular" 35). This is certainly true of much of the courtly lyric poetry of the *Cancionero* corpus (Gerli 14). And while many of the middle-class *letrados* – educated courtiers and functionaries – who wrote this poetry consciously upheld the poetic values of the nobility (Boase 7–8, 72, and 81), others (and especially those who did not depend on royal patronage) parodied or subverted medieval ideals of love and sexual behaviour. In the late Middle Ages, the class system of Aragonese (and Castilian) society was in flux, and saw an increasingly influential middle-class made up of merchants, notaries and clergymen (Hillgarth 2:68–9). Some of these were authors who produced works undermining courtly and ecclesiastical standards for sexual behaviour. Juan Ruiz, Archpriest of Hita in neighbouring Castile during the fourteenth century, famously lampooned the doctrines of both clerical celibacy (Eisenberg 252) and courtly love (Deyermond 69–70) in the *Libro de buen amor*.[9] In the following century, the physician Jaume Roig chronicled the fruitless quest of a self-made Valencian burgher to marry happily in a scathing satire of bourgeois life titled the *Spill* or *Llibre de les dones* (the *Mirror*, or *Book of Ladies*, ca. 1450) (Wacks 196–200). This trend is anticipated in the thirteenth-century Andalusi Arabic *Hadith Bayad wa-Riyad*, a tale narrated by a go-between woman whose clients flaunt courtly convention both in their behaviour and in their verse (Robinson, *Medieval Andalusian Courtly Culture* 2). These authors pointed out the irrelevance of idealized codes of sexual behaviour in a new world in which mercantile culture threatened aristocratic values. In Castilian, this intrusion of a mercantile middle-class sensibility into the world of courtly love found its culmination in the *Celestina*, or "Tragicomedy of Calisto and Melibea," by the *converso* lawyer Fernando de Rojas, published as the fifteenth century drew to a close. Calisto's efforts to carry out the ideals of courtly love in a world where the old rules no longer apply make for excellent broad comedy and biting social satire (Severin, *Tragicomedy* 23–4).

Like his Christian counterparts who portrayed the failure of courtly values in a world governed more by money than by aristocratic ideals of romantic love, Benvenist portrays the conflict between mercantile society and medieval Rabbinic ideals of love and marriage. The Jewish doctrine of *onah* (conjugal rights) holds that a married woman is entitled to regular sexual relations, and that a man who cannot provide this has no business getting married (Biale 92–5; Rosen, *Unveiling Eve* 122). These conjugal rights of women are guaranteed in both Torah (Exodus 21:10) and Talmud (Ketubot 61b–62, Cohen, *Holy Letter* 66–7), and the *Iggeret Hakodesh* or *Holy Letter*, a thirteenth-century Hispano-Hebrew treatise on conjugal love, is quite explicit on the topic of a man's duty to his wife. He must engage in foreplay both verbal and physical (S. Cohen, *Holy Letter* 140–3), must allow her ample time to become aroused before engaging in intercourse, and should allow her to climax first (S. Cohen, *Holy Letter* 144–5).[10] The rich but impotent Efer is unable to fulfill these obligations, and must resort to an aphrodisiac of which he receives a fatal overdose. As in the *Libro de buen amor* and the *Celestina*, the protagonists rely on technology (potions and aphrodisiacs)[11] to remedy their shortcomings in affairs of the "heart," both with tragic results (Schirmann actually refers to the work as a "tragi-comedy"; Schirmann and Fleischer 6).

These works reflect an important change in the literary discourse and practices of love. Whereas the works of Juan Ruiz, Jaume Roig, and Fernando de Rojas point out the impossibility of living out ecclesiastic and courtly ideals of love in a post-feudal society, Benvenist depicts the interference of mercantile values with Rabbinic ideals of conjugal duty. This would place *Efer ve-Dinah* in step with Castilian and Catalan reactions to the realities of middle-class life. This trend in Castilian and Aragonese Jewish authors goes as far back as the *Disciplina clericalis* of the *converso* Petrus Alfonsi (early twelfth century), in which stories of merchants abound, but the nobleman "scarcely makes an appearance" (Hermes 6). In the following century, authors of Hispano-Hebrew *maqamat* parodied the excesses of bourgeois life (in particular as practiced by women) as a distraction from a life of pious study (Wacks 231–5). One may read Dinah as a metaphor for the materialism that Shlomo Da Piera denounces in the *conversos* who – in his opinion – had sold out their community. This allegorical reading resonates with the literary debate on woman that flourished in Spain in Hebrew in the twelfth and thirteenth centuries (Pagis, "Poetic"; T. Fishman; Rosen, *Unveiling Eve* 103–23; Jacobs), and in Castilian and Catalan in the fourteenth and fifteenth (Matulka 5–37; Tapia and Cruz; Archer, *Misoginía, Problem*).

The debate on women in Christian Iberia spans the literature of the Virgin cult, the various pro- and anti- feminist works of the time, including the Castilian *Corbacho* of Alfonso Martínez de Toledo (the Archpriest of Talavera), and the Valencian *Spill* or *Mirror* of Jaume Roig. In Hebrew, it is represented by texts such as Judah ibn Shabbetai's *Minhat Yehudah, Soneh Hanashim* (*The Offering of Judah the Misogynist*) and *Ezrat Hanashim* by an author known only as Isaac. In some of these texts, as in *Efer ve-Dinah*, the woman is symbolic of man's weakness before the temptations of the secular world (Hamilton 64). We also therefore read the debate as an allegory of contemporary social problems. For example, in Ibn Shabbetay's *Minhat Yehudah*, the misogynist Zerah is tempted away from his studies by the beautiful young Ayala, whose physical beauty and honeyed rhetoric make short work of Zerah's vow of scholarly celibacy. As in *Efer ve-Dinah*, the fleshly pleasures represented by the beautiful young woman are ultimately the ruin of the protagonist, who is duped into marrying not the beautiful Ayala, but the hag Ritzpah (Ibn Shabbetay 2:25, ll. 583–98). This literary topos reflected an ongoing debate within the Iberian Jewish community over the moral dangers of intellectual assimilationism and materialism that came to a head in the Maimonidean controversy of the mid-thirteenth century (Septimus 61–74; Dobbs-Weinstein; Hamilton 72). In this way, Dinah is part of a tradition of allegorical temptresses who embody the seductions and false promises of the material world as opposed to the durable rewards of Torah study and good works. What sets Dinah apart from other temptresses in medieval tradition is that she is in no way complicit in the scheme to use her beauty to separate Efer from his money. Her natural right to a happy marriage with a man who can fulfill her needs falls prey to her father's greed and Efer's arrogance.

Unlike Ibn Shabbetay's Ayala, who is merely a decoy used to lure Zerah away from his studies, Dinah ultimately bends to her father's will and, in marrying Efer, joins the ranks of the unhappily married young girls of vernacular Romance tradition. In both oral tradition and in literary genres that draw heavily upon it, the theme of the young girl married to the much older man is well-represented in medieval Romance literature. There are examples in the *Lais* of Marie de France (109–12), as well as in French *chansons de malmariées* (Doss-Quinby et al. 151–64; Tomaryn Bruckner, Shepard and White 130–3). The theme is especially well-represented in Spanish tradition as the *malmaridada* or *malcasada* ("mis-married young girl"), several of whom appear in popular songs preserved in *cancioneros*, compilations of courtly poetry, from the late fifteenth and early sixteenth centuries (Frenk Alatorre 103–13, nos. 223–44; Rodríguez Puértolas 345–6). In the popular

Spanish ballad of *La bella malmaridada*, the young bride's husband cheats on her, she retaliates by taking a lover of her own, and when her husband finds out, he kills her. The ballad probably dates back to the thirteenth or fourteenth century, and first appeared in print in the mid-sixteenth century (Sepúlveda fol. 258). In Sephardic oral tradition, it has persisted into the twentieth century (Alvar 167, no. 213). Students of Spanish literature will also recognize the theme of *La bella malmaridada* from the mid-seventeenth-century play by Lope de Vega bearing the same title (*Bella*), or perhaps from the very popular novella by Cervantes, *El celoso extremeño* (*The Jealous Man from Extremadura*), in which a frustrated younger wife of a much older and obsessively jealous husband smuggles a lover into the house, to great comic effect (*Novelas* 97–135).

Less known are the contributions of Sephardic writers from Christian Iberia to the literature of the *malmaridada*. Roughly contemporary with *Efer ve-Dinah*, a Judeo-Catalan wedding song, *Piyyut Na'eh* or *Festive Hymn*, lampoons the *malmari-dada* theme, with a Talmudic twist (Hebrew words in italics):

He broke the law "*Do not profane woman*" when he gave
his daughter to an *old man*, who made her a *whore*.
The *old man* lay down at *the head of the bed*;
the *girl* woke him up with great *vigor*.
The *old man* said to her: "Are you a *slut*?
Money and clothes you will have, but no *sex*!"

Al tehal·lel[12] passà qui primer donà
sa filla al *zaqén*, qui la·n féu *zoná*.
El *zaqén* se'n va a colgar al *roš ha-mità*
La *ne`arà* lo desperta am gran *geburà*
Lo *zaqén* li·n diu: "Que n'ès tu *sotà*?
Šéer we-kesut n'hauras, mas no pas `*onà*!"   (Riera i Sans 17)

Here the girl's plight is similar to that of Dinah: she is forced to marry a man who cannot perform his conjugal duty (Benvenist 173 n 264). We have seen that Rabbinic tradition guarantees a married woman sexual gratification. Furthermore, a man who will not or cannot gratify his wife sexually is partially responsible for any adultery resulting from his wife's frustration. This understanding of the sexual rights of married women informs Jewish interpretations of the *malmari-dada* theme, in which older, less-qualified grooms are taken to task for their vanity and arrogance. Vidal Benvenist's novelization of the *malmaridada* theme in *Efer ve-Dinah* is exactly contemporary with this song, is likewise predicated on a woman's right to sexual gratification within her marriage, and likewise ridicules the older groom for not providing it. Benvenist's treatment of the *malmaridada* is a decid-edly Jewish, literary take on a theme quite prevalent in the Hispanic and Romance world.[13]

The final vernacular tradition to which *Efer ve-Dinah* responds is of biblical origin. Benvenist named Dinah for the biblical Dinah (Genesis 24:1–31), the only daughter of Jacob, who is raped by Shehem, prince of the Canaanite city of the same name. In retaliation for Shehem's affront to the family's honour, Dinah's brothers Shimon and Levi destroy the city and put all its male inhabitants to the sword. This story apparently resonated deeply with the famous Spanish sense of honour, and was novelized in the medieval ballad "El robo de Dina," ("the rape of Dinah") (Benardete et al. 12). Not surprisingly, Lope de Vega also wrote a play based on the ballad (*Robo*). Several of Lope's plays, including *La bella malmaridada* and *El Robo de Dina*, were based on popular ballads, and this suggests that the bal-lad of the Rape of Dinah was popular with both Christian and Jewish audiences before and after the 1492 Expulsion. In all likelihood, Benvenist chose the name Dinah for his protagonist in homage to the Dinahs of his vernacular tongue, as well as to the biblical original.

Benvenist's tale of an ill-fated marriage occupies a unique space in the Hebrew and Romance literatures of its time. Linguistically, Benvenist is in keeping with the conservative ideological program of the Zaragoza poets, but his adaptation of the Hispano-Romance *malmaridada*, his critique of bourgeois morality, his par-ticipation in the current vernacular literary debate on woman, and his nod to the Hispanic ballad tradition of the Rape of Dinah all indicate that he was very much a Hispanic author in addition to a Jewish one. And despite the open disdain of some of his peers for the literary uses of the vernacular, Benvenist's use of con-temporary thematic material, some of it drawn directly from the oral tradition of his own speech community, places him squarely among the vernacular writers of his day.

NOTES

1 Preliminary research for this essay was conducted while I was a Harry Starr Fellow at the Harvard Center for Jewish Studies in Spring 2006. Many thanks to Suzanne Akbari and Karla Mallette for providing the initial forum for these ideas at the *Persistence of Philology* symposium. I am also grateful to Profs. Michelle M. Hamilton (University of California at Irvine) and Matti Huss (Hebrew University) for their comments, as well as to the anonymous reviewer who made several thoughtful and thought-provoking suggestions.

2 See also Jonathan Decter's comments about the *Sefer Ha-meshalim* (*The Book of Parables*) of Yaaqob ben Elazar vis-à-vis the European romance narrative (149–56).

3 See Yassif 345. His description of the Hebrew novellas in *Sefer Ha-maasim* might equally apply to *Efer ve-Dinah*: "The romantic quality of the novella, its treatment of matters of the heart and sexual propriety (or lack thereof) as determined by Jewish norms, all revolve around the figure of the woman" (346).

4 Translations of primary texts are mine unless indicated otherwise.

5 Compare to Ibn Shabbetay's parody of the traditional reading of the ketubah in *Minhat Yehudah* (Schirmann, *Hebrew Poetry in Spain and Provence* 2:79–80; Huss, *Don Vidal Benvenist's Tale of Efer and Dinah* 2:24–5; Navarro Peiro 185; Davidson 11).

6 Something along the lines of rimshots and catcalls from the crowd, meaning the dowry that she brings is her own nubile self. Here the Aramaic *karnah* (horn) denotes the horn blown as an instrument, but also connotes the horns Efer will wear as the impotent old husband to a beautiful young wife (Benvenist 174 n. 264).

7 On the tradition of allegory in Jewish literature and in particular in Hebrew *maqamat*, see Drory, "Maqama" 202–3.

8 In the *Libro de buen amor* (*Book of Good Love*), however, the tenor of Ruiz's moral message is much more ambivalent, whereas Benvenist is explicit about his sincere moral agenda.

9 Ruiz also anticipates Benvenist's critique of bourgeois culture's threat to conjugal responsibility in the episode of the painter Pitas Payas, who is cuckolded when he leaves his wife alone during an extended business trip (477b).

10 Compare with the Christian discussion of the Pauline "debt" in which the husband's conjugal duties are viewed as a concession (to nature) (Feldman 64) rather than as a commandment, as in Judaism (Feldman 62). Brundage notes that even the relatively enlightened Aquinas viewed marital sex as "a source of moral and spiritual impurity" (448), and that in Benvenist's day most Catholic theologians held that "sexual pleasure in marriage should be feared and shunned" (503).

11 Dorothy Severin ("Relationship") argues that the *alcahuetas* (go-betweens) in both *Libro de buen amor* and *Celestina* use love potions in order to win the "hearts" of their respective clients' love objects. Recipes for several such potions can be found in the pages of the Hebrew *Sefer Ahavat Nashim* (*Book of the Love of Women*; thirteenth-century, circulated in fifteenth-century Spain) (*El Libro de amor de mujeres* 35–9).

12 "Do not profane thy daughter, to cause her to be a whore" (Leviticus 19:29).

13 See Eli Yassif's comments on the assimilation of gender folk novellas into Jewish religious and literary culture (346).

14 The Shadow of Islam in Cervantes's "El Licenciado Vidriera"

LEYLA ROUHI

Ideally, the reader of these lines will have read the novella by Miguel de Cervantes titled "El Licenciado Vidriera" ("The Glass Graduate"). For the benefit of those who have not, a brief plot summary follows:

While travelling, two upper-class students find a young boy sleeping by the banks of the river Tormes. They inquire as to his origin and the reason for his solitude, to which he responds that he does not remember the name of his birthplace, but that he wishes to go to Salamanca to find a good master and to study. Moved by his responses, the two students take him in and facilitate his studies in Salamanca, where he excels as a student to the point of achieving some fame for his intellect. At this stage of his life he calls himself Tomás Rodaja. As an adult, travelling on his own, he meets an army captain and tours Italy with him in the capacity of soldier. Upon his return to Spain he moves back to Salamanca and continues his studies until he obtains a degree in law. A mysterious woman described as "altogether wily and artful" ["de todo rumbo y manejo" (*Novelas* 2:115; trans. *Exemplary Stories* 112)] becomes infatuated with him but fails to charm him; a Morisca counsels the woman to give a love philter disguised inside a quince to Tomás in the hope of securing his love. Not only does the quince not arouse love in him, but it makes Tomás very ill. After a violent sickness, Tomás recovers physically but loses his sanity. He becomes convinced that he is made of glass, and expresses great concern that he may break. In the meantime, he begins to offer witty and incisive aphorisms to all who come into contact with him, some of whom refer to him as "Señor Vidriera" ("Mr. Glass"; he gives himself the name "Licenciado Vidriera," "The Glass Graduate"), though the narrator continues to call him Rodaja. He becomes famous for his peculiar madness and his intriguing and cutting statements on all aspects of society. Eventually, a monk of the Order of San Jerónimo cures him, and Tomás takes on the name Rueda. But few people remain interested in Tomás in his recovered sane form. He moves back to

Flanders (where he had lived for some time), becomes a soldier again, and dies there.

This novella – like all Cervantes's writings – has inspired much debate amongst scholars regarding possible sources and meanings. Critics have commented on numerous facets of the story: its fragmented yet oddly symmetrical structure, the possible shapes of its thematic unity, the meanings of Rodaja's three names, and the aphorisms he offers, to name just a few (see El Saffar; Shipley; Friedman; King; Avalle-Arce; Casalduero; Molho; Riley). This article will explore an aspect of the tale that has seldom been discussed in previous criticism. Alongside *Don Quijote* and a number of other texts by Cervantes, this novella contains a reference to a member of the Morisco community.[1] The mention is brief and does not come close to the much more fleshed-out characterizations in some other Cervantine texts. In fact, the appearance is so minimal that it does not even occupy a whole sentence. Yet in "El Licenciado Vidriera" the intervention of a Morisca does seem to have serious implications for the tale as well as for the place of Islam in Cervantes's writings.

The repercussions of the Morisca's advice are far-reaching, particularly in view of the brevity of the episode that reports the act. This takes up twenty-seven lines, and neither the Morisca nor the love-sick woman she advises is heard of again:

> It was at that time that a wily and artful lady happened to arrive in the city. All the birds in the neighborhood immediately flocked to the bait and fell into her snare, and there was not a student in the place who did not pay her a visit. They told Tomás that this lady claimed to have been to Italy and Flanders, and so in order to find out whether he knew her, he paid her a visit. The consequence of this encounter was that she fell in love with Tomás but he, unaware of the effect he had on her, would not have set foot in her house again if he had not been dragged there by others. To cut a long story short, she revealed her feelings to him and offered him her worldly wealth. However, since he was more attached to his books than to other forms of entertainment, he did not return the lady's affections in the slightest. When she saw herself scorned and, in her own eyes, despised, and realized that she could not conquer the resistance of Tomás's will by any common or ordinary means, she resolved to seek out other methods which she considered more effective and capable of satisfying her desires. So, on the advice of a Moorish woman she gave Tomás a so-called love potion in a Toledan quince, believing that it gave her the power to force his will to love her, as if there existed in the world some herb or spell or incantation capable of bending our free will. The people who administer such love-inducing drinks and aphrodisiac foods are known as poisoners, for they do no less than poison the people who eat and drink them, as experience has demonstrated on many different occasions.

Tomás ate the quince at such a fateful moment that he immediately began to shake from head to foot as if he were having a fit, and lost consciousness for many hours, at the end of which he regained his senses but seemed to have lost his wits. He stuttered and stammered that a quince he had eaten had killed him and he named the person who gave it to him. When the officers of the law were informed of the incident they went in search of the culprit. She, however, seeing how badly her plan had gone awry, had made herself scarce and was never seen again. (*Exemplary Stories* 112–13)

[Sucedió que en este tiempo llegó a aquella ciudad una dama de todo rumbo y manejo. Acudieron luego a la añagaza y reclamó todos los pájaros del lugar, sin quedar *vademecum* que no la visitase. Dijéronle a Tomás que aquella dama decía que había estado en Italia y en Flandes, y por ver si la conocía, fue a visitarla, de cuya visita y vista quedó ella enamorada de Tomás; y él, sin echar e ver en ello, si no era por fuerza y llevado de otros, no quería entrar en su casa. Finalmente, ella le descubrió su voluntad y le ofreció su hacienda; pero como él atendía más a sus libros que a otros pasatiempos, en ninguna manera respondía al gusto de la señora, la cual, viéndose desdeñada y, a su parecer, aborrecida, y que por medios ordinarios y comunes no podía conquistar la roca de la voluntad de Tomás, acordó de buscar otros modos, a su parecer; más eficaces y bastantes para salir con el cumplimiento de sus deseos. Y así, aconsejada de una morisca, en un membrillo toledano dio a Tomás unos destos que llaman hechizos, creyendo que le daba cosa que le forzase la voluntad a quererla; como si hubiese en el mundo yerbas, encantos ni palabras suficientes a forzar el libre albedrío; y así, las que dan estas bebidas o comidas amatorias se llaman venéficas; porque no es otra cosa lo que hacen sino dar veneno a quien lo toma, como lo tiene mostrado la experiencia en muchas y diversas ocasiones.

Comió en tal mal punto Tomás el membrillo, que al momento comenzó a herir de pie y de mano como si tuviera alferecía, y sin volver en sí estuvo muchas horas, al cabo de las cuales volvió como atontado, y dijo con lengua turbada y tartamuda que un membrillo que había comido le había muerto, y declaró quién se le había dado. La justicia, que tuvo noticia del caso, fue a buscar la malhechora; pero ya ella, viendo el mal suceso, se había puesto en cobro, y no pareció jamás.] (*Novelas* 2:115–16)

As mentioned earlier, the Morisca does not even inspire a full sentence: the text says of her only that the scorned lady of the tale was "advised by a Moorish woman" ["aconsejada de una morisca"]. Few scholars have focused on the actual Morisca who provides the love potion, though the quince itself has been the object of some discussion, and in this respect the generally unsavory reputation of Morisca healers and go-betweens in Cervantes's time is often invoked as well

(Redondo; Simó; Schindler and Jiménez). The seventeenth-century reader would have made a number of associations relevant to Moriscos and magic, likely involving Moriscas as sorceresses or unqualified pseudo-healers, craftily producing fake spells and philters for gullible women. These kinds of practices were dismissed increasingly by qualified physicians and the erudite classes as ineffectual at best and harmful at worst (Caro Baroja; García Ballester; Perry). The story, as though confirming such dismissals, turns away from "la dama de todo rumbo y manejo" as well as the Morisca, rejects the idea of a love potion as absurd, and focuses instead on the illness and subsequent condition of Tomás, who calls himself "el Licenciado Vidriera." The rest of the tale centers upon his peculiar behaviour and his fame. Likewise, the description of the cure in the hands of the monk occupies a small space, and the tale is wrapped up on a laconic note. Thus, the causes of the two most transformative moments of his life occupy surprisingly little space in the narrative.

Scholars have identified two factors in particular that play a significant role in the narrative strategy of the novella as well as the formation of Tomás's identity: repression and fragmentation. Felipe Ruan has shown the reliance of the narrative structure on fissures and faults. Through a careful reading, Ruan posits that lacunae and fragmentation create a kind of movement in this story that does not appear to have a specific direction, deliberately going everywhere yet nowhere. Rodaja/Rueda's indeterminate origin, the chance encounters that change his life, the directionless aphorisms that he produces, all suggest to Ruan that the tale is a process without foundation, and as such dramatizes Cervantes's own assertion in his introduction to the *Novelas ejemplares* that: "In my stories, I have forged a path / by which the Castilian language can / dabble with decorum in nonsense" ["Yo he abierto en mis novelas un camino / por do la lengua castellana puede / mostrar con propiedad un desatino" (*Viaje del Parnaso* 304)]. Thus, for Ruan, the aimlessness and absence of origin that one perceives in the story underscore the fact that finality and origin are rendered invalid by the narrative, precisely to show the "desatino" ("nonsense") about which Cervantes has spoken. Likewise, Álvaro Molina names Cervantes's poetics as one of glass, focusing on "issues related to fragility and fractures, interpolation and interruptions, and the breach of *decorum* with the resulting interferences of life and literature" (Molina 9). Both scholars make convincing cases for fracture and fissure, as well as a certain aimlessness, as the very core of the narrative project in this tale. George Shipley acknowledges a fundamental limitation in the tale, yet alerts the reader to the split between the fictional narrator whom he qualifies as "incurious and inattentive" and the real Miguel de Cervantes, "who sought repeatedly in his art to teach us to be wary of the coercive authority of narrators" (Shipley 38). The narrator's "grievous errors of commission and omission" are "in need of re-ordering" by us, the readers (Shipley 7).

The critic Elaine Bunn explains the idea of repression in the novella using a Jungian frame of analysis. Bunn shows that the tale offers two sides, the conscious and the unconscious, showcasing fully what is masculine, yet allowing the feminine, "the private, sensual, erotic, affective world," to show up only indirectly and to remain always in a state of being hidden from the surface (Bunn 122). Noting that Tomás "consistently identifies with and advances patriarchal and masculine values and represses the affective, the feminine, and his own sexuality," Bunn suggests that the two women "challenge him to acknowledge that part of himself that up to that point he had been able to exclude from consciousness and systematically repress" (Bunn 124). This, precisely, is the Jungian "shadow": "that part of the personality which has been repressed for the sake of the ego ideal. Since everything unconscious is projected, we encounter the shadow in projection – in our view of 'the other fellow'" (Bunn 124). For Bunn then, these two women represent all that is repressed in Tomás, even if there has been a "subtle feminine presence" in his life, say in the shape of the kinds of books he chooses to take with him on his travels (Bunn 129). Thus, the two women "are libidinous, he is rigidly scrupulous; if they are Eros, Tomás is logos. They are the seductive Eves who offer the forbidden fruit. These also liminal figures represent his shadow, his personal unconscious threatening to reveal itself" (Bunn 130).

Yet alongside repression, the novella also offers exposure. In his period as a madman, "[n]o one is spared [his] verbal commentary" (Friedman 59). The tale uncovers a parade of professions, characters, and patterns of behaviour, all of which receive Tomás's opaque commentary, in need of deciphering. Through Tomás's pronouncements, the novella focuses on the tension between an impossibility of direct communication that coexists oddly with the transparency of that which is being said. Edmund L. King deciphers one such passage, illuminating a segment that is "not the least puzzling of the many insufficiently explained passages" of the tale (King 99).

> On one occasion, while Tomás was passing through the cloth-market of Salamanca, a female draper said to him, "My heart grieves for your misfortune, Mister Graduate, but what can I do, for I cannot weep?"
>
> Choosing his words very carefully, he turned to her and said, "Daughters of Jerusalem, weep for yourselves and for your children."
>
> The draper's husband understood the malicious thrust of his words and said to him, "Brother Graduate of Glass," for this is what he called himself, "you're more of a rogue than a madman." (*Exemplary Tales* 115)

> [Pasando, pues, una vez por la ropería de Salamanca, le dijo una ropera:
>
> —En mi ánima, señor Licenciado, que me pesa de su desgracia; pero ¿qué haré, que no puedo llorar?

Él se volvió a ella, y muy mesurado le dijo:

—*Filiae Hierusalem, plorate super vos et super filios vestros.*

Entendió el marido de la ropera la malicia del dicho, y díjole:

—Hermano Licenciado Vidriera — que así decía él que se llamaba —, más tenéis de bellaco que de loco.] (*Novelas* 119)

This might be, as some have argued, a reference to the illegitimate children borne by the "ropera." But King shows convincingly that here, Tomás indicates that he knows she is a Jew (or a *converso*) and "this is why [the husband] calls Tomás more of a scoundrel than a madman. For, in view of the contemporary attitude towards *conversos*, what greater mischief could Tomás do than to raise such a terrible suspicion?" (King 102) Here we have an example of a potentially risky truth uttered by the madman: Tomás uncovers an element that exists in society, but by official accounts should not be there. Edward H. Friedman observes that

> the potion awakens a dormant mental capacity and brings about another way of life. While studies had earlier made him detached from society, the imagined physical factor now isolates the licentiate from the world he so ably criticizes. In his fragile state, his voice provides his only source of power against a people more used to force of arms than of expression. (Friedman 55)

Friedman notes that when Tomás is cured, a "figurative silence" is imposed on him by none other than a member of the Church, the monk of the Order of San Jerónimo (Friedman 56). The critic explains that the three identities of Tomás each entails a different engagement with society. As Rodaja (in his early incarnation), he is isolated from society intellectually; as the Glass Graduate, he is physically disconnected; when he is cured, he enters a third identity as Rueda, whereupon he is no longer isolated nor detached, but he "elicits no response from the society he wishes to enter" (Friedman 56). This third identity, while it is his most complete, also points towards his demise, as explained eloquently by Friedman: "If development of the third identity signifies a new awakening, it is an awakening to a realization of defeat and a final doom" (Friedman 56). For Friedman, the novella does in fact have "a modulated inner structure" that traces the progressions of a life; the story is "the account of a process of growth — mental, emotional, and physical" (Friedman 58).

The interpretations invoked above show that the novella is deeply concerned with the repression of what is (supposedly) unwanted, and its narrative progress is characterized by an apparent aimlessness — a passage from beginning to end marked by many gaps — and a journey from an illness that creates exposure to a cure that, oddly, brings about silence. It also strives to reveal the hidden through Vidriera's cryptic aphorisms. Interestingly, one can see in all of this an echo of the

Morisco experience. If the story traces the trajectory of a transformation in one man's puzzling identity, it also allows room to recall another such transformation in the Morisco question.

For many Moriscos, life in the sixteenth and seventeenth centuries underwent a similar kind of movement. The ever-increasing pressure on various Morisco communities in Castile, though varied in scope and degree, brought about a scrutiny of their origins, identity, activities, and supposed identity, especially by official Christian discourse (García Arenal; Perry). Sweeping generalizations regarding Moriscos are not a possibility, for after the fall of Granada their situation depended largely on the region and the structures of power in operation at any given time; however, there can be little doubt that in general the circle tightened around them and their identity was increasingly described by official rule as undesirable and impure. To quote Mary Elizabeth Perry, their "difference" soon began to be expressed as "deviance" (Perry 47), and regardless of what they did – for some did genuinely convert and integrate into Old Christian society – they were always under suspicion (Perry 80). The complication, best articulated by literature, arose from the fact that they were born and raised in Spain, and thus the descriptions of their identity and their behaviour in law and literature did register – albeit unconsciously – the shifts in their integration, detachment, separation, and belonging to society. The development of fiction on Moorish themes – portraying the Moor as valiant and noble if a little impulsive – or the Ricote episode in *Don Quijote* are examples of fiction's engagement with the tremendous discomfort with the Morisco's place in society. These genres and episodes problematized and fantasized the Moor or Morisco, but always drew attention one way or another to the fact that this identity was a part of Spanish history and society: as enemy, friend, convert or suspect. Thus, the Moriscos can be said to have moved through the sixteenth and seventeenth centuries in trajectories that, like that of Tomás, described paradoxical and uncomfortable points of belonging and alienation. The main difference, of course, is that Tomás moves in linear fashion from one point to the next, whereas the socio-political reality of Morisco life meant a much less neat progression between forms of inclusion and exclusion.

The novella's simultaneous stifling and uncovering can be recognized in the presence of Islam in post-Reconquista Christian Spain. In much the same way that "El Licenciado Vidriera" nudges the reader towards the fissures of the tale and the hidden, repressed presences of Tomás's world, the Islamic past of Spain surfaces through numerous monuments, texts, and artefacts of Christian Spain, often visible only through fissures or as a shadow. It is the uncanny: an awareness of the familiarity of something that is, nonetheless, projected as foreign or unfamiliar. In this case, it has to do with the persistence of non-Christian elements in a framework (official discourse) that wishes to purge and disregard these elements.

In spite of resistance from some corners, the process of showing the non-Christian dimensions of Christian art in early modern Spain is today becoming increasingly familiar and common. It is no longer considered subversive nor innovative to perceive the hybrid, multi-cultural identity of canonical Romance texts, and to show how they try either to repress or manifest in coded form their debt to non-Christian tropes or influences. However, this contemporary scholarly trend is far removed from practices of half-a-century ago, not to mention Cervantes's own time. That is, the discomfort and erasure of the Morisca's presence in "El Licenciado Vidriera" are indicative of a larger anxiety in Cervantes's writing – evidenced also by the Ricote episode in *Don Quijote* and the references to non-Christians in "El coloquio de los perros" – about what to do with the reality of an increasingly xenophobic Spain.

Tomás's cure and his supposed reintegration into society act as metaphors of this unease. Critics such as Friedman have read the ending of the novella in several ways, noting the possibility that it does not, in fact, offer a reintegration at all. As mentioned, the ending is unusually brief, almost abrupt. The sense of closure is undermined, to quote Ruan again, by a kind of dissonance that once again points out everything that is omitted throughout the tale: we never find out who Tomás's real family is, and his sane being does not represent a complete and whole self (Ruan 159). He changes identities, and, unable to gain recognition from the community now that he has recovered his reason, leaves Spain. This silence concerning his origins could be another fissure in the narrative, or it "might be due to a mature rejection of the traditional norms of evaluating self-worth and acknowledging personal success" (Bunn 134).

The refusal to allow Tomás a full and traditional "happy ending" echoes an anxiety on the narrative's part that even after a cure, things are not entirely fine. The parallel with the Morisco experience is again compelling: just as the monk's cure fails to restore Tomás – and we do not even know who the real Tomás is – the measures to cleanse society and restore it to an original purity (through the Inquisition or the imminent expulsion of Moriscos) will not provide the wholeness of society for which official Spain might have hoped.

Note that this parallel is by no means explicit, nor does this essay wish to make a watertight case for a point-for-point and therefore simplistic correspondence between Tomás and Moriscos. Rather, it is worth noticing the uncanny echo of minority experience in Tomás's trajectory: the issues of belonging, alienation, and integration raised by Tomás's case recall those of the Islamic and Morisco presence in Spain in Cervantes's time, suggesting not so much that Cervantes had this specific parallel in mind, but rather that these questions were almost impossible to escape when attempting to represent life in art. Naturally, alienation and integration are a staple of all fiction and not exclusive to Cervantes; the shadow of Islam comes into focus with the fragmented presence of the Morisca and her magic quince.

The Morisca's brief appearance suggests at first sight that she is a blocking character, and a minor one at that; yet the decisive impact of her advice, taken alongside other disturbing fragmentations and disproportions in a text that keeps attempting to create symmetry in the stages of Tomás's life, implies otherwise. The shadow of Islam in the novella is projected through the Morisca, who remains, uncomfortably, on the margins of the text, yet establishes an important framework for the tale. The half-complete clause in which she makes her one and only appearance points at something that ought to have already disappeared but still remains, a part of the fabric of society that cannot be purged, however strenuous the effort to wash it out.

The Morisca is the instrument of Tomás's bizarre entry into society, while a Christian monk is the instrument of his exit from it. The Morisca opens, and the Christian closes: in between, a Spaniard with no fixed name and no origin circulates in the world like the wheel that is suggested by his two names, and exposes "the fundamental ambivalence of madness, this other face of reason and of wisdom, united to them by a relationship of reversibility" (Redondo 39). So, if the Morisca is the shadow of Islam, the cure can be thought of as an expulsion of the unwanted poison and insanity (the imminent expulsion of the Moriscos) that, instead of leading to a fully satisfactory ending, leads to a refusal of closure and completeness.

Ruth El Saffar has suggested that Don Quixote and the Glass Graduate – Cervantes's two famous madmen – represent the intellectual's effort to challenge society, but that the intellectual "is an alienated being whose will to make direct contact with the society from which he has at the same time wished to escape is condemned to failure" (El Saffar 60). Of importance is El Saffar's notion that the quince only exaggerates what was already in Tomás: an unease with the self, and a quest to use knowledge as "a means to disarm reality of its persistent corrosion of life and health and personal integrity" (El Saffar 57). To this, and drawing on the writings of Américo Castro and Stephen Gilman, she adds that this desperation might echo a New Christian (i.e., convert) attitude (El Saffar 60). Certainly if one were to subscribe to the views of Castro, Gilman, Francisco Márquez Villaueva and the many other scholars who see Cervantes's poetics as one of subversion and protest against Inquisitorial attitudes, the shadow of Islam would gain even more prominence in the novella. The quince and the Morisca, in this light, will have mobilized a frustration and a despair that were already present but are now exaggerated in the form of the Glass Graduate.

"El Licenciado Vidriera" describes a trajectory of belonging and alienation that contains an overarching anxiety about beginnings as well as a cynical engagement with endings. Equating illness with insight and cure with dissatisfaction, it sets up a model for the analysis of supposedly undesirable versus seemingly desirable elements in the life of one Tomás Rodaja/Rueda. As this essay argues, Cervantes's description of this life bears an uncanny resemblance to an entirely plausible description of another life, that of the Moriscos on the Iberian Peninsula. As tidy as the stages of Tomás's life as well as the causes and effects of his trajectory appear to be, the novella soon demonstrates that all sequencing is subject to dispute and all causes are subordinated to latent factors that precede them. The Morisca appears briefly as a wrongdoer and as the apparent cause of the insanity; but the insanity turns out to be integrally connected with Tomás's previous personality, not to mention a curious blessing. Stripped of her causal power, the Morisca now becomes a shadow of Islam in the tale, asking the reader to associate her fragmented presence with another story being told in Spain at the same time as the story of Rodaja: a tale of the uncertain origins of Moriscos, their confused integration, and metaphors of contamination and purity imposed by official discourse on situations that contained neither purity nor contamination.

The shadow of glass, as all physicists know, is invisible except around the edges. The Glass Graduate's frail and transparent body casts just such a shadow on his surroundings as he walks through Salamanca, and the name of this largely invisible shadow could well be Islam.

NOTE

1 "Morisco" is the term often used to describe New Christians (converts) of Moorish, i.e., Muslim extraction in Iberia. However, the term needs to be used with some caution. As L.P. Harvey explains, in Spanish it can mean anything that is broadly Moorish – for example, a musical instrument. In such a sense it does not relate to the idea of a Muslim who has converted to Catholicism, but it can also mean the latter more specifically (Harvey 202).

15 "The Finest Flowering": Poetry, History, and Medieval Spain in the Twenty-First Century

MARÍA ROSA MENOCAL

One of the last things written by Edward Said before his death in December 2002 was a bittersweet article on Spain for a popular travel magazine, *Travel and Leisure*. "For me, and indeed for many Arabs," he writes near the beginning, "Andalusia [*sic*] still represents the finest flowering of our culture. That is particularly true now, when the Arab Middle East seems mired in defeat and violence, its societies unable to arrest their declining fortunes, its secular culture so full of almost surreal crisis, shock and nihilism" (Said, "Andalusia's Journey" 181).[1] The whole of Said's article veers back and forth between pride in the incomparable achievements of moments like tenth-century Umayyad Cordoba and anger, directed first and foremost against "the self-destructive demise of the Andalusian kings and their *tawa'if*" – which he explicitly compares to "present-day Arab disunity and consequent weakness," pointing out the inescapable linguistic resonance and connection between the Andalusian *muluk al-tawa'if* (the *taifa*s, or city-states, of the eleventh century) and the warring confessional sects (*tawa'if*) of the Lebanese civil wars of our own age.

One is tempted to see this late essay of Said's in the context of that long tradition in Arabic letters which William Granara, adopting Bakhtin's figure, has called the "Andalusian chronotope." Said himself here muses briefly on this powerful literary tradition; among other things, he quotes the "Andalusian Ode" of the Palestinian poet Mahmoud Darwish. In this tradition, the figure of a long-gone al-Andalus can be evoked by the poet or novelist to reflect not on the past, but rather on the present and the future of his own society and times. But Said is not writing in that Arabic literary tradition, but rather speaking to a non-academic American public. And his contemplation of the meaning of the history of Islamic Spain is part of a surprisingly widespread phenomenon, in our times, of interest in medieval Spain. Medieval Spain has become relevant, even chic. A field that was a backwater in literary studies until not so long ago – indeed, until the very beginning of the twenty-first century – has come out of its traditional obscurity and into the limelight. At the same time, concerns that were once almost exclusively those of Arab writers – Just what does al-Andalus mean? Can its image help shape a better future? – have become the concerns of a much broader public in the West.

All of this has happened thanks to the mostly tragic political events on the world stage at the beginning of the twenty-first century, beginning with 9/11. Needless to say, these dramatic episodes are profoundly rooted in the history of the twentieth century; it is not as if the searing conflict between Arabs and Israelis, or the problems of Muslim communities inside Europe, or, indeed, the kinds of hostilities manifest in 9/11 were not around before the turn of the twenty-first century – during all those years when medieval Spain was not fashionable at all, when al-Andalus was a name unfamiliar even to some medievalist colleagues. But, clearly, we are now on the other side of a "perfect storm" of events which seem to have defined the beginnings of the twenty-first century, including Osama bin Laden's own evocation of what he called the "tragedy of al-Andalus" in a number of his post-9/11 communiqués,[2] and the choice of Spain itself as a target for a large-scale terrorist attack in March of 2004, after which again the ghost of medieval Spain was explicitly evoked.[3] Whatever the causes, the dramatic shift is undeniable. We now inhabit a previously improbable universe in which the history of medieval Spain is widely perceived – either openly or covertly – as tied to the political dramas of our times, and as a history that can thus shed light on and perhaps even provide guidance in the most searing political problems of the twenty-first century.

And this is true across the full political spectrum – as Said's emotionally charged piece makes perfectly clear, as is revealed in Bin Laden's dramatically different notion of the virtues of al-Andalus. For Bin Laden, and for many others who know little about the actual history of the time and place, al-Andalus evokes an Islamic presence in Europe imagined to have been pure and hegemonic: a moment of presumably merciless dominion over Christians and Jews, "when we used to truly adhere to Islam" (as Bin Laden says in one of his broadcasts). This is a history that lends itself with greater ease than most to a remarkable range of interpretations, including the most contradictory. This is either the age of *convivencia* or *reconquista*, to put it at its most blunt and facile. It is either about how the three Abrahamic religions fruitfully co-existed or about how, in truth, they could not. Virtually every political lesson can potentially be extracted from the tale. And although, like many of us who work in the field of medieval Spain, I now frequently find myself asked to comment on the lessons that this medieval universe provides for our own times, I do not believe that beyond a handful of pieties and self-evident generalizations there is much conventional political wisdom to be had here – certainly not of that easy or unambiguous kind which is what audiences seem to want, distilled to a sound bite or a 300-word newspaper editorial or even to a *New Yorker* article.

But there are other kinds of insights to be had here, and all sorts of reasons to take advantage of the prominence that, thanks to a series of tragic events, medieval Spain has lately acquired. These are our fifteen minutes, for those happy few of us who have long fought a seemingly impossible battle to make others see (among many other things) how central to the transmission of culture in the West medieval Spain was. And so it seems vital to use them as effectively as we can – occasionally for a general public, but especially inside the academy, dwelling on what we might think of as the "morals" of the story for literary and cultural studies, those that can be drawn from our knowledge of medieval Spain. And I do mean "Spain" rather than al-Andalus – thus an anachronistic "Spain," in all its pre-national lack of coherence and uniformity, encompassing that ever-shifting al-Andalus but also much more: the Christian kingdoms (usually feuding amongst themselves), the immensely varied community of Sefarad. Indeed, this is the first and perhaps most significant lesson: the notion that the components of "al-Andalus" can be meaningfully isolated from each other is an insidious one, no matter the motivation.

But before addressing the ways in which our modern-language disciplinary boundaries make medieval Spain so difficult to study – which I will return to briefly later – let me instead go down a different road. Let us return to Said's angry analogy between the eleventh-century *taifa*s and the Lebanese civil wars, an association that makes explicit the most unavoidable paradox, for those of us who are students first and foremost of the literature and only secondarily of the political history. It was in the *taifa*s – and not in unified, prosperous and relatively peaceful Cordoba – that Andalusian poetic culture achieved its greatest glories. The comparison is conventionally made (and it is not a bad one) with the Italian Renaissance, when individual city-states had murderous attitudes towards each other, yet out of political chaos great cultural achievement arose.

But whether we use that particular analogy or another, whether we focus on the eleventh century or another moment (there is no shortage of instances in which cultural achievement and political well-being correspond not at all, or correspond inversely), the overriding question is one that medieval Spain forces us to confront explicitly: just what is the relationship of literature (and other aesthetic forms) to politics, to *history* as it is usually understood? This is, of course, a vast question; but if you get your fifteen minutes it seems just that they should be spent on big questions – not in order to provide more of those facile political answers, but rather to establish what the interesting big questions are and how they might be pursued. And medieval Spain is a gold mine of such big questions, in some measure for those same reasons that now make it a gold mine of political relevance.

I had a very telling encounter a couple of years ago, when I delivered a series of talks in Cairo on "the memory of al-Andalus." During the first talk I showed a series of slides of some of the arresting buildings of medieval Spain, including a number of those churches and synagogues built in what is commonly called the "Mudejar" or Islamicizing style.[4] And I read excerpts from some of the poetry of the moment: the new Hebrew poetry (a poetry created by Jewish poets whose native language was Arabic, and informed by a profound symbiosis with Arabic poetry)[5] as well as some of the great bilingual poetry, which Romance permeates and in which it is explicitly inscribed into the Arabic tradition, and vice versa. This display of medieval Spain's profoundly hybrid culture prepared the audience for the second part of my presentation, when I would talk about why the memory of this past had been so assiduously and lovingly cultivated by so many different constituencies, by Palestinians like Darwish and Said, but also by the late nineteenth-century Ashkenazi Jews who built synagogues in what is conventionally called the "Moorish" or "Moorish revival" style. These and many other cultural monuments speak loudly to the stunningly complex interaction of the three faiths, and how aesthetically, intellectually and even spiritually productive those interactions were.

But at the end of that first talk, a young woman stood up and said: "This is all well and good and indeed very lovely, these buildings, this poetry ... but where are the real people, and their real history?" I was taken aback, and replied suggesting that poetry and buildings *were* a part of our reality. But of course the underlying question – or one of the potential implied questions – is not to be dismissed lightly. On the one hand, I have little sympathy for what might be termed the pseudo-Marxist version of the question: the notion that poetry and fine buildings belong only to the privileged, and that in writing their history we are ignoring that of the "real people." But on the other hand, the question asks us to contemplate the relationship of culture to the other spheres that constitute history. And this challenge is fundamental, especially so at a moment like this: a moment of sometimes-dramatic disciplinary changes in the academy, and a moment at which people are looking at the different histories we are writing – whether they are architectural or literary or musical – as guideposts for an understanding of a culture at large, sometimes even of our own culture at large, its present, its future. The concluding sentence of Said's essay for *Travel and Leisure* says it as directly as one can: medieval Spain "enacted an earlier version of our own hybrid world, one whose borders were also thresholds, and whose multiple identities formed an enriched diversity." And in our academic universe, at the beginning of the twenty-first century, the question of what poetry (using this word now as shorthand for the aesthetic overall) has to do with the rest of society, and with the histories of societies, is fundamental to the ongoing redefinition of literary studies. The changes at hand have brought us very far indeed from where we were when talking about anything other than the "text itself" was virtually forbidden in literature departments – not so long ago, in the last part of the twentieth century.

What does it mean – to take just one currently controversial example – to talk about a "Golden Age" in Jewish culture in the Islamic polities of eleventh- and twelfth-century Spain, when we know (as it is now *de rigeur* to point out explicitly) that *dhimma* status is not social or political equality, and when we know that persecutions and indeed massacres of Jews took place during this period? Perhaps this was the gist of the question from the young woman in Cairo. If a handful of men (dead white males, no less) wrote great poetry, what does that tell us about the lives of ordinary people? What does poetry, in sum, have to do with social issues? Just what do metrical patterns and the shapes of arches tell us about *la realidad histórica* – the "reality on the ground" – to use that wonderful expression coined by the great theoretician of the Spanish symbiosis, Américo Castro? He would say they told us a great deal: Castro was himself first and foremost a literary historian of the Spanish "Golden Age," not that of the Jews of the eleventh century, but rather of the very different *Siglo de Oro* of the sixteenth and seventeenth centuries in Spain. It is more than just a curiosity in the biography of this scholar who so radically transformed how we understand medieval "Spain" to note that he did not start out as a medievalist at all, and that in fact he was not a historian, properly speaking, although it would be difficult to argue that anyone has had a greater impact on how the history of the period is perceived or the terms in which it is argued. And his first epiphanies about the remarkable cultural and religious mixes of the Middle Ages in the peninsula, about the profound hybridity of all of Spanish identity, came from his readings of much later literature – most prominently Cervantes's masterpiece, *Don Quixote*: literature in which he sensed that the Spaniards were struggling with a past that was being eradicated in their *Siglo de Oro*.

This *Siglo de Oro* or "Golden Age," we must surely note, coincides almost perfectly with the horrors of the Inquisition, the terrible history of the Moriscos whose tragic final expulsions come in the years between the publication of parts I and II of Cervantes's masterpiece, and the more-often-than-not brutal colonization of the Americas, to mention just the highlights. So on the one hand the best and perhaps most frustrating answer to the question of what constitutes "Golden Ages" is to note that the term denotes not a political or social but rather an aesthetic judgment: these periods have to do with the triumphs of literature or philosophy or architecture or music or some combination of these or of other aesthetic forms. And these achievements may or may not take place in what we would consider anything like ideal social or political circumstances. Make a list of your own favourites, those times and places that produced books we still read, buildings we imitate, ideals to which we aspire: Periclean Athens, Jeffersonian democracy, Renaissance Florence. And then ask yourself whether the social realities of those moments are up to our minimal standards, let alone whether they are utopian by our early-twenty-first century measures. And yet this is the most common criticism leveled again medieval Spain: "The *dhimma* isn't really equal protection under the law, is it?" "If there were massacres of Jews, how can you call it the 'Golden Age'?"

But of course one of the vexing things about great art is that it is sometimes made by terrible people. One of Said's great passions in life was Wagner – or, rather, his music; and Said ended up embroiled, as many Wagnerites do, in sometimes bitter and politically charged discussions about the terrible man and his wonderful music. And sometimes great art is made not by terrible people but by boring people, or perhaps even by wonderful people, but under terrible or at least imperfect social and historical circumstances, especially by our own exacting standards, which all too often we tacitly assume to be historically and geographically transcendent ideals. If we measure and define the achievements of an age by its cultural profile, perhaps (this is certainly what some would argue) we are making statements *only* about the cultural artefacts, and not really, or not necessarily, about the culture within which they were created. Yet there is a great deal more to it than that, and if there were not – if we were to argue that there is nothing more than a random connection between aesthetic achievements and other aspects of history – then we would be back at ground zero: circa 1965 structuralism, or 1975 deconstruction, with nothing left outside the "text itself."

However, thanks to the persistence of philology, we no longer work in those times and places; and in the search for both contemporary and historical meaning, the role that poetry plays (and once again I mean "poetry" as shorthand, to evoke all the art forms) is perhaps the most difficult one, and thus the most indispensable: poetry reveals the sometimes unbearable contradictions that political and ideological discourse rarely tolerates. Américo Castro's insights about the profound intermarriage of the different peoples of Spain during the medieval centuries were based on his readings of the turmoil that lies just beneath the surface of the most canonical works of Castilian literature in later centuries, when Spain had seemingly become "purely Christian" and monolingual, quite the opposite of what it had once been. For Castro, the brilliance of the many masterpieces of this later period came from the veiled writerly struggles with the many repressions of the moment: those of society, and those of the memory of the earlier period. So perhaps literature does indeed tell us a history – or histories, really – that other kinds of historical records obscure. We might even say that those of us who are historians of the aesthetic forms are also writing what Cervantes would slyly call a *verdadera historia*, a true (hi)story.

Indeed, in attempting to get a sense of the texture and tenor of a historical period, we might ask why we should privilege the evidence of other forms – of documents overtly expressing church or state ideology, for example – over that of poetry: not because those other kinds of documents and memories are not themselves true reflections, but rather because they may speak *no more* truthfully or revealingly about *la realidad histórica* than the poetic forms do. Consider, for example, the tough *reconquista* ideology articulated in the highly influential histories of Rodrigo Jimenez de Rada, his notion that Spain is defined in the crusade-like struggle to expel the Moors: do his strident assertions about Christian identity tell us what life and culture and even politics were really about at the turn of the thirteenth century, in the ascendant kingdom of Castile? Or is that reality revealed as truthfully – perhaps more truthfully – in the interweaving of Arabic and Latin on the walls of the Castilian church of San Román, a church that Rodrigo himself consecrated in 1221; or in the gown in which Rodrigo was buried, with its elaborately embroidered kufic border – a gown that was itself one of many gifts exchanged between Castilians and Andalusians? Such gifts speak to wars and treaties – but also to cultural longing and shared tastes.

The best answer is the most Abelardian, the most medieval: to accept both the "yes" and the "no," to become so comfortable with the paradoxes that we can assume them as necessary. We should not play the role of normative exegetes to mystical poetry, trying to make poetry adhere to the rules set by the lawmakers. Sometimes laws reflect the values and the normative realities of a society; but sometimes poetry does a better job of it, telling a very different story and one which is at least as true. Much of the challenge and the pleasure of our work is to be able to dwell on these contradictions, rather than attempt to reconcile them or imagine that only one of them can really be true. So – much as the great theoreticians of literary deconstruction did – we should be attentive to the power of paradox and the revelations that lie in contradictions, scrutinizing the vast yes-and-no-ness of the cultures of medieval Spain. Thus we can grasp the exemplariness of phenomena such as the flourishing of Arabic poetry in the politically disastrous eleventh century, the homoerotic lyrics of some of the most revered rabbis, or the *Mudejar* or "Islamicizing" architecture of the Christian-warrior Castilians who, although mostly remembered as the leaders of the wars to expel the Muslims from the peninsula, were at the same time the engineers of the pluralistic and multilingual society of the Toledo where the Arabic library was translated, first into Latin – thereby transforming intellectual life throughout Latin Christendom – and then into Castilian. And Castilian, we must surely note, as the new written language of this culture born in supposed intractable opposition to Islam, is a language literally born out of Arabic: out of those translations from Arabic not just of words but of approaches to the universe. These kinds of vivid contradictions speak to the special properties of poetry, the arts and intellectual life, and to what these forms tell us that political and religious documents cannot or will not. At the heart of the difference with the high theory of the last decades of the twentieth century is the assumption that we are also able to learn and teach things about "history itself" from the study of the unruly arts. We are necessarily readers not just of the "poetry itself" but also of the culture that made possible the aesthetic forms of the moment, and we thus learn things about society from aesthetic forms that would otherwise be unknowable.

Susan Sontag articulated some of this notion in one of her posthumously published essays (like Said's essay on Spain, a late meditation, written in the shadow of impending death): "A great writer of fiction, by writing truthfully about the society in which she or he lives, cannot but help evoke (if only by their absence) the better standards of justice and truthfulness that we have the right (some would say the duty) to militate for in the necessarily imperfect societies in which we live" (Sontag 213). I would modify this very slightly and note that those "better standards of justice and truthfulness" necessarily do exist in a culture; but often enough only the poets, the musicians and the painters can really express them. Poets, Percy Shelley famously said in his "Defence of Poetry," are the unacknowledged legislators of the world. Like other legislators', sometimes their efforts succeed and other times (perhaps most of the time) they do not. Obviously, the *Quixote* – despite its poignant lament for what Spain had become, and despite the tears it openly sheds in some of its chapters for the various social catastrophes at hand – did not change the course of political affairs. It certainly did not prevent the expulsion of the Moriscos (which Cervantes in some of his writing openly advocated) any more than Ibn Zaydun's *Nuniyya* or the *muwashshahat* – or any of the great Arabic poetry of the eleventh century – prevented the disintegration of the *taifa*s that led to their colonization by the Almoravids. The irony, generally accepted these days, is that the Almoravids were powerfully affected by the aesthetic and other values of the Andalusians – values they originally decried and sought to reform.

Just what does a rhyme or metrical form or the shape of an arch reveal about the shifting relationships of different strands of a culture with each other? A great deal, perhaps: our lives and values are in some measure shaped by the aesthetics of our universe. And a society is itself necessarily affected – again, in some measure – by the presence of those aesthetic monuments that it has produced through reading books, hearing music, praying in churches with Arabic writing on their walls. And we must acknowledge that this whole universe of aesthetic forms in turn shapes, either through reaction or imitation, the next generation's aesthetics and thus some part of its values – unless we still cling to the belief that there is little or nothing beyond the "text itself" and that the aesthetics of the text carry little or no social or political or historical value; or that, even if they do, it is not our job as readers of literature to worry about those. Philology persists in telling us otherwise.

But it was not so long ago that this was the orthodox view in literary studies, and along with it came a parallel, new orthodoxy: that the languages of the modern nations are the natural or best divisions for institutionalized literary study. But while the notion that the aesthetic is divorceable from the historical has become irrelevant in many quarters, the hold of the national over the literary is, if anything, more powerful than it has ever been. And here, once again, medieval Spain provides a powerful specimen: a marvellous philological proof-text that forces us to question the conventional pieties, so utterly incomprehensible is it inside that paradigm. With its spectacularly complex literary history, involving half a dozen intertwined languages, and with an extraordinary array of texts that then spill out of the peninsula to reshape "western culture" – the troubadour song traditions, the intellectual ferment of Paris in the thirteenth century, the framed tales of Boccaccio and Chaucer, to name only the most unarguable – medieval Spain deserves to be on centre stage and exploited, not only for its political and historical relevance but perhaps even more so for the ways in which it can help us redefine what literary studies could and should be in the twenty-first century. Indeed, the philological lessons are far less ambiguous than the social ones; and philology, especially Romance philology, has long been the holdout against the various tyrannies in literary studies in the last half of the twentieth century.

Philology has always been about meaning, and about the human struggle to find meaning that literary texts chronicle. Sometimes that might be an intensely personal and existential matter; but mostly, no matter how private, it is inextricably bound up with the culture and history of the artefact. Language itself, after all, is culturally and temporally bound – which is what philology teaches us, very directly. At the same time, Romance philology has long been a field capacious and historical enough to embrace the study of Arabic – or just about any other language, whether Romance or not. For some of us, Arabic was part of our training because Arabic was unambiguously a part of the Romance world during the medieval period. "Romance," in that expression, is both less and more than a technical linguistic demarcation – and in any event, as Hans Ulrich Gumbrecht has brilliantly showed (Gumbrecht, "Un Souffle d'Allemagne"), Romance philology was the anti-national-philology, the creation of the nationless nineteenth-century Germans, so dramatically different from their national, and nationalizing, counterparts. What makes a broad study of medieval Spain possible is that exilic philological paradigm so vividly on display in Erich Auerbach's *Mimesis*, which begins with a reading of a Hebrew and a Greek text, and ends with a reading of twentieth-century English. Auerbach, towards the end of his life, would make the point explicitly when he wrote "our philological home is the earth: it can no longer be the nation."[6]

Medieval Spain, at the beginning of the twenty-first century, presents us with a vivid opportunity to reassert the enduring value of that poignant observation – a statement informed by the history of Auerbach's exile, and iconic of some of the most profound tragedies of the twentieth century. In his "Eleven Planets over the Last Andalusian Sky" – the long poem sometimes referred to as his Andalusian *qasida*, or ode – Mahmoud Darwish writes: "And in the end we will ask ourselves: 'Was Andalus here or there? On the land? Or in the poem?'" The poet's reluctant answer is that even if it was once in the land, its difficult beauty and truth can only endure in the poem (or the novel, the building, the music). Poetry, the text itself, can indeed speak to us truthfully, powerfully, about history itself. Sometimes – and this a man like Cervantes, who was both a man of the "real world" and of letters, would surely tell us – it is the only authentic historical memory. Often enough it is the best.

NOTES

1 Said's use of the word "Andalusia" for "al-Andalus," or more simply "Andalus," the original Arabic name for the Islamic lands of the Iberian peninsula, reflects some of the considerable awkwardness of terminology that plagues discussions of medieval Spain. "Andalusia" is no doubt a contamination of "Andalus" with the contemporary Spanish "Andalucía." This autonomous region in the south encompasses many of the most famous cities and sites of al-Andalus but is far from coterminous with the medieval polities, which themselves varied enormously in both time and space – encompassing the majority of the peninsula at one extreme, in the early centuries, but reduced to the lone city of Granada at the other. The confusion with the modern southern region provoked by using "Andalusia" to talk about the medieval obscures the fact (among others) that notable northern cities – such as Saragossa or Toledo – were long vital parts of al-Andalus.

2 The story in the *New York Times* on 9 October 2001 reports on Bin Laden's widely watched televised speech soon after 9/11, and includes the following paragraph: "In the same broadcast, Ayman al-Zawahiri, Mr. bin Laden's deputy and the leader of the Islamic Jihad group, vowed that 'the tragedy of al-Andalus' would not be repeated. He was referring to the period widely considered the Islamic golden age in Andalusia, in

Spain, that ended in the ignominy of Muslims being driven out of Europe by Christian armies in the fifteenth century" (Sachs).

3   The terrorist cell in the Madrid suburb that carried out the attacks at Atocha station identified itself as "the brigade situated in al-Andalus" and, in a public message reconstructed after the cell was stormed, talked about Spain as the "land of Tariq ibn Ziyad." An excellent recounting of much of this can be found in the "Reporter at Large" article by Lawrence Wright in *The New Yorker*, an illuminating narrative of the Madrid bombings which includes the following:

Less than a month after 9/11, Osama bin Laden and his chief lieutenant, Dr. Ayman al-Zawahiri, had appeared on Al Jazeera. "We will not accept that the tragedy of al-Andalus will be repeated in Palestine," Zawahiri said, drawing an analogy between the expulsion of the Moors from Iberia and the present-day plight of the Palestinians. The use of the archaic name al-Andalus left most Spaniards nonplussed. "We took it as a folkloric thing," Ramón Pérez-Maura, an editor at ABC, told me. "We probably actually laughed." This January, bin Laden issued a "Message to the Muslim People," which was broadcast on Al Jazeera. He lamented the decline of the Islamic world: "It is enough to know that the economy of all Arab countries is weaker than the economy of one country that had once been part of our world when we used to truly adhere to Islam. That country is the lost al-Andalus."

4   Mudejar derives from the Arabic word *mudajjan*, or "those left behind": i.e., the Muslims who remained in ancestral territories after they were ruled by Christians. It was adopted as a term to describe the Islamicized architectural style that both Christians and Jews used widely for many centuries. The original and in some quarters still tacit assumption was that the corps of Muslim craftsmen and builders in Christian territories were the agents of such a style, a view that obscures the extent to which this was in fact not an "Islamic" style but rather a shared building tradition in the peninsula. For a fuller discussion see Dodds, Menocal and Balbale.

5   Our access to and understanding of this body of poetry has recently been incomparably enriched with the publication of Peter Cole's anthology of translations – *The Dream of the Poem*, a luminous title taken from one of the Andalusian odes of Mahmoud Darwish, which is also quoted by Said in his "Andalusia's Journey" article. Andalus, says Darwish, "might be here or there, or anywhere … a meeting place of strangers in the project of building human culture … It is not only that there was a Jewish-Muslim co-existence, but that the fates of the two peoples were similar … Al-Andalus for me is the realization of the dream of the poem" (Cole vii). It is unfortunate that neither such quality translations, nor such a comprehensive anthology of any kind of translations, exists for the great corpus of Hispano-Arabic poetry, even though that extended body of poetic work includes some of the most spectacular examples of "courtly

love" as well as the hybrid Andalusian song forms – the muwashshaha and the zajal – that to this day are sung throughout North Africa.

6 This phrase appears in an essay lovingly translated by Edward Said (Auerbach, "Philology and Weltliteratur" 17) and remembered in Said's own writings (Said, *The World, the Text, and the Critic* 7). For an extended discussion of these and closely related issues see Menocal, *Shards of Love*, especially "The Inventions of Philology."

16 Boustrophedon: Towards a Literary Theory of the Mediterranean

KARLA MALLETTE

I.

Literary historians have arrived late to the Mediterranean, a fact which the observer of modern intellectual history might find baffling. Economic historians, social historians and anthropologists – with all their concern for the verifiable and the falsifiable and the quantifiable – have their Mediterranean. They debate the valence of the term and its transhistorical validity; but the Mediterranean exists in their disciplines as a regional lens and a disciplinary modifier. And classicists use the rubric "Mediterranean" to refer to the Semitic, Greek, and Latin cultures, including the literatures, of the region.[1] The sea would seem to be a natural field of play for literary historians: ripe with metaphorical possibility, a map with a trackless void at its centre, theory-ready. Yet we have not tried to formulate a theory of the Mediterranean.

The reason for our resistance to Mediterranean thinking, I believe, is self-evident. It goes to the heart of what it means to view literary history regionally rather than nationally. To think the Mediterranean as a literary historical category means to propose a unity that transcends – for however brief a moment – the cultural differences that fragment the Mediterranean region. It requires us to join together shores which God has put asunder. We typically think of religious difference as the most decisive of the cultural distinctions that fragment the Mediterranean. The divide between Islam and Christianity bisects the Mediterranean Sea; the northern shore of the Mediterranean may be defined – with a notorious lack of geographic precision – as western (albeit differently western) because it is Christian (that is, Catholic Christian). And the southern and eastern edges of the sea constitute the near shores of the Islamic "Orient." But philology teaches us that language is the first and most potent orthodoxy. The most fundamental cultural rift in the Mediterranean is the breach between language written from left to right and language written from right to left.

The word *boustrophedon* – the word comes from a Greek adverb which means "turning like oxen pulling a plough" – refers to a style of writing, used in archaic texts and inscriptions, in which the text runs from left to right and from right to left in alternate lines. This mode of writing possesses undeniable advantages. The eye need not jump at the end of each line to the opposite margin. Boustrophedon script – if its proponents are to be believed – promotes a more seamless interface with the text. And because it does not impose a jump in the line of vision, it encourages the flow of thought.[2] I use the word *boustrophedon* in the title of this essay to suggest any number of physical, historical, intellectual and linguistic turns, returns and reversals relevant to the themes of this book. Not all the essays collected here concern *literary* history; Suzanne Akbari and I share a conviction that literary historians may learn valuable lessons from scholars working on parallel questions in other disciplines. We maintained a steady focus on the *medieval* Mediterranean, but also included essays on more recent topics which we, as medievalists, found engaging, provocative, and useful. We are both primarily Europeanists, trained in the early history of the languages and literary traditions of modern Europe. But we have come to understand that Europe (to follow in the grand tradition of riffing on Prince Metternich's pronouncement concerning Italy) is a geographical expression. During the Middle Ages, one cannot think "Europe" without thinking the Mediterranean. This final essay will reflect on the task of thinking the Mediterranean in a literary context – not with the aim of framing a theory of the Mediterranean, but rather of posing some of the questions that might animate such a theory and thus suggesting what it might look like.

In his magisterial work on the Mediterranean, Fernand Braudel cites a letter from a Spanish monarch to her brother. Referring to the slow pace of communicating by hand-delivered letters in the Mediterranean of the sixteenth century, she complains about "lo que se pierde en ir y venir" (Braudel, *Mediterranean World* 1:355). What is "lost in the coming and going" in our standard narratives of medieval literary history is the nature of the relations among the linguistic communities of the Mediterranean: Arabic, Latin and Romance along with a host of territorially coterminous languages, including (but not exclusively) Hebrew, Turkish, Armenian, and Greek. The essays in this volume attempt nothing so audacious; who, after all, could claim to take into account the Babelian complexity of the Mediterranean in its entirety? Our strategy here is more focused. Attention to the linguistic specificities of medieval textual traditions is the honed blade of the knife we use to attack the Gordian knot of medieval Mediterranean literary history. The exquisitely crafted handle of this knife, well-worn with use, is the scholarly tool kit we use to analyse the history, the intellectual traditions upon which we as scholars depend: the methodological practices, the editions and reference works we need to construct a historical narrative. And – to drive the metaphor home – the tang that connects blade to handle is a single scholarly intervention: María Rosa Menocal's seminal first book, *The Arabic Role in Medieval Literary History*. In that work, Menocal threw down a gauntlet; Hispanists and, beyond the Iberian peninsula, medieval literary scholars in general still respond to her provocation. It was in order to take stock of the first twenty-five years of scholarship in the arena Menocal staked out in that book that Suzanne Akbari and I convened the conference where most of these essays were first presented. And this collection continues in that spirit, using the Iberian peninsula as a Mediterranean in microcosm in order to assess the successes and address the failures of a quarter century of scholarship on medieval Mediterranean literary history.

We hope, however, that our tactical decision will not be understood as an admission of defeat. Medieval Mediterranean linguistic complexity presents a peculiarly thorny challenge, but not a fatal difficulty for the literary historian. In her introductory essay to this volume, Suzanne Akbari discusses the work of one of the most innovative scholars in literary studies of the last two decades, Franco Moretti. The specifics of Moretti's research strategies have limited application for the medieval literary historian. He works with a vast corpus of digitized texts in a limited scope of modern languages. We who are working across multiple languages, dead and living, and are working with the manuscript traditions that predated the era of modern print will not be able to yoke machines to our service as Moretti does. In other ways, however, Moretti can serve as a crucial model, and (I believe) can help us to face down the problem of linguistic complexity in particular. His intellectual modesty, his willingness to adopt scientific methods for humanistic research (advancing knowledge through hypothesis and experimentation, working with a team of researchers), and, most importantly, his lucid acceptance of the implications of complex systems theory for the humanities make him an immensely important point of reference for the medieval literary historian. The medieval literary record displays prodigious complexity in at least three senses, each of them investigated in the essays in this volume: it is linguistically multiple; its languages are hybrid and unstable; it is witnessed in a diverse and discordant manuscript tradition. If we are to make coherent sense of this complexity, we do well to study closely Moretti's exemplary efforts to "map the labyrinth" – to borrow Akbari's felicitous description of the implications of Moretti's work for Mediterranean literary studies. This final essay takes a preliminary step in that direction, turning away from the Iberian promontory to look out over the choppy confusion of a sea of languages and ask what theoretical moves might help us to recuperate the literary history of what Dante termed the "discordanti liti" (*Paradiso* IX, 85) – the *dissonant shores* – of the Mediterranean.

II.

"Utinam essem bonus grammaticus. Non aliunde discordiae in religione pendent quam ab ignoratione grammaticae."

Joseph Justus Scaliger (quoted in Pfeiffer 116)

In his magnificent study of the European discovery of Sanskrit letters, *The Oriental Renaissance*, Raymond Schwab placed a discriminating emphasis on the second half of his title. (Edward Said would tell much the same story but would emphasize the first component of Schwab's formula: the production of the Orient as abject and alien, rather than the regenerative power of its discovery by Europeans.) Schwab saw the philological labours of the nineteenth century that made Sanskrit literary history available to Europeans as the logical culmination of the centrifugal force of the Renaissance. The fall of Greek Constantinople to the Ottoman Turks in 1453 provoked an exodus of Greek scholars from the eastern Empire and placed texts and teachers within the reach of the scholars of the Christian west: western Europe acquired, for the first time since the collapse of the Roman Empire, the ability to read the works of Greek antiquity in the original, rather than by means of transmission through Arabic. Nineteenth-century philology would bring to fruition the intellectual expansionism that began with Renaissance Humanism, using a bouquet of new scientific methodologies to decipher both the linguistic cultures of antiquity and the languages of the Orient. *The Oriental Renaissance* traces the expansion of philology beyond its birthplace and its first field of play, culminating with the acquisition of Sanskrit, another achievement of the European nineteenth century: "For so long merely *Mediterranean*," Schwab wrote, "humanism began to be *global*" (Schwab 4–5; emphasis added).

The rhythm of waves of expansion that Schwab describes – from the Mediterranean to the Near East to the Indian subcontinent – feels familiar, as if philology embodied the inexorable march of discovery and conquest so central to these last centuries of human history. But European intellectual history is, of course, more complex. The scope of the Mediterranean comprehended by a European intelligentsia has waxed and waned over time, reflecting the perceived relevance of other cultures and the perceived capacity of European scholars to master them. Consider, for instance, the fate of Greek. Unknown in western Europe during the Middle Ages, the Greek language experienced its first vogue during the fifteenth and sixteenth centuries, but then went through a period of decline when Greek literacy all but vanished in Europe. Thus, for instance, Europeans produced sixteen editions of Homer during the eighty-one years between 1525 and 1606, and only one during the 153 years between 1606 and 1759 (Bagnani 109). During the nineteenth century – which witnessed the flowering of classics scholarship in general and of philological study in particular, as a method of interpreting the textual production of antiquity – Greek literacy soared. Europeans began to generate the editions of ancient texts with their meticulous critical apparatuses that we consider the epitome of the *modern* edition.

In the same way, European knowledge of Arabic has undergone dramatic tidal fluctuations. During the late Middle Ages, Arabic *signified* in both a commercial and intellectual sense. Qualified translators Latinized Arabic scientific texts and composed economic and military correspondence for European traders and kings. And in places like the Iberian and Italian peninsulas, Christian traders, diplomats and monarchs might be expected to acquire at least a smattering of Arabic themselves in order to transact their business. The general population did not, of course, read Arabic. But the pseudo-kufic inscriptions found on late medieval coinage and architectural monuments demonstrate the potency of the language as signifier even for an audience incapable of reading it. The end of the Middle Ages saw an increasing segregation of Muslim and Christian populations. Following the expulsions of the Arab populations of Sicily and the Iberian peninsula, following the consolidation of European control of the northern Mediterranean and Ottoman control of the southern and eastern shores, the sense of the proximity of the Arabic language and its relevance to European concerns was lost. And the advances of the Renaissance gradually superseded the sciences that translations of Arab natural philosophers had made available to Europeans. By the end of the fifteenth century, Arab communities in the northern Mediterranean had been dispersed; European attempts to extend military power over the eastern Mediterranean had (momentarily) ceased; Europe was in possession of Greek, and no longer needed Arabic as an intermediary to gain access to the philosophical texts of Greek antiquity. Thus – to cite a provincial but useful gauge of changing intellectual fashions – while Dante had consigned Arab philosophers and an Arab governor (Ibn Rushd, Ibn Sina, Salah al-Din) to the relative comfort of his Limbo, Petrarch (anticipating subsequent intellectual history, here as so often) considered the Arabs to be beneath his notice. "The Arabs!" he wrote to a friend. "I hate the whole lot ... You know them as doctors; I know them as poets. Nothing more insipid, nothing softer, nothing more limp, nothing more obscene ... I will not be persuaded that any good can come from Arabia."[3] The economic, social and cultural links that bound Muslims and Christians, speakers of Arabic and the Romance languages, lived on in marginal forms, as outsider culture: the Barbary corsairs (many of them Christian renegades), Los Plomos del Sacromonte (the Lead Books of Sacromonte, late sixteenth-century inventions claiming to be ancient Christian documents in Arabic), Giuseppe Vella's late eighteenth-century forgery of Arabic documents relating the history of medieval Sicily. At the same time, mainstream Europeans began to perceive the culture of the Arabs as inert and irrelevant, the antithesis of the modern.

The spirit of commercial and colonial enterprise of the late eighteenth and nineteenth centuries put the southern and eastern shores of the Mediterranean on the map once again, literally as well as figuratively. In a discussion of the evolution of maritime geography during the eighteenth century, Christopher Drew Armstrong points out that eighteenth-century geographers considered the existing maps of the Mediterranean to be unreliable, and the sea to be relatively unknown.[4] Imagine: the birthplace of marine navigation placed on the list of territories yet to be charted! But, in fact, the new science of astronomy had changed the standards of maritime knowledge. The portolans which had served the merchants and corsairs of the fourteenth century did not satisfy the exacting mind of the eighteenth century; the Mediterranean was all to be discovered. During the eighteenth century, too, the Knights of the Order of Saint John in Malta – the heirs of the venerable Hospitalers – still received the sons of the aristocratic families of Europe, both Catholic and Protestant, and sent them on caravans against the Barbary corsairs. In earlier centuries popes and statesmen had painted the skirmishes between the corsairs of Malta and the Barbary Regencies as the final chapter of the crusades. But by the eighteenth century those glory days were far in the past; now, in order that they might not interrupt shipping, the Grand Masters in Malta communicated the dates and routes their fleets would follow to the captains of Tunisian and Tripolitan fleets. The Grand Tour of the late eighteenth and nineteenth century was, in essence, born in these Disneyland versions of the caravans of the Maltese corsairs.[5] And, finally, with the rebirth of philology as a positivistic science, the nineteenth century would see the generation of the first great European dictionaries of Arabic and the first exhaustive European grammars of Arabic.[6] An era of translation of common texts (to use a discursive metaphor) and circumnavigation of a common sea (turning to a geographical metaphor) had been forgotten. The expansionist sentiment and the philological methods of textual interpretation of the eighteenth and nineteenth centuries reawakened European recognition of the Arab shores of the Mediterranean, this time as an object of scientific study (and colonial rule).

The opening years of the twenty-first century would transform this dynamic. I scarcely need note the chain of events that have realigned relations between the Arab world and Europe over the last decade. Indeed, given the pace of developments, history would undoubtedly outrun any summary attempted here by the time this publication appears in print. Suffice it to say that again a combination of military, economic, and cultural pressures has narrowed the distance between the northern and southern shores of the Mediterranean. We generally assume that modern colonial investments sparked and shaped European knowledge of Arabic (the language, the history, the culture). But the truth is more complex. We should trace our contemporary entanglement with the Arab world to the medieval Mediterranean, indeed to the emergence of Islam and thus of Arab culture as a player in global history. The Arab world is implicated in European history, and the European world in the history of the Arabs. Both civilizations take part in the culture of comprehension which – obeying a tidal rhythm of ebb and flow – has historically traversed the Mediterranean.

It is this discursive Mediterranean that literary historians have yet to chart. And for this task we need a strategy of textual interpretation that will allow us to read diverse textual traditions with precision, yet without losing sight of the larger cultural context in dialogue with which texts are produced. Philology has – for more than two millennia – provided passionate readers with the instruments they need to undertake such exacting textual analysis. But more recently, Philology has been drawn into a marriage of convenience with the European nationalisms, and this has dulled her senses somewhat – or, at least, has predisposed her to see the grand sweep of history in a certain light. In order to read the medieval Mediterranean seriously and accurately, it may be necessary to unlearn some of the lessons that our teachers (and, in truth, the structure of the modern university) have taught us. As the essays in this volume attest, it is, in the first instance, inaccurate to call oneself a "Hispanist" or an "Italianist" when one's primary task as a scholar is to disentangle the history of an era that predated the Spanish or the Italian nation by some centuries. Even the term "comparatist" may lead us astray: by calling oneself a "comparatist," one implies that there may be some other way to read a textual record, a state of linguistic singularity and purity from which one's own readings depart. Certainly during the Middle Ages nobody wrote in the language he spoke; bilingualism was the price of literacy.

The most fundamental task to be achieved, however, and perhaps the most difficult, is the unlearning of a pseudo-scientific taxonomy that posits a radical and "natural" distinction between the Semitic and the Indo-European languages. As students, we learn to use the branching tree to chart relations between languages and textual traditions, and we use ramification to model linguistic change over time. And these metaphors serve to demonstrate the relatedness of the Indo-European languages and the radical alterity of the Semitic. But the history of communications between the Semitic and the Latin-Romance "families" in the Mediterranean should help literary historians to recognize that our trees and their ramifications are metaphors, not scientific theorems, and should encourage us to forge new metaphors in order to produce a fuller, more accurate account of this history. The Hebrew, the Greek, the Latin, the Arabic, the Turkish, the Armenian, along with the relevant vernaculars, did interact with each other in the medieval Mediterranean: they translated each other, glossed each other, calqued each other, transliterated each other; they appeared side by side in texts and inscriptions. And it seems at once redundant and essential to point out that the people who spoke those languages interacted with each other as well. If the metaphors that we use to characterize pre-modern literary history misrepresent or fail to represent these connections and communications, we need to replace them.

For philologists, a return to the Mediterranean is a return to the primal scene: to the terrain where the cultural foundations of the three monotheisms were set, and where the instruments we use to interpret those cultures were created. The complexity of the medieval Mediterranean allows philology to fulfill its original promise of constructing an instrument of intelligibility for mediating between discrete linguistic and discursive fields. The most significant obstacle to thinking a literary Mediterranean is, I believe, neither religious nor cultural. It is linguistic. Or rather, because the impasse is linguistic, it is also religious and cultural; language is the first and most potent orthodoxy. "Would that I were a good *grammaticus*," wrote the Humanist scholar Scaliger (see the epigraph cited above); "all religious discord arises from ignorance of *grammatica*." Scaliger understood *grammatica* in the sixteenth-century sense. In this passage it signifies not only the ligaments and musculature of languages, but also the rudiments of textual criticism and the techniques of textual interpretation; that is, it signifies the foundations of human knowledge and, not coincidentally, of philology as well. The process of becoming a good *grammaticus* begins simply: by memorizing paradigms, by working one's mouth into strange shapes in order to pronounce the sounds of a new language, by not fearing – to paraphrase another great philologist – the diversity of peoples and epochs.[7] A good *grammaticus* of the medieval Mediterranean might begin by recognizing those truths which scholars have, for ideological reasons, learned to disregard: the Mediterranean teaches us that the crucible of literary modernity was linguistic complexity, rather than unity and singularity. And it shows us that the fates of Arabic and Latin-Romance letters have been entangled for some centuries in a culture of comprehension that does not preclude periodic episodes of incomprehension – and, at its most decadent, ignorance and aggression.

III.

Ma se 'l latino e 'l greco
parlan di me dopo la morte, è un vento ...

Petrarch, Canzoniere 264, 68–9 (page 331)

[But if Latin and Greek
speak of me after I die, it is but a breeze ...]

Can we, in fact, speak of a *literary* history of the Mediterranean, without viewing the literature as (merely) an adjunct to the political or social or religious history of the region? *Is* there a literary Mediterranean? I will hazard a description of one characteristic aspect of Mediterranean literature during the Middle Ages in particular, a quality that the essays in this volume have studied with a particularly keen interest and focus. The literary traditions of the medieval Mediterranean are marked by the coexistence of multiple languages and by play between linguistic systems – each, by a curious and at times perilous paradox, defining itself as singular, while implicitly acknowledging and at times explicitly relying on the historical witness of others. Was there ever a writer more monolingual than Petrarch? Of course, in late medieval Italy, to be "monolingual" meant to limit oneself to a single linguistic paradigm (rather than a single language): to a written *grammatica* (in Petrarch's case Latin) and a local vernacular (in Petrarch's case Tuscan Italian). And in Petrarch's Italy the vernacular remained fluid, without a monolithic written form; the *Questione della Lingua* would be resolved only many centuries in the future. One imagines Petrarch carrying the banner of his Tuscan Italian into exile with him – a poetic Italian *koinê* created by Dante, whose masterpiece Petrarch famously claimed never to have read – and honing it in Avignon, in the linguistic cacophony of the papal court, and in his sylvan retreat at Vaucluse. He kept a steady focus on a painstakingly constructed Latin antiquity; he adored Ovid's verse and esteemed Virgil's; he emulated the round periodic sentences of Cicero, Tacitus and Livy and the moral heft of Augustine's prose. And yet his gestures of refusal and denial veil his awareness of what he professed not to know: the poetry of the Arabs and of Dante. Recent scholarship has suggested, ever more convincingly, that his claim to know the poetry of the Arabs was based on study of Hermannus Alemannus's translation of Averroës's commentary on Aristotle's *Poetics*, which included Latin renderings of a number of passages from the Arab poets (and even a handful of phrases from the Qur'an).[8] In the "sea of languages" navigated by the essays in this book, even literary traditions that claim a religious or cultural primacy may concede their contingency in unguarded moments, or when they feel their position is unassailable. Indeed, even Arabic – the language in which God created the world – admitted its boundedness, when it imported a school of natural philosophy from the Greeks and imaginative literature from the Persians.

Literary historians need not only technical vocabulary and historical narratives – of the sort that recent scholarship has begun to generate – but also a reservoir of images to describe the dynamic of simultaneous dependency and denial that characterized relations between linguistic-literary paradigms in the medieval

Mediterranean. Most metaphors are expendable. They are typically situational; they do not typically survive when transplanted out of the textual setting for which they were designed. Some, however, possess the capacity to regenerate themselves, text after text and even generation after generation. See, for instance, the philologist's metaphorical tree, used to picture phylogenetic relations between languages – its ramifications invariably read as a two-dimensional representation of evolution, a narrative that weds science and history. It is easy to assume that the arboreal representation of language development is of antique vintage. In fact, the image was a product of nineteenth-century scientism: philologist August Schleicher pioneered it after reading Darwin's comments about the pseudo-genealogical evolution of language, during the 1860s.[9] And John Tolan's essay in this volume considers Richard Bulliet's metaphorical response to another potent metaphor, Samuel Huntington's "Clash of Civilizations." Bulliet's "sibling civilizations," like the genealogical tree, uses the human family metaphorically to represent a non-genealogical relation. It deploys the relative specificity of the noun *sibling* against the vapid *clash*, but leaves the equally problematic noun *civilization* untouched.

So, too, for millennia the image of oxen plowing has served to represent the act of writing. The earliest-known written text in Italian, a ninth-century marginal manuscript inscription known as the "Indovinello Veronese" or *Veronese riddle*, runs as follows: "He drove on the oxen, plowed the white field, held a white ploughshare, and sowed black seed" ["Se pareba boves alba pratalia araba & albo versoria teneba & negro semen seminaba"]. This charming marginal vignette is, of course, a scribal self-portrait: the ox driver is the writer who recorded the riddle, guiding his quill (the white ploughshare) over the page (the white field) and sowing ink (the black seed). And the image is scarcely unique to the Italian peninsula.[10] The technical term *boustrophedon* mines an identical vein of associations. It represents the act of writing as laborious, fruitful, and above all tactile and sensual. Our age has lost the association between the act of writing and the senses of touch and of smell. An era when paper was made from old bed sheets and underclothes and ink was distilled from the lees of wine, black amber, nut-galls, or fish glue would be more likely to associate writing with a substance as gamey and chunky, as full of worms and seedlings, as earth. It would be convenient for us – in the interests of writing the Mediterranean – if the ancients had used the image of ships *plowing the waves* as a metaphor for writing. We would possess an abundant supply of off-the-rack epigraphs and maritime and naval metaphors to spice our literary histories. We could, above all, describe the ships threading the shores of the Mediterranean – like a boustrophedon text, its lines weaving from left to right and from right to left – and knitting together the sea's "dissonant shores." But for obvious reasons the metaphor does not answer. The ships that plow the waves leave no trail to represent the trace of writing. Keats, who came to the Mediterranean to die of consumption, evoked the image of the sea as amnesiac writing surface in his epitaph: "Here lies one whose name was writ in water."

If the oxen no longer signify, however, the helical path they trace in order to generate meaning still speaks to a twenty-first-century readership. See, for instance, the memorable image that begins a recent essay by Moroccan writer Abdelfattah Kilito, who recalls al-Jahiz's description of an imam preaching to a bilingual audience: to the Arabs sitting on his right, the imam spoke in Arabic; he then turned to translate his words into Persian for the Persians seated on his left (Kilito 22–3). This is the boustrophedon movement once again: a linguistic about-face when one reaches the border (of the page or the sea); a translation so spontaneous and irresistible that original and translation form a seamless whole, and no language can be thought without its other lest the integrity of the text be lost.

The Mediterranean has demanded such compulsive acts of translation with an intermittent urgency. Kilito argues that from the mid-nineteenth century, Arab poets and novelists have written with the notion that what they write will ultimately be translated into the European languages; they write with translation in mind (Kilito 18–20). So, too, the modern reader of Arabic literature "soon connects [the Arabic work], directly or indirectly, to a European text. He is necessarily a comparatist, or we could say a translator" (Kilito 16). And so, finally, literary historians might learn to think the integrity of literary history in the Mediterranean basin, without transforming the Mediterranean into a multicultural Shangri-La (indeed, in the twenty-first century – when metaphors may be effortlessly weaponized – such quaint formulations have become untenable), but rather in recognition of the bald facts of intellectual history. We might work to construct a historical narrative that recognizes the intellectual investments shared between the Arabo-Islamic and Romance-Christian worlds – and beyond, embracing also the Hebrew, the Syriac or Arab or Armenian or Greek Christian, the Turkish Ottoman, and so on – as a necessary context for the literary history of the states of the Mediterranean littoral. At the least, we might cultivate a more robust plurilingualism in order to understand literary history more accurately. American academics, though we are less invested in narratives of European national history than are Europeans themselves, are hamstrung by our disciplines' fetishization of "native or near-native fluency" in a single target language. And economic developments in the academic marketplace seem likely to increase this tendency in the future. Yet the literary history we seek to understand would be better-served by scholarship with linguistic breadth in place of depth; and the end of modernity and of the modern nation state may yet return us to a quasi-medieval linguistic actuality, encouraging adequate knowledge of lingua franca/vernacular constellations of languages rather than intimate knowledge of a single mother tongue.

I close this brief excursus on Mediterranean letters by citing an essay by a man of letters who, like Petrarch, crossed the Mediterranean while clinging tenaciously to literary monolingualism: Albert Camus, who in his *discours d'ouverture* at the Maison de la Culture in Algiers celebrated the Mediterranean "qui nous entoure" as "un pays vivant, plein de jeux et de sourires" (that is, the Mediterranean "that surrounds us" is "a living country, full of games and smiles"; Camus 1321). It is useful to remember when reading these words – which seem so fresh, the product of a distant and more ingenuous age – that Camus spoke them in 1937, and in conscious resistance to the use of particularly malignant forms of nationalism by German and Italian fascists. I pass over the richest ironies of Camus's deployment of Mediterranean identity against national identity (the fact that Camus, Algerian by birth, seems flummoxed by the challenge of integrating Arabs into his Mediterranean; the place that the Mediterranean held in the image bank of the Italian fascists in particular) in order to relish his choice of words. *Games and smiles*: How did Camus mean his audience to understand this particular concatenation of terms? Did he intend to evoke the thoughtless joy of the clichéd Sicilian or Spanish or Greek peasant, the *dolce far niente* that has been converted to callisthenic philosophy by Club Med? And why did he describe the sea as encircling us, when it is evident to the most casual observer that it is rather we who surround it?

I prefer to give his words a more vigorous reading, and indeed the context in which Camus wrote them makes any less-nuanced interpretation impossible. Camus wrote with the peculiar and paradoxical combination of cynicism and tenacity that is another of the clichés of Mediterranean culture. His notion of play – of *jeu* and *sourire* – in this phrase is akin to Derrida's (also, it seems worth noting, Algerian by birth). At the very least, Camus recognizes that the Mediterranean "qui nous entoure" lacks a centre (or rather that *we* whom it surrounds, who observe it and write it, constitute its centre); it lacks a structural integrity (of the sort that fascists might co-opt in the name of nationalist orthodoxy); it multiplies, generating and regenerating its heterodoxies, and not playing favourites among them. The literatures of the Mediterranean certainly did not invent the notion of a poetics of semantic play; that urge is global. But a peculiar kind of play seems altogether typical of (if not unique to) the region: a poetics of plurilingualism, a literary tradition that at once asserts its primacy and assumes (even, at times, laboriously constructs) a parallel linguistic universe in which parallel literary traditions evolve in parallel languages. In this textual universe, as Kilito suggests, to read is to translate; the reader is by definition a comparatist: no position of monolingualism exists with reference to which linguistic complexity might situate itself. This landscape of linguistic difference, and the compulsive *ir y venir* between the sea's incommensurable shores that it entails, is constitutive of the literary traditions of the Mediterranean, which have demonstrated tirelessly the insufficiency of literary systems bounded by monolingualism. It remains to be seen whether a new generation of historians can generate a critical vocabulary to catalogue the linguistico-literary heterodoxies of the sea, without retreating to the cold comfort of dissonant orthodoxies.

NOTES

1 For an interesting perspective on the recent Mediterranean vogue among classicists, see Susan E. Alcock's article on the incidence of the appearance of the word "Mediterranean" in the titles of serials over the last forty years (Alcock).

2 In fact, boustrophedon script possesses at least one contemporary proselytizer: see the boustrophedon web site at http://traevoli.com/boust/ (accessed 30 March 2009).

3 Petrarch, Sen. XII, 2; [*Senilium*]:241; my translation. See Petrarch, *Letters of Old Age* 2:471–2 for a published translation.

4 Here, for instance, Joseph-Bernard, Marquis de Chabert, argues the necessity of a navigational initiative to the Académie des Sciences in 1766: "Although the Mediterranean was the theatre of the first navigators, it is not for all that better known; one can even say that this branch of marine geography has remained until our age the most imperfect of all and that which has the greatest need of being rectified" (quoted in C.D. Armstrong 250; my translation).

5 For a discussion of this fascinating chapter in Maltese history see Freller.

6 Thus, for instance, Silvestre de Sacy's grammar (published in 1810) and the dictionaries of Lane (1863–93) and Dozy (1877–81).

7 In his study of the Latin literary tradition of the Middle Ages, Erich Auerbach wrote: "Not only the scholars and critics among us, but also a large and steadily growing section of the general public, have ceased to be frightened by the diversity of peoples and epochs" (Auerbach, *Literary Language* 11).

8 On the vexed question of Petrarch and the poetry of the Arabs, see Bodenham; Burnett, "Petrarch and Averroes" and "Learned Knowledge"; and my *European Modernity and the Arab Mediterranean*, 34–64.

9 On Schleicher and the use of arboreal imagery to represent relations between languages and language change, see Koerner.

10 Remember, for instance, Chaucer's lines: "I have, God wot, a large field to ere; / And wayke been the oxen in my plough" (*Canterbury Tales*, "The Knight's Tale" 28–9).

Bibliography

Primary Sources

Adelard of Bath. *Quaestiones naturales*. Ed. M. Müller. Münster: Aschendorff, 1934. *Beiträge zur Geschichte der Philosophie und Theologie des Mittelalters* 31.2.

Amari, Michele. *Biblioteca arabo-sicula*. Lipsia: F.A. Brockhaus, 1857.

al-Andalusi, Sa'id ibn Ahmad. *Tabaqat al-umam*. Ed. Louis Cheiko. Beirut: Al-Matba'a al-kathulikiyya lil-aba' al-yasu'iyyin, 1912.

Andrés, Juan. *Dell'origine, de' progressi, e dello stato attuale d'ogni letteratura*. 8 vols. Parma: Stamperia Reale, 1785–1822.

Ariosto, Ludovico. *Orlando Furioso*. Ed. Cesare Segre. Milan: Mondadori, 1990.

Barber Lightfoot, Joseph, ed. and trans. *The Apostolic Fathers*. 2nd ed. 5 vols. London and New York: Macmillan, 1885–90.

Barbieri, Giovanni Maria. *Dell'origine della poesia rimata*. Modena: Società Tipografica, 1790.

[*Bayad y Riyad*]. *Historia de los amores de Bayad y Riyad, una chantefable oriental en estilo persa (Vat. ar. 368)*. Trans. and ed. Aloysius R. Nykl. New York: Hispanic Society of America, 1941.

al-Bayati, Abdal Wahhab. *Love, Death and Exile*. Trans. Bassam K. Frangieh. Washington: Georgetown University Press, 1990.

Benoît de Sainte-Maure. *Le Roman de Troie*. Ed. Léopold Constans. 6 vols. Paris: Société des Anciens Textes Français, 1904–12.

Benveniste, Vidal. *Melitsat `Efer ve-Dinah*. Ed. Matti Huss. Jerusalem: Magnes, 2003.

Birgitta of Sweden. *Life and Selected Revelations*. Ed. Marguerite Tjader Harris. Trans. Albert Ryle Kezel. New York: Paulist Press, 1990.

Bonaventure. *Decem Opuscula ad Theologiam Mysticam Spectantia*. Ed. PP. Collegii S. Bonaventurae. 5th ed. Rome: Quaracchi, 1965.

Bosone da Gubbio. *L'Avventuroso Ciciliano*. Ed. G.F. Nott. Milan: Giovanni Silvestri, 1834.

Bosone da Gubbio. *Avventuroso ciciliano.* Ed. Roberto Gigliucci. Rome: Bulzoni, 1989.

Brunetto Latini. *Tresor.* Ed. Pietro Beltrami, Paolo Squillacioti, Plinio Torri, and Sergio Vatteroni. Turin: Einaudi, 2007.

Burton, Richard F., ed. *The Thousand Nights and a Night.* 10 vols. London: privately printed, 1885.

Camoens, Luis de. *Camoens, The Lyricks.* Trans. Richard F. Burton. 2 vols. London: Bernard Quaritch, 1884.

Camoens, Luis de. *Os Lusiadas (The Lusiads).* Trans. Richard F. Burton. Ed. Isabel Burton. 2 vols. London: B. Quaritch, 1880.

de Caulibus, Johannes. *Meditationes Vitae Christi.* Trans. and ed. M. Stallings-Taney. Turnhout: Brepols, 1997.

Cervantes Saavedra, Miguel de. *Exemplary Stories.* Trans. Lesley Lipson. Oxford: Oxford University Press, 1998.

Cervantes Saavedra, Miguel de. *Novelas ejemplares.* Ed. Juan Bautista Avalle-Arce. 3 vols. Madrid: Clásicos Castalia, 1982. Rpt. ed. Harry Sieber. Madrid: Cátedra, 1998.

Cervantes Saavedra, Miguel de. *Viaje del Parnaso. Novelas ejemplares.* 2 vols. Madrid: Víctor Saiz, 1878. 2: 259–362.

Les chansons mozarabes: les vers finaux (kharjas) en espagnol dans les muwashshahs arabes et hébreux. Ed. Samuel Stern. Palermo: U. Manfredi, 1953. Università di Palermo, Istituto di filologia romanza, Collezione di testi l.

Le Charroi de Nîmes: Chanson de geste du Cycle de Guillaume d'Orange. Ed. Claude Lachet. Paris: Gallimard, 1999.

Chrétien de Troyes. *Cligès.* Ed. Charles Méla and Oliver Collet. Paris: Le Livre de Poche, 1994.

Chrétien de Troyes. *Le Conte du graal.* Ed. Charles Méla. Paris: Le Livre de Poche, 1990.

Cohen, Seymour J., trans. and ed. *The Holy Letter: A Study in Jewish Sexual Morality.* Northvale, NJ: Jason Aronson, 1993.

Conquerors and Chroniclers of Early Medieval Spain. Ed. Kenneth Baxter Wolf. Liverpool: Liverpool University Press, 1990.

Constanza de Castilla. *Book of Devotions/Libro de Devociones y oficios.* Ed. Constance L. Wilkins. Exeter: University of Exeter Press, 1998.

Corpus de la antigua lírica popular hispánica (siglos XV a XVII). Ed. Margit Frenk Alatorre. Madrid: Castalia, 1987.

Corpus scriptorum Muzarabicorum. Ed. Juan Gil. 2 vols. Madrid: Instituto Antonio de Nebrija, 1973.

Crescas de Caylar. "Provençal Esther Poem." Ed. Susan Milner Silberstein. "The Provençal Esther Poem Written in Hebrew Characters c. 1327 by Crescas de Caylar: Critical Edition." Diss. University of Pennsylvania, 1973.

Daniel of Morley. *Philosophia.* Ed. G. Maurach. *Mittellateinisches Jahrbuch* 14 (1979): 204–53.

Dante Alighieri. *La Commedia secondo l'antica vulgata.* Ed. Giorgio Petrocchi. 4 vols. Milan: Mondadori, 1966–7.

[*Doncella Teodor*]. *Narrativa popular de la Edad Media: Doncella Teodor, Flores y Blancaflor, París y Viana*. Ed. Victor Infantes and Nieves Baranda. Torrejón de Ardoz: AKAL, 1995.

Don Vidal Benvenist's Tale of Efer and Dinah [Hebrew]. Ed. Matti Huss. Jerusalem: Y.L. Magnes, Hebrew University, 2003.

Durandus, William. *Guillelmi Duranti Rationale divinorum officiorum*. Ed. A. Davril and T.M. Thibodeau. Turnholt: Brepols, 1995–2000.

Fada'il al-andalus wa-ahliha. Ed. Salah al-Din al-Munajjad. Beirut: Dar al-Kitab al-Jadid, 1968.

[*Flores y Blancaflor*]. *Narrativa popular de la Edad Media: Doncella Teodor, Flores y Blancaflor, París y Viana*. Ed. Victor Infantes and Nieves Baranda. Torrejón de Ardoz: AKAL, 1995.

de Flores, Juan. *Grimalte y Gradissa*. Ed. Pamela Waley. London: Tamesis, 1971.

de Flores, Juan. *La historia de Grisel y Mirabella*. Ed. Pablo Alcázar López and José A. González Núñez. 1529. Granada: Editorial Don Quijote, 1983.

Frayre de Joy e Sor de Plaser. Nouvelles Courtoises occitanes et françaises. Ed. Suzanne Thiolier-Méjean and Marie-Françoise Notz-Grob. Paris: Livre de Poche, 1997. 206–59.

Hebrew Poetry in Spain and Provence [Hebrew]. Ed. Jefim Schirmann. 4 vols. 1956. Jerusalem: Mosad Bialik, 2006.

Hermann of Carinthia. *De essentiis*. Ed. and trans. Charles Burnett. Leiden: Brill, 1982.

al-Himyari Abu al-Walid. *Al-Badi' fi wasf al-rabi'*. Ed. 'Ali Ibrahim Kurd. Damascus: Dar Sa'd al-Din, 1997.

al-Himyari, Muhammad ibn 'Abd Allah. *Al-Rawd al-mi'tar fi khabar al-aqtar*. Ed. Evariste Levi-Provençal. Cairo: Lajnat al-ta'lif wa al-tarjama wa al-nashr, 1937.

Hispano-Arabic Poetry: A Student Anthology. Ed. James T. Monroe. Berkeley: University of California Press, 1974.

Ibn al-Khatib, Lisan al-Din. *Mufakharat malaqa wa-sala*. Ed. A.M. al-'Abbadi. Alexandria [n.p.]: 1958.

Ibn al-Qatta' al-Siqilli. *Al-durra al-khatira fi shu'ara' al-jazira*. Ed. Bashir Bakkush. Beirut: Dar al-gharb al-islami, 1995.

Ibn 'Arabi, Muhyi al-Din. *Al-Futuhat al-makkiya*. Vol. 1. Ed. Ahmad Shams al-Din. Beirut: Dar al-Kutub al-'Ilmiyah, 1999.

Ibn 'Arabi, Muhyi al-Din. *Fusus al-hikam*. Ed. 'Abd Allah 'Afifi. Beirut: Dar al-Kitab al-'Arabi, 1980.

Ibn 'Arabi, Muhyi al-Din. *Tarjuman al-ashwaq*. Beirut: Dar Sadir, 1998.

Ibn 'Ezra', Moses. *Kitab al-muhadara wal-mudhakara*. Ed. Abraham S. Halkin. Jerusalem: Meqize Nirdamim, 1975.

Ibn Fadl Allah al-'Umari. *Masalik al-absar fi mamalik al-amsar*. Eds. Fuat Sezgin and Eckhardt Neubauer. 30 vols. Frankfurt: Ma'had Ta'rikh al-'Ulum al-'Arabiyya wa-l-Islamiyya/Publications of the Institute for the History of Arabo-Islamic Sciences, Series C, Facsimile Editions, 1988–2001.

Ibn Gabirol, Solomon. *Secular Poems*. Ed. H. Brody and J. Schirmann. Jerusalem: Schocken Institute, 1974.

Ibn Hamdis, 'Abd al-Jabbar. *Diwan*. Ed. Ihsan 'Abbas. Beirut: Dar Sadir, 1960.

Ibn Hayyan, Abu Marwan Hayyan ibn Khalaf. *Al-Sifr al-thani min kitab al-muqtabas al-Ibn Hayyan al-Qurtubi*. Ed. Mahmud 'Ali Makki. Tahqiq al-turath 3. Riyad: Markaz al-Malik Faysal lil-Buhuth wa-l-Dirasat al-Islamiyya, 2003.

Ibn Hazm, Abu Muhammad Ali ibn Ahmad. *Rasa'il Ibn Hazm al-Andalusi*. Ed. Ihsan 'Abbas. 4 vols. Beirut: al-Mu'assasa al-'Arabiyya li–l-Dirasat wa-l-Nashr, 1981.

Ibn Jubayr, Muhammad. *Rihla*. Beirut: Dar Sadir, 1964.

Ibn Khafajah. *Diwan Ibn Khafajah*. Ed. Mustafa Ghazi. Alexandria: Al-Ma'arif, 1960.

Ibn Khaldun. *Al-Muqqadima*. Tunis: al-Dar al-Tunisiyya li–l-Nashr, 1989.

Ibn Khaldun. *The Muqaddimah: An Introduction to History*. Trans. Franz Rosenthal. 3 vols. Princeton: Princeton University Press and Bollingen Foundation, 1967.

Ibn Sasson, Shmuel. *Sefer Avnei Hashoham*. Ed. Hayyim Chamiel. Jerusalem: Hotsa'at Mahbarot Lesifrut, 1962.

Ibn Shabbetai, Judah ben Isaac. *'Minhat Yehudah', "Ezrat ha-nashim' ve-''En mishpat*. Ed. Matti Huss. 2 vols. Jerusalem: Hebrew University, 1991.

al-Isbahani, Abu al-Faraj. *Kitab al-aghani*. 4th ed. Vols. 1–16. 1927. Cairo: al-Hay'at al-Misriyya al-'Ammah lil-Ta'lif wa-l-Tarjamah wa-l-Nashr, 1963. Vol. 17. Ed. 'Ali Muhammad al-Bajawi. Vol. 18. Ed. 'Abd al-Karim Ibrahim al-'Izbawi. Cairo: al-Hay'at al-Misriyya al-'Ammah lil-Ta'lif wa-l-Tarjamah wa-l-Nashr, 1970. Vol. 19. Ed. 'Abd al-Karim Ibrahim al-'Izbawi. Cairo: al-Hay'at al-Misriyya al-'Ammah lil-Ta'lif wa-l-Tarjamah wa-l-Nashr, 1972. Vol. 20. Ed. 'Ali al-Najdi Nasif. Vol. 21. Ed. 'Abd al-Karim Ibrahim al-'Izbawa and Mahmud Muhammad Ghunaym. Vol. 22. Ed. 'Ali al-Siba'i, 'Abd al-Karim Ibrahim al-'Izbawi and Mahmud Muhammad Ghunaym. Vol. 23. Ed. 'Ali al-Siba'i. Vol. 24. Ed. 'Abd al-Karim Ibrahim al-'Izbawi and 'Abd al-'Aziz Matar. Cairo: Al-Hay'at al-'Misriyyah al-'Ammah li–l-Kitab, 1972–4.

Isidore of Seville. *Etymologies. The "Etymologies" of Isidore of Seville*. Trans. Stephen A. Barney, et al. Cambridge: Cambridge University Press, 2006.

Isidore of Seville. *Etymologies. Isidori Hispalensis Episcopi Etymologiarum sive Originum Libri XX*. Ed. W.M. Lindsay. 2 vols. 1911. Oxford: Clarendon Press, 1985.

Isidore of Seville. *History of the Goths, Vandals and Suevi*. Trans. Guido Donini and Gordon B. Ford, Jr. 2nd ed. Leiden: E.J. Brill, 1970.

Jaufre Rudel. *Il canzoniere di Jaufre Rudel*. L'Aquila [Italy]: Japadre, 1985.

Judeo-Spanish Ballads from New York. Ed. Meir José Benardete, Samuel G. Armistead, and Joseph H. Silverman. Berkeley: University of California Press, 1981.

Leopardi, Giacomo. *Opere*. Ed. Giovanni Getto. Milan: Mursia, 1975.

El Libro de amor de mujeres. Ed. and trans. Carmen Caballero Navas. Granada: Universidad de Granada, 2003.

Llull, Ramón. *The Art of Contemplation*. Trans. and ed. E. Allison Peers. 1925. San Francisco: Ignatius Press, 2002.

Llull, Ramón. *Llibre d'Amic i Amat*. Ed. Albert Soler i Llopart. Barcelona: Editorial Barcino, 1995.

Ludolph of Saxony. *Vita Jesu Christi: ex Evangelio et approbatis ab Ecclesia Catholica doctoribus sedule collecta*. Ed. L.M. Rigollot. 4 vols. Paris: Apud Victorem Palme, 1870.

al-Maqqari, Shihab al-Din Ahmad ibn Muhammad. *Analectes sur l'histoire et la littérature des Arabes d'Espagne*. 2 vols. Leiden: E.J. Brill, 1855–61. Amsterdam: Oriental Press, 1967.

al-Maqqari, Shihab al-Din Ahmad ibn Muhammad. *Nafh al-tib min ghusn al-andalus al-ratib*. Ed. Ihsan 'Abbas. 8 vols. Beirut: Dar Sadir, 1968.

Marie de France. *Lais*. Ed. Alfred Ewert. Oxford: Basil Blackwell, 1944.

Marie de France. *Les Lais de Marie de France*. Ed. Jean Rychner. Paris: Honoré Champion, 1973.

al-Marrakushi, 'Abd al-Wahid. *Kitab al-mu'jib fi talkhis akhbar al-maghrib*. Ed. Reinhart Pieter Anne Dozy. 2nd ed. Amsterdam: Oriental Press, 1968.

Misoginía y defensa de mujeres: Antología de textos medievales. Ed. Robert Archer. Madrid: Cátedra, 2001.

Al-Nawawi. *An-Nawawi's Forty Hadith: An Anthology of the Sayings of the Prophet Muhammad*. Trans. Ezzedin Ibrahim and Denys Johnson-Davies. Cambridge: Cambridge University Press, 1997.

Nietzsche, Friedrich. "We Philologists." Trans. John M. Kennedy. *The Complete Works of Friedrich Nietzsche*. Vol. 8. London: T.N. Foulis, 1911. 104–90.

[París y Viana]. *Narrativa popular de la Edad Media: Doncella Teodor, Flores y Blancaflor, París y Viana*. Ed. Victor Infantes and Nieves Baranda. Torrejón de Ardoz: AKAL, 1995.

Perfet, Isaac ben Sheshet. *Responsa*. 2 vols. Jerusalem: Jerusalem Institute, 1992.

[Peter of Cluny] Petrus Venerabilis. *Liber contra sectam, sive haeresim Saracenorum and Summa totius haeresis Saracenorum. Schriften zum Islam*. Ed and trans. Reinhold Glei. Corpus Islamo-Christianum, Series Latina 1. Alternberg: CIS-Verlag, 1985.

Petrarch, Francesco. *Canzoniere*. Ed. Gianfranco Contini. Turin: Einaudi, 1966.

Petrarch, Francesco. *Lettres de la viellesse (Rerum senilium)*. 4 vols. Paris: Belles Lettres, 2002–6.

Petrarch, Francesco. *Rerum senilium libri*. Ed. Elvira Nota. Italian trans. Ugo Dotti. 2 vols. Turin: Aragno, 2004.

Petrus Alfonsi. "Epistola ad Peripateticos." *Petrus Alfonsi and his Medieval Readers*. Ed. and trans. John Tolan. Gainesville: University Press of Florida, 1993. 163–81.

Pico della Mirandola, Giovanni. *On the Dignity of Man, On Being and the One, and Heptaplus*. Indianapolis: Hackett, 1998.

Da Piera, Shelomo ben Meshullam. *Diwan*. Ed. Simon Bernstein. New York: Alim, 1941.

Poe, Edgar Allan. *The Complete Works of Edgar Allan Poe*. Ed. James A. Harrison. 17 vols. New York: Society of English and French Literature, 1902.

Poesía Cancioneril Castellana. Ed. Michael Gerli. Madrid: Akal, 1994.

Raimbaut de Vaqueiras. *The Poems of the Troubadour Raimbaut de Vaqueiras*. Ed. Joseph Linskill. The Hague: Mouton, 1964.

Raimon Vidal de Besalú. *The "Razos de Trobar" of Raimon Vidal and Associated Texts*. Ed. John H. Marshall. London: Oxford University Press, 1972.

Riera i Sans, Jaume, ed. *Cants de noces dels jueus catalans*. Barcelona: Curial, 1974.

Ruiz, Juan. *El libro de buen amor*. Ed. Alberto Blecua. Madrid: Cátedra, 1992.

Al-Saraqusti, Abu al-Tahir Muhammad ibn Yusuf. *Al-Maqamat al-luzumiyya*. Ed. Hasan al-Warakili. Rabat: Manshurat 'Ukaz, 1995.

Schirmann, Jefim, ed. *Hebrew Poetry in Spain and Provence* [Hebrew]. 4 vols. 1956. Jerusalem: Mosad Bialik, 2006.

Schirmann, Jefim, ed. *New Hebrew Poems from the Genizah*. [Hebrew] Jerusalem: Israel Academy of Sciences and Humanities, 1965.

Schlegel, Friedrich. *Kritische Friedrich Schlegel Ausgabe*. Vol. 2. Ed. Ernst Behler, Jean Jacques Anstett, and Hans Eichner. Munich: Schöningh, 1967.

Sepúlveda, Lorenzo de, ed. *Romances nuevamente sacados de historias antiguas de la crónica de España*. Antwerp, 1551.

Sercambi, Giovanni. *Novelle inedite*. Ed. Rodolfo Renier. Bologna: Forni, 1971.

Songs of the Women Troubadours. Ed. Matilda Tomaryn Bruckner, Laurie Shepard, and Sarah White. New York: Garland, 1995.

Songs of the Women Trouvères. Ed. Eglal Doss-Quinby, et al. New Haven: Yale University Press, 2001.

Al-Tabari. *The Early 'Abbasi Empire*. Trans. John Alden Williams. 2 vols. Cambridge: Cambridge University Press, 1988.

Ten Hispano-Arabic Strophic Songs in the Modern Oral Tradition: Music and Texts. Ed. Benjamin M. Liu and James T. Monroe. University of California Publications in Modern Philology 125. Berkeley: University of California Press, 1989.

Uc Faidit. *The "Donatz Proensals" of Uc Faidit*. Ed. John H. Marshall. London: Oxford University Press, 1969.

Vega, Lope de. *La bella malmaridada o la cortesana*. Ed. Christian Andrès. Madrid: Clásicos Castalia, 2001.

Vega, Lope de. "El Robo de Dina: Comedia famosa." *Parte veinte y tres de las Comedias de Lope Felix de Vega Carpio*. Ed. Pedro Coello. Madrid: Maria de Quiñones, 1638. ff. 118v–55.

Vico, Giambattista. *New Science*. Trans. David Marsh. London: Penguin, 2001.

Secondary Works

Aarsleff, Hans. *From Locke to Saussure: Essays on the Study of Language and Intellectual History*. Minneapolis: University of Minnesota Press, 1982.

Abrahams, Israel. *Jewish Life in the Middle Ages*. New York: Atheneum, 1981.

Abulafia, David. "Mediterraneans." In Harris, *Rethinking the Mediterranean* 64–93.

Akasoy, Anna. "Convivencia and Its Discontents: Interfaith Life in Al-Andalus." *International Journal of Middle East Studies* 42.03 (2010): 489–99. http://dx.doi .org/10.1017/S0020743810000516.

Akbari, Suzanne Conklin. "The Diversity of Mankind in *The Book of John Mandeville.*" *Eastward Bound: Travel and Travellers, 1050–1500.* Ed. Rosamund Allen. Manchester: Manchester University Press, 2004. 156–76.

Akbari, Suzanne Conklin. *Idols in the East: European Representations of Islam and the Orient, 1100–1450.* Ithaca: Cornell University Press, 2009.

Akbari, Suzanne Conklin, and Amilcare A. Iannucci, eds. *Marco Polo and the Encounter of East and West.* Toronto: University of Toronto Press, 2008.

Alcock, Susan E. "Alphabet Soup in the Mediterranean Basin: The Emergence of the Mediterranean Serial." In Harris, *Rethinking the Mediterranean* 314–36.

Alfonso, Esperanza. "Constructions of Exile in Medieval Hebrew Literature: Between Text and Context." *Mikan* 1 (2000): 85–96.

Alfonso, Esperanza. *Islamic Culture through Jewish Eyes: Al-Andalus from the Tenth to Twelfth Century.* London: Routledge, 2008.

Alfonso, Esperanza. "The Uses of Exile in Poetic Discourse: Some Examples from Medieval Hebrew Literature." *Renewing the Past, Reconfiguring Jewish Culture: From Al-Andalus to the Haskalah.* Ed. Ross Brann and Adam Sutcliffe. Philadelphia: University of Pennsylvania Press, 2003. 31–49.

Allen, Roger, and D.S. Richards, eds. *Cambridge History of Arabic Literature: Arabic Literature in the Post-Classical Period.* Cambridge: Cambridge University Press, 2006. http://dx.doi.org/10.1017/CHOL9780521771603.

Allony, Nehemiah. "The Reaction of Moses Ibn Ezra to `Arabiyya." *Bulletin of the Institute of Jewish Studies* 3 (1975): 19–40.

Altmann, Barbara K., and F. Regina Psaki. "Considering Holy War in the *Charroi de Nîmes.*" *Medium Ævum* 65 (2006): 247–72.

Alvar, Manuel. *Poesía tradicional de los judíos españoles.* Mexico City: Porrúa, 1966.

Alves, Hélio J.S. "Post-Imperial Bacchus: The Politics of Literary Criticism in Camões Studies, 1940–2001." Special issue on *Post-Imperial Camões,* ed. João Ricardo Figueiredo. *Portuguese Literary and Cultural Studies* 9 (2002): 95–106.

Amer, Sahar. "Integrating Multiculturalism in the Medieval Studies Classroom: The Challenge of the New Millennium. (A Short Reflection, a Pedagogical Methodology, and a Select Bibliography)." *Medieval Perspectives* 15.2 (2000): 61–80.

Amin, Samir. *Eurocentrism.* Trans. Russell Moore. New York: Monthly Review Press, 1989.

Amouric, H., G. Demians d'Archimbaud, and L. Vallauri. "De Marseille au Languedoc et au Comtat Venaissin: Les chemins du vert et du brun." *Le Vert et le brun: de Kairouan à Avignon, céramique du Xe au XVe siècle.* Marseille: Musées de Marseille; Paris: Réunion des musées nationaux, 1995. 185–201.

Amsterdamska, Olga. *Schools of Thought: The Development of Linguistics from Bopp to Saussure.* Dordrecht: D. Reidel, 1987.

Andrés-Gallego, José. "El problema (y la posibilidad) de entender la historia de España." *Historia de la historiografía española.* Ed. José Andrés-Gallego. Madrid: Ediciones Encuentro, 1999. 297–338.

Anidjar, Gil. *"Our Place in al-Andalus": Kabbalah Philosophy Literature in Arab Jewish Letters.* Stanford: Stanford University Press, 2002.

Anrich, Ernst, ed. *Die Idee der deutschen Universität. Die fünf Grundschriften aus der Zeit ihrer Neubegründung durch klassischen Idealismus und romantischen Realismus.* Darmstadt: Wissenschaftliche Buchgesellschaft, 1956.

Ara Gil, Clementina-Julia. *Escultura Gótica en Valladolid y su Provincia.* Valladolid: Institución Cultural Simancas, 1977. 64–120.

Araya, Guillermo. *El pensamiento de Américo Castro. Estructura intercastiza de la historia de España.* Madrid: Alianza, 1983.

Arazi, Albert. "*Al-hanin ila l-awtan* entre la Gahiliyya et l'Islam. Le Bedouin et le citadin reconciliés." *Zeitschrift der Deutschen Morgenlandischen Gesellschaft* 143 (1993): 287–327.

Arbuckle, John. "August Schleicher and the Linguistics/Philology Dichotomy. A Chapter in the History of Linguistics." *Word* 26.1 (1970): 17–31.

Archer, Robert, ed. *Misoginía y defensa de mujeres: Antología de textos medievales.* Madrid: Cátedra, 2001.

Archer, Robert, ed. *The Problem of Woman in Late-Medieval Hispanic Literature.* London: Tamesis, 2004.

Arie, Rachel. "Notes sur la maqama andalouse." *Hesperis Tamuda* 9.2 (1968): 204–5.

Armstrong, John Alexander. *Nations Before Nationalism.* Chapel Hill: University of North Carolina Press, 1982.

Asensio, Eugenio. "Américo Castro historiador: Relexiones sobre *La realidad histórica de España*." *Modern Language Notes* 81 (1966): 602–7.

Asín Palacios, Miguel. *Shadhilíes y Alumbrados.* Madrid: Ediciones Hiperión, 1990.

Aslanov, Cyril. *Le Français au Levant, jadis et naguère: à la recherche d'une langue perdue.* Paris: Honoré Champion, 2006.

Aubry, Elizabeth. *Historical Facts for the Arabian Musical Influence: Studies in the Music of the Middle Ages.* London, W.: Reeves, 1930.

Aubry, Elizabeth. *The Music of the Troubadours.* Bloomington: Indiana University Press, 1996.

Auerbach, Erich. "Figura." *Scenes from the Drama of European Literature.* 1938. Minneapolis: University of Minnesota Press, 1984. 11–76.

Auerbach, Erich. *Literary Language and Its Public in Late Latin Antiquity and in the Middle Ages.* 1965. Princeton: Princeton University Press, 1993.

Auerbach, Erich. *Mimesis: The Represenation of Reality in Western Literature.* Trans. Willard R. Trask. 1953. Princeton: Princeton University Press, 1991.

Auerbach, Erich. "Philology and Weltliteratur." Tr. Edward Said and Maire Said. *Centennial Review* 13 (1969): 1–17.

al-Azmeh, Aziz. "Northerners in Andalusi Eyes." *The Legacy of Muslim Spain.* Ed. Salma Khadra Jayyusi. Leiden: E.J. Brill, 1994. 259–72.

Backman, Clifford. *The Worlds of Medieval Europe*. New York: Oxford University Press, 2003.

Baer, Yitzhak [Fritz]. *Die Juden im Christlichen Spanien: Erster Teil Urkunden und Regesten*. 2 vols. 1929. London: Gregg International Publishers, 1970.

Baer, Yitzhak [Fritz]. *A History of the Jews in Christian Spain*. Trans. Louis Schoffman. 2 vols. Philadelphia: Jewish Publication Society, 1978.

Bagnall, Roger S. "Egypt and the Concept of the Mediterranean." In Harris, *Rethinking the Mediterranean* 339–47.

Bagnani, Gilbert. "Winckelmann and the Second Renascence, 1755–1955." *American Journal of Archeology* 59 (1955): 107–18.

Bahti, Timothy. "Vico, Auerbach, and Literary History." *Philological Quarterly* 60 (1981): 235–55. Rpt. in *Vico: Past and Present*. Vol 2. Ed. Giorgio Tagliacozzo. Atlantic Highlands, NJ: Humanities Press, 1981. 97–114.

Baker, Denise N. "The Privity of the Passion." In Bartlett and Bestul, 85–106.

Barbour, Stephen. "Nationalism, Language, Europe." *Language and Nationalism in Europe*. Ed. Stephen Barbour and Cathie Carmichael. Oxford: Oxford University Press, 2000. 1–17.

Barkaï, Ron, ed. *Chrétiens, musulmans et juifs dans l'Espagne médiévale: De la convergence à l'expulsion*. Paris: Cerf, 1994.

Bartlett, Anne Clark, and Thomas H. Bestul, eds. *Cultures of Piety: Medieval English Devotional Literature in Translation*. Ithaca: Cornell University Press, 1999.

Bédier, Joseph. *La tradition manuscrite du* Lai de l'Ombre: *Réflexion sur l'art d'éditer les anciens textes*. Paris: Champion, 1929.

Beiser, Frederick. *The Romantic Imperative: The Concept of Early German Romanticism*. Cambridge: Harvard University Press, 2003.

Benardete, Meir José, Samuel G. Armistead, and Joseph H. Silverman, eds. *Judeo-Spanish Ballads from New York*. Berkeley: University of California Press, 1981.

Bennett, Jill. "Stigmata and Sense Memory: St. Francis and the Affective Image." *Art History* 24.1 (2001): 1–16. http://dx.doi.org/10.1111/1467-8365.00247.

Berkey, Jonathan. *The Transmission of Knowledge in Medieval Cairo: A Social History of Islamic Education*. Princeton: Princeton University Press, 1992.

Berlin, Isaiah. *Against the Current: Essays in the History of Ideas*. New York: Viking Press, 1980.

Berlin, Isaiah. *Three Critics of the Enlightenment: Vico, Hamann, Herder*. Ed. Henry Hardy. Princeton: Princeton University Press, 2000.

Bernstein, Simon. *By the Rivers of Sefarad*. Tel Aviv: Mahbarot le-Sifrut, 1956.

Bertoni, Giulio. "L' 'Istituto di Filologia Romanza di Roma.'" *Cultura neolatina* 1 (1941): 5–13.

Bestul, Thomas. *Texts of the Passion: Latin Devotional Literature and Medieval Society*. Philadelphia: University of Pennsylvania Press, 1996.

Biale, David. *Eros and the Jews*. New York: Basic Books, 1992.

Birnbaum, Jean. "Polémique sur les 'racines' de l'Europe." *Le Monde des Livres*. 25 April 2008.

Bisaha, Nancy. *Creating East and West: Renaissance Humanists and the Ottoman Turks.*
Philadelphia: University of Pennsylvania Press, 2004.

Bisaha, Nancy. "Petrarch's Vision of the Muslim and Byzantine East." *Speculum* 76.2
(2001): 284–314. http://dx.doi.org/10.2307/2903448.

Blachère, Régis. "Étude sémantique sur le nom 'maqama'." *Al-Mashriq* 47 (1953): 646–52.

Blair, Sheila S., and Jonathan M. Bloom. *The Art and Architecture of Islam, 1250–1800.* New
Haven: Yale University Press, 1994.

Bloom, Jonathan. *Arts of the City Victorious: Islamic Art and Architecture in Fatimid North
Africa and Egypt.* New Haven: Yale University Press, 2007.

Boase, Roger. *The Troubadour Revival: A Study of Social Change and Traditionalism in Late
Medieval Spain.* London: Routledge and Kegan Paul, 1978.

Bodenham, C.H.L. "Petrarch and the Poetry of the Arabs." *Romanische Forschungen* 94
(1982): 167–78.

Bonebakker, Seeger A. "Some Medieval Views on Fantastic Stories." *Quaderni di studi arabi*
10 (1992): 21–43.

Boon, Jessica. "The Agony of the Virgin: The Swoons and Crucifixion of Mary in
Sixteenth Century Castilian Passion Treatises." *Sixteenth Century Journal: Journal of Early
Modern Studies* 38.1 (2007): 3–26.

Borlandi, Franco. "Alle origini del libro di Marco Polo." *Studi in onore di Amintore Fanfani.*
Vol. 1. Milano: Giuffrè, 1962. 107–47.

Boswell, John. *Christianity, Social Tolerance, and Homosexuality: Gay People in Western Europe
from the Beginning of the Christian Era to the Fourteeth Century.* Chicago: University of
Chicago Press, 1980.

Boswell, John. *The Royal Treasure: Muslim Communities under the Crown of Aragon in the
Fourteenth Century.* New Haven: Yale University Press, 1977.

Bouchard, Constance Brittain. *"Every Valley Shall Be Exalted": The Discourse of Opposites in
Twelfth-Century Thought.* Ithaca: Cornell University Press, 2003.

Boyd, Carolyn P. *Historia Patria. Politics, History, and National Identity in Spain, 1875–1975.*
Princeton: Princeton University Press, 1997.

Brann, Ross. *The Compunctious Poet: Cultural Ambiguity and Hebrew Poetry in Medieval Spain.*
Baltimore: Johns Hopkins University Press, 1991.

Brann, Ross. "Constructions of Exile in Hispano-Hebrew and Hispano-Arabic Elegies."
Israel Levin Jubilee Volume. Ed. T. Rosen and R. Tsur. Tel Aviv: Tel Aviv University Press,
1994. 45–61.

Brann, Ross. Forthcoming. "Inscribing the Mediterranean Journey: Two Paradigmatic
Twelfth-Century Texts from Iberia." *The Medieval Mediterranean and the Origins of the
West.* Ed. Sharon Kinoshita and Brian Catlos. Valencia: University of Valencia Press.

Brann, Ross, Angel Saenz-Badillos, and Judit Targarona. "The Poetic Universe of Samuel
Ibn Sasson, Hebrew Poet of Fourteenth-Century Castile." *Prooftexts* 16 (1996): 75–103.

Braudel, Fernand. *The Mediterranean and the Mediterranean World in the Age of Philip II*. 1949. Trans. Siân Reynolds. 2nd ed. 2 vols. New York: Harper & Row, 1976.

Braudel, Fernand. *Les Mémoires de la Méditerranée: Préhistoire et antiquité* (Paris: Editions de Fallois, 1998). Trans. Siân Reynolds as *Memory and the Mediterranean*. New York: Knopf, 2001.

Breisach, Ernst. *Historiography: Ancient, Medieval, Modern*. 2nd ed. Chicago: University of Chicago Press, 1994.

Brodie, Fawn. *The Devil Drives: A Life of Sir Richard Burton*. New York: Norton, 1967.

Brobjer, Thomas H. "Nietzsche's View of the Value of Historical Studies and Methods." *Journal of the History of Ideas* 65.2 (2004): 301–22. http://dx.doi.org/10.1353/jhi.2004.0025.

Brothers, Cammy. "The Renaissance Reception of the Alhambra: The Letters of Andrea Navagero and the Palace of Charles V." *Muqarnas* 11 (1994): 79–102. http://dx.doi.org/10.2307/1523211.

Brown, Catherine. "The Relics of Menéndez Pidal: Mourning and Melancholia in Hispanomedieval Studies." *La Corónica* 24.1 (1995): 15–41.

Bruckner, Matilda Tomaryn, Laurie Shepard, and Sarah White, eds. *Songs of the Women Troubadours*. New York: Garland, 1995.

Brugnolo, Furio. *Plurilinguismo e lirica medievale da Raimbaut de Vaqueiras a Dante*. Rome: Bulzoni, 1983.

Brundage, James A. *Law, Sex, and Christian Society in Medieval Europe*. Chicago: University of Chicago Press, 1987.

Bulliet, Richard W. *The Case for Islamo-Christian Civilization*. New York: Columbia University Press, 2004.

Bunn, Elaine. "Fashioning Identities in 'El licenciado Vidriera.'" *Cervantes: Bulletin of the Cervantes Society of America* 24.1 (2004): 119–36.

Burman, Thomas E. *Reading the Qur'an in Latin Christendom, 1140–1560*. Philadelphia: University of Pennsylvania Press, 2007.

Burnett, Charles. "Adelard of Bath and the Arabs." *Rencontres de cultures dans la philosophie médiévale: traductions et traducteurs de l'antiquité tardive au XIVe siècle*. Ed. Jacqueline Hamesse and Marta Fattori. Louvain: Institut d'Études Médiévales de l'Université Catholique de Louvain, 1990. 89–107.

Burnett, Charles. "Learned Knowledge of Arabic Poetry, Rhymed Prose, and Didactic Verse from Petrus Alfonsi to Petrarch." *Poetry and Philosophy in the Middle Ages: A Festschrift for Peter Dronke*. Ed. John Marenbon. Leiden, New York: Brill, 2001. 29–53.

Burnett, Charles. "Petrarch and Averroes: An Episode in the History of Poetics." *The Medieval Mind: Hispanic Studies in Honour of Alan Deyermond*. Ed. Ian MacPherson and Ralph Penny. Woodbridge, England: Tamesis, 1997. 49–56.

Burton, Isabel. *The Life of Captain Sir Richard F. Burton*. 2 vols. New York: Appleton, 1893.

Burton, Richard F. *Camoens: His Life and his Lusiads*. 2 vols. London: Bernard Quaritch, 1881.

Burton, Richard F. *Scinde; or, the Unhappy Valley*. 2 vols. London: Richard Bentley, 1851.

Butterfield, Ardis. *The Familiar Enemy: Chaucer, Language and Nation in the Hundred Years War*. Oxford: Oxford University Press, 2009.

Cabré, Miriam. "Italian and Catalan Troubadours." *The Troubadours: An Introduction*. Ed. Simon Gaunt and Sarah Kay. Cambridge: Cambridge University Press, 1999. 127–40.

Camille, Michael. "Mimetic Identification and Passion Devotion in the Later Middle Ages: A Double-sided Panel by Meister Francke." *The Broken Body: Passion Devotion in Late Medieval Culture*. Ed. A.A. MacDonald, H.N.B. Ridderbos, and R.M. Schlusemann. Mediaevalia Groningana 21. Groningen, The Netherlands: Egbert Forsten, 1998. 183–210.

Caro Baroja, Julio. *Vidas mágicas e Inquisición*. Madrid: Istmo, 1992.

Carrete Parrondo, Carlos. "Los judíos de Castilla en la Baja Edad Media." *España, Al-Andalus, Sefarad: Síntesis y nuevas perspectivas*. Ed. Felipe Maíllo Salgado. Salamanca: University of Salamanca, 1988. 143–51.

Casalduero, Joaquín. *Sentido y forma de las "Novelas ejemplares."* Madrid: Gredos, 1969.

Castro, Américo. *Dos ensayos*. Mexico City: Porrúa, 1956.

Castro, Américo. *Ensayo de historiología: Analogueías y diferencias entre hispanos y musulmanes*. New York: Franz C. Feger, 1950.

Castro, Américo. *España en su historia: cristianos, moros y judíos*. 2nd ed. Barcelona: Crítica, 1983.

Castro, Américo. *Origen, ser y existir de los españoles*. Madrid: Taurus, 1959. Rpt. in *Los españoles. Cómo llegaron a serlo*. In *Sobre el nombre y el quién de los españoles*. 1965. Madrid: Taurus, 1985.

Castro, Américo. *La realidad histórica en España*. 2nd ed. Mexico City: Porrúa, 1962.

de Castro y Castro, P. Manuel, OFM. "La Reforma en Castilla." *Archivo Ibero-Americano* 17 (1957): 120–73.

Catlos, Brian. "Cristians, musulmans i jueus a la Corona d'Arago medieval: Un cas de 'conveniencia'." *L'Avenc* 236 (2001): 8–16.

Catlos, Brian. *The Victors and the Vanquished: Christians and Muslims of Catalonia and Aragon, 1050–1300*. Cambridge: Cambridge University Press, 2004. http://dx.doi.org/10.1017/CBO9780511496424.

Cerquiglini, Bernard. *In Praise of the Variant: A Critical History of Philology*. Trans. Betsy Wing. Baltimore: Johns Hopkins University Press, 1999.

de Certeau, Michel. *Heterologies*. Trans. Brian Massumi. Minneapolis: University of Minnesota Press, 1986.

Chamberlain, Michael. *Knowledge and Social Practice in Medieval Damascus, 1190–1350*. Cambridge: Cambridge University Press, 1994.

Cigni, Fabrizio. "La ricezione della letteratura francese nella Toscana nord-occidentale." *Fra toscanità e italianità*. Ed. Edeltraud Werner and Sabine Schwarze. Tübingen, Basel: Francke, 2000. 71–108.

Clark, Elizabeth A. *History, Theory, Text: Historians and the Linguistic Turn.* Cambridge, MA: Harvard University Press, 2004.

Cochran, Terry. *Twilight of the Literary: Figures of Thought in the Age of Print.* Cambridge: Harvard University Press, 2005.

Cohen, Jeffrey Jerome, ed. *Cultural Diversity in the British Middle Ages.* New York: Palgrave, 2008. http://dx.doi.org/10.1057/9780230614123.

Cohen, Jeffrey Jerome. "On Saracen Enjoyment: Some Fantasies of Race in Late Medieval France and England." *Journal of Medieval and Early Modern Studies* 31.1 (2001): 113–46. http://dx.doi.org/10.1215/10829636-31-1-113.

Cohen, Jeffrey Jerome, ed. *The Postcolonial Middle Ages.* New York: Palgrave, 2000. http://dx.doi.org/10.1057/9780230107342.

Cohen, Mark R. "The Neo-Lachrymose Conception of Jewish Arab History." *Tikkun* 6 (1991): 55–60.

Cole, Peter. *The Dream of the Poem: Hebrew Poetry from Muslim and Christian Spain, 950–1492.* Princeton: Princeton University Press, 2007.

Constable, Olivia Remie. "Is *Convivencia* Dangerous?" Address. 40th International Congress on Medieval Studies. Western Michigan University, Kalamazoo, MI. 5 May 2005.

Convivencia.net. Sponsored by BibleLands.com. 30 May 2007. www.convivencia.net.

Cornish, Alison. "Translatio Galliae: Effects of Early Franco-Italian Literary Exchange." *Romanic Review* 97 (2006): 309–30.

Cornish, Alison. *Vernacular Translation in Dante's Italy: Illiterate Literature.* Cambridge: Cambridge University Press, 2010. http://dx.doi.org/10.1017/CBO9780511734762.

Corriente, Federico. "Tres mitos contemporáneos frente a la realidad de Alandalús: romanticismo filoárabe, 'cultura Mozárabe' y 'cultura Sefardí'." *Orientalismo, exotismo y traducción.* Cuenca: Ediciones de la Universidad de Castilla-La Mancha, 2000. 39–47.

Crane, Susan. *Insular Romance: Politics, Faith and Culture in Anglo-Norman and Middle English Literature.* Berkeley, Los Angeles, London: University of California Press, 1986.

Croce, Benedetto. *La Filosofia di Giambattista Vico.* Bari: Laterza e Figli, 1911.

Curtin, Philip D. *Cross-Cultural Trade in World History.* Cambridge: Cambridge University Press, 1984. http://dx.doi.org/10.1017/CBO9780511661198.

Curtius, Ernst. *European Literature and the Latin Middle Ages.* Trans. Willard R. Trask. 1948. Princeton: Princeton University Press, 1991.

Dagenais, John, and Margaret R. Greer. "Decolonizing the Middle Ages: Introduction." *Journal of Medieval and Early Modern Studies* 30.3 (2000): 431–48. http://dx.doi .org/10.1215/10829636-30-3-431.

Davidson, Israel. *Parody in Jewish Literature.* 1907. New York: AMS Press, 1966.

Davis, Kathleen. *Periodization and Sovereignty: How Ideas of Feudalism and Secularization Govern the Politics of Time.* Philadelphia: University of Pennsylvania Press, 2008.

Decter, Jonathan P. *Iberian Jewish Literature: Between al-Andalus and Christian Europe.* Bloomington: Indiana University Press, 2007.

Delcorno Branca, Daniela. *Tristano e Lancillotto in Italia: studi di letteratura arturiana.* Ravenna: Longo, 1998.

Denis, Françoise. "Landscape and Nostalgia in Andalusian Hebrew Poetry." *Prooftexts* 24 (2004): 135–66.

Denis, Françoise. "Les Sarrasins dans *Gui de Bourgogne*: Plaisirs du cliché et approches du réel." *L'épopée médiévale: Actes du XVe Congrès international Rencesvals, Poitiers, 21–27 août 2000.* Civilisation Médiévale 13. Poitiers: Centre d'Etudes Supérieures de Civilisation Médiévale, 2002. 1: 177–86.

Deyermond, Alan D. "Some Aspects of Parody in the *Libro de buen amor*." *Libro de buen amor Studies.* Ed. G.B. Gybbon-Monypenny. London: Tamesis, 1970. 53–78.

Díaz, Elías. "La Institución Libre de Enseñanza en la España del nacional-catolicismo." *Historia Internacional* 16 (1976): 69–78.

Díaz Esteban, Fernando. "El 'Debate del cálamo y las tijeras,' de Sem Tob Ardutiel, don Santo de Carrión." *Revista de la Universidad de Madrid* 18 (1969): 61–102.

Dobbs-Weinstein, Idit. "The Maimonidean Controversy." *History of Jewish Philosophy.* Ed. Daniel H. Frank and Oliver Leaman. London: Routledge, 1997. 331–49.

Dodds, Jerrilynn D., María Rosa Menocal, and Abigail Krasner Balbale. *The Arts of Intimacy: Christians, Jews, and Muslims in the Making of Castilian Culture.* New Haven: Yale University Press, 2008.

Doñate Sebastià, José María, and José Ramón Magdalena Nom de Deu. *Three Jewish Communities in Medieval Valencia.* Jerusalem: Magnes, 1990.

Doron, Aviva. "'Dios, haz que el rey se apiade de mí.' Entrelazamiento de lo sacro y lo profano en la poesia hebrea-toledana en el trasfondo de la poesía cristiana-española." *Sefarad* 46 (1986): 151–60.

Doron, Aviva. "New Trends in the Conception of Hebrew Poetry in Thirteenth and Fourteenth-Century Spain in Relation to Spanish Literature." *Encuentros and Desencuentros: Spanish Jewish Cultural Interaction Throughout History.* Ed. Carlos Carrete Parrondo, et al. Tel Aviv: University of Tel Aviv Publishing Projects, 2000. 213–39.

Doron, Aviva. *A Poet in the King's Court: Todros Halevi Abulafia, Hebrew Poetry in Christian Spain.* Tel Aviv: Dvir, 1989.

Doss-Quinby, Eglal, et al., eds. *Songs of the Women Trouvères.* New Haven: Yale University Press, 2001.

Droit, Roger-Pol. "Et si l'Europe ne devait pas ses savoirs à l'Islam?" *Le Monde des Livres.* 4 April 2008.

Drory, Rina. "The Maqama." In Menocal, Scheindlin, and Sells, 190–210.

Drory, Rina. "Words Beautifully Put: Hebrew vs. Arabic in Tenth-Century Jewish Literature." *Genizah Research After 90 Years: The Case for Judeo-Arabic.* Ed. Joseph Blau and Stefan Reif. Cambridge: Cambridge University Press, 1992. 53–66.

Duby, Georges. *The Three Orders: Feudal Society Imagined.* Trans. Arthur Goldhammer. Chicago: University of Chicago Press, 1980.

Durán Velasco, José F. "Reflexiones y digresiones en torno a la mitificación de Al-Andalus." *El saber en Al-Andalus: textos y estudios.* Ed. Ildefonso Garijo Galán, et al. Vol. 3. Seville: University of Seville, 2001. 135–68.

Eco, Umberto. *A Theory of Semiotics.* 1976. Bloomington: Indiana University Press, 1979.

Edwards, Robert. "Exile, Self and Society." *Exile in Literature.* Ed. Maria-Ines Lagos-Pope. Lewisburg: Bucknell University Press, 1988. 15–31.

Einbinder, Susan L. "A Proper Det: Medicine and History in Crescas Caslari's *Esther.*" *Speculum* 80.2 (Apr 2005): 437–63. Medline:16021768.

Einbinder, Susan L. *No Place of Rest: Jewish Literature, Expulsion, and the Memory of Medieval France.* Philadelphia: University of Pennsylvania Press, 2009.

Eisenberg, Daniel. "Juan Ruiz's Heterosexual 'Good Love'." *Queer Iberia: Sexualities, Cultures, and Crossings from the Middle Ages to the Renaissance.* Ed. Josiah Blackmore and Gregory S. Hutcheson. Durham: Duke University Press, 1999. 250–74.

El-Hibri, Tayeb. *Reinterpreting Islamic Historiography.* Cambridge: Cambridge University Press, 1999. http://dx.doi.org/10.1017/CBO9780511497476.

El Saffar, Ruth. *Novel to Romance.* Baltimore: Johns Hopkins University Press, 1974.

Elden, Stuart. *The Birth of Territory.* Chicago: University of Chicago Press, 2013.

Elinson, Alexander E. *Looking Back at al-Andalus: The Poetics of Loss and Nostalgia in Medieval Arabic and Hebrew Literature.* Leiden: E.J. Brill, 2009.

Elukin, Jonathan. *Living Together, Living Apart. Rethinking Jewish-Christian Relations in the Middle Ages.* Princeton: Princeton University Press, 2007.

Emery, Ed, ed. *Muwashshah: Proceedings of the Conference on Arabic and Hebrew Strophic Poetry and Its Romance Parallels.* 8–10 October 2004, School of Oriental and Asian Studies, University of London. London: RN Books, 2006.

Enderwitz, Susanne. "Homesickness and Love in Arabic Poetry." *Myths, Historical Archetypes and Symbolic Figures in Arabic Literature.* Ed. Angelika Neuwirth, et al. Beirut: Franz Steiner Verlag, 1999. 59–70.

Engels, Josef. "Philologie Romane–Linguistique–Études Littéraires." *Neophilologus* 37.1 (1953): 14–24. http://dx.doi.org/10.1007/BF01514392.

Epalza, Mikel de. "Les études arabes en Espagne: institutions, chercheurs, publications." *Annuaire de l'Afrique du Nord* 15 (1976): 1015–29.

Español, Francesca. "Los descendimientos hispanos." *La Deposizione legnea in Europa: L'immagine, il culto, la forma.* Ed. Giovanni Sapori and Bruno Toscano. Rome: Electa, 2004. 511–54.

Ettinghausen, Richard, Oleg Grabar, and Marilyn Jenkins-Madina. *The Art and Architecture of Islam, 650–1250.* New Haven: Yale University Press, 2001.

Fanjul, Serafín. *Al-Andalus contra España. La forja del mito.* Madrid: Siglo XXI de España Editores, 2000.

Fanjul, Serafín. *La quimera de al-Andalus.* Madrid: Siglo XXI de España Editores, 2004.

Faria e Sousa, Manuel de. *Lusiadas de Luis de Camoens.* Madrid: Ivan Sanchez, 1639.

Farmer, Henry George. *Historical Facts for the Arabian Musical Influence.* Studies in the Music of the Middle Ages. London: W. Reeves, 1930.

Farmer, Henry George. *A History of Arabian Music to the XIIIth Century.* 1929. London: Luzac Oriental, 1994.

Feldman, David M. *Birth Control in Jewish Law: Marital Relations, Contraception, and Abortion as Set Forth in the Classic Texts of Jewish Law.* New York: New York University Press, 1968.

Ferris, Paul Wayne, Jr. *The Genre of Communal Lament in the Bible and the Ancient Near East.* Atlanta: Scholars Press, 1992.

Fierro, Maribel. *'Abd al-Rahman III: The First Cordoban Caliph.* Oxford: One World Publications, 2005.

Fierro, Maribel. *La heterodoxia en al-Andalus durante el periodo Omeya.* Madrid: Instituto Hispano-Arabe de Cultura, 1987.

Fierro, Maribel. "Women as Prophets in Islam." *Writing the Feminine: Women in Arab Sources.* Ed. Manuela Marín and Randi Deguilhem. London: I.B. Tauris, 2002. 183–99.

Fishman, Joshua A. *Language and Nationalism; Two Integrative Essays.* Rowley, MA: Newbury House Publishers, 1973.

Fishman, Talya. "A Medieval Parody of Misogyny: Judah Ibn Shabbetai's *Minhat Yehudah, Soneh Hanashim.*" *Prooftexts: A Journal of Jewish Literary History* 8.1 (1988): 89–111.

Folena, Gianfranco. *Culture e lingue nel Veneto medievale.* Padua: Editoriale Programma, 1990.

Fontan, Élisabeth, and Hélène Le Meaux. *La Méditerranée des Phéniciens.* Paris: Somogy, 2007.

Fowden, Garth. *Empire to Commonwealth: The Consequences of Monotheism in Late Antiquity.* Princeton: Princeton University Press, 1994.

Franco Mata, Ángela. "El Crucifijo de Oristano (Cerdeña) y su influencia en el área mediterránea catalana-italiana: Consideraciones sobre la significación y origen del Crucifijo gótico doloroso." *Boletín del Mueso e Instituto "Camón Azmar"* 25 (1989): 5–64.

Franco Mata, Ángela. "El crucifijo gótico de la iglesia del convento de San Pablo de Toledo y los crucifijos góticos dolorosos castellanos del siglo XIV." *Archivo Español de Arte* 223 (1983): 220–41.

Frank, Robert Worth, Jr. "*Meditationes Vitae Christi*: The Logistics of Access to Divinity." *Hermeneutics and Medieval Culture.* Ed. Helen Damico and Patrick Gallagher. Albany: State University of New York Press, 1990. 39–49.

Freitag, Ulrike. "The Critique of Orientalism." *Companion to Historiography.* Ed. Michael Bentley. London: Routledge, 2002. 620–39.

Freller, Thomas. "'Adversus Infideles': Some Notes on the Cavalier's Tour, the Fleet of the Order of Saint John, and the Maltese Corsairs." *Journal of Early Modern History* 4 (2000): 405–30.

Frenk Alatorre, Margit, ed. *Corpus de la antigua lírica popular hispánica (siglos XV a XVII).* Madrid: Castalia, 1987.

Friedman, Edward H. "Conceptual Proportion in Cervantes' 'El Licenciado Vidriera'." *South Atlantic Bulletin* 39.4 (November 1974): 51–9. http://dx.doi.org/10.2307/3198230.

Fück, Johann. *Die arabischen Studien in Europa bis in den Anfang des 20. Jahrhunderts.* Leipzig: Otto Harrassowitz, 1955.

Fulton, Rachel. *From Judgment to Passion: Devotion to Christ and the Virgin Mary, 800–1200.* New York: Columbia University Press, 2002.

Gabrieli, Francesco. "Arabi di Sicilia e arabi di Spagna." *Dal mondo dell'Islam.* Naples: Riccardo Ricciardi Editore, 1954. 88–108.

Gabrieli, Francesco. *Dal Mondo dell'Islam.* Milan: Riccardo Ricciardi, 1956.

Gabrieli, Francesco. "Petrarca e gli Arabi." *Al-Andalus* 42 (1977): 241–8.

Gadamer, Hans-Georg. *Truth and Method.* 2nd rev. ed. Trans. Joel Weinsheimer and Donald G. Marshall. New York: Continuum, 1994.

Gallois, William. "Andalusi Cosmopolitanism in World History." *Cultural Contacts in Building a Universal Civilization: Islamic Contributions.* Ed. Ekmeleddin Ihsanoglu. Istanbul: O.I.C. Research Centre, 2005. 59–109.

Ganim, John. "Cosmopolitanism and Medievalism." *Exemplaria* 22.1 (2010): 5–27. http://dx.doi.org/10.1179/104125710X12670926011716.

Ganim, John. *Medievalism and Orientalism: Three Essays on Literature, Architecture and Cultural Identity.* New York: Palgrave Macmillan, 2005.

García Arenal, Mercedes. Introduction. *Al-Andalus allende el atlántico.* Ed. Mercedes García Arenal. Granada: Ediciones Unesco/Legado Andalusí, 1997. 23–34.

García Ballester, Luis. *Los moriscos y la medicina: un capítulo de la medicina y la ciencia marginadas en la España del siglo XVI.* Barcelona: Editorial Labor, 1984.

García Casar, María Guencisla. "¿Américo Castro, historiador del judaísmo español?" *El legado de los judíos al occidente eruopeo: De los reinos hispánico a la monarquía española. Cuartos encuentros judaicos de Tudela, 11–13 de Septiembre de 2000.* Ed. F. Miranda. Pamplona: Universidad Pública de Navarra, 2002. 75–82.

García Gómez, Emilio. "Primer centenario del nacimiento de Don Julián Ribera Tarragó." *Al-Andalus* 23 (1958): 207–9.

García Oro, José. *El Cardenal Cisneros: vida y empresas.* 2 vols. Madrid: Biblioteca de Autores Cristianos, 1992–3.

García Oro, José. *La reforma de los religiosos españoles en tiempo de los Reyes Católicos.* Valladolid: Instituto Isabel la Católica de Historia Ecclesiastica, 1969.

Garulo, Teresa. "La Nostalgia de al-Andalus: Genesis de un Tema Literario." *Qurtuba* 3 (1988): 47–63.

Gaunt, Simon. "Can the Middle Ages Be Postcolonial?" *Comparative Literature* 61 (2009): 160–76.

Gaunt, Simon. "*Desnaturat son li Frances*: Language and identity in the twelfth-century Occitan epic." *Tenso* 17.1 (2002): 10–31. http://dx.doi.org/10.1353/ten.2002.0008.

Gaunt, Simon. *Love and Death in Medieval French and Occitan Courtly Literature: Martyrs to Love*. Oxford: Oxford University Press, 2006. http://dx.doi.org/10.1093/acprof: oso/9780199272075.001.0001.

Gaunt, Simon. *Marco Polo's* Le Devisement du Monde*: Narrative Voice, Language and Diversity*. Cambridge: D.S. Brewer, 2013.

Gaunt, Simon. "Sexual difference and the metaphor of language in a troubadour poem." *Modern Language Review* 83.2 (1988): 297–313. http://dx.doi.org/10.2307/3731681.

Gaunt, Simon. "Translating the Diversity of the Middle Ages: Marco Polo and John Mandeville as 'French' Writers." *Australian Journal of French Studies* 46.3 (2009): 235–48. http://dx.doi.org/10.3828/AJFS.46.3.235.

Gerber, Jane. "Reconsiderations of Sephardic History: The Origins of the Image of the Golden Age of Muslim-Jewish Relations." *Solomon Goldman Lectures* 4 (1985): 85–93.

Gerli, E. Michael. "Inventing the Spanish Middle Ages: Ramón Menéndez Pidal, Spanish Cultural History, and Ideology in Philology." *La Corónica* 30.1 (2001): 111–26. http:// dx.doi.org/10.1353/cor.2001.0022.

Gerli, Michael, ed. *Poesía Cancioneril Castellana*. Madrid: Akal, 1994.

Gildenhard, Ingo. "Philologia Perennis? Classical Scholarship and Functional Differentiation." Gildenhard and Ruehl. 161–203.

Gildenhard, Ingo, and Martin Ruehl, eds. *Out of Arcadia: Classics and Politics in Germany in the Age of Burckhardt, Nietzsche and Wilamowitz*. London: University of London Institute of Classical Studies, 2003.

Gjesdal, Kristin. "Hermeneutics and Philology: A Reconsideration of Gadamer's Critique of Schleiermacher." *British Journal for the History of Philosophy* 14.1 (2006): 133–56. http://dx.doi.org/10.1080/09608780500449206.

Glick, Thomas. "Darwin y la filología española." *Boletín de la Institución Libre de Enseñanza*, 2nd series 12 (1991): 35–41.

Glick, Thomas. *Islamic and Christian Spain in the Early Middle Ages: Comparative Perspectives on Social and Cultural Formation*. Princeton: Princeton University Press, 1979.

Goitein, S.D. *A Mediterranean Society: The Jewish Communities of the Arab World as Portrayed in the Documents of the Cairo Geniza*. 6 vols. Berkeley: University of California Press, 1967–93.

Goldziher, Ignacz. "The Spanish Arabs and Islam: The Place of the Spanish Arabs in the Evolution of Islam Compared with the Eastern Arabs." *The Muslim World* 53.4 (1963): 281–6. Rpt. in *Gesammelte Schriften*. Vol. 1. Ed. Joseph Desomogyi. Hildesheim: G. Olms Verlag, 1967. 370–423.

Gómez-Martínez, José Luis. *Américo Castro y el origen de los españoles: Historia de una polémica*. Madrid: Gredos, 1975.

Gossman, Lionel. *Basel in the Age of Burckhardt: A Study in Unseasonable Ideas*. Chicago: University of Chicago Press, 2000.

Gossman, Lionel. *Between History and Literature*. Cambridge, MA: Harvard University Press, 1990.

Gouguenheim, Sylvain. *Aristote au Mont-Saint-Michel: Les racines grecques de l'Europe chrétienne.* Paris: Seuil, 2008.

Goytisolo, Juan. "Américo Castro en la España actual." *Américo Castro y la revisión de la memoria (El Islam en España).* Ed. Eduardo Subirats. Madrid: Libertarias, 2003. 23–37.

Goytisolo, Juan. "Convivencia con el Islam." *Revista de Occidente (Madrid, Spain)* 263 (April 2003): 7–17.

Graetz, Heinrich. *A History of the Jews.* 6 vols. Philadelphia: Jewish Publication Society, 1946.

Grafton, Anthony. "'Man muß aus der Gegenwart heraufsteigen': History, Tradition, and Traditions of Historical Thought in F. A. Wolf." *Aufklärung und Geschichte. Studien zur deutschen Geschichtswissenschaft im 18. Jahrhundert.* Ed. Hans Erich Bödeker, et al. Göttingen: Vandenhoeck and Ruprecht, 1986. 416–29.

Granara, William. "*Extensio Animae*: The Artful Ways of Remembering 'Al-Andalus'." *Journal of Social Affairs* 19.75 (2002): 45–72.

Granara, William. "Nostalgia, Arab Nationalism, and the Andalusian Chronotope in the Evolution of the Modern Arabic Novel." *Journal of Arabic Literature* 36.1 (2005): 57–73. http://dx.doi.org/10.1163/1570064053560648.

Granara, William. "Remaking Muslim Sicily: Ibn Hamdis and the Poetics of Exile." *Edebiyat* 9 (1998): 167–98.

Gregory, Derek. *Geographical Imaginations.* Cambridge: Blackwell, 1994.

Grieve, Patricia. *Floire and Blancheflor and the European Romance.* Cambridge: Cambridge University Press, 1997. http://dx.doi.org/10.1017/CBO9780511585470.

Grotzfeld, Heinz. "The Age of the Galland Manuscript of the *Nights.*" *The Arabian Nights Reader.* Ed. Ulrich Marzolph. Detroit: Wayne State University Press, 2006. 105–21.

Grotzfeld, Heinz. "The Manuscript Tradition of the Arabian Nights." *The Arabian Nights Encyclopedia.* Ed. Ulrich Marzolph and Richard van Leeuwen. 2 vols. Santa Barbara, Calif.: ABC-CLIO, 2004. 1:17–21.

Gumbrecht, Hans Ulrich. "A Philological Invention of Modernism: Menéndez Pidal, García Lorca, and the Harlem Renaissance." *The Future of the Middle Ages: Medieval Literature in the 1990s.* Ed. William D. Paden. Gainesville: University Press of Florida, 1994. 32–49.

Gumbrecht, Hans Ulrich. *The Powers of Philology: Dynamics of Textual Scholarship.* Urbana, Chicago: University of Illinois Press, 2003.

Gumbrecht, Hans Ulrich. "'Un Souffle d'Allemagne ayant passé': Friedrich Diez, Gaston Paris, and the Genesis of National Philologies." *Romance Philology* 40 (1986–7): 1–37.

Gysseling, Maurits, and A.F.C. Koch. "Het 'Fragment' van het tiende-eeuwse Liber Traditionum van de Sint-Pitersabdij te Gent." *Bulletin de Commission Royale d'Histoire* 113 (1948): 253–312.

Hacking, Ian. "Locke, Leibniz, Language and Hans Aarsleff." *Synthese* 75.2 (1988): 135–53. http://dx.doi.org/10.1007/BF00872975.

Hamburger, Jeffrey. "'To Make Women Weep': Ugly Art as 'Feminine' and the Origins of Modern Aesthetics." *Res* 31 (1997): 9–33.

Hames, Harvey. *The Art of Conversion: Christianity and Kabbalah in the Thirteenth Century*. Leiden: Brill, 2000.

Hames, Harvey. "Conversion via Ecstatic Experience in Ramon Llull's *Llibre del gentil e dels tres savis*." *Viator* 30 (1999): 181–200.

Hämeen-Anttila, Jaakko. *Maqama: A History of a Genre*. Wiesbaden: Harrassowitz, 2002.

Hamilton, Michelle M. *Representing Others in Medieval Iberia*. New York: Palgrave Macmillan, 2007. http://dx.doi.org/10.1057/9780230606975.

Harris, Lucian. "Fatimid ewer sells for £220,000 in provincial British auction." *The Art Newspaper*. 10 September 2008. http://www.theartnewspaper.com/articles/Islamic-sleeper-priced-at-100-in-January-to-be-auctioned-for-3-million-in-October/16118.

Harris, Max. *Aztecs, Moors, and Christians: Festivals of Reconquest in Mexico and Spain*. Austin, TX: University of Texas Press, 2000.

Harris, W.V., ed. "The Mediterranean and Ancient History." In Harris, *Rethinking the Mediterranean* 1–42.

Harris, W.V., ed. *Rethinking the Mediterranean*. Oxford, New York: Oxford University Press, 2005.

Harvey, L.P. "The Political, Social and Cultural History of the Moriscos." *The Legacy of Muslim Spain*. Ed. Salma Khadra Jayyusi and Manuela Marín. Leiden: Brill, 1992. 201–35.

Haug, Walter, and Burghart Wachinger. *Die Passion Christi in Literatur und Kunst des Spätmittelalters*. Tübingen: Max Niemeyer, 1993.

Heidegger, Martin. *Basic Writings*. Ed. David F. Krell. New York: Harper Collins, 1977.

Heijkoop, Henk, and Otto Zwartjes. *Muwaššah, Zajal, Kharja: Bibliography of Strophic Poetry and Music from al-Andalus and Their Influence in East and West*. Leiden: Brill, 2004.

Heller-Roazen, Daniel. "Des altérités de la langue: plurilinguismes poétiques au Moyen Âge." *Littérature* 130.2 (2003): 75–96. http://dx.doi.org/10.3406/litt.2003.1800.

Helsloot, Niels. *Een korte geschiedenis van de rede*. Münster: Nodus, 1998.

Henkel, Jacqueline M. *The Language of Criticism: Linguistic Models and Literary Theory*. Ithaca: Cornell University Press, 1996.

Hermes, Eberhard. "The Author and His Times." *The Disciplina Clericalis of Petrus Alfonsi*. Trans. P.R. Quarrie. Berkeley: University of California Press, 1977. 3–102.

Hess, Steven. "'Castilian Hegemony': Linguistics and Politics in *Orígenes del Español*." *La Corónica* 24.2 (1996): 114–22.

Hillgarth, Jocelyn N. *The Spanish Kingdoms, 1250–1516*. 2 vols. Oxford: Clarendon Press, 1976.

Hinojosa Montalvo, José. *The Jews of the Kingdom of Valencia: From Persecution to Expulsion, 1391–1492*. Jerusalem: Magnes Press, 1993.

Hitti, Philip K. *A History of the Arabs*. 10th ed. London: MacMillan-St Martin's Press, 1970.

Hodgson, Marshall G.S. *Rethinking World History: Essays on Europe, Islam and World History*. Cambridge: Cambridge University Press, 1993.

Hoffman, Eva R., ed. *Late Antique and Medieval Art of the Mediterranean World.* Malden, MA: Blackwell, 2007.

Hofstetter, Michael. *The Romantic Idea of a University: England and Germany, 1770–1850.* New York: Palgrave, 2001. http://dx.doi.org/10.1057/9780230510739.

Holsinger, Bruce. "The Color of Salvation: Desire, Death, and the Second Crusade in Bernard of Clairvaux's *Sermons on the Song of Songs.*" *The Tongue of the Father: Gender and Ideology in Twelfth-Century Latin.* Ed. David Townsend and Andrew Taylor. Philadelphia: University of Pennsylvania Press, 1998. 156–86.

Holsinger, Bruce. *Neomedievalism, Neoconservatism, and the War on Terror.* Chicago: Prickly Paradigm Press, 2007.

Holtus, Günter, and Peter Wunderli. *Franco-Italien et épopée franco-italienne. Grundriss des Romanischen Litteraturen des Mittelalters*, vol. 1.2 fasc. 10. Heidelberg: Universitätsverlag Winter, 2005.

Horden, Peregrine, and Nicholas Purcell. *The Corrupting Sea: A Study of Mediterranean History.* Oxford: Blackwell, 2000.

Horden, Peregrine and Nicholas Purcell. "Four Years of Corruption: A Response to the Critics." In Harris, *Rethinking the Mediterranean* 348–75.

Horden, Peregrine, and Nicholas Purcell. "The Mediterranean and 'the New Thalassology'." *American Historical Review* 111.3 (June 2006): 722–40. http://dx.doi .org/10.1086/ahr.111.3.722.

Howard, Deborah. *Venice and the East: The Impact of the Islamic World on Venetian Architecture, 1100–1500.* New Haven: Yale University Press, 2000.

Hughes, Andrew. *Late Medieval Liturgical Offices: Resources for Electronic Research: Sources and Chants.* Toronto: Pontifical Institute of Mediaeval Studies, 1996.

Humboldt, Alexander von. *Cosmos: A Sketch of a Physical Description of the Universe.* Trans. E.C. Otté. London: Henry G. Bohn, 1849.

Huntington, Samuel. *The Clash of Civilizations and the Remaking of the World Order.* New York: Simon and Schuster, 1996.

Huss, Matti. Introduction. *Don Vidal Benvenist's Tale of Efer and Dinah.* [Hebrew] Jerusalem: Y.L. Magnes, Hebrew University, 2003. 3–146.

Hutcheson, Gregory S., and Josiah Blackmore. Introduction. *Queer Iberia: Sexualities, Cultures, and Crossings from the Middle Ages to the Renaissance.* Ed. Gregory S. Hutcheson and Josiah Blackmore. Durham: Duke University Press, 1999. 1–19.

Ibn 'Abd Allah Shushtari, 'Ali. *Poesía estrófica (cejeles y/o muwassahat) atribuida al místico granadino As-Sustari: siglo XIII d.C.* Ed. F. Corriente. Madrid: Consejo Superior de Investigaciones Científicas, Instituto de Filología, Departamento de Estudios Arabes, 1988.

Iggers, George G. *Historiography in the Twentieth Century: From Scientific Objectivity to the Postmodern Challenge.* Hanover, NH: Wesleyan Universitcy Press, 1997.

Infantes, Victor, and Nieves Baranda, eds. *Narrativa popular de la Edad Media: Doncella Teodor, Flores y Blancaflor, París y Viana.* Torrejón de Ardoz: AKAL, 1995.

Irwin, Robert. *The Arabian Nights: A Companion.* London: Allen Lane, 1994.

Isaac, Benjamin. *The Invention of Racism in Classical Antiquity.* Princeton: Princeton University Press, 2004.

al-Jabiri, Mohammad 'Abid. *Arab-Islamic Philosophy: A Contemporary Critique.* Trans. Aziz Abbassi. Austin: Center for Middle Eastern Studies, 1999.

Jacobs, Jason, and Sharon Kinoshita. "Ports of Call: Boccaccio's Alatiel in the Medieval Mediterranean." *Journal of Medieval and Early Modern Studies* 37.1 (2007): 163–95. http://dx.doi.org/10.1215/10829636-2006-014.

Jacobs, Jill. "'The Defense Has Become the Prosecution': *Ezrat HaNashim*, a Thirteenth-century Response to Misogyny." *Women in Judaism: A Multidisciplinary Journal* 3.2 (2003): 1–9.

Jacoby, David. "Silk in Western Byzantium before the Fourth Crusade." *Trade, Commodities, and Shipping in the Medieval Mediterranean.* Aldershot: Ashgate Variorum, 1997.

Jansen, Philippe, Anneliese Nef, and Christophe Picard, eds. *La Méditerrannée entre pays d'Islam et monde latin.* Paris: SEDES, 2000.

Jarausch, Konrad. *Students, Society, and Politics in Imperial Germany.* Princeton: Princeton University Press, 1982.

Jaspers, Karl. *Die Idee der Universität.* 1946. Rev. ed. trans. H.A.T. Reiche and H.F. Vanderschmidt. Boston: Beacon Press, 1959.

Jewers, Caroline. *Chivalric Fiction and the History of the Novel.* Gainesville: University of Florida Press, 2000.

Jones, Alan. "Eppur si muove." *La Corónica* 12.1 (1983): 45–70.

Jones, Alan. "Sunbeams from Cucumbers? An Arabist's Assessment of the State of Kharja Studies." *La Corónica* 10.1 (1981): 38–53.

Jubb, Margaret. "The Crusaders' Perception of Their Opponents." *Palgrave Advances in the Crusades.* Ed. Helen Nicholson. Houndsmill, Basingstoke: Palgrave Macmillan, 2005. 225–44.

Kassin, Leon Jacob. "A Study of a Fourteenth-Century Polemical Treatise ADVERSUS JUDAEOS." Diss. Columbia University, 1969.

Kay, Sarah. *The Chansons de Geste in the Age of Romance: Political Fictions.* Oxford: Clarendon, 1995. http://dx.doi.org/10.1093/acprof:oso/9780198151920.001.0001.

Kennedy, Dane. *The Highly Civilized Man: Richard Burton and the Victorian World.* Cambridge, Massachusetts: Harvard University Press, 2005.

Kennedy, Hugh. *The Early Abbasid Caliphate: A Political History.* London: Croom Helm, 1981.

Kilito, Abdelfattah. *Thou Shalt Not Speak My Language.* Trans. Waïl S. Hassan. Syracuse, New York: Syracuse University Press, 2008.

King, Edmund L. "A Note on 'El Licenciado Vidriera.'" *Modern Language Notes* 69.2 (1954): 99–102. http://dx.doi.org/10.2307/3039798.

Kinoshita, Sharon. "Almería Silk and the French Feudal Imaginary: Toward a 'Material' History of the Medieval Mediterranean." *Medieval Fabrications: Dress, Textiles, Clothwork, and Other Cultural Imaginings*. Ed. E. Jane Burns. New York: Palgrave Macmillan, 2004. 165–76.

Kinoshita, Sharon. "Fraternizing with the Enemy: The Crusader Imaginary in *Raoul de Cambrai*." *L'épopée médiévale: Actes du XVe Congrès international Rencesvals, Poitiers, 21–27 août 2000*. Civilisation Médiévale 13. Poitiers: Centre d'Etudes Supérieures de Civilisation Médiévale, 2002. 2: 695–703.

Kinoshita, Sharon. *Medieval Boundaries: Rethinking Difference in Old French Literature*. Philadelphia: University of Pennsylvania Press, 2006.

Kinoshita, Sharon. "'Noi siamo mercatanti cipriani': How To Do Things in the Medieval Mediterranean." In *The Age of Philippe de Mézières: Fourteenth-Century Piety and Politics between France, Venice, and Cyprus*. Ed. Renate Blumenfeld-Kosinski and Kiril Petkov. The Medieval Mediterranean. Leiden: Brill, 2001. 41–60.

Kinoshita, Sharon. "Political Uses and Responses: Orientalism, Postcolonial Theory, and Cultural Studies." *MLA Approaches to Teaching the Song of Roland*. Ed. William W. Kibler and Leslie Z. Morgan. New York: Modern Language Association, 2006. 269–80.

Kobler, Franz. *Letters of Jews through the Ages*. 2 vols. New York: East and West Library, 1978.

Koerner, Konrad. "On Schleicher and Trees." *Biological Metaphor and Cladistic Classification: An Interdisciplinary Perspective*. Ed. Henry M. Hoenigswald and Linda F. Wiener. Philadelphia: University of Pennsylvania Press, 1987. 109–13.

Kokovtzov, Pavel K. *Evrejsko-Xazarskaja Perepiska v X vieke*. Leningrad: Izd-vo Akademii nauk SSSR, 1932.

Krueger, Roberta. "Romance." *The New Oxford Companion to Literature in French*. Ed. Peter France. Oxford, New York: Oxford University Press, 1995. 707–9.

Krueger, Roberta. *Women Readers and the Ideology of Gender in Old French Verse Romance*. Cambridge: Cambridge University Press, 1993.

Krug, Rebecca. "The Fifteen Oes." In Bartlett and Bestul, 107–17.

Lacan, Jacques. *Encore: Le Séminaire, livre XX*. Paris: Editions du Seuil, 1975.

Lachmann, K.K.F.W. *Kleinere Schriften*. Ed. J. Vahlen. Berlin: G. Reimer, 1876.

Ladero Quesada, Miguel Ángel. Introduction to Serafín Fanjul, *Al-Andalus contra España*. 5th ed. Madrid: Siglo XXI, 2000. xi–xiv.

Laird, Andrew. "Figures of Allegory from Homer to Latin Epic." *Metaphor, Allegory, and the Classical Tradition*. Ed. G.R. Boys-Stones. Oxford: Oxford University Press, 2003. 151–76. http://dx.doi.org/10.1093/acprof:oso/9780199240050.003.0008.

Lampert-Weissig, Lisa R. *Medieval Literature and Postcolonial Studies*. Edinburgh: Edinburgh University Press, 2010.

Lazarus-Yafeh, Hava. *Intertwined Worlds: Medieval Islam and Bible Criticism*. Princeton: Princeton University Press, 1992.

Leaman, Oliver. *Moses Maimonides*. London: Routledge, 1990.

Léglu, Catherine. *Multilingualism and Mother Tongue in Medieval French, Occitan, and Catalan Narratives*. University Park: Pennsylvania State University Press, 2010.

Lehmann, Winfred P. "Philology to Linguistics: Constructive to Literary Study." *South Central Review* 1.1/2 (1984): 131–40. http://dx.doi.org/10.2307/3189245.

Leupin, Alexandre. *La Passion des idoles*. Paris: Harmattan, 2000.

Lévi-Provençal, E. "La 'Description de L'Espagne' d'Ahmad al-Râzî: Essai de reconstitution de l'original arabe et traduction française." *Al-Andalus* 18 (1953): 51–108.

Lightfoot, Joseph Barber, trans. and ed. *The Apostolic Fathers*. 2nd ed. 5 vols. London and New York: Macmillan, 1885–90.

Lipton, Sara. "'The Sweet Lean of His Head': Writing About Looking at the Crucifix in the High Middle Ages." *Speculum* 80.4 (2005): 1172–1208.

Liu, Benjamin M., and James T. Monroe, eds. *Ten Hispano-Arabic Strophic Songs in the Modern Oral Tradition: Music and Texts*. University of California Publications in Modern Philology 125. Berkeley: University of California Press, 1989.

Loiseau, Julien and Gabriel Martinez-Gros. "Une démonstration suspecte." *Le Monde des Livres* 25 April 2008.

López Baralt, Luce. *Huellas del Islam en la literatura española: De Juan Ruiz a Juan Goytisolo*. Madrid: Hiperión, 1985.

López Baralt, Luce. "Simbología mística musulmana en San Juan de la Cruz y en Santa Teresa de Jesús." *Nueva Revista de Filología Hispánica* 30.1 (1981): 21–91.

López Baralt, Luce. *A zaga de tu huella: La enseñanza de las lenguas semíticas en Salamanca en tiempos de san Juan de la Cruz*. Madrid: Editorial Trotta, 2006.

López García, Bernabé. "Arabismo y orientalismo en España: Radiografía y diagnóstico de un gremio escaso y apartadizo."*Awraq: Estudios sobre el mundo árabe e islámico contemporáneo*. Supp. to vol. 11 (1990): 35–69.

López García, Bernabé. "Enigmas de al-Andalus: una polémica." *Revista de Occidente* 224 (Jan. 2000): 31–50.

López García, Bernabé. "30 años de arabismo español: el fin de la almogaravía científica (1967–1997)." *Awraq: Estudios sobre el mundo árabe e islámico contemporáneo* 18 (1997): 11–48.

Lopez-Morillas, Consuelo. "Hispano-Arabic Studies in the New Millenium: The United States and Canada." *Al-Masaq* 16.2 (September 2004): 241–61. http://dx.doi.org/10.10 80/0950311042000269855.

Lovell, Mary. *A Rage to Live: A Biography of Richard and Isabel Burton*. New York: Norton, 1998.

Lusignan, Serge. *La Langue des rois au Moyen Âge: le français en France et en Angleterre*. Paris: Presses Universitaires de France, 2004.

Maccoby, Hyam. *Judaism on Trial: Jewish-Christian Disputations in the Middle Ages*. Portland: Vallentine Mitchell, 1996.

Madariaga, Rosa María de. "En Torno a al-Andalus: extrapolaciones históricas y utilizaciones abusivas." *Orientalismo, exotismo y traducción*. Cuenca: Ediciones de la Universidad de Castilla-La Mancha, 2000. 81–9.

Mahdi, Muhsin. "From History to Fiction: The Tale Told by the King's Steward in *The Thousand and One Nights*." *The Thousand and One Nights in Arabic Literature and Society*. Ed. Richard G. Hovannisian and Georges Sabagh. Cambridge: Cambridge University Press, 1997. 78–105.

Mahdi, Muhsin. "The Sources of Galland's *Nuits*." *The Arabian Nights Reader*. Ed. Ulrich Marzolph. Detroit: Wayne State University Press, 2006. 122–36.

Mahdi, Muhsin. *The Thousand and One Nights*. 1984. Leiden: Brill, 1995.

Makdisi, George. *The Rise of Colleges: Institutions of Learning in Islam and the West*. Edinburgh: Edinburgh University Press, 1981.

Makdisi, George. *The Rise of Humanism in Classical Islam and the Christian West with Special Reference to Scholasticism*. Edinburgh: Edinburgh University Press, 1990.

Makki, Mahmud 'Ali. "Egypt and the Origins of Arabic Spanish Historiography: A Contribution to the Study of the Earliest Sources for the History of Islamic Spain." Trans. Michael Kennedy. *The Formation of Al-Andalus*. Ed. Maribel Fierro and Julio Samsó. Aldershot: Ashgate Variorum, 1988. 173–233.

Mallette, Karla. *European Modernity and the Arab Mediterranean*. Philadelphia: University of Pennsylvania Press, 2010.

Mallette, Karla. "Misunderstood." *New Literary History* 34.4 (2003): 677–97. http://dx.doi.org/10.1353/nlh.2004.0008.

Malkiel, Yakov. "Filología española y lingüística general." *Actas del primer Congreso internacional de hispanistas*. Ed. F. Pierce and C.A. Jones. Oxford: Dolphin, 1964. 107–26.

Mann, Vivian B., Jerrilyn D. Dodds, and Thomas F. Glick, eds. *Convivencia: Jews, Muslims, and Christians in Medieval Spain*. New York: G. Braziller in association with the Jewish Museum, 1992.

Manzanares de Cirre, Manuela. *Arabistas españoles del siglo XIX*. Madrid: Instituto Hispano-Árabe de Cultura, 1971.

Manzano Moreno, Eduardo. "La creación de un esencialismo: la historia de al-Andalus en la visión del arabismo español." *Orientalismo, exotismo y traducción*. Cuenca: Ediciones de la Universidad de Castilla-La Mancha, 2000. 23–37.

Manzano Moreno, Eduardo. "The Creation of a Medieval Frontier: Islam and Christianity in the Iberian Peninsula, Eighth to Eleventh Centuries." *Frontiers in Question: Eurasian Borderlands 700–1700*. Ed. Daniel Power and Naomi Standen. London: Palgrave MacMillan, 1999. 32–54.

Marchand, Suzanne L. *Down from Olympus: Archaeology and Philhellenism in Germany, 1750–1970*. Princeton: Princeton University Press, 1996.

Marcó i Dachs, Lluís. *Los judíos en Cataluña*. Barcelona: Ediciones Destino, 1985.

Marcus, Ivan. "Beyond The Sephardic Mystique." *Orim* 1 (1985): 35–53.

Marichal, Juan. "Américo Castro y la crítica literaria del siglo XX." *Estudios sobre la obra de Américo Castro*. Ed. Pedro Laín Entralgo. Madrid: Taurus, 1971. 329–47.

Marín, Manuela. "Arabistas en España: Un asunto de familia." *al-Qantara* 13 (1992): 379–93.

Marín, Manuela. "Historical Images of al-Andalus and Andalusians." *Myths, Historical Archetypes and Symbolic Figures in Arabic Literature*. Ed. Angelika Neuwirth, et al. Beirut: Franz Steiner Verlag, 1999. 409–21.

Marín, Manuela, and Joseph Pérez. "'L'Espagne des Trois Religions': Du Mythe aux Réalités." *Revue du Monde Musulman et de la Méditerranée* 63–4.1 (1992): 23–7 http:// dx.doi.org/10.3406/remmm.1992.1535.

Marín Gelabert, Miquel Ángel. *Los historiadores españoles en el franquismo, 1948–1975. La historia local al servicio de la patria*. Zaragoza: Prensas Universitarias de Zaragoza, 2005.

Martínez Gázquez, José. *La Ignorancia y negligencia de los latinos ante la riqueza de los estudios árabes*. Barcelona: Real Academia de Buenas Letras, 2007.

Martínez Martínez, María Jesus. "El Santo Cristo de Burgos y los Cristos Dolorosos articulados." *Boletín del Seminario de Estudios de Arte y Arqueología* 69–70 (2003–4): 207–46.

Martínez Montávez, Pedro. "Lectura de Américo Castro por un arabista: apuntes e impresiones." *Revista del Instituto Egipcio de Estudios Islámicos en Madrid* 22 (1983–4): 21–42.

Martínez Montávez, Pedro. "Sobre el aún 'desconocido'arabismo español del siglo XIX." *Ensayos marginales de arabismo*. Madrid: Instituto de Estudios Orientales y Africanos, 1977. 3–22.

Al-Mas'udi. *The Meadows of Gold: The Abbasids*. Trans. and ed. Paul Lunde and Caroline Stone. London, New York: Kegan Paul, 1989.

Matulka, Barbara. *The Novels of Juan de Flores and Their European Diffusion: A Study in Comparative Literature*. New York: Columbia University Press, 1931.

Meddeb, 'Abd al-Wahhab. "La trace, le signe." *L'image dans le monde arabe*. Ed. G. Beaugé and J.-F. Clément. Paris: CNRS Éditions, 1995. 107–24.

Ménard, Philippe. *Marco Polo: à la découverte du monde*. Paris: Glénat, 2007.

Menéndez Pidal, Ramón. *La Chanson de Roland y el neotradicionalismo: Orígenes de la épica románica*. Madrid: Espasa-Calpe, 1959.

Menéndez Pidal, Ramón. *El Cid en la historia*. Madrid: Jiménez y Molina, 1921.

Menéndez Pidal, Ramón. *Manual elemental de gramática histórica española*. 1904. 6th rev. ed. Madrid: Espasa-Calpe, 1941.

Menéndez Pidal, Ramón. *Orígenes del español. Estado lingüístico de la península ibérica hasta el siglo XI*. Madrid: Imprenta de la librería y casa editorial Hernando, 1927.

Menocal, María Rosa. *The Arabic Role in Medieval Literary History: A Forgotten Heritage*. Philadelphia: University of Pennsylvania Press, 1987.

Menocal, María Rosa. "Beginnings." *The Cambridge History of Spanish Literature*. Ed. David T. Gies. Cambridge: Cambridge University Press, 2004. 58–74. http://dx.doi .org/10.1017/CHOL9780521806183.005.

Menocal, María Rosa. *The Ornament of the World: How Muslims, Jews, and Christians Created a Culture of Tolerance in Medieval Spain*. Boston: Little, Brown, 2002.

Menocal, María Rosa. *Shards of Love: Exile and the Origins of the Lyric*. Durham: Duke University Press, 1994.

Menocal, María Rosa. "Visions of Al-Andalus." In Menocal, Scheindlin, and Sells, 1–24.

Menocal, María Rosa, Raymond P. Scheindlin, and Michael Sells, eds. *The Literature of Al-Andalus*. Cambridge: Cambridge University Press, 2000.

Meyer, Paul. "Nouvelles catalanes inédites." *Romania* 13 (1884): 264–84.

Meyer-Lübke, Wilhelm. *Introducción a la lingüística románica*. Trans. and notes by Américo Castro. 2nd ed. Madrid, 1926.

Meyerson, Mark D. *The Muslims of Valencia in the Age of Fernando and Isabel: Between Coexistence and Crusade*. Berkeley: University of California Press, 1991.

Meyerson, Mark D., and Edward D. English, eds. *Christians, Muslims, and Jews in Medieval and Early Modern Spain: Interaction and Cultural Change*. Notre Dame: University of Notre Dame Press, 2000.

Meyuhas Ginio, Alisa, and Carlos Carrete Parrondo, eds. *Creencias y culturas. Congreso Internacional Encuentro de las Tres Culturas (9th: 1995: Universidad de Salamanca)*. Salamanca: Universidad Pontificia de Salamanca; Universidad de Tel-Aviv, 1998.

Mickle, William Julius. *The Lusiads or The Discovery of India: An Epic Poem*. Oxford: Jackman and Lister, 1776.

Millás Vallicrosa, José María. "Literatura hebraicoespañola." *Historia general de las literaturas hispánicas*. Ed. Guillermo Díaz Plaja. Barcelona: Barna, 1949. 145–93.

Minervini, Laura. "La lingua franca mediterranea: Plurilinguismo, multilinguismo, pidginizzazione sulle coste del Mediterraneo tra tardo medioevo e prima età moderna." *Medioevo Romanzo* 20 (1996): 231–301.

Minervini, Laura. "Tradizioni linguistiche e culturali negli Stati Latini d'Oriente." *Medioevo romanzo e orientale: Oralità, scrittura, modelli narrativi*. Ed. Antonio Pioletti and Francesca Rizzo Nervo. Messina: Rubettino, 1995. 155–72.

Mishra, Vijay, and Bob Hodge. "What Was Postcolonialism?" *New Literary History* 36.3 (2005): 375–402. http://dx.doi.org/10.1353/nlh.2005.0045.

Mitre Fernández, Emilio. "La historiografía sobre la Edad Media." *Historia de la historiografía española*. Madrid: Ediciones Encuentro, 1999. 67–115.

Molho, Maurice. "'Una dama de todo rumbo y manejo': para una lectura de 'El licenciado Vidriera'." *Erotismo en las letras hispánicas: aspectos, modos, y fronteras*. Ed. Luce López-Baralt and Francisco Márquez Villanueva. Mexico City: El Colegio de México, 1995. 387–406.

Molina, Álvaro. "Glass Characters and Glass Fictions: The Poetics of 'El curioso impertinente' and 'El licenciado Vidriera.'" *Mester* 25.1 (1996): 5–29.

Molina i Figueras, Joan. *Arte, devoción y poder en la pintura tardogótica catalana*. Murcia: Universidad de Murcia, Servicio de Publicaciones, 1999.

Monroe, James. "Américo Castro y los estudios arabistas." *Estudios sobre la obra de Américo Castro*. Ed. Laín Entralgo and Andrés Amorós. Madrid: Taurus, 1971. 349–64.

Monroe, James T, ed. *Hispano-Arabic Poetry: A Student Anthology*. Berkeley: University of California Press, 1974.

Monroe, James T. *Islam and the Arabs in Spanish Scholarship (Sixteenth Century to the Present)*. Leiden: Brill, 1970.

Monroe, James T. "Maimonides on the Mozarabic Lyric: A Note on the *Muwaššaha*." *La Corónica* 17.2 (1989): 18–32.

Monroe, James T. "¿Pedir peras al olmo? On Medieval Arabs and Modern Arabists." *La Corónica* 10.2 (1982): 121–47.

Monteiro, George. *The Presence of Camões: Influences on the Literature of England, America, and Southern Africa.* Lexington: University Press of Kentucky, 1996.

Moretti, Franco. *Graphs, Maps, Trees.* London, New York: Verso, 2005.

Morris, Bridget, and Veronica O'Mara, eds. *The Translation of the Works of St. Birgitta of Sweden into the Medieval European Vernaculars.* The Medieval Translator 7. Turnhout: Brepols, 2000.

Morrison, James. "Vico's Principle of Verum is Factum and the Problem of Historicism." *Journal of the History of Ideas* 39.4 (1978): 579–95. http://dx.doi.org/10.2307/2709443.

Muhlack, Ulrich. "Historie und Philologie." *Aufklärung und Geschichte: Studien zur deutschen Geschichtswissenschaft im 18. Jahrhundert.* Ed. Hans Erich Bödeker, et al. Göttingen: Vandenhoeck and Ruprecht, 1986. 49–81.

Müller-Sievers, Helmut. "Reading Evidence: Textual Criticism as Science in the Nineteenth Century." *Germanic Review* 76.2 (2001): 162–71. http://dx.doi.org/10.1080/00168890109601552.

Munro, John H.A. *Textiles, Towns and Trade: Essays in the Economic History of Late-Medieval England and the Low Countries.* Variorum Collected Studies series CS 442. Aldershot, Hampshire: Ashgate, 1994.

Murrin, Michael. "First Encounter: The Christian-Hindu Confusion When the Portuguese Reached India." *Portuguese Literary and Cultural Studies* 9 (2003): 189–202.

Myers, Robert Edwards. "The Language of Camões: Modern Readers of The Lusiads and the Exclusion of Portuguese from the Western Canon." Diss. Yale University, 1995.

Navarro Peiro, Ángeles. *Narrativa hispanohebrea: siglos XII–XV: introducción y selección de relatos y cuentos.* Córdoba: El Almendro, 1988.

Nichols, Stephen G. "Introduction: Philology in a Manuscript Culture." *Speculum* 65.1 (1990): 1–10. http://dx.doi.org/10.2307/2864468.

Nichols, Stephen G. "The Medieval Author, An Idea Whose Time Hadn't Come." *The Author in Medieval French Literature.* Ed. Virginie Greene. London: Palgrave MacMillan, 2006. 77–102.

Nichols, Stephen G. "Philology and Its Discontents." *The Future of the Middle Ages: Medieval Literature in the 1990s.* Ed. William D. Paden. Gainesville: University Press of Florida, 1994. 113–41.

Nichols, Stephen G. "Philology in Auerbach's Drama of (Literary) History." *Literary History and the Challenge of Philology.* Ed. Seth Lerer. Stanford: Stanford University Press, 1996. 63–77.

Nicolopulos, James. *The Poetics of Empire in the Indies: Prophecy and Imitation in* La Araucana *and* Os Lusíadas. University Park: Pennsylvania State University Press, 2000.

Nirenberg, David. *Communities of Violence. Persecution of Minorities in the Middle Ages.* Princeton: Princeton University Press, 1996.

Nirenberg, David. "Hope's Mistakes [review of Jonathan Elukin, *Living Together, Living Apart: Rethinking Jewish-Christian Relations in the Middle Ages*]." *New Republic* [New York, N.Y.] 13 February 2008. 46–50.

Nirenberg, David. "Islam and the West: Two Dialectical Fantasies." *Journal of Religion in Europe* 1.1 (2008): 3–33. http://dx.doi.org/10.1163/187489208X285459.

Noorani, Yaseen. "The Lost Garden of Al-Andalus: Islamic Spain and the Poetic Inversion of Colonialism." *International Journal of Middle East Studies* 31.2 (1999): 237–54. http://dx.doi.org/10.1017/S0020743800054039.

Norris, H.T. "Fables and Legends." *Abbasid Belles-Lettres.* Ed. Julia Ashtiany, T.M. Johnstone, J.D. Latham, R.B. Serjeant, and G. Rex Smith. Cambridge: Cambridge University Press, 1990. 136–45.

Novikoff, Alex. "Between Tolerance and Intolerance in Medieval Spain: An Historiographic Enigma." *Medieval Encounters* 11.1 (2005): 7–36. http://dx.doi .org/10.1163/157006705775032834.

al-Nowaihi, Magda M. *The Poetry of Ibn Khafaja: A Literary Analysis.* Leiden: Brill, 1993.

Nykl, Aloysius R., trans. and ed. *Historia de los amores de Bayad y Riyad, una chantefable oriental en estilo persa (Vat. ar. 368).* New York: Hispanic Society of America, 1941.

The Oxford English Dictionary. Oxford University Press. 10 December 2007.

Pagis, Dan. "Dirges on the Persecutions of the Year 5151 in Spain." [Hebrew]. *Tarbiz* 37 (1968): 355–73.

Pagis, Dan. *Hebrew Poetry of the Middle Ages and the Renaissance.* Berkeley: University of California Press, 1991.

Pagis, Dan. *Innovation and Tradition in Secular Hebrew Poetry: Spain and Italy.* Jerusalem: Keter Israel Jerusalem, 1976.

Pagis, Dan. "The Poetic Polemic on the Nature of Women." *Jerusalem Studies in Hebrew Literature* 9 (1986): 259–300.

Pancaroglu, Oya. *Perpetual Glory: Medieval Islamic Ceramics from the Harvey B. Plotnick Collection.* Chicago: Art Institute of Chicago, 2007.

Park, Katharine. "The Meanings of Natural Diversity: Marco Polo on the 'Division' of the World." *Texts and Contexts in Ancient and Medieval Science: Studies on the Occasion of John E. Murdoch's Seventieth Birthday.* Ed. Edith Sylla and Michael McVaugh. Leiden: Brill, 1997. 134–47.

Pasquali, Giorgio. *Storia della tradizione e critica del testo.* Florence: Felice le Monnier, 1952.

Paterson, Linda. *Troubadours and Eloquence.* Oxford: Clarendon Press, 1975.

Patterson, Lee. "On the Margin: Postmodernism, Ironic History, and Medieval Studies." *Speculum* 65.1 (1990): 87–108. http://dx.doi.org/10.2307/2864473.

Penelas, Mayte. "Hispano-Arabic Studies in the New Millenium: Spain." *Al-Masaq* 16.2 (2004): 227–39. http://dx.doi.org/10.1080/09503110420002698466.

Pereda, Felipe. "El debate sobre la imagen en la España del siglo XV: Judíos, cristianos y conversos." *Anuario Arte* 24 (2002): 59–79.

Pereda, Felipe. *Las imágenes de la discordia. Política y poética de la imagen sagrada en la España del cuatrocientos.* Madrid: Marcial Pons, 2008.

Peretz, Yitzhak. Introduction. Trans. Judah al-Harizi. *Mahberot I'ti'el.* Ed. Yitzhak Peretz. Tel Aviv: Ha-Rav Kuk, 1950. iii–xl.

Pérez, Joseph. "Chrétiens, Juifs et Musulmans en Espagne. Le mythe de la tolérance religieuse (VIIIe–XVe siècle)." *L'histoire* 137 (Oct. 1990): 8–17.

Perry, Mary Elizabeth. *The Handless Maiden: Moriscos and the Politics of Religion in Early Modern Spain.* Princeton: Princeton University Press, 2005.

Pfeiffer, Rudolph. *History of Classical Scholarship from 1300 to 1850.* Oxford: Clarendon Press, 1976.

Piemontese, Angelo Michele. "Il Corano latino di Ficino e i corani arabi de Pico e Monchates." *Rinascimento (Florence, Italy)* 36 (1996): 226–73.

Pierce, Frank. "The Place of Mythology in the *Lusiads.*" *Comparative Literature* 6.2 (1954): 97–122. http://dx.doi.org/10.2307/1768486.

Pinault, David. *Story-Telling Techniques in the Arabian Nights.* Leiden: Brill, 1992.

Pinault, David. "*A Thousand and One Nights*: A History of the Text and Its Reception." Allen and Richards. 270–91.

Pirot, François. *Recherches sur les connaissances littéraires des troubadours occitans et catalans des XIIe et XIIIe siècles.* Barcelona: Réal Academia de Buenas Letras, 1972.

Pollock, Sheldon. "Cosmopolitan and Vernacular." *Cosmopolitanism.* Ed. Carol A. Breckenridge, Sheldon Pollock, Homi K. Bhabha, et al. Durham: Duke University Press, 2002. 15–53.

Pollock, Sheldon. *The Language of the Gods in the World of Men: Sanskrit, Culture, and Power in Premodern India.* Berkeley, Los Angeles: University of California Press, 2006.

Portolés, José. *Medio siglo de filología española (1896–1952). Positivismo e idealismo.* Madrid: Cátedra, 1986.

Pound, Ezra. "For a New Paideuma." *The Criterion,* January 1938. Rpt. in *Selected Prose, 1909–1965.* Ed. William Cookson. London: Faber and Faber, 1973. 254–9.

del Pozo Coll, Patricia Sela. "La devoción a la hostia consagrada en la Baja Edad Media castellana: Fuentes textuales, materiales e iconográficas para su estudio." *Anales de Historia del Arte* 16 (2006): 12–58.

del Pozo Coll, Patricia Sela. "Un gesto litúrgico poco frecuente: La ocultación parcial de la patena bajo los corporales: Relaciones entre texto e imagen a finales de la Edad Media." *Cultura y Mentalidades: de la antigüedad al siglo XVII (Nuevas Investigaciones).* Ed. Nicolas Ávila Seoane. Colección "Temas Históricos." Madrid: Castellum, 2007. 11–42.

de Puelles Benítez, Manuel. *Educación e ideología en la España contemporánea.* Barcelona: Editorial Labor, 1980.

de la Puente, Juan. *Tomo primero de la convivencia de las dos monarquias catolicas, la de la Iglesia Romana y la del imperio español, y defensa de la precedencia de los Reyes Católicos de España a todos los Reyes del mundo.* [N.p.]: [n.pl.], 1612.

Puerta Vílchez, José Miguel. *Historia del pensamiento estético árabe: al-Andalus y la estética árabe clásica.* Madrid: Ediciones Akal, 1997.

Purcell, Nicholas. "The Boundless Sea of Unlikeness? On Defining the Mediterranean." *Mediterranean Historical Review* 18.2 (2003): 9–29. http://dx.doi.org/10.1080/09518960 32000230462.

Quettat, Mahmoud. *La musique arabo-andalouse: l'empreinte du Maghreb.* Paris: Éditions el-Ouns, 2000.

Quettat, Mahmoud. *La musique classique du Maghreb.* Paris: Sindbad, 1980.

Quint, David. *Epic and Empire: Politics and Generic Form from Virgil to Milton.* Princeton: Princeton University Press, 1993.

Rajan, Balachandra. *Milton and the Climates of Reading: Essays.* Toronto: University of Toronto Press, 2006.

Rajan, Balachandra. *Under Western Eyes: India from Milton to Macaulay.* Durham, N.C.: Duke University Press, 1999.

Ranke, Leopold von. *Geschichten der romanischen und germanischen Völker von 1494 bis 1514.* Leipzig, 1885.

Ranke, Leopold von. *The Secret of World History. Selected Writings on the Art and Science of History.* Ed. and trans. Roger Wines. New York: Fordham University Press, 1981.

Rashed, Roshdi, ed. *Histoire des sciences arabes.* 3 vols. Paris: Seuil, 1997.

Ray, Jonathan. "Beyond Tolerance and Persecution: Reassessing Our Approach to Medieval *Convivencia.*" *Jewish Social Studies* 11 (2005): 1–18.

Redondo, Agustín. "La folie du cervantin 'Licencié de verre,' (traditions, contexte historique et subversion)." *Visages de la folie, études réunies et présentées par Augustin Redondo et André Rochon.* Paris: Université de Paris III - Sorbonne Nouvelle, 1981. 33–44.

Reill, Peter Hanns. "Philology, Culture and Politics in Early Nineteenth Century Germany." *Supplement to Romance Philology* 30.2 (1976): 18–29.

Remensnyder, Amy G. "Christian Captives, Muslim Maidens, and Mary." *Speculum* 82.3 (2007): 642–77. http://dx.doi.org/10.1017/S0038713400010277.

Renan, Ernst. *L'avenir de la science. Pensées de 1848.* Paris, 1890.

Renan, Ernst. *Histoire générale et système comparé des langues sémitiques.* Paris, 1858.

Renevey, Denis. "Household Chores in *The Doctrine of the Hert*: Affective Spirituality and Subjectivity." *The Medieval Household in Christian Europe, c. 850–c. 1550: Managing Power, Wealth, and the Body.* Ed. Cordelia Beattie, Anna Maslakovic, Sarah Rees Jones, Felicity · Riddy, P.J.P. Goldberg, and Jane Grenville. Turnhout: Brepols, 2003. 167–85.

Renzi, Lorenzo. "Il francese come lingua letteraria e il franco-lombardo: l'epica carolingia nel Veneto." *Storia della cultura Veneta I: Dalle origini al trecento.* Ed. Girolamo Arnaldi and Gianfranco Folena. Vicenza: Neri Pozza Editore, 1976. 563–89.

Reynolds, Dwight F. "Al-Maqqari's Ziryab: The Making of a Myth." *Journal of Middle Eastern Literatures* 11.2 (2008): 155–68. http://dx.doi.org/10.1080/14752620802223756.

Reynolds, Dwight F. "*A Thousand and One Nights*: A History of the Text and Its Reception." In Allen and Richards, 270–91.

Reynolds, Dwight F. "Musical Aspects of Ibn Sana' al-Mulk's *Dar al-Tiraz*." In Emery, 211–27.

Reynolds, Dwight F. "Popular Prose in the Post-Classical Period." In Allen and Richards, 245–69.

Ribera y Tarragó, Julián. *Discursos leídos ante la Real Academia Española en la recepción pública del Señor D. Julián Ribera y Tarragó el día 26 de mayo de 1912*. Madrid: Ibérica, 1912.

Ribera y Tarragó, Julián. *Historia de la música árabe medieval y su influencia en la española*. Madrid: Editorial Voluntad, 1927.

Ribera y Tarragó, Julián. *Music in Ancient Arabia and Spain; being La música de las Cantigas*. Trans. and abridged by Eleanor Hague and Marion Leffingwell. London: H. Milford; Oxford: Oxford University Press; Stanford: Stanford University Press, 1929.

Ribera y Tarragó, Julián. *La música andaluza medieval y las canciones de trovadores, troveros y minnesinger*. Madrid: Tipografía de la Revista de Archivos, 1923–5.

Ribera y Tarragó, Julián. *La música de las cantigas: estudio sobre su orígen y su naturaleza*. Madrid: Tipografía de la Revista de Archivos, 1922.

Ridao, José María. "L'Arabisme dans l'Université espagnole." *Revue d'Études Palestiniennes* 15 (1996): 64–8.

Ridao, José María. "El oscurantismo reverenciado." *El País*. 24 February 2002.

Ridao, José María. "Reflexión sobre el arabismo español." *Quimera* 157 (1997): 56–60.

Riley, E.C. "Cervantes and the Cynics ('El licenciado Vidriera' and 'El coloquio de los perros')." *Bulletin of Hispanic Studies* 53.3 (1976): 189–99. http://dx.doi.org/10.1080/1475382762000353189.

Ringer, Fritz K. *The Decline of the German Mandarins: The German Academic Community, 1890–1933*. Cambridge: Harvard University Press, 1969.

Riquer, Martin de. *Història de la literatura catalana*. 4 vols. Barcelona: Ariel, 1964.

Robinson, Cynthia. *In Praise of Song: The Making of Courtly Culture in Al-Andalus and Provence, 1005–1134 A.D.* Leiden: Brill, 2002.

Robinson, Cynthia. "Les Lieux de la lyrique: Pour une esthétique 'jardinière' de la lyrique mystique andalouse du XIIIe et XIVe siècles." Address. "L'Espace lyrique méditerranéen." Nantes, France: University of Nantes, 26 March 2004.

Robinson, Cynthia. *Medieval Andalusian Courtly Culture in the Mediterranean: Hadith Bayad wa-Riyad*. London: Routledge, 2007.

Robinson, Cynthia. "Preaching to the Converted: Valladolid's *Cristianos Nuevos* and the *Retablo de Don Sancho de Rojas* (1415 A.D.)." *Speculum* 83.1 (2008): 112–63. http://dx.doi.org/10.1017/S0038713400012434.

Robinson, Cynthia. Forthcoming. "El Retablo de Miraflores romanzado o, ¿qué significa ser un Van der Weyden en Castilla?" *Gótico y Frontera. En busca de nuevos paradigmas para el estudio del gótico hispano.* Ed. Rocío Sánchez Ameijeira. Murcia: Nausícaa.

Robinson, Cynthia. "Seeing Paradise: Metaphor and Vision in Taifa Palace Architecture." *Gesta* 36 (1997): 145–55.

Robinson, Cynthia. "Trees of Love, Trees of Knowledge: Toward the Definition of a Cross-Confessional Current in Late-Medieval Iberian Spirituality." *Medieval Encounters* 12.3(2006): 388–435. http://dx.doi.org/10.1163/157006706779166101.

Rodríguez Magda, Rosa María. *Inexistente Al Ándalus. De cómo los intelectuales reinventan el Islam.* Oviedo: Nobel, 2008.

Rodríguez Puértolas, Julio. *Poesía crítica y satírica del siglo XV.* Madrid: Clásicos Castalia, 1989.

Rosen, Tova. "The Muwashshah." In Menocal, Scheindlin, and Sells, 165–89.

Rosen, Tova. *Unveiling Eve: Reading Gender in Medieval Hebrew Literature.* Philadelphia: University of Pennsylvania Press, 2003.

Rossetti, Dante Gabriel. *The Early Italian Poets, From Ciullo d'Alcamo to Dante Alighieri (1100–1200–1300). In the Original Metres Together with Dante's Vita Nuova.* 1861. Ed. Sally Purcell. Berkeley: University of California Press, 1981.

Roth, Cecil. "A Hebrew Elegy on the Martyrs of Toledo, 1391." *Gleanings: Essays in Jewish History, Letters, and Art.* New York: Hermon Press, 1967. 91–118.

Roth, Norman. *Conversos, Inquisition, and the Expulsion of the Jews from Spain.* Madison: University of Wisconsin Press, 2002.

Roth, Norman. *Daily Life of the Jews in the Middle Ages.* Westport, CT: Greenwood Press, 2005.

Rothstein, Edward. "Was the Islam of Old Spain Truly Tolerant?" *New York Times.* 2 Sept. 2003, late ed.: B9.

Ruan, Felipe. "Carta de guía, carto-grafía: Fallas y fisuras en 'El licenciado Vidriera.'" *Cervantes* 20.2 (2000): 151–62.

Ruggles, D. Fairchild. *Gardens, Landscapes and Vision in the Palaces of Islamic Spain.* University Park: Pennsylvania State University Press, 2000.

Rushdie, Salman. "Hobson-Jobson." *Imaginary Homelands: Essays and Criticism, 1981–1991.* London: Penguin, 1992. 81–3.

Sachs, Susan. "A Nation Challenged: The Videotape; Bin Laden Images Mesmerize Muslims." *New York Times,* 9 October 2001. Electronic.

Sáenz-Badillos, Angel. "Šelomoh Bonafed at the Crossroad of Hebrew and Romance Cultures." *Encuentros and Desencuentros: Spanish Jewish Cultural Interaction Throughout History.* Ed. Carlos Carrete Parrondo, et al. Tel Aviv: University of Tel Aviv Publishing Projects, 2000. 343–79.

Sáenz-Badillos, Angel. "Šelomoh Bonafed, último gran poeta de Sefarad." *eHumanista* 2 (2002).

Safran, Janina M. *The Second Umayyad Caliphate: The Articulation of Caliphal Legitimacy in Al-Andalus.* Harvard Middle Eastern Monographs 33. Cambridge: Harvard University Press, 2000.

Said, Edward. 2002. "Andalusia's Journey." *Travel and Leisure*, December 2002: 178–94.

Said, Edward. *Humanism and Democratic Criticism.* New York: Columbia University Press, 2004.

Said, Edward. *Orientalism.* 1978. New York: Pantheon Books/Random House, 2003.

Said, Edward. *The World, the Text, and the Critic.* Cambridge, MA: Harvard University Press, 1983.

Saleh, Walid. "The Female as a Locus of Apocalyptic Anxiety in Medieval Sunni Islam." *Myth, Historical Archetypes and Symbolic Figures in Arabic Literature.* Ed. Angelika Neuwirth and Maher Jarrar. Beirut: Deutschen Morgenländischen Gesellschaft, 1996. 121–42.

Saleh, Walid. "A Fifteenth-Century Muslim Hebraist: Al-Biqa'i's Bible Treatise and His Defense of Using the Bible to Interpret the Qur'an." *Speculum* 83 (2008): 629–54.

Saleh, Walid. *In Defense of the Bible: A Critical Edition and an Introduction to al-Biqāʻī's Bible Treatise.* Leiden: Brill, 2008. http://dx.doi.org/10.1163/ej.9789004168572.i-224.

Sánchez Albornoz, Claudio. *España, un enigma histórico.* Buenos Aires: Sudamericana, 1956.

Scheindlin, Raymond P. "Secular Hebrew Poetry in Fifteenth-Century Spain." *Crisis and Creativity in the Sephardic World.* Ed. Benjamin R. Gampel. New York: Columbia University Press, 1997. 25–37.

Scheindlin, Raymond P. *Wine, Women, and Death: Medieval Hebrew Poems on the Good Life.* Philadelphia: Jewish Publication Society, 1986.

Schelsky, Helmut. *Einsamkeit und Freiheit: Idee und Gestalt der deutschen Universität und ihrer Reformen.* Düsseldorf: Bertelsmann Universitätsverlag, 1971.

Schindler, Carolina María, and Alfonso Martín Jiménez. "El licenciado Avellaneda y *El licenciado Vidriera.*" *Hipertexto* 3 (2006): 81–100.

Schirmann, Jefim, and Ezra Fleischer. *Studies on Hebrew Poetry in Christian Spain and Southern France.* [Hebrew] 4 vols. Jerusalem: Y.L. Magnes, 1997.

Schleicher, August. *Die Sprachen Europas in systematischer Übersicht.* Bonn: Koenig, 1850.

Schlözer, August. "Von den Chaldäern." *Repertorium für biblische und morgenländische Literatur* 8 (1781): 131–76.

Schorsch, Ismar. "The Myth of Sephardic Supremacy." *Leo Baeck Institute Yearbook* 34.1 (1989): 47–66. http://dx.doi.org/10.1093/leobaeck/34.1.47.

Schwab, Raymond. *The Oriental Renaissance: Europe's Rediscovery of India and the East, 1680–1880.* Trans. Gene Patterson-Black and Victor Reinking. New York: Columbia University Press, 1984.

Sells, Michael. *Mystical Languages of Unsaying.* Chicago: University of Chicago Press, 1994.

Septimus, Bernard. *Hispano-Jewish Culture in Transition: The Career and Controversies of Ramah.* Cambridge, MA: Harvard University Press, 1982.

Severin, Dorothy Sherman. "The Relationship between the *Libro de buen amor* and *Celestina*: Does Trotaconventos Perform a *Philocaptio* Spell on Doña Endrina?" *A Companion to the Libro de buen amor*. Ed. Louise M. Haywood and Louise O. Vasvári. London: Tamesis, 2004. 123–7.

Severin, Dorothy Sherman. *Tragicomedy and novelistic discourse in Celestina*. Cambridge: Cambridge University Press, 1989. http://dx.doi.org/10.1017/CBO9780511898013.

Shatzmiller, Maya. *The Berbers and the Islamic State: The Marinid Experience in Pre-Protectorate Morocco*. Princeton: Markus Weiner, 2000.

Shipley, George A. "Garbage In, Garbage Out: 'The Best of Vidriera.'" *Cervantes: Bulletin of the Cervantes Society of America* 21.1 (2001): 5–41.

Silberstein, Susan Milner. "The Provençal Esther Poem Written in Hebrew Characters c. 1327 by Crescas de Caylar: Critical Edition." Diss. University of Pennsylvania, 1973.

Silva Maroto, María Pilar. *Pintura hispanoflamenca castellana, Burgos y Palencia: Obras en tabla y sarga*. 3 vols. Valladolid: Junta de Castilla y León, Consejería de Cultura y Bienestar Social, 1990.

Simó, Lourdes. "Los 'tósigos de amor' en las novelas de Cervantes." *Espéculo: Revista de estudios literarios* 29 (March–June 2005): http://www.ucm.es/info/especulo/numero29/tosigos.html.

Sims, James. "Camoens' *Lusiads* and Milton's *Paradise Lost*: Satan's Voyage to Eden." *Papers on Milton*. Ed. Philip M. Griffith and Lester F. Zimmerman. Tulsa: University of Tulsa Press, 1969. 36–46.

Sims, James. "Christened Classicism in *Paradise Lost* and the *Lusiads*." *Comparative Literature* 24.4 (1972): 338–56. http://dx.doi.org/10.2307/1769461.

Siraisi, Nancy. *Avicenna in Renaissance Italy: The Canon and Medical Teaching in Italian Universities after 1500*. Princeton: Princeton University Press, 1987.

Smith, Jane I., and Yvonne Y. Haddad. "The Virgin Mary in Islamic Tradition." *Muslim World* 79.3–4 (1989): 161–87. http://dx.doi.org/10.1111/j.1478-1913.1989.tb02846.x.

Soifer, Maya. "Beyond Convivencia: Critical Reflections on the Historiography of Interfaith Relations in Christian Spain." *Journal of Medieval Iberian Studies* 1.1 (2009): 19–35. http://dx.doi.org/10.1080/17546550802700335.

Sontag, Susan. *At the Same Time: Essays and Speeches*. Ed. Paolo Dilonardo and Anne Jump. New York: Farrar, Straus and Giroux: 2007.

Spiegel, Gabrielle M. "'Getting Medieval': History and the Torture Memos." *Perspectives on History* 46 (September 2008): 3–6.

Spitzer, Leo. *Linguistics and Literary History: Essays in Stylistics*. New York: Russell and Russell, 1962.

Stearns, Justin. "Representing and Remembering al-Andalus: Some Historical Considerations Regarding the End of Time and the Making of Nostalgia." *Medieval Encounters* 15 (2009): 355–74.

Steiner, George. *After Babel: Aspects of Language and Translation*. 1975. Oxford: Oxford University Press, 1998.

Stern, Samuel M, ed. *Les chansons mozarabes: les vers finaux (kharjas) en espagnol dans les muwashshahs arabes et hébreux.* Università di Palermo, Istituto di filologia romanza, Collezione di testi 1. Palermo: U. Manfredi, 1953.

Stetkevych, Suzanne Pinckney. *Abu Tammam and the Poetics of the 'Abbasid Age.* Leiden: Brill, 1991.

Stetkevych, Suzanne Pinckney. "The Poetics of Ceremony and the Competition for Legitimacy: Al-Muhannad al-Baghdadi, Muhammad ibn Shukhays, Ibn Darraj al-Qastallî, and the Andalusian Ode." *The Poetics of Islamic Legitimacy: Myth, Gender and Ceremony in the Classical Arabic Ode.* Bloomington: Indiana University Press, 2002. 241–82.

Stillman, Norman. "Myth, Counter-Myth, and Distortion." *Tikkun* 6.3 (May-June 1991): 60–4.

Stock, Brian. "The Middle Ages as Subject and Object: Romantic Attitudes and Academic Medievalism." *New Literary History* 5.3 (1974): 527–47. http://dx.doi.org/10.2307/468359.

Subirats, Eduardo. "Américo Castro Secuestrado." *El Mundo.* 11 September 2001. Rpt. in *Américo Castro y la revisión de la memoria (El Islam en España).* Ed. Eduardo Subirats. Madrid: Libertarias, 2003. 215–18.

Tapia, Muriel, and María Cruz. *Antifeminismo y subestimación de la mujer en la literatura medieval castellana.* Cáceres: Editorial Guadiloba, 1991.

Targarona Borrás, Judit. "Los últimos poetas hebreos de Sefarad: Poesía hebrea en el mundo románico." *Revista de Filología Románica* 19 (2002): 249–68.

Targarona Borrás, Judit, and Raymond P. Scheindlin. "Literary Correspondence Between Vidal Benvenist Ben Lavi and Solomon ben Meshulam de Piera." *Revue des Etudes Juives* 160.1 (2001): 61–133. http://dx.doi.org/10.2143/REJ.160.1.186.

Terés, Elias. "Textos poéticos arabes sobre Valencia." *Al-Andalus* 30 (1965): 291–307.

Thiolier-Mejean, Suzanne. *Une Belle au Bois dormant médiévale: Frayre de Joy et Sor de Plaser, nouvelle d'oc du XIVe siècle.* Paris: Presses de l'Université de Paris-Sorbonne, 1996.

Thiolier-Mejean, Suzanne. "Le langage du perroquet dans quelques textes d'Oc et d'Oïl." *Le Plurilinguisme au Moyen Âge: Orient-Occident de Babel à la langue une.* Ed. Claire Kappler and Suzanne Thiolier-Méjean. Paris: L'Harmattan, 2009. 267–99.

Thiolier-Mejean, Suzanne. "Le motif du perroquet dans deux nouvelles d'oc." *Miscellanea Mediaevalia: Mélanges offerts à Philippe Ménard.* Ed. J. Claude Faucon, Alain Labbé and Danielle Quéruel. 2 vols. Paris: Champion, 1998. 2: 1355–75.

Timpanaro, Sebastiano. "Angelo Mai." *Aspetti e figure della cultura ottocentesca.* Pisa: Nistri-Lischi, 1980. 225–71.

Toews, John E. "Intellectual History after the Linguistic Turn: The Autonomy of Meaning and the Irreducibility of Experience." *American Historical Review* 92.4 (1987): 879–907. http://dx.doi.org/10.2307/1863950.

Tolan, John. "Aristophane à Mont Saint Michel? Les écueils de la recherché identitaire." In *L'Islam médiéval en terres chrétiennes: science et idéologie.* Ed. Max Lejbowicz. Villeneuve d'Ascq: Presses Universitaires du Septentrion, 2008. 45–58.

Tolan, John. *Petrus Alfonsi and his Medieval Readers.* Gainesville: University Press of Florida, 1993.

Tolan, John. "Reading God's Will in The Stars: Petrus Alfonsi and Raymond de Marseille Defend The New Arabic Astrology." *Revista Española de Filosofía Medieval* 7 (2000): 13–30.

Tolan, John. "Saracen Philosophers Secretly Deride Islam." *Medieval Encounters* 8 (2002): 185–208. Rpt. in Tolan, *Sons of Ishmael,* 113–32.

Tolan, John. *Sons of Ishmael: Muslims through European Eyes in the Middle Ages.* Gainesville: University Press of Florida, 2008.

Trésors fatimides du Caire. Cat. exp. Paris, Institut du monde arabe, 1998. Ghent: Snoeck-Ducaju & Zoon, 1998.

Trexler, Richard C. "Being and Non-Being: Parameters of the Miraculous in the Traditional Religious Image." *The Miraculous Image in the Late Middle Ages and Renaissance: Papers from a Conference Held at the Accademia di Danimarca in Collaboration with the Bibliotheca Hertziana (Max-Planck-Institut für Kunstgeschichte), Rome, 31 May–2 June 2003.* Ed. Erik Thunø and Gerhard Wolf. Rome: "L'Erma" di Bretschneider, 2004. 15–28.

Turner, R. Steven. "The Growth of Professorial Research in Prussia, 1818–1848 – Causes and Context." *Historical Studies in the Physical Sciences* 3 (1971): 137–82.

Uebel, Michael. *Ecstatic Transformation: On the Uses of Alterity in the Middle Ages.* New York: Palgrave, 2005.

Uhlig, Claus. "Auerbach's 'Hidden' (?) Theory of History." *Literary History and the Challenge of Philology.* Ed. Seth Lerer. Stanford: Stanford University Press, 1996. 36–49.

Uitti, Karl. "Philology." *The Johns Hopkins Guide to Literary Theory and Criticism.* Ed. Michael Groden and Martin Kreiswirth. Baltimore: Johns Hopkins University Press, 1994. 567–73.

Useem, John, and Ruth Hill Useem. *The Western-Educated Man in India: A Study of his Social Roles and Influence.* New York: Dryden, 1955.

Valcke, Louis. *Pic de la Mirandole: Un itinéraire philosophique.* Paris: Les Belles Lettres, 2005.

van Bekkum, Wout. "O Seville! Ah Castile!: Spanish-Hebrew Dirges from the Fifteenth Century." *Hebrew Scholarship and the Medieval World.* Ed. Nicholas De Lange. Cambridge: Cambridge University Press, 2001. http://dx.doi.org/10.1017/CBO9780511627996.012.

van Liere, Katherine Elliot. "The Missionary and the Moorslayer: James the Apostle in Spanish Historiography from Isidore of Seville to Ambrosio de Morales." *Viator* 37 (2006): 519–43.

Le Vert et le brun: de Kairouan à Avignon, céramique du Xe au XVe siècle. Marseille: Musées de Marseille; Paris: Réunion des musées nationaux, 1995.

Vidal, César. *España frente al Islam. De Mahoma a Ben Laden.* Madrid: La Esfera de los libros, 2004.

Viguera, María Jesús. Introduction to Francisco Codera, *Decadencia y desaparición de los almorávides en España.* Pamplona: Urgoiti, 2005. i–cxxxvii.

Vitullo, Juliann. *The Chivalric Epic in Medieval Italy.* Gainesville, Fl.: University of Florida Press, 2000.

Warren, Michelle R. "The Noise of Roland." *Exemplaria* 16.2 (2004): 277–304.

Wartburg, F.W. von. *Franzözisches Etymologisches Wörterbuch*. 25 vols. Tübingen: Niemeyer, 1925–2005.

Wacks, David A. *Framing Iberia: Maqamat and Frametale Narratives in Medieval Spain*. Leiden: Brill, 2007. http://dx.doi.org/10.1163/ej.9789004158283.i-279.

Wasserstein, David. *The Rise and Fall of the Party-Kings: Politics and Society in Islamic Spain, 1002–86*. Princeton: Princeton University Press, 1985.

Watson, Oliver. *Ceramics from Islamic Lands*. New York: Thames and Hudson, 2005.

Webster, Susan Verdi. *Art and Ritual in Golden-Age Spain: Sevillian Confraternities and the Processional Sculpture of Holy Week*. Princeton, N.J.: Princeton University Press, 1998.

Wellek, Rene. "Auerbach and Vico." *Vico: Past and Present*. Ed. Giorgio Tagliacozzo. Atlantic Highlands, N.J.: Humanities Press, 1981. 85–96.

Wellek, Rene. "Auerbach's Special Realism." *Kenyon Review* 16.2 (1954): 299–307.

Wellek, Rene. *Theory of Literature*. 3rd ed. New York: Harcourt, Brace, and Co, 1984.

White, Hayden. "Croce's Criticism of Vico." *Giambattista Vico: An International Symposium*. Ed. Giorgio Tagliacozzo and Hayden White. Baltimore: Johns Hopkins University Press, 1969. 379–90.

White, Hayden. *Metahistory: The Historical Imagination in Nineteenth-Century Europe*. 1973. Baltimore: Johns Hopkins University Press, 1993.

Whitfield, Susan. "The Perils of Dichotomous Thinking: A Case of Ebb and Flow Rather than East and West." *Marco Polo and the Encounter of East and West*. Ed. Suzanne Conklin Akbari and Amilcare A. Iannucci. Toronto: University of Toronto Press, 2008. 247–61.

Whitman, James. "Nietzsche in the Magisterial Tradition of German Classical Philology." *Journal of the History of Ideas* 47.3 (1986): 453–68. http://dx.doi.org/10.2307/2709663.

Wolf, Kenneth Baxter. *Conquerors and Chroniclers of Early Medieval Spain*. Liverpool: Liverpool University Press, 1990.

Wolf, Kenneth Baxter. "Convivencia in Medieval Spain: Brief History of an Idea." *Religion Compass* 3.1 (2009): 72–85. http://dx.doi.org/10.1111/j.1749-8171.2008.00119.x.

Wright, Lawrence. "The Terror Web." *The New Yorker*, 2 August 2004. Electronic.

Yassif, Eli. *The Hebrew Folktale: History, Genre, Meaning*. Bloomington: Indiana University Press, 1999.

Zago, Ester. "*Frayre de Joy e Sor de Plaser* re-examined." *Fabula* 24 (1983): 269–74.

Zeigler, Johanna E. *Sculpture of Compassion: The Pietà and the Beguines in the Southern Low Countries, c.1300–c.1600*. Brussels: Institut historique belge de Rome; Turnhout: Brepols, 1992.

Ziolkowski, Jan. "What Is Philology?" *On Philology*. Ed. Jan Ziolkowski. University Park: Pennsylvania State University Press, 1990. 1–12.

Ziolkowski, Theodore. *German Romanticism and its Institutions*. Princeton: Princeton University Press, 1990.

Žižek, Slavoj. *The Ticklish Subject: The Absent Centre of Political Ontology*. London, New York: Verso, 1999.

Zumthor, Paul. *La Mesure du monde*. Paris: Seuil, 1993.

Zwartjes, Otto. *Love Songs from al-Andalus: History, Structure and Meaning of the Kharja*. Leiden: Brill, 1997.

Contributors

Suzanne Conklin Akbari is Professor of English and Medieval Studies at the University of Toronto, and works on the intersection of comparative literature and intellectual history. Her books are on optics and allegory (*Seeing Through the Veil*, 2004), European views of Islam and the Orient (*Idols in the East*, 2009), travel literature (*Marco Polo*, 2008), and somatic history (*Ends of the Body*, 2012). She is currently writing *Small Change: Metaphor and Metamorphosis in Chaucer and Christine de Pizan*, and is a co-editor of the *Norton Anthology of World Literature*.

Ross Brann is the Milton R. Konvitz Professor of Judeo-Islamic Studies at Cornell University. He is the author of *The Compunctious Poet: Cultural Ambiguity and Hebrew Poetry in Muslim Spain* (1991), recipient of the National Jewish Book Award in Sephardic Studies, and *Power in the Portrayal: Representations of Muslims and Jews in Islamic Spain* (2002), and has edited four volumes of essays on the intersection of Jewish and Islamic cultures. He is currently at work on *Andalusi Moorings: Al-Andalus and Sefarad as Tropes of Muslim and Jewish Culture*.

Simon Gaunt is Professor of French Language and Literature at King's College London, where he is also currently Head of the School of Arts and Humanities. His publications include *Martyrs to Love: Love and Death in Medieval French and Occitan Courtly Literature* (2006) and *The Cambridge Companion to Medieval French Literature* (with Sarah Kay; 2008). He is Principal Investigator on the AHRC-funded collaborative project Medieval Francophone Literary Culture outside France and his next book, *Marco Polo's* Le Devisement du Monde: *Narrative Voice, Language, and Diversity*, will appear in 2013.

William Granara is Professor of Arabic at Harvard University where he teaches Arabic language and literature and directs the program in modern Middle Eastern languages. He has translated several novels from Arabic into English: *The Earth-quake* by Tahir Wattar (2000), *Granada* by Radwa Ashour (2004), and *The Battle of Poitiers* by Jurji Zaydan (2012). In addition to his writings on modern Arabic litera-ture, he researches the literature and culture of medieval Muslim Sicily. Among his recent articles are "Fragments of the Past: Reconstructing Palermo's Jewish Neighborhood, 973–1492" (2010) and "Rethinking Muslim Sicily's Golden Age: Poetry and Patronage at the Fatimid Kalbid Court" (2008).

Paulo Lemos Horta is a scholar of world literature, currently interested in the cross-cultural collaborations that influenced *A Thousand and One Nights* and the reception of the works of sixteenth-century Portuguese author Luis de Camoes. He is co-editing a volume for the MLA series *Approaches to Teaching World Litera-ture*. He is Assistant Professor of Literature at New York University Abu Dhabi.

Sharon Kinoshita, Professor of Literature and co-director (with Brian Catlos) of the Center for Mediterranean Studies at the University of California, Santa Cruz, is the author of *Medieval Boundaries: Rethinking Difference in Old French Literature* (2006) and the co-author of *Thinking through Chrétien de Troyes* (2011) and *Marie de France: A Critical Companion* (2012). She is currently working on a translation of and accompanying monograph on Marco Polo's *Le Divisement du monde*; co-editing (with Peregrine Horden) the *Blackwell Companion to Mediterranean History*; and com-pleting a study provisionally entitled *The Case for Medieval Mediterranean Literature*.

Karla Mallette, Professor of Italian and Near Eastern Studies at the University of Michigan, is author of *The Kingdom of Sicily, 1100–1250: A Literary History* (2005) and *European Modernity and the Arab Mediterranean: Toward a New Philology and a Counter-Orientalism* (2010). She has published articles on medieval Italian and Arabic literature, philology and Mediterranean Studies, and is currently at work on a project entitled *Lingua Franca in the Mediterranean*.

María Rosa Menocal was the author of *The Arabic Role in Medieval Literary His-tory: A Forgotten Heritage* (1987), *Writing in Dante's Cult of Truth: From Borges to Boc-caccio* (1991), *Shards of Love: Exile and the Origins of the Lyric* (1994), *The Ornament of the World: How Muslims, Christians, and Jews Created a Culture of Tolerance in Medieval Spain* (2002), which has been translated into eleven languages, and *The Arts of Intimacy: Christians, Jews and Muslims in the Making of Castilian Culture* (co-authored with art historian Jerrilynn Dodds and Arabist and historian Abigail Krasner Bal-bale; 2008). She co-edited *The Literature of Al-Andalus* in the Cambridge History of Arabic Literature series with Raymond Scheindlin and Michael Sells, and was Director of the Whitney Humanities Center at Yale University.

Dwight Reynolds is Professor of Arabic Language and Literature in the Department of Religious Studies at the University of California, Santa Barbara. He is the author of *Heroic Poets, Poetic Heroes: The Ethnography of Performance of an Arabic Oral Epic Tradition* (1995), editor and co-author of *Interpreting the Self: Autobiography in the Arabic Literary Tradition* (2001), co-editor of *The Garland Encyclopedia of World Music Volume VI: The Middle East* (2002) and editor of the "Music" section for the *Encyclopaedia of Islam* (3rd edition). He has conducted field research on Andalusian musical traditions in Algeria, Egypt, Lebanon, Morocco, Spain, Syria, and Tunisia.

Cynthia Robinson is Professor of Islamic and Medieval Art in the Department of Art History and Visual Culture at Cornell University. She is author of *In Praise of Song: The Making of Courtly Culture in al-Andalus and Provence, 1065–1135 A.D.* (2002), *Three Ladies and a Lover: Mediterranean Courtly Culture through the Text and Images of the "Hadith Bayad wa Riyad," an Andalusi Manuscript* (2006), and *Imagining the Passion in a Multiconfessional Castile: The Virgin, Christ, Devotions, and Images in the Fourteenth and Fifteenth Centuries* (2013). Robinson is currently editor of *Medieval Encounters*.

Leyla Rouhi is John T. and John B. McCoy Professor of Romance Languages at Williams College in Massachusetts. Her recent publications include essays on Cervantes in *Islamicate Sexualities: Translations across Temporal Geographies of Desire* (edited by Kathryn Babayan and Afsaneh Najmabadi, 2008), *In the Light of Medieval Spain* (edited by David Coleman and Simon Doubleday, 2008), and *Writing Out of Limbo: International Childhoods, Global Nomads and Third Culture Kids* (edited by Gene Bell-Villada and Nina Sichel, 2011). She was guest co-editor with María Judith Feliciano and Cynthia Robinson of the special issue of the journal *Medieval Encounters* titled *Interrogating Iberian Frontiers* 12.3 (2006). She is currently working on a number of projects, including a Persian translation of *Don Quijote*.

Walid A. Saleh is Associate Professor of Religion at the University of Toronto. He is the author of *The Formation of the Classical Tafsir Tradition* (2004) and *In Defense of the Bible* (2008), and is finishing an introduction to the history of Quranic interpretation (*tafsir*). Saleh has published on the Bible and Psalms in Islam, and is also working on the history of the medieval super-commentary literature (*hashiya*) and the curriculum of the madrasa.

Ryan Szpiech received his graduate training at Yale University under María Rosa Menocal. He is currently Assistant Professor of Spanish in the Department of Romance Languages and Literatures and the Department of Judaic Studies at the University of Michigan. He has published *Conversion and Narrative: Reading and*

Religious Authority in Medieval Polemic (2013), as well as articles on authors such as Pablo de Santa María, Anselm Turmeda, Abner of Burgos, and Ramon Martí. He is currently editing a book of essays on medieval exegesis and polemical writing and is co-editing a critical edition of the *Pugio Fidei* (Dagger of Faith) by Ramon Martí. He is also part of an international research project entitled "The Intellectual and Material Legacies of Late-Medieval Sephardic Judaism: An Interdisciplinary Approach," supported by the European Research Council. Beginning in summer 2013, he will be editor of *Medieval Encounters*.

John Tolan is Professor of Medieval History at the University of Nantes (France) and author of numerous articles and books in medieval history and cultural studies, including *Petrus Alfonsi and His Medieval Readers* (1993), *Saracens: Islam in the Medieval European Imagination* (2002), *Sons of Ishmael: Muslims through European Eyes in the Middle Ages* (2008), *Saint Francis and the Sultan: The Curious History of a Christian-Muslim Encounter* (2009), and (with Gilles Veinstein and Henry Laurens) *Europe and the Islamic World* (2012). He currently is director of a major project funded by the European Research Council, "RELMIN: The legal status of religious minorities in the Euro-Mediterranean world (5th–15th centuries)" (www.relmin.eu).

David A. Wacks is Associate Professor of Spanish in the Department of Romance Languages at the University of Oregon. His research centres on the interaction of the Romance, Hebrew, and Arabic literary traditions in medieval Iberia. He is the author of *Framing Iberia: Frametale and Maqama Narratives in Medieval Spain* (2007) and co-editor of *Wine, Women, and Song: Hebrew and Arabic Literature in Medieval Iberia* (2004). He is currently working on a book-length study on diaspora in Sephardic literature (1200–1700).